A Maritime History
of the United States

Studies in Maritime History
William N. Still, Jr., Editor

A Maritime History of the United States

The Role of America's Seas and Waterways

by K. Jack Bauer

University of South Carolina Press

Copyright © UNIVERSITY OF SOUTH CAROLINA 1988

Published in Columbia, South Carolina, by the
University of South Carolina Press

FIRST EDITION

Manufactured in the United States of America

Library of Congress Cataloging-in-Publication Data

Bauer, K. Jack (Karl Jack), 1926–
  A maritime history of the United States.

  (Studies in maritime history)
  Bibliography: p.
  Includes index.
  1. Merchant marine—United States—History.
2. Merchant ships—United States—History.   3. Shipping—
United States—History.   4. Inland water transportation—
United States—History.   5. United States. Navy—
History.   I. Title.   II. Series.
HE745.B38   1988   387.5'0973   87-19190
ISBN 0-87249-519-1

To the Memory of My Friends

Samuel Eliot Morison (1887–1976)
and
John Rowen Lyman (1915–1977)

Two of America's great maritime historians

CONTENTS

Illustrations

Maps

PREFACE

Earth is the water planet. Oceans cover three-quarters of its surface, and even on the remaining portion mankind finds dry-shod movement hampered. Streams, lakes, and arms of the sea circumscribe his area of domain. Since prehistoric times, homo sapiens has sought to utilize the waterways of the planet for movement, food, and raw materials. The varying success achieved in that quest has been a significant factor in the rise and decline of regions, nations, and civilizations. In few areas can this be seen more strikingly than in the history of the United States.

The history of the discovery and exploration of the American shoreline is a maritime story; so is the account of the settlement of the coastal, tidewater plains. The early economic growth of the new nation sprang largely from the sea and from the rivers; the factors that controlled the direction and rate of flow of settlement in the great central heartland of the country were intimately related to the rivers, lakes, and canals that traversed the Mississippi Basin. The massive industrialization of the late nineteenth century had its foundations in the waters of the Great Lakes, the coal tipples of Hampton Roads, the timber wharves of Maine and the Pacific Northwest, as well as the teeming piers of New York, New Orleans, San Francisco, and half a hundred smaller ports.

Today, when overseas raw material sources and energy conservation assume ever increasing importance, waterborne transport must play an expanding role. The laws of physics favor water carriage of bulky goods since the force necessary to move a floating body through water is appreciably less than that needed to push it through any other medium. As a result the salt and fresh waters of the nation carry the shipping that hauls the bulk of our raw materials and over a quarter of our energy. Without their cargoes we would quickly die as a nation. So, if Americans have tended to forget their debt to the sea and other waterways or overlook their growing dependence on them, they dare not continue averting their eyes. The continuation of the world Americans know is tied to the rational use of the waterways of the nation and globe.

Contemporary Americans, often cut off from the visual impact of a busy port or an active river and misunderstanding the significance of frequently prosaic watercraft, too often ignore the maritime role in their country's development and fail to realize its importance in the nation's survival. The tug with a rusty sand barge churning its way up the Potomac in the shadow of the Lincoln Memorial is as important to the nation's survival as many of the deliberations carried on in the cluttered hearing rooms of the Capitol. The tanker lumbering through the swell beneath the red span of the Golden Gate Bridge is as significant as much of the research being carried on in the Berkeley Hills ahead. The massive "thousand footer" on Lake Superior hauling taconite from the mines of the Mesabi is as valuable to the life of the country as the decisions being made in the communications centers of Chicago.

Too often the histories upon which Americans rely to describe and interpret the United States' rise to global economic and political dominance slight the role of maritime affairs. This book is an effort to correct that oversight by depicting the maritime impact on the history of the United States. As such it not only traces the role played by the oceans in the development of the country but also those of the navigable inland waterways like lakes, rivers, streams, and canals without which settlement beyond the coastal plains would have been nearly impossible.

If the reader gains an understanding of the tremendous importance of maritime affairs in the history of the nation and a glimmering of the role that they play today the book will be a success. Of course, that maritime role is not the sole determinant of American history. It is but one of a number of factors that have shaped the course of events and the culture of the nation's inhabitants. Yet, in some periods, notably those prior to the Civil War, maritime affairs played a major role in shaping events and thoughts.

After 1860, as the nation's attention turned inward, the visible impact of maritime affairs declined as settlement flowed into areas beyond the heads of navigation on the western rivers and as few raw materials arrived from overseas. Today the trend has reversed as the United States develops ever greater dependence on foreign trade and raw materials and as increasing quantities of materials and finished goods move domestically by water.

By design this book tells a civilian story. The contributions of the Navy and the other uniformed services to the American maritime tradition are numerous and important but they nearly always have been separate and distinct from the concerns discussed in this book. Even so, the decline of United States participation in the world's maritime life during the late twentieth-century threatens to make the services the sole repository of the American maritime tradition. Neither is this book the definitive study of the maritime impact on the United States. Too many gaps exist in our knowledge of the maritime history of the nation to permit that. If it points maritime historians in the direction of areas in need of study the book will have fulfilled one of its objectives. Formal documentation through footnotes has been eliminated as too distracting but the concluding bibliographical essay serves both to indicate the major sources used and to suggest where readers may pursue their particular interests in greater detail.

Many people have had a hand in the preparation of this study. Most obvious are the librarians, especially those at Rensselaer Polytechnic Institute, the State University of New York at Albany, Union College, Williams College, Mariners Museum, the Troy Public Library, and the Navy Department Library where the bulk of the research took place. Other valuable help has been cheerfully offered by the staffs of the National Archives, Naval Historical Center, Maine Maritime Museum, Peabody Museum of Salem, National Maritime Museum, New York State Historical Society, and the Institute for Great Lakes Research. To them all goes my deepest appreciation.

No author could have had better advice from his confrères than I have had on this manuscript. The late Samuel Eliot Morison offered valuable suggestions for an approach and lent strong moral support in the formative period. John Lyman read most of an early draft before his untimely death and in his usual careful way pointed out where facts and conclusions strayed. Benjamin W. Labaree, John H. Kemble, and Richard J. Wright read chapters. I am indebted to them for catching errors, suggesting better interpretations, and pointing out areas ignored. Dean C. Allard, Paolo E. Coletta, Benjamin F. Gilbert, and Richard W. Turk contributed other advice, support, and information during the gestation period of this study. The final manuscript owes its existence and form to the persistent prodding of William N. Still, Jr. It was Bill Still's gentle pressure that forced me back to the project when other more immediate ones sought to draw me elsewhere. Individually and collectively they proved once again that the leaders of the discipline deserve their position. For the errors that remain they bear no responsibility; those rest squarely on the author.

The manuscript was typed with their usual grace and efficiency by Margaret A. McLeod, Carol Halder, Tina Gendron, and Sandy Charette of the Department of Science and Technology Studies at Rensselaer Polytechnic Institute. Earle W. Jackson of the University of South Carolina Press, shepherded the book through its final stages with gentleness and efficiency. Portions of the research for this study were conducted under a grant from Rensselaer.

It is conventional to thank one's wife for her assistance. In this instance it is not conventional. My wife, Dorothy Sargent Bauer, has not only once again proven herself to be the most careful and incisive of editors but she has cheerfully endured endless hours of visits to museums, libraries, and other repositories. This book, like all my others, is truly a collaborative work.

With these notes entered on the pilot chart, I bid you bon voyage.

K. Jack Bauer

42°43′30″N, 73°39′45″W
July 1986

A Maritime History
of the United States

Chapter One

A NEW WORLD EMERGES

IF THE EARTH IS THE WATER PLANET, THEN NORTH AMERICA IS THE water continent. The Great Lakes form an eighth sea stretching inland for nearly a third of its breadth while the Mississippi River system alone drains an area of 1,231,000 square miles. The Hudson-Mohawk, the Susquehanna-Juniata, Chattahoochee, Rio Grande, Colorado, Sacramento, Columbia, Yukon, and Mackenzie River systems, along with many others, drain smaller regions while offering no less valuable services to their watersheds.

As the last of the Ice Ages retreated towards its Arctic birthplace and the ancestors of the American Indian began their trek across the land bridge to Alaska, the topography of North America as we know it today began to appear. The southward flowing Mississippi system formed, and the Great Lakes began to take shape. Indians, moving southward along the eastern foothills of the Rocky Mountains, spread throughout the central core of the continent and spilled across the Appalachian barrier onto the Atlantic Coastal plain while others edged farther south into Mexico and the southern coastal plains. Eddies of movement found passages through the western mountains onto the Pacific coastal plains and river valleys.

As the Indians adapted to their new homes in the plains and in the forests they learned to use the streams for food and transportation. Fishing is one of man's oldest occupations. Undoubtedly the migrants brought it with them from Asia, and they practiced it wherever the streams offered hope of a meal. Massive shell heaps along the Maine and Cape Cod coasts attest to the fact that the Indians there discovered and consumed shellfish in great quantities.

The wanderers developed craft to carry them along and across the streams and lakes while those who reached the coast modified the boats for use in coastal waters. On the plains, buffalo herds not only provided food, clothing, and fuel but also skins for bull boats. Those nearly round skimming dishes were made by stretching buffalo hides over light wooden frames. They could be disassembled when not in use and easily carried, which was an important attribute for wide-ranging hunters. In the northern birch forests other

The Indians of the coastal plains and the Great Lakes basin developed several different types of craft. The Northwest tribes commonly used large dugouts for fishing, travel, and ceremonial occasions. Salmon, whether speared from a boat or from shore, formed a large part of their diet. Office of War Information Photograph Courtesy of the National Archives

Indians laced the bark of the paper birch over an elongated spruce or cedar frame to produce the canoe. Although primarily a Canadian product, it also took form in the hands of the forest Indians in northern New England and New York. Farther south the natives developed various forms of dugouts while on the West Coast skin craft also appeared. The coastal tribes in the Northwest produced wooden-hulled craft large enough even to be used for whaling. Although both the northwestern and the northeastern Indians covered long distances in their trading and warmaking expeditions and other coastal tribes sometimes ventured out to offshore islands, North American Indians developed no extensive maritime interests.

The reverse is true of the first Europeans who we are confident actually visited the Americas. During the tenth century three restless groups of Scandinavian seafarers lived on the northern fringes of European civilization. As early as the ninth century they began to move outwards, driven by overpopulation, political upheavals, and a love of adventure. The Swedes advanced eastward into Russia as traders and settlers; the Danes moved into Britain, France, and the Low Countries as conquerors; while the Norse reached out to the Faroes and Ireland (ca. 800); to Iceland (874), where Irish monks had preceeded them; and to Greenland (986).

The Norse voyages were epic trips by sailors who were the premier navigators of the Western world of their day. The American trips were made in the broad-beamed *knarr,* a 50–60-foot-long trading vessel propelled by a large square sail—not the long, sleek, oared craft that generations of American schoolbook illustrators have drawn for us. The latter were warcraft, not used for exploration. The Norse navigated by a relatively simple method. They sailed north until the North Star reached a predetermined height, and then they sailed along that meridian, using the location of the star on the starboard beam by night and the sun's azimuth by day to check direction. Since they had developed a method of roughly checking latitude by means of a "sun shadow board," the Norse could make longer deepwater voyages than any other European sailors of the period.

In 986 a trading skipper, Biarni Heriulfson, bound for the new Greenland settlements, missed Cape Farewell and sighted an unknown coast farther west, probably Labrador or Baffin Island, but possibly Newfoundland. Not being endued with an inquisitive nature, Heriulfson did not tarry to explore the new land but hurried on to Greenland. His report caught the attention of Leif Ericsson. In 1000 or 1002 Ericsson, after securing a commission from King Olaf Trygvesson of Norway, visited the new land. He established a short-lived base settlement at L'Anse aux Meadows on the northwest coast of Newfoundland. Ericsson remained but a short time before returning to the relative hospitality of Greenland. The L'Anse site passed into the hands of his half brother Thorvald, who visited in 1004–5. Thorfinn Karlsevni followed with a third settlement in 1009–12 and apparently returned for a final time in 1013. The natives proved hostile, and since the Norse had no military advantage they could not maintain themselves in the new country. Indeed, until the introduction of gunpowder no European settlers had the technological advantage necessary to offset the numerical one of the natives.

The Norse settlers' problems with hostile natives not only caused the sites to be abandoned but erased further thoughts of colonization. Few knowledgeable scholars give credence to alleged Norse artifacts like the Kensington Stone or the rune stones scattered about in Maine, Massachusetts, and Arizona. These have proven to be either the product of overambitious imaginations or modern rock carvers. However, since additional Norse expeditions probably did visit North America before the collapse of the Greenland settlement in the fourteenth century, valid remains may yet appear.

1. The Age of Discovery

In spite of tantalizing wisps of evidence that evaporate upon pursuit like low-lying mists and clouds, there is no proof of other visits to the New World before Christopher Columbus. Why then did the discovery from which the history of the Western Hemisphere stems occur at the end of the fifteenth century? It occurred because all the elements necessary for the discovery did not appear until then. During the thirteenth century Mediterranean seamen began to venture into the Atlantic. They probably sighted both the Azores and Madeira and certainly rediscovered the Canary Islands. By the middle of the following century European travelers had traversed Africa north of the Sahara as well as the western part of that desert.

The pioneer travelers not only added to European awareness of the world but helped lift the fog bank of intellectual apathy that enveloped the continent as an aftermath of the Dark Ages. Nearly all the travelers were merchants seeking new markets. Their activity signaled the beginnings of an economic revival. As trade increased so did the availability of capital with which to finance additional expeditions. The expanding economy hastened the formation of new and stronger central governments whose presence and support were necessary if large-scale explorations and their exploitations were to occur. During the fourteenth and fifteenth centuries strong, vibrant national states in the full vigor of their youth arose in Portugal, Spain, France, and England.

Intellectually important was the midfifteenth-century shift in the concept of the world held by the educated portion of the European populace. They came to view the world as a single entity and the seas as a waterway to all places. This concept acquired increased significance after the Turks disrupted the traditional caravan routes to the Orient. Psychologically, if not practically, the concern intensified after the loss of Constantinople in 1453, which not only demolished the last vestiges of the Eastern Empire but opened southeastern Europe to the infidel invader. Many Europeans soon concluded that if a secure route to the Orient could be found it had to be seaborne and that the first nation to establish such a route would win a prize of great value.

To use the waterways efficiently fifteenth-century seamen had to learn mathematics and astronomy and understand the physical universe. Initially they relied on the ancient scientists like the second-century A.D. Egyptian Claudius Ptolemy. His *Geography,* first translated into Latin about 1406, appeared in print in 1475. Ptolemy divided his spherical world into 360 degrees but underestimated its size by two-sevenths. Even worse, he overestimated the length of the Eurasian continent by 46 percent. Nevertheless, Ptolemy's book and its accompanying maps became the geographical basis for Renaissance scholars and remained the standard study for a century after Columbus.

Advances in navigation and cartography during the later fifteenth century, as well as improved sailing direction, enabled mariners to find their way with reasonable confidence to any point on an unfamiliar coast. This capability to observe and record position, at least in latitude, was indispensable to a mariner willing to direct those who followed to the places he had seen.

Most of these advances originated in Portugal, where a school of navigation flourished at Sagres after about 1430. It formed a part of the attempt by Prince Henry the Navigator to explore a route around Africa. His navigators developed a method of navigation called *altura* by which a captain sailed due south until he reached a given latitude before turning east for the African coast. The captains, therefore, required both an accurate means of determining their latitude and an improved acquaintance with mathematics. The earliest instrument to do this satisfactorily was the quadrant. It allowed the mariner to measure the elevation of the North Star by observing it through a pair of pinholes and then reading the point at which a plumbline cut a 90° scale. In daytime, latitude could be determined by measuring the angle of the sun at zenith and comparing this with a printed table, much as a modern navigator takes his noon shot. The quadrant, which first appeared about 1456, was an awkward instrument ill fitted for use on a tossing ship. Early in the sixteenth century it gave way to the more sophisticated sea-astrolabe and cross-staff. They, in turn, yielded later in the century to the English-developed Davis Quadrant or back-staff. Few mariners in the fifteenth and early sixteenth centuries, however, ever mastered astronomical navigation because of the cumbersome instruments then available. Most, like Christopher Columbus, relied on dead reckoning, often with great accuracy. From the little we know of their navigational techniques it seems clear that most navigators sailed north or south along the known European coast and then headed west to the new continent, essentially as had the Norsemen five centuries earlier.

Means of determining direction had been known since medieval times. The Norse probably possessed the lodestone, a magnatized needle floating on a card in water, but apparently did not greatly rely on it. The compass was known in Europe as early as the thirteenth century and came into general use during the following hundred years. Cheaply constructed and easily used, the magnetized compass probably contributed more to the voyages of discovery than any other single instrument.

The Dutch evolved a method of determining the speed of a vessel through the water by timing the passage of a floating piece of wood *(loog)* between two marks on a vessel's rail. About 1574 the English discovered that if a wooden chip was attached to a string with a knot every seven fathoms, the number of knots to pass through the fingers in a minute would indicate how many sea miles or knots would be traveled in an hour. Naturally, the book in which speed and changes in courses were registered came to be called the log book.

As important as the new navigation instruments were in the exploitation of the discovery of America, they could not have been used had not naval architecture taken long strides forward in the fifteenth century. In northern Europe the *knarr* of the Norse had evolved into the cog, a single-masted, square-sailed cargo carrier sturdy enough to traverse the rough northern waters. She sported a sternpost rudder. With the appearance of the sternpost rudder during the late twelfth century, naval architecture moved forward rapidly since it eliminated the long steering oar and made possible larger vessels, more accurate steering, and simplified tacking. Nevertheless, the cog was a difficult vessel to handle since she lacked a headsail to balance the craft and keep her on course. Moreover, since she was square-sailed she made little headway against unfavorable winds.

For their African voyages the Portuguese developed the two- and three-masted lateen-rigged caravels. They were fast, strong, easily handled, and beat to the windward nearly as well as a modern yacht. Before the wind the caravels were unhandy, so later versions acquired a square foresail. During the fifteenth century other builders, probably in the Bay of Biscay, introduced a large mixed-rigged type that came to be known as the carrack. It normally set square sails on the fore- and mainmasts and lateen ones on the mizzen. By the end of the century a spritsail, a square sail set on the sprit, or as we say today bowsprit, served as a headsail to assist in steering. Some craft added a fourth mast, a lateen-rigged bonaventure mizzen, on the stern.

Although the new rigs had yet to offer the best sail arrangement for the Atlantic crossing, the vessels were reasonably handy craft that permitted sailors to make long voyages in relative safety and comfort. Without such vessels no extended exploration was possible nor could the discoveries be exploited since the craft had to carry both supplies to feed the crew and enough cargo to make the voyage economically feasible.

Once seamen began to understand the wind system of the Atlantic, passages became easier. As a general rule the steadiest winds are those between 30° north and 30° south latitude, i.e., between the Canary Islands and St. Augustine, Florida, on the north and Porto Alegre, Brazil, and South Africa to the south. Masses of air continually settle at about 30° (the horse latitudes), which produce high barometric pressures but little wind. Closer to the equator steady trade winds blow, northeast in the Northern Hemisphere and southeast in the Southern. The collision of the two systems at the equator results in a zone of doldrums while the air on the polar side of the horse latitudes becomes unstable and stormy when it collides with the colder polar air. Land masses alter the wind patterns somewhat since winds tend to converge on hot areas and blow away from cold ones. This produces tropical monsoons as well as the phenomena of onshore afternoon breezes and offshore night breezes familiar to coastal residents.

Portugal took the lead in prospecting the all-water route to the Orient. Not only did she occupy a geographically favored position on the southwest corner of Europe but she had acquired a strong central government early in the fifteenth century and unlike Spain had avoided Moorish conquest. During the fifteenth century, Portugal developed an export trade in salt, fish, wine, olive oil, fruit, cork, and hides with Flanders, England, Morocco, and various Mediterranean ports. This provided both the nautical experience and the financial capital for voyages of discovery. The militant Christianity that locked the Portuguese in a perpetual war with the Moslems also drove them in search of the mythical Prestor John, whose Christian empire lay somewhere beyond the Sahara and who was expected to join in one final Crusade to free the Holy Places from the heathen. The Portuguese soon discovered that religious motives blended smoothly with economic ones since the same activities that led to Prestor John also pointed to the spices of the Orient with a stop enroute for the gold of Guinea.

The Portuguese began their search for the water route around Africa about 1419 with the rediscovery of Madeira. By 1434, Portuguese sailors reached the Azores and had rounded Cape Bojador in Rio de Oro, which marked the southern limit of the known Atlantic. This caused Pope Martin V to bestow on Portugal all the lands to be discovered in Africa and India. During the fifth decade of the century Portuguese seamen pressed on to the Cape Verde Islands. In 1482 the Portuguese built the great Castle of São Jorge on the Gold Coast, which gave them control of the substantial gold and slave trade of the region. The final step in the conquest of West Africa came early in 1488 when Bartholomeu Dias rounded the Cape of Good Hope. Nine years later Vasco da Gama's successor expedition sailed for India. The delay apparently resulted from the vain efforts of unrecorded expeditions to find a better route down the African coast.

The great empire that the Portuguese seized in East Asia falls outside the scope of this book but is important because it represents a significant aspect of the expansion of European power and influence contemporaneous with the discovery and settlement of the Americas. The empires on the other side of the globe are too often forgotten by Americans blinded by the flashes of their own history. Lest we forget, between 1509 and 1557 the Portuguese established a line of fortified posts, stretching from Zanzibar to Macao, that won them control of the Indian Ocean, the Malacca pepper trade, and the sole Western contact with China. Pepper dominated their commerce with the Orient. The Portuguese imported an average of roughly six million pounds per year throughout the sixteenth century. Portugal's dominance was short lived. Her population was too small to permit her a successful defense of the immense Asiatic commercial empire. By the middle of the following century it had succumbed to the assaults of Turkish, Dutch, and English raiders.

2. Christopher Columbus

While the Portuguese struggled to reach around Africa to the fabled East, other Europeans considered the possibility that it could be approached by sailing westward. The discovery of the Azores broke the bounds of the Atlantic and carried Europeans a third of the way across it. In England the merchants of Bristol who traded with both Iceland and Portugal became interested in the supposed islands to the west and may actually have reached North America in 1481, although we have no conclusive evidence. If they did find the New World the Bristol seamen made no effort to exploit their discovery except perhaps to fish the teeming grounds off Newfoundland.

It remained for a doggedly determined Genoese seaman and visionary to "discover" the New World. Whether or not others preceded Christopher Columbus to the Americas is unimportant in any practical sense since the history of the Western Hemisphere as we know it stems from the 1492 voyage. That Columbus came from Genoa is not surprising since the city-state had both a tradition of explorers and a noted school of mapmakers. Columbus went to sea at an early age and about 1476 moved to Portugal. Some five years later he became interested in the westward passage to the Orient and corresponded with the famed Florentine geographer Paolo Toscanelli, who estimated the distance to China at only 5,000 miles, a mere 72 percent error. When Columbus himself calculated the distance he reduced it a further 5 percent. He under-estimated the length of a degree by one quarter and stretched the Eurasian Continent to 253° instead of the correct 131°. As a result he placed Japan in the West Indies and the coast of China in Chicago. Whether Columbus's miscalculation played a significant role in the rejection of his request to the Portuguese crown for support we do not know since the refusal officially came on other grounds.

After the rebuff Columbus moved to Spain and spent the next six years vainly trying to gain royal support, largely because the Spanish court concentrated all its interest, energy, and money on the final campaign against the Moors. Not until the seizure of Granada in 1492 did Ferdinand and Isabella agree to support Columbus. Actually the rulers risked little, since the money for the expedition came from merchants in the port of Palos from which Columbus sailed on August 3, 1492. His three vessels were unexceptional trading craft. The *Santa Maria* was a carrack of about 100 tons burden or 85 feet over all. The *Pinta,* a lateen-rigged caravel, could carry about 60 tons and the little *Niña,* also lateen rigged, about 50. The latter two craft had a square foresail added during the stop at the Azores. After a relatively easy but slow crossing of 71 days came the cry of *"Tierra, tierra"* [land, land] as the lookout sighted the New World at what is probably Watlings Island in the Bahamas. Safely passing through the difficult waters of the Bahamas, Columbus reached Cuba, which he identified as Japan, and sailed on to the north shore of Hispaniola, where he lost the *Santa Maria.* Leaving the Caribbean on January 4, 1493, the survivors crowded into the two smaller craft battled a stormy midwinter crossing before staggering into Lisbon on March 4, and Palos eleven days later.

The enthusiasm generated by the successful voyage ensured that a large fleet of seventeen vessels assembled at Cadiz for a triumphal second voyage to the Indies. Sailing on September 25, 1493, the squadron made landfall at Dominica in the Windward Islands on November 3. Running north and west up the inside of the Windwards and Puerto Rico, Columbus led his force to the fort at Navidad, where he had left a garrison on the first voyage. But they had perished. Establishing a new settlement farther eastward, Columbus explored the south coast of Cuba and Jamaica. His project quickly deteriorated. The site of the settlement proved to be poorly chosen and unhealthy. The settlers soon became disgruntled, while the Indians rose in revolt. Moreover, gold was scarce and China yet unvisited.

Leaving orders for the settlement to move to what we know today as Santo Domingo, Columbus returned to Spain in 1496. It took him two years to raise the money to outfit a third expedition. Trying a more southerly route than before, he made a miserable, hot midsummer crossing of two months before sighting Trinidad, which offered naked Indians but no representatives of the Great Khan. He next sighted the South American coast but quickly realized that it was not just another of the seemingly endless string of islands that had prevented his reaching the mainland of Asia. Hastening on to Santo Domingo he found conditions horrible and his settlers near revolt. Sent back to Spain in 1500, Columbus won his freedom but could not return to the Caribbean for two years. His four vessels were driven by storms past Jamaica and towards the Cuban coast before finally running across the Caribbean to the Bay Islands, off modern Honduras. In what must have been one of the worst of Columbus's numerous miserable voyages the vessels worked their way down the coast in a seemingly endless series o rainstorms while searching for a passage to the Indian Ocean. Finally abandoning that quest, Columbus with the two remaining vessels limped eastward as far as Jamaica before shipworms destroyed the craft. The survivors waited nearly a full year for rescue. In 1504 Columbus returned to Spain only to die two year later in relative obscurity.

While Columbus struggled unsuccessfully to find his passage to India, other explorers from Spain enlarged the knowledge of the world he had found. In 1499–1500 Alonso de Ojeda and Amerigo Vespucci explored the South American coast as far as the bulge of Brazil while Columbus's old shipmate Vicente Yannez Pinzón discovered the Amazon River. During a 1500–1501 voyage Rodrigo de Bastidas examined the coast between the Gulfs of Maracaibo and Darien. Eight years later Pinzón and Juan Días de Solís extended the known coast to Yucatan. In 1508 Sebastian de Ocampo circumnavigated Cuba, and five years later Juan Ponce de León discovered Florida and explored the peninsula from approximately Daytona Beach in the east to the Caloosahatchee River in the west.

Alonso Alvárez de Pineda in 1518 traced the northern shore of the Gulf of Mexico from Florida to the Panuco River and entered the Mississippi River. That same year Juan de Grijalva filled in the knowledge of the coast southward to Yucatan. Three years later Francisco de Gordillo extended Spanish acquaintanceship with the Atlantic Coast as far as South Carolina.

The disastrous attempt by Páfilo de Narváez to establish a Spanish settlement in Florida during 1527 plays a significant role in American maritime history. When the settlement at modern St. Petersburg failed, the survivors built five small brigantines on the shores of Tampa Bay that were the earliest craft built by Europeans within the confines of the United States. Despite shipwreck and incredible hardships four survivors reached Mexico safely in 1536. Their tales of rich inland cities led to both Hernando de Soto's expedition of 1539–43 and that of Francisco Coronado in 1540–42. The first wandered through the southeast, rediscovered the Mississippi River, and on its banks built a fleet of "bergantinas" in which they made their way back to Mexico. Support for the second included the deposit of supplies at the head of the Gulf of California by vessels sailing from Acapulco.

Slowly but surely Spanish navigators determined the coastline of Central and South America. Their efforts culminated in Ferdinand Magellan's circumnavigation of the globe. The shape of the northern coastline would come later.

3. A Northern Continent Appears

The northern coastline became known through the explorations of a large group of seamen—French, English, Spanish, Dutch, and Portuguese—whose motivations are difficult when not impossible to determine. The earliest was by the Venetian John Cabot. It appears that Cabot, like Columbus, underestimated the distance to the Orient, but we know very little about his voyage. While we do not know whether the Bristol merchants for whom he worked had prior knowledge of the continent across the Atlantic or whether it was a surprise, we do know that in 1496 Cabot received a royal grant from Henry VII of England for a voyage westward.

Embarking on a 50-ton craft called *Matthew,* Cabot departed Bristol about May 20, 1497, sailed north and west to Dursey Head, Ireland, before steering out into the Atlantic. Following the same system of navigation that the Norse and Columbus had used, Cabot ran west, always keeping the North Star on his starboard beam. Holding to roughly 51°30′, he made a landfall on June 24 somewhere between Cape Breton Island and the Strait of Belle Isle, most likely Cape Degrat at the north end of Newfoundland. Cabot explored the Newfoundland coast for about four weeks before returning home in early August. The following year he made a second voyage from which he did not return. Although the information on the Cabot voyages is scant and much of that distorted by his son Sebastian, who may well be as consummate a liar as most modern historians believe, the discovery of the northern continent set in motion other expeditions.

Despite the appreciably shorter distances involved if a route to the Orient could be found in the higher latitudes, the exploitation of Cabot's discovery was limited in comparison to that stemming from Columbus's. This illustrates a relatively overlooked aspect of the age of discovery: only a handful of explorers sought the passage to China. Most hoped for immediate riches and power through the location of gold and jewels or the establishment of control over a large, productive area. The northern continent quickly demonstrated that it lacked either immediate wealth or power.

In 1500–1508 at least seven Portuguese or Bristol-based voyages sought to enlarge upon the Cabot discoveries but returned with so little of value that English interest waned, especially after Henry VIII came to the throne. Since the Iceland fisheries supplied the English with ample fish for the remainder of the sixteenth century little incentive existed to exploit the only known natural resource of North America. Breton, Portuguese, and a handful of other fishermen did follow up the voyages of discovery by sailing their shallops and smacks to the waters off Newfoundland and the Grand Banks, which teemed with cod. Whether these voyages resulted from the Cabot discoveries or from even earlier knowledge we do not know. Nor do we know when the first fishermen appeared on the Banks. Some Bretons were there by 1504. So much Grand Banks cod reached Portugal, however, that two years later the government placed a 10 percent duty on fish coming from the New World, the first discriminatory tariff directed at American produce.

Although the rate of exploration declined it did not vanish, and in 1521 the Portuguese navigator João Alvares Fagundes planted a settlement at Ingonish on Cape Breton Island. It was the first attempt at permanent settlement by Europeans on North America since the Norse. The colony lasted only eighteen months before being broken up by local Indians and the hostile Breton fishermen who dominated the nearby waters. At that time the Bretons themselves maintained forty of fifty huts along the coast that they used when tending their flake yards, repairing their vessels, or trading with the Indians. None of the huts appear to have been permanently occupied.

The decade of the 1520s saw the final closing of the gaps in knowledge of the outline of the Atlantic coast of North America. King Francis I of France sent Giovanni da Verrazzano, a well-educated minor Italian nobleman and experienced mariner, to search the American coast for the elusive passage to the Orient. Sailing in the 100-ton carrack *Dauphine,* Verrazzano reached the coast near Cape Fear, North Carolina, about March 1, 1524. Fearful that he was approaching the edge of the Spanish domain he headed the *Dauphine* north, close enough to shore to detect any breaks in the coast. Although his craft safely traversed the treacherous waters of the Carolina Banks and set a party ashore at Kitty Hawk, her lookouts failed to detect both Hampton Roads and Delaware Bay. On April 17 the *Dauphine* entered New York harbor only to be driven to sea by an approaching storm. Continuing north she passed Block Island and entered Narragansett Bay but tarried little before heading east. After skirting Cape Cod, Verrazzano turned north, sighting the Maine coast near Casco Bay. Passing on to Mount Desert Island the explorer sailed eastward again, missing the Bay of Fundy and most of Nova Scotia. Verrazzano continued his course along the Newfoundland coast to Fogo Island before heading home to Dieppe, where the *Dauphine* dropped anchor on July 8. During his four months of cruising through unknown waters Verrazzano added as much as any single explorer to the knowledge of the east coast of North America but failed to find the sought-after Northwest Passage.

Neither did Estevan Gómez, a Portuguese sailing for the king of Spain. Gómez had been a member of Magellan's expedition but had mutinously turned back in the Strait of Magellan. Nevertheless, he secured command of an expedition to seek the Northwest Passage. The original Spanish intention had been to dispatch Gómez in 1523 in order to precede Verrazzano, but the expedition was not ready until a year later. Sailing west from Corunna, Gómez reached the American coast somewhere on Cape Breton Island in February 1525. He looked into the Gulf of St. Lawrence but concluded that it would be as impractical a passage as he considered Magellan's to be and worked south. Gómez sailed closer inshore

The model of Hudson's *Half Moon* in the Museum of the City of New York offers an excellent view of the type of vessel in which the explorers of the early seventeenth century sailed. Photograph courtesy of the Museum of the City of New York

than Verrazzano and found much that the French had overlooked. He discovered Prince Edward Island; the Gut of Canso; traced the Nova Scotia coast; crossed the Bay of Fundy; fetched Mount Desert; and followed the narrow Eggemoggin Reach to the head of Penobscot Bay. After ascending the Penobscot River perhaps as far as modern Bangor, he continued down the coast, sighted Cape

Ann, and rounded Cape Cod. He cruised probably as far as New-port, Rhode Island, before turning his caravel eastward towards Spain. Gómez's charts are extremely accurate, and his feat of dis-covering the narrow and obscure Eggemoggin Reach is little short of amazing. Yet he has missed the recognition that Verrazzano and a host of later and lesser pilots have received in American history books.

Since other Spanish expeditions, notably that of Luis Vásquez de Ayllón, filled in the area between Florida and Verrazzano's land-fall, the east coast of North America was known in general outline within forty years of Columbus's first voyage. So well charted was the coast that in 1536 an enterprising Englishman brought sixty tourists to Newfoundland.

More important was the clear evidence that, unless some care-less mariner had missed it or its opening was extremely small, no passage to the Orient existed through either of the Americas. Al-though for another hundred years men would thrust explorative needles into the larger waterways in hopes of finding the elusive route, most attention shifted northward, to the passages opening westward out of Davis Strait and Baffin Bay. At the end of the sixteenth century, English sailors under Martin Frobisher and John Davis ventured into those iceberg-infested waters without success. Neither Henry Hudson, Robert Bylot, nor William Baffin, who fol-lowed in the first two decades of the seventeenth century, had greater success although they penetrated farther north and west. The Northwest Passage remained one of those impossible dreams that drew men into the unknown until 1906, when Roald Amund-sen completed his epic passage.

In 1533 Francis I prevailed upon the pope to interpret the bull that divided the world between Spain and Portugal as applying only to lands known when it was issued. This permitted France to establish colonies on lands still to be discovered. To find those sites and to establish fishing bases, Francis lent support to Jacques Car-tier, who in the summer of 1534 explored the Bay of St. Lawrence as far as Gaspé Bay and Anticosti Island. The following year he followed the St. Lawrence River as far as the Lachine Rapids. To the high hill dominating the north shore of the river behind the rapids he gave the name that it has carried to the present, Mont Royal. Cartier wintered at Quebec, where he heard fanciful Indian tales of riches to be found in a kingdom that lay up the Saguenay

River. The stories spurred further exploration but not until 1541 did the king authorize a permanent settlement.

With an easy Northwest Passage clearly nonexistent, interest in North America slumped during the remainder of the sixteenth century. Britain was too preoccupied with internal problems and those arising from Henry VIII's voracious appetite for wives to expend energy or interest in further scouting of the New World; even her fishermen retired from the Grand Banks. The French, embroiled in the Religious Wars, had less opportunity while Portugal and Spain found their energies too absorbed in digesting the spoils of their earlier conquests to seek new routes to the East.

Nevertheless, some explorers still managed to contribute to mankind's knowledge of the world. A few like Francis Drake did so as an accidental benefit from other activities. The West Coast of the United States and Canada lay so far from areas usually visited that exploration came late in the period of discovery. The Spanish traversed the west coast of Mexico after the founding of Acapulco, but most of their efforts were directed southward towards Central America and Peru. Hernando Cortés in 1522 laid plans to explore the Pacific coast. He established a shipyard near Acapulco in order to build a craft to seek a strait closer than Magellan's, but when the vessel was finally completed after five years it was diverted to the Far East. In 1532 a pair of vessels under Diego Hurtado de Mendoza vanished while searching for California. Despite these setbacks Cortés persisted, and in 1535–40 his lieutenant Francisco de Ulloa explored the Gulf of California and sailed up the west coast of Baja California as far as the Isla de Cedros. During 1540 Hernando de Alarcón, carrying supplies for Coronado, ascended the Colorado River at least to its junction with the Gila. More important was the voyage two years later of Juan Rodgríquez Cabrillo and Bartolomé Ferrelo looking for a northwest passage. They touched Alta California at San Diego, passed Los Angeles Bay, slipped through the Santa Barbara Channel, rounded Point Conception, entered Monterey Bay, but missed the Golden Gate. While sailing as far north as Point Arena, other Spanish did not continue their probing, since none of the expeditions found riches.

Not until the development of the Manila galleon trade in the last half of the sixteenth century did even limited interest in California reappear. The paucity of concern in large part stemmed from the same factor that caused the great galleons to skirt the coast—the prevailing southerly wind and the Japan current, which sped vessels southward but sentenced them to difficult days of tacking when they beat a course northward.

It was the Manila galleon with its valuable cargo of specie and oriental goods that attracted Sir Francis Drake and sent him on the first English circumnavigation of the globe in 1577–80. After his successful attack on the galleon, Drake visited California and took possession of the future golden state in the name of Queen Elizabeth. Once he had repaired his ship, he headed across the Pacific and the treasure of the Orient. The English did not follow up on Drake's claim until the end of the eighteenth century, and the Spanish ignored the region until the time of the American Revolution. By then the Russians, employing an international group of sea captains, notably the Dane Vitus Bering, had laid a strong claim to Alaska and had begun to extend their control south to California.

Although Juan de Fuca may have reached Vancouver Island in 1592 and Sebastian Vizcaíno beat his way up the coast at least as far as Monterey ten years later, the first Spanish settlers did not arrive until 1769. They came overland, and one of the ironies of California history is that Gaspar de Portola discovered San Francisco Bay while searching the shore for a point to rendezvous with his supply vessels. Everyone before him, viewing the narrow and indistinct entrance from the sea, had missed it. In 1774 Juan Pérez explored the coast north of Monterey, entered Nootka Sound, and ran as far north as the Queen Charlotte Islands off modern British Columbia. The following year three Spanish expeditions scoured the California and Northwest coasts. Juan Manuel de Ayala took the *San Carlos* through the Golden Gate to make the initial seaborne arrival in San Francisco Bay; Juan Francisco de Bodega y Quadra pushed north to Alaska; and Bruno Heceta discovered the Columbia River. The Spanish kept their discoveries so secret that the river had to be rediscovered two decades later.

In 1776 Captain James Cook brought the English flag to the West Coast again, entering Nootka Sound but missing the strait of Juan de Fuca. Two years later Cook began his famed North Pacific voyage, which took him to Hawaii and into the Bering Strait, which he hoped would open into the Northwest Passage. Unfortunately, he turned back before realizing that the strait is indeed the western outlet of the passage. Other Englishmen and Spaniards probed the Northwest Coast in the area of Vancouver Island. The three expeditions of George Vancouver in 1792–94 traced the detail of the Strait of Juan de Fuca and Puget Sound.

While by 1525 the general outline of the east coast of the New World was clear to Europeans, that of the west had to await another two and a half centuries. Even after the preliminary reconnaissance had been completed much exploration was needed on both coasts before their details could be entered on charts. But enough was known to permit settlement.

4. Settlers Arrive

The first phase of the history of colonial North America ended about 1550 with the general examination of the East Coast completed and hope for the existence of a northwest passage through the continent nearly extinguished. Although a handful of Englishmen continued to search for an Arctic passage throughout the early seventeenth century, most other Europeans abandoned it.

The quest for the Northwest Passage lay behind the first English colonizing effort. Sir Humphrey Gilbert secured a patent for a colony that he planned to place at the mouth of the yet to be discovered Northwest Passage. He launched his search in 1583, taking possession of Newfoundland, only to be lost on the return voyage. The patent passed into the hands of his half brother Walter Raleigh. The latter abandoned the Northwest Passage concept and sent out an expedition that reported an attractive location on the quiet waters behind the outer islands of the North Carolina coast. Raleigh entrusted the initial settlement, 1585–86, to Ralph Lane. As it turned out, the site at Roanoke was poorly chosen for it had no nearby deepwater anchorage. Moreover, the settlers soon aroused the animosity of the local Indians and had to be evacuated by Sir Francis Drake, enroute home from a raid in the Caribbean.

In 1587 Raleigh sent out a second group under John White, who has left us excellent drawings of the Indians he encountered. Although the earlier colonists found Roanoke a poor location and Raleigh had directed settlement along the Chesapeake, the colonists reoccupied the old site. White returned to England to arrange for resupply, but before he could return the Spanish Armada sailed and all English attention turned towards that threat. Not until 1590 did a relief expedition depart, and by then it was too late. The colonists had disappeared, an early proof of the truism that in a maritime environment a settlement must have continuing contact with the outside world to survive.

While some of the expeditions sent out in search of the lost colony ventured into hitherto unknown regions, English interest in North America waned. After the turn of the seventeenth century, however, other Englishmen resumed the search of the coast, especially along that of northern New England.

The earliest was Bartholomew Gosnold. In 1602 he charted the coast of lower Maine and Massachusetts, including the islands of Buzzards Bay and assigned Cape Cod and Martha's Vineyard their names. The following year Martin Pring in the *Speedwell* studied the coast farther north and sailed up the Piscataqua River. Samuel de Champlain, operating from a base at the short-lived French settlement of St. Croix on the Maine-New Brunswick border, sketched the coast with great accuracy as far south as Cape Cod, an area covered in even greater detail by George Weymouth while searching for a possible site for an English Catholic refuge. These additions to the knowledge of the New England coast soon appeared on contemporary maps but attracted little popular attention. The English voyages, however, did excite interest in a group of London and Plymouth merchants who formed a trading-colonizing company that took the name of Raleigh's ill-fated settlement, Virginia.

The Virginia Company was a peculiarly seventeenth-century organization. It consisted of two separate companies operating under a single charter. One largely London-based group revived Raleigh's colonization project. It planted a settlement at Jamestown, Virginia, in 1607. Although it faced much the same problems as Raleigh's colony, Jamestown survived thanks to better leadership and an open supply line to the mother country. Despite its dependence upon its ability to ship produce to England, Virginia never developed a strong deepwater tradition. A singleminded concentration on tobacco permitted its trade to pass into other hands. Most of the cargo carriers that hauled the tobacco to market were English although, as time passed, vessels from the northern and middle colonies carried an increasing share. Most of the plantations established in the first century of Virginia's history lay along her 3,300 miles of tidal streams and navigable rivers. Those often busy waterways carried nearly all the produce grown and goods imported. The river orientation also explains why modern automobile-borne tourists approach the surviving James and Potomac River plantations from the rear.

The Virginians appreciated the value of the coastal trade and the threat that both the Dutch and French settlements farther north represented. In 1613 Thomas Argall in the *Treasurer* sailed to Mount Desert on the Maine coast to frustrate French efforts to plant a colony there. Shortly after the founding of Massachusetts Bay, a Virginia craft appeared to trade a cargo of corn, and within ten years a lively exchange developed between the two dissimilar British commonwealths. Even New Haven, which had only limited maritime aspirations, had a vessel trading with Virginia by 1635. Although the size of the exchange is difficult to estimate from the scanty surviving records we know that the intercolonial trade of Virginia contributed significantly to her early economic health.

The second Virginia Company group, the Plymouth Company, fastened its attention on New England. In 1607 the Plymouth investors dispatched a party under George Popham to Sagadahoc (modern Popham Beach) near the mouth of the Kennebec River in Maine. Under the direction of a London shipwright named Digby the hardy band constructed "a faire pinnace of thirty tons" which they christened *Virginia*. She is frequently called the first vessel built in the United States, which she was not. At least seven craft built by Spanish and French mariners along the southern coast antedated her. After one winter along the Maine coast the colonists fled, but the *Virginia* traded between the mother country and her namesake colony for another twenty years.

The two most common small craft employed by the early colonists both for trade and fishing were the pinnace and shallop. The shallop was a large ship's boat, usually 30 feet or less long, suitable for navigation in sheltered waters where it could be either sailed or rowed. Occasionally one would make a solo transatlantic crossing, but most did so as the tender to a larger vessel. Whenever possible the mother vessel carried her shallop either on deck or in the hold. If space or tackle to stow her on board was absent the shallop might be towed, although this often caused its loss in a storm. Some shallops were brought to the New World knocked down for assembly on arrival, like the one belonging to the *Mayflower*. Others, of course, were built from scratch ashore. Over the years the term came to signify any smaller open- or half-decked craft, irrespective of rig. The pinnace was a larger but still lightly built craft also used as a tender and coastal vessel. Like shallop, the term indicated size rather than rig.

While the English struggled to establish colonies in New England and maintain one in Virginia, the Dutch planted themselves in between. In 1609 Henry Hudson, an Englishman sailing for the Dutch East India Company in search of a Northeast Passage above Russia, ran into such ice that his crew refused to continue. He altered his course to America to make his landfall near Penobscot Bay. In late August he discovered Delaware Bay and on September 3 entered New York Bay. He spent ten days there before heading up the river that came to bear his name in hopes of finding in it a passage to the Orient. Hudson sailed his *Half Moon* to within a few miles of the present site of Albany. He sent boat expeditions farther upstream, but the freshwater and a shoaling river made it clear that this was not the passage he sought. On the other hand, Hudson had found a land of great trading potential, which his employers promptly exploited.

While Hudson sailed north on his fateful voyage into Hudson's Bay the Dutch sent out a second expedition. It acquired furs from the Indians along the Hudson River. Business developed so rapidly that in 1613 the Dutch established a post below Albany to handle that trade. Late that year one of their vessels burned off Manhattan Island, but the crew under Adraen Block built a 45-foot, 16-ton replacement, the "yacht" *Onrust*. During the spring of 1614 Block sailed her through the "Hellgat" to explore the north shore of Long Island Sound, enter the Connecticut and Thames rivers, sight Montauk Point, Block Island, and bestow the name Rood upon the chief island in Narraganset Bay. From there the Dutchman and his crew visited Nantucket and swept around the forearm of Cape Cod to touch at both Plymouth and Nahant before returning to Manhattan. The *Onrust,* on a second trip, without Block, ascended the Delaware River about as far as Philadelphia.

These trading and exploring successes caused the formation of the United New Netherland Company and in 1621 the Dutch West India Company. The latter held a monopoly of trade with South Africa, America, the West Indies, and the Far East. During the 1620s the Dutch planted trading settlements in New York Harbor, at Gloucester, New Jersey, on the Delaware, and at Albany on the Hudson River. In 1633 they pushed eastward to establish a trading post at Fort Good Hope (Hartford, Connecticut). New Amsterdam on Manhattan Island quickly became the trading center of the middle coast. Not only did it funnel the furs collected by the Hudson and Delaware River trades to Holland but it developed a sizable commerce with the surrounding English colonies. Shipbuilding continued sporadically, reaching a peak in 1631 with the construction of the *Nieuw Nederland,* a mammoth 600-ton* vessel that was the largest merchant craft built in North America for 150 years.

Meanwhile, mercantilistic-thinking Englishmen revived interest in New England. The colonies appeared to be potential sources for naval stores, timber, iron, potash, copper, and other raw materials; delicacies like oranges, lemons, spices, silk, and wines; and a market for English goods, although the latter would not be fully recognized until late in the century. The immediate cause of the revival was a 1614 voyage along the New England coast by John Smith, the former Virginia strong man. At Monhegan Island he found fishermen already in residence and the open ground there in use as flake yards. Fish were so plentiful that Smith's crew quickly caught and dried 40,000 and corned another 7,000. While some of his crew prepared the catch, Smith cruised the coast as far south as Cape Cod, making a careful chart that has given us such place names as Penobscot River, Massachusetts, New England, Charles River, Plymouth, and Cape Ann. After his return from the reconnaissance Smith loaded a chartered vessel with a cargo of fish for Spain, placed a second cargo for the English market in his own vessel, and headed for home. The six-month voyage cleared £1,500, an immense profit for that day.

While such successful fish shipments were not unique, the real impact of Smith's voyage grew out of the flowery testimonial that he wrote of the lands he had seen. It appeared in 1616 as *Description of New England,* one of the earliest land-development sales pitches for American real estate. The report prompted a series of New England settlements. One was that made in 1620 at Plymouth by the congregation of Separatists, known today as the Pilgrims. They had expected to settle within the lands of the London branch of the Virginia Company but found themselves brought instead to the area with the domains of the Plymouth faction. Whether the change of location was wrought by a corrupt ship captain or an

---

*The most commonly used formula for tonnage was: length on deck less ³/₅ of maximum beam × maximum beam × depth (or half of the maximum beam), the product being then divided by 94.

arrangement between the mariners, the leaders of the settlers, and the Plymouth group we do not know.

Plymouth, alone of the initial New England settlements, was not conceived as a maritime settlement although out of necessity it quickly developed such a capacity. The Pilgrims initially earned the money to repay the English capitalists who had financed their voyage through fishing but soon turned to fur trade with the Maine and Connecticut Indians as more lucrative. As early as 1624 Plymouth recruited a ship carpenter in England who built them a pair of shallops and a lighter. Three years later other enterprising Pilgrims built a pinnace on the shores of Buzzards Bay for the growing trade with the New Netherlands. That commerce grew so large that the colony considered digging a canal across Cape Cod. Although the canal proved to be beyond the capabilities of the Plymouth settlers, it attests to the volume of their coastal trade even in the first third of the seventeenth century.

Another apparent result of the Smith voyage was King James I's land grant of land between the middle New Jersey coast and Newfoundland along with a monopoly of offshore fishing to Sir Ferdinando Gorges and a group of associates known as the Council for New England. They promptly slapped a tax on all fish caught in their waters—which the fishermen, not surprisingly, refused to pay. Since there was no way for the Council for New England to enforce its levy, Parliament killed the monopoly.

By the start of the decade of the 1620s, a large number of fishermen sought cod in the waters of the Northeast coast. In the summer of 1622 thirty craft operated out of the island of Damariscove, Maine. Wintering-over settlements existed there and on Monhegan. As a rule fishermen did not winter on the mainland because of the danger from Indians, who had begun assaults on fishing craft that year. Although there were no settlements along the Maine coast between the Piscataqua and Penobscot Bay before 1620, permanent fishing stations with flake yards appeared in the next few years at the Isle of Shoals, Kittery Point, Saco, Stratton Island, Richmond Island, Sagadahoc, Damariscove, Pemaquid, New Harbor, Monhegan, St. George, and Matinicus. The largest of these—operated on Richmond's Island off Cape Elizabeth by John Winter—may have built vessels as early as 1630. During the 1620s a number of similar small settlements sprang up around Massachusetts Bay.

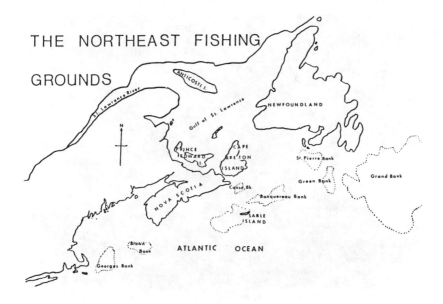

THE NORTHEAST FISHING GROUNDS

When John Smith visited outer Boston harbor he reported that French traders were already established and that the area received regular visits by Plymouth merchants bound to and from the small settlement at Salem. It remained for Miles Standish and the crew of a Plymouth shallop actually to enter the inner harbor in September 1621. Shortly afterwards a fishing station appeared on the south shore at Hull. In 1623 the first settlers gathered at Weymouth, Chelsea, Charlestown, and on the slopes of Beacon Hill on the Boston peninsula. That year saw the Dorchester Company establish a short-lived settlement on Cape Ann while the following year the Pilgrims added one at Gloucester. None of these posts was large although a new settlement at Salem in 1629 included half a dozen master shipbuilders.

Undoubtedly none of these hardy settlers was prepared for the invasion of their domains in 1630 by the 900 Puritans under John Winthrop who settled on the Boston peninsula and at Charlestown, Medford, Watertown, Roxbury, and Dorchester. That one movement, the largest that had yet occurred, changed the complexion of the coastal settlements. Within a year trade with Virginia began, and the first Dutch traders arrived from New

The reproduction of a seventeenth-century shallop designed by William
A. Baker for Plimoth Plantation. She represents the type of vessel upon
which the colonists relied for coastal trade and for inshore exploration.
Photograph courtesy of Plimoth Plantation

Amsterdam. Both exchanges grew, as did trade with Maryland. In
1634 Massachusetts imported 10,000 bushels of corn from Virginia, shipping fish south in return. The New Netherlands trade
was even greater. It reached such a value that in 1642 Massachusetts had to regulate the circulation of Dutch coins. Nor were the
other New England settlements slow in entering the intercolonial
trade. New Haven traded with Virginia as well as New Amsterdam.
The latter brought knowledge of the lucrative Delaware River fur
trade and set in motion an abortive attempt to tap the riches of that
area that nearly wrecked the economy of New Haven. Nevertheless, in none of the colonies did the intercolonial trade ever reach
the scale of that with Europe or the West Indies.

5. Establishing a Maritime-Based Economy

Although the natural wealth of the waters lapping at their landings
might seem to make it only natural for the Puritans to turn to the

sea, it was not. Most of them came from the cities or the farming areas, not coastal England. Many of the leaders were men of trade who thought in terms of commerce with the mother country and other colonies without realizing that the staple crops of New England swam close offshore and raised their towering green heads all around them. Moreover, geography dictated that much of the communication within the expanding Massachusetts Bay colony be by water since the eastern settlements scarcely reached thirty miles inland after a century, and most of the larger villages still crouched beside the sea or a tidal stream. It does not follow, however, that the maritime interests of the early settlers were restricted to salt water. Sometimes they wandered inland. The Pilgrim leaders of Plymouth directed that creeks and rivulets be bridged or provided with canoe ferries. As traffic developed, dugouts replaced the fragile canoes. Not only were the new craft larger but they were less likely to give their passengers the bath that they probably needed. In Massachusetts a ferry reportedly plied between Chelsea and Charlestown in 1631, and others appeared elsewhere as the need arose.

Although most Virginians traveled along, rather than across, their rivers, a ferry operated between Norfolk and Portsmouth in 1636. As settlements pushed inland the House of Burgesses encouraged the ferry service across the numerous unbridgeable streams of the Tidewater by exempting ferrymen from public or county levies, service in the militia, acting as constables, impressment, or highway work. But control of ferrymen, their fares, and their service came to be a curse to most governments while the quality of that service was consistently denounced by travelers.

As plantations expanded farther and farther inland along the banks of coastal streams, more and more produce moved to the ports by flatboats and other rough-hewn one-way craft. The flatboats were too ungainly to move upstream and too unhandy to be safe in unsheltered waters, but they drifted on the current very well. When the route faced current or when portages were necessary, the Indian canoe remained, as it would for two centuries more, the best vehicle. On long lake and river voyages the flat-bottomed bateau offered more economical transportation. It was widely used both by fur traders and the military.

Along the Connecticut River a different development took place. The settlers along its banks employed pole boats, 20–30 feet long, 3–5 feet wide, and 2–3 feet deep, that drew less than a foot when loaded with cargo and a 4- to 8-man crew. Like their larger cousins, which would appear two centuries later on the western rivers, they were propelled by a crewman planting a spike-tipped pole in the bottom and, with the pole braced solidly against his shoulder, walking to the stern, or by having the crew members thrust their poles into the bottom, in unison generally, one side at a time like a gang of canoe paddlers.

In the more settled areas canals occasionally overcame local transportation or navigation problems. During the midseventeenth century, Massachusetts workmen dug two small waterways, one at the head of tidal action on the Charles River at Watertown and a second connecting the Charles and the Neponset in Dedham. They may have been power canals; the record is not clear. We have already noted the early Pilgrim interest in a canal across Cape Cod. In 1690 William Penn proposed a more extensive work to connect the Schuylkill and Susquehanna rivers in Pennsylvania and actually had a route surveyed. The canal, however, waited until 1762 but even then proved too large an undertaking for the colony.

The exploitation of the great New England forests took three forms: (1) cutting of timber for fuel; (2) cutting of timber for lumber; and (3) shipbuilding. The first involved very little maritime activity until the trees in the immediate area of settlement became exhausted. That point arrived sooner than most modern readers might expect since the average household in colonial times consumed 30–60 cords of wood a year. Boston's 1,300 homes in 1689 would have consumed 14,000–15,000 trees in a year. When local sources gave out, hauling firewood became a very important coastal trade. In 1706 Gloucester had 30–50 sloops carrying wood to market. Trees also became houses, furniture, and containers. Since the West Indies sugar planters exhausted most of the native forests, or destroyed them to make way for cane fields, early in the seventeenth century the islands imported nearly all their barrels as well as their building timber. Both came almost exclusively from New England, the barrels being shipped disassembled as shooks.

It took no monumental insight to recognize that shipbuilding could contribute substantially to the economic health of the new settlements. In planning for the settlement of Massachusetts, Governor John Winthrop insisted that trained shipwrights form part of the initial group. He quickly put them to work fashioning a trading vessel. On July 4, 1631, the 30–40-ton bark *Blessing of the Bay* took to the waters of the Mystic River at Medford. In the next four years five other craft joined her, and by the end of the decade Boston, Dorchester, Scituate, and Salem as well as Plymouth; New Haven and New London in Connecticut; and Newport in Rhode Island had all constructed vessels. The Massachusetts authorities actively supported shipbuilding. In 1639 they exempted ship-wrights from military service and two years later the General Court passed legislation regulating the industry. In 1644 the ship-builders formed a guild with the full blessing of the colony.

Salem took the early lead in shipbuilding. Richard Hol-lingsworth built an extremely large (300-ton) ship there in 1641. At least four other substantial yards operated there between 1659 and 1677. One was that of William Stevens, an impractical perfec-tionist who before his transfer to the New World had acquired a reputation as the best builder in England. Boston became a major competitor after 1641. Between 1697 and 1702, the peacetime years between King William's and Queen Anne's wars, Boston yards turned out an average of 15 craft a year totaling 1,024 tons. The Merrimack River yards at Newbury and Haverhill entered pro-duction about 1670, the same year that those along the North River on the South Shore started operation. A century before inde-pendence Massachusetts boasted 30 craft between 50 and 100 tons and about 500 smaller ones. At the end of the seventeenth century Governor the Earl of Bellamont wrote: "I believe I may venture to say there are more good vessels belonging to the town of Boston than to all Scotland and Ireland, unless one should reckon the small craft, such as herring boats."

Once established, shipbuilding grew rapidly as an industry be-cause of the availability of large trees in the nearby forests. New England white oak, 3- to 8-feet thick at the butt, 60–80 feet tall, proved itself to be excellent building material. It was heavy but tough, elastic, and durable. In the early years builders often used only the heart of the tree while ignoring the outer, less durable parts. As white oak became scarcer during the years immediately preceding the Revolution, American builders turned to the more expensive but superior southern live oak. Yellow or pitch pine came into wider use in the eighteenth century, especially in the South, for planking. On the other hand, northern white pine was preferred for masts, spars, and deck planking.

The coastal trade sailed on craft no larger than a medium-sized modern yacht. Most were rigged as ketches or sloops, but during the eighteenth century newer rigs began to dominate. Schooners appeared early in the century, the earliest reported at Boston in 1716. Contrary to Gloucester folklore, the rig was not a 1713 invention of Captain Andrew Robinson. Two-masted, fore- and aft-rigged vessels existed much earlier. It may be that what was unique about Robinson's vessel was her hull lines rather than rig, although the concept was not unknown. Modern readers should remember that "schooner" during the eighteenth century almost always described what today we call a topsail schooner, i.e., one fitted with a square foretopsail.

Not only do schooners begin to appear during the eighteenth century but so does the hermaphrodite brig that in colonial usage indicated a brig fore and aft rigged on the main. The very similar brigantine set square main topsails. The two rigs are often confused, and not by modern writers alone. The eighteenth century also saw the appearance of the snow, a brig with her spanker set on a separate mast stepped immediately aft of the main much like the Spencer mast of the nineteenth century. Eighteenth-century owners built few three-masted vessels or ships. The ship rig normally was reserved for long-distance vessels, which needed a maximum driving power.

Colonial vessels were not only small but were quickly and cheaply put together. In 1700 American builders produced about 4,000 tons of shipping at approximately 60 percent of the cost of building in European yards. At the end of the colonial period, 1769–71, American yards averaged about 35,000 tons a year at prices around £3–4 per ton while British builders could not operate profitably below £5–7. As early as 1724 Thames shipwrights attempted unsuccessfully to limit importation of colonial-built craft. Their fear was real. British owners purchased so many vessels that at the outbreak of the Revolution 2,342 vessels, 30 percent of the British merchant marine, were American built. That in turn meant that approximately three-quarters of the commerce of the colonies was carried in vessels of their own construction.

Colonial vessels had a reputation in Britain for poor construction and rapid decay because of the general use of inadequately seasoned timbers. It is difficult to test the validity of the accusation. Apparently the colonial vessels lacked the finish of their English counterparts, but most British owners and builders also believed that English oak was both stronger and more durable than its American cousin. The 2,962 vessels passing through New York customs between 1715 and 1765 averaged 4.7 years in age with only 9.4 percent being over 10 years old. Although the figures show no significant age differentiation in average age between vessels built in different colonial regions, English vessels were older than the colonial ones. When archeologists have finished work on the Browns Ferry, South Carolina, vessel we will know much more about second-quarter eighteenth-century colonial American vessels.

One difficulty historians have in assessing the importance of shipbuilding in colonial times is a shortage of statistics, but the surviving information is at least indicative. It shows that after 1750 Virginia increased her construction until she ranked only behind New England in output. This presumably reflects the decline in accessibility of northern white oak stands and the shift to live oak even though it cost about 50 percent more to build at Norfolk than in New England. In 1769 the colonies produced 389 vessels, 276 of them schooners or sloops, with a tonnage of 20,001. The distribution of building among the colonies that year can be seen in table 1–1.

Table 1–1. Shipbuilding, 1769

Colony	No. of vessels	%	Tonnage	%
New Hampshire	45	11.5	2,452	12.2
Massachusetts	137	35.2	8,013	40.0
Rhode Island	39	10.0	1,428	7.1
Connecticut	50	12.8	1,542	7.7
New York	19	4.8	955	4.7
New Jersey	4	0.1	83	0.4
Pennsylvania	22	5.6	1,469	7.3
Maryland	20	5.1	1,344	6.7
Virginia	27	6.9	1,269	6.3
North Carolina	12	3.0	607	3.0
South Carolina	12	3.0	789	3.9
Georgia	2	0.5	50	0.2

Source: Winthrop L. Marvin, The American Merchant Marine (New York, 1902), 8.

Total tonnage rose in the succeeding years, but the proportions of colony of origin changed only slightly.

Shipbuilding consumed more wood than any other use except heating. Since a wooden ship required 400–500 board feet of lumber per ton, this means that in the late colonial era, when production averaged about 20,000 tons annually, shipbuilders used between 8 and 10 million board feet per year. This translates into 16,000–20,000 trees. It is not surprising that the industry exhausted local timber supplies and enterprising builders began to move away from the centers of population. Thomas Clark and Thomas Lake of Boston established a trading post and shipyard on the Kennebec River in Maine during the 1650s, but few other builders went that far afield for another century. By 1742, however, 40 square-rigged vessels had come down the ways at various points along the Maine coast.

The shipment of masts for the Royal Navy came to prominence in the eighteenth century. American white pine trees made good masts. While they were not as strong as Baltic firs, they were larger and could be fashioned into one-piece masts up to thirty inches in diameter. Although the first masts were exported to England in 1634 the Royal Navy did not adopt them until the Dutch War of 1652–54 cut off Baltic supplies. In 1685 the establishment of the post of surveyor of pines and timber marked the start of a campaign by the Crown to enforce its claim to the large pines for the future use of the Royal Navy. Although the Massachusetts Charter of 1691 reserved all trees two feet or more in diameter at a foot above the ground for the Crown and in 1711 Parliament extended the provisions to all the colonies north of New Jersey, the colonists showed less than veneration for the broad arrow that after 1729 marked the royal trees. In practice the prohibition was difficult to enforce since the number of inspectors was far too few to cover all the great forests of New England and New York.

Mast harvesting was a particularly profitable trade since a 33- to 36-inch mast sold for £95–115 and an exceptionally large one might be worth £1,600. The center of the trade was Portsmouth, New Hampshire, although masts were occasionally shipped from Virginia and from the Connecticut River valley in the seventeenth century. In 1670 Portsmouth shippers sent ten cargoes to Britain, and within thirty years the great trees had to be sought as far as twenty miles inland. Because of this denuding of the Piscataqua watershed and a bad forest fire in 1761, the center of mast shipment moved north to Falmouth (modern Portland), Maine, by 1772. That year the Maine port shipped 382 masts, 69 bowsprits, and 451 spars. Even the Casco Bay forests had limits, and by the outbreak of the Revolution the mast merchants were already moving eastward to the shores of the Kennebec and Penobscot rivers.

Another basic wood product employed in shipbuilding was tar. It had been one of the commodities that the Jamestown settlers were to produce, but the initial efforts to secure it from the Virginia forests failed. Very little, except for local consumption, was refined before 1704. A more concerted effort occured in 1709–10 when the British government settled a group of Palatine German refugees at Newburgh on the Hudson River and at the nearby Livingston Manor. Unfortunately, the refugees knew little about their new profession and were so bitterly unhappy over arrangements that the colony broke up within three years, having produced almost no tar.

In an effort to develop a source of naval stores outside the Baltic, Parliament in 1704 put a £4-per-ton bounty on tar or pitch exported to the mother country. This caused such a massive tapping of the southern pitch pine forests that by 1715 England drew 25,000 barrels, half her annual consumption, from the colonies. The shipments rose to an average of 61,000 barrels over the next nine years, but when the bounty was discontinued in 1725 so was production. Four years later, therefore, Parliament reenacted a £2 4s. to £4 bounty. By 1733 shipments were back up to 63,500 barrels. Although the bounties brought the cost of colonial-produced naval stores above those originating in the Baltic, most imperial leaders were satisfied since it ensured a British-controlled supply and aided the Empire's balance of trade.

Soon after settlement, the Massachusetts colonists opened trade with the West Indies. It developed rapidly. While to the New Englanders it offered a means of offsetting their unfavorable balance of trade with the mother country, to their southern trading partners it soon became a lifeline. The economics of plantation agriculture dictated that the West Indies planters concentrate their efforts on exportable crops to the exclusion of forestry and food production. Although the West Indies plantations initially grew cotton and tobacco, by the second quarter of the seventeenth century nearly all the islands switched to sugar.

We do not know when the first traders from the mainland colonies visited the sugar islands, but that trade was well established in 1640. That year eleven vessels left from New England ports with cargoes of lumber for the islands. Other products soon followed. Before long, fish and grain from New England and the middle colonies fed the slaves who worked the plantations while New England lumber built their shanties and formed barrels and hogsheads.

As early as 1676 Boston could claim to be "the mart town of the West Indies." It was the need to coin and record the bullion and currency that the trade garnered that provided the impulse for the establishment of a Massachusetts mint in 1652. Moreover, the efforts of British officials to enforce the prohibitions of the Navigation Acts and to collect the high duties imposed by them were nullified by the flagrant obstructions erected by the Boston merchants and the local authorities. Whether this created a tradition of ignoring disadvantageous regulations is a matter of dispute among historians, but it cannot have failed to have impact.

Although the trade with the British sugar islands continued throughout the colonial period, the French islands took on greater importance after 1713. The Peace of Utrecht in that year gave the English control of Newfoundland and Nova Scotia, the fishing

A View of the City of Boston the Capital of New England.

Boston's strong tie to the sea is evident in this 1759 engraving. The Massachusetts port was the largest city in English America. Official U.S. Navy Photograph

grounds off their coasts, and the flake yard sites along them. This allowed the New Englanders access to the most adventageously located combination of fish and drying yards yet available to them. In 1717 the French authorities threw open the ports of their islands to American shipping. There trade transmuted the salted fare into more sugar and molasses than the Yankee traders thought possible. Since the French sugar prices were appreciably lower than the British, the price of rum fell. In Massachusetts alone, sixty-three distilleries produced rum. In short order it replaced beer and cider as the favorite American beverage and supplanted French brandy as the staple trade article in the Guinea slave trade.

In order to protect the domestic brandy industry the French government halted the importation of rum and reexport of sugar. That brought the cost of sugar on the French islands down to about half of the British planters' price. As a result the Americans turned even more heavily to French sources for their sugar and molasses. In 1731, for instance, Boston imported enough French molasses to make 1,600,000 gallons of rum. The English sugar planters used their strong influence in Parliament to secure a new, prohibitively high tariff on the French products in 1733. The new rates, 9d. per gallon on rum, 6d. on molasses, and 5s. per hundredweight on sugar, were too high and never seriously enforced by the American customs officials. Moreover, the total sugar production of the British islands was only about an eighth of that consumed by the North American market.

Even during the French and Indian War the northern colonists continued to trade food to the French sugar growers for sugar not elsewhere available. As a part of the gradual tightening of economic controls that followed the war, the Sugar Act of 1764 forbade the importation of foreign rum and raised the duty on sugar to £1 7s. per hundredweight. Despite these changes the colonial trade with Martinique and the Môle-St.-Nicolas in Santo Domingo continued undiluted down to the Revolution.

As the seventeenth century progressed, trade tended to concentrate in a handful of ports: Boston, Newport, New York, Philadelphia, and Charleston. Moreover, New Hampshire, Connecticut, New Jersey, and Delaware maintained few craft, and most of those served local customers who needed contact with the major ports. Between the larger harbors regularly sailing traders spun a web of

interlocking trade connections—personal and commercial relations that served as the initial lines of communication during the
crisis that led to the American Revolution.

By 1698 Massachusetts registered 171 vessels averaging 49.4
tons. Those craft were twice the size of those hailing from elsewhere along the New England shore but small compared to the
125–150 tons of the English transatlantic traders. Moreover, although the actual size of colonial vessels increased during the next
century, Boston craft consistently averaged twice the size of other
American-owned traders. This suggests that Boston owned a substantial number of deepwater vessels. Surviving statistics indicate
that the ownership was widely scattered, although no one should
conclude that the colonists practiced economic democracy. By
1700 the Boston merchants were the wealthiest single economic
group in the colonies except for the Virginia and Maryland tobacco
planters, whose capital was absorbed in land and slaves.

Some conception of the volume of trade that those vessels
represented can be found in the customs house records. Between
June 1714 and June 1719 a total of 390 vessels cleared Boston for
other American ports and about the same number for Britain. Further evidence of the significance of the coastal trade to Boston
appears in the record of imports during a single week in 1741: 200
bushels of peas, 180 bushels of beans, 534 barrels of flour, 291
barrels of beef, 278 barrels of pork, and 79 barrels of rice.

Although Roger Williams's settlement at Providence grew into
a respectable town in size, the commercial power of Rhode Island
lay at Newport. Closer to the sea than Providence and with a harbor entrance free of shoals, Newport grew into one of the three
largest cities on the Atlantic coast in the years immediately preceding the Revolution. Its wharves stretched for a full mile, and its
customs house handled over 600 entrances and clearances a year,
200 of them for foreign voyages including those of a line sailing
regularly to London. In 1764 Rhode Island had 34 vessels engaged
in transatlantic trade, 150 sailing to the West Indies, and 352 engaged in coastal commerce. Most of Newport's wealth derived
from the West Indies and African trades and the port's leadership
as a rum-distilling center. The speculative nature of Newport's
trade helped attract the earliest organized Jewish community in
the colonies and gave rise to the first major American Jewish merchant, Aaron Lopez. If the early acceptance of Jews indicated the
laissez-faire cultural atmosphere of Newport, the port's activity
in the slave trade pushed that freedom to its ethical limits. Yet

Newport never shrank from its blackbirding role until after the Revolution.

Perhaps nowhere is the danger inherent in the sea-based economies of the early colonial period more dramatically evident than in the decline of New Haven. Never an economically strong entity, the Bible republic on Long Island Sound suffered a pair of nearly fatal blows. In 1646 Captain George Lamberton's "Great Shippe" disappeared on a voyage to England with a cargo of silver, hides, furs, and grain worth £5,000, which represented 20 percent of the colony's wealth. That voyage had been an attempt to recoup the devastating losses suffered in the abortive attempt to compete with the Dutch and Swedes for the fur trade of the Delaware River valley. The twin blows left New Haven so impoverished that it could not even send a representative to London in 1662 to argue the case against its absorption by Connecticut.

The growth of the maritime trade of the colonies south of Connecticut was less pronounced. New York's expansion was hobbled by its slow population growth and the trading restrictions imposed by both its Dutch and English overlords. The colony's primary exports of furs, cereals, provisions, animals, lumber, and whale oil found a restricted market in Britain. Yet when traders turned towards the West Indies they quickly felt the competition of the well-entrenched New England merchants. Even so, especially after 1685, the southern islands welcomed the flour, provisions, and lumber sent from the port at the mouth of the Hudson.

By the end of the century New York had established herself as the chief wheat-growing and -exporting colony, a position that she would soon share with Pennsylvania. Between 1678 and 1694 New York possessed a monopoly of flour bolting and breadstuff packing for the West Indies trade. During those years the population of New York City doubled, and 85 additional vessels joined the city's merchant fleet. After 1730 New York added an intercolonial trade in refined sugar. Even so, New York's intercolonial trade remained small well into the eighteenth century. New York had the good fortune to receive official assistance in building up its shipping. After 1715 all New York-built vessels, no matter where owned, were exempted from the colony's tonnage duties. Although it created little additional work for the colony's shipwrights, the legislation established a precedent for tax preferences.

Philadelphia's history differed. Although not settled until 1681, Penn's city almost immediately took to the water. A shipyard appeared within two years, and an export trade quickly developed. By the middle of the eighteenth century Pennsylvania sent wheat, flour, bread, corn, meat, butter, lumber, and iron to the West Indies in exchange for the standard colonial fare of rum, sugar, coin, and bills of exchange. Philadelphia also shipped provisions to Honduras in exchange for mahogany, lignum vitae, and logwood. Some of these tropic woods joined hides, rum, sugar, naval stores, copper, and iron as exports to England, but others can be found in the furniture crafted by Philadelphia master carpenters. Philadelphia vessels returned from Britain with manufactured goods and bond servants. Wheat, bread, and iron flowed to Lisbon, Madeira, and the Canaries in return for wines, oils, salt, Far Eastern goods, and coin. An interesting quadrangular trade sprang up with Rotterdam in which Philadelphia vessels ran down the coast to Charleston, South Carolina, to load rice for England and then skipped across the North Sea to Rotterdam to embark German immigrants who generally paid for their passage with 3–5 years of bound service.

In 1750 Philadelphia's 320 foreign trade arrivals overtook that of New York (302) but lagged far behind Boston's more than 562. Within another two decades Philadelphia had firmly established herself as the second port in the colonies. It is scarcely surprising, therefore, that when the Continental Congress in 1775 and 1776 decided to outfit a naval squadron it turned to the merchant fleet of the City of Brotherly Love for the bulk of those vessels. Nor is it surprising that in 1776 the Congress relied on Philadelphia shipyards for the largest group of the newly authorized frigates.

The tobacco colonies' early West Indies traffic flowed through Barbados as an exchange of foodstuff for sugar. That exchange remained small because both Virginia and Maryland concentrated on exporting tobacco and furs rather than foodstuff and forest products. Not until the eighteenth century did grain export to the West Indies give both colonies a significant second crop. Following the settlement of the valley of Virginia and the shift of many tidewater plantations, like George Washington's Mount Vernon, to grain production, Virginia moved into the forefront of wheat growing, and now somnambulant ports like Falmouth and Dumfrees became major grain-shipment points.

Although the Virginians and the Marylanders exported some produce in locally owned vessels, the bulk moved outward in craft having Old and New England hail ports. By 1770 the external trade of Virginia and Maryland, composed nearly exclusively of tobacco and grain, totaled about £600,000, or £6 per person, in the two colonies. This represented roughly three and a half times the per capita export average for the United States in 1914.

North Carolina, the third largest tobacco-growing colony, suffered from a shortage of deepwater ports capable of direct export. Therefore, nearly all of her trade had to move through middlemen. The Dutch in New Amsterdam handled the bulk of her trade. This was one of the reasons behind the Navigation Act of 1650. That law froze the Dutch out of the trade with the result that nearly all of it passed into New England hands or flowed south to the mercantile houses of Charleston.

In all the southern colonies a large proportion of the overseas trade loaded at the wharves of individual plantations since the larger establishments could fill the holds of one or two cargo carriers. On the other hand, because the plantations tended to be relatively self-sufficient they generated less local coastwise shipping than did northern farms. Trade with the northern colonies grew slowly since they produced little that the southerners needed. Even when the New Englanders offered a product desired by the plantation owners, like rum, it could frequently be imported as easily from the West Indies. Conversely, except for tobacco, the southern colonies produced little to attract northern buyers.

Throughout much of the colonial period the tobacco and rice colonies piled up favorable balances of trade. Virginia, for instance, in 1760–69 imported an average of £1,000 worth of sugar per year, a quarter of that much of molasses, and slightly less than £450 per year worth of rum. In the same period the colony's tobacco exports averaged £382,000 per year, and the overseas shipments of corn totaled £42,000, and that of wheat £23,000. In this period the Virginians imported almost no fish. To the limited degree that fish appeared on the plantation tables, or in slave huts, it was locally caught.

Statistical studies of colonial trade show that shuttle voyages consistently dominated sailings and that vessels seldom shifted among routes, apparently because of unfamiliarity with infrequently visited ports. This needs to be kept in mind because we have been bombarded since childhood with tales of the triangular trade. That mystical maritime economic activity had a hazy origin and at best only a limited importance south of Long Island Sound. Nevertheless, it contributed significantly to the economic health of New England. Its economic basis lay in the exclusion or heavy taxation in Britain of colonial fish, grains, and salted provisions. Some enterprising merchants therefore turned to "double trading" or following a triangular route in which New England grain, pork, fish, staves, and lumber flowed to the southern islands in exchange for sugar, molasses, cotton, and tropical woods. The new cargo could then be traded in Britain for staples and manufactured goods.

As shippers grew more sophisticated so did the triangular trade. Aaron Lopez favored shipping fish, grain, and lumber to Spain, Portugal, or Gibraltar; carrying Spanish textiles, citrus fruits, wine, and salt to the West Indies; and there exchanging part of the cargo for molasses for the return voyage to Newport. Best known, of course, was the rum to Africa, slaves to the West Indies, sugar to New England triangle. Other routes developed, two of the most common involving fish and lumber to the West Indies, sugar to Britain, and English goods back home to New England; or fish to an Iberian port, wine or specie to England, and manufactured goods back to New England. Innumerable variations existed that depended upon the ingenuity and contacts of the merchant and his captain.

6. Slaving

The least attractive area of colonial maritime activity, not only to modern Americans but also the earlier ones, was slave trading. Since the trade in later years was clandestine, it is difficult to locate reliable figures upon which to build a clear understanding of the role played by American merchants and mariners.

Slavery throughout most of the colonial period carried no strong opprobrium and appeared to many in the colonies to be the best answer to the chronic shortage of unskilled workers. The failure of the Spanish efforts to use Indian slaves on Hispaniola brought the first Negro slaves to the Americas at the start of the sixteenth century.

Although Negro slaves formed part of the population of many of the Spanish settlements within the present United States, the earliest slave traders to ply the coast were probably Dutch. It should be remembered, moreover, that even within the English colonies Negroes were not alone in being held in bondage. Indentured servants served in bond until they worked off the cost of their passage, and not all of them entered the arrangement willingly. Others were criminals bound to their masters for life. Nevertheless, it was only the Negroes who were legally placed in perpetual slavery, a custom initiated by Virginia in 1661 and adopted by other colonies later. The earliest recorded American slaver, the *Desire* of Salem, in 1638 transported seventeen Pequot Indians for sale in the West Indies. She returned with a partial cargo of Negro slaves.

The first identified American vessel to import slaves from Africa was the *Rainbow* in 1645. She brought back to Boston a pair who had been kidnapped rather than purchased. That so offended the Puritan officials' sense of propriety that they set them free and ultimately returned them home. Both British and colonial slave trade remained limited until after the chartering of the Royal African Company in 1672. Since the company had a monopoly of the trade on the African west coast English, colonial traders had either to buy slaves from the company, trade illegally, or secure their cargoes on the east coast. By 1698, however, it became clear that the Royal African Company could not supply the market, and the trade opened to all English vessels.

In 1713, after the Royal African Company secured the *asiento* (contract) to supply slaves to Spanish America, 40,000–100,000 persons a year made the Middle Passage from Africa to the West Indies. Most of the half who survived the crossing and the "seasoning" process in the West Indies went to the Spanish possessions and the sugar islands, but some came to the North American colonies. In 1700 the importation of slaves into the southern colonies totaled not more than 1,000. A quarter of a century later it approached 2,500, and that figure doubled after 1740. As the demands in the older tobacco-raising regions declined, other areas, notably the South Carolina rice and indigo plantations, absorbed ever greater numbers after 1764. To put the matter in a different perspective, the British North American colonies in 1714 contained 59,000 slaves; in 1764 approximately 298,000; while the census of 1790 counted 697,897.

Many of the slaves reaching the continental colonies arrived from the West Indies, but reliable statistics are lacking on the proportions of direct and indirect shipment. The available figures suggest that the proportion of direct importation from Africa increased rapidly during the eighteenth century, probably passing 50 percent between 1720 and 1750. The South Carolina rice and indigo planters, for instance, preferred Senegambian slaves who could survive better there and imported nearly 95 percent of their slaves directly. As far as its impact on the development of the country is concerned, whether or not slave shipments were direct or indirect had little effect. What had effect was the appearance of the slaves and the maritime industry that their movement created.

How large was the traffic? We have reports of as many as 100 vessels from Boston and Newport on the Middle Passage between Africa and the West Indies in the decade after 1698. We know that rum quickly supplanted French brandy as the staple of the slave trade in the Gold Coast after being introduced by Rhode Island shippers in 1723. One Rhode Island skipper complained in 1736 that there were 18 other craft trying to buy slaves in the same area in which he operated and that they had flooded the market with rum. Be that as it may, the demands of the African trade clearly helped develop the thriving rum industry of pre-Revolutionary Massachusetts and Rhode Island. Boston began the American blackbirding with assistance from Salem, Portsmouth, New London, Newport, and Bristol. By the eve of the Revolution, Newport was most active although nearly all Rhode Island shipping families participated. In 1770 the Rhode Islanders had 150 vessels working the slave routes.

Most colonial slave vessels, irrespective of home port, sailed the Middle Passage. Few plied regularly between the West Indies and the mainland colonies. The vast majority of slaves imported from the southern islands traveled on the regular traders sailing between the northern colonies and the Caribbean. While one freighter might carry as many as thirty slaves as her entire cargo, more commonly they embarked a smaller number as part of a mixed cargo.

Very little occurred before the Revolution to inhibit the slave trade. Rhode Island in 1708 taxed imported Negroes £3, using the proceeds for public works such as paving Newport's streets. The following year New York imposed a similar tax on Negroes arriving from ports outside Africa. That appears to have been, as one might suspect, an effort to strengthen direct trade rather than to inhibit the importation of slaves. The first colony to attempt to halt the trade was Pennsylvania, which in 1712 placed a prohibitive £20 duty on imported Negroes.

7. Navigation Acts and the American Revolution

Nowhere could the American of the Revolutionary period turn without being reminded of his proximity to the seas, lakes, and rivers. Much of his food came from or via the water; his exports found their markets by water; manufactured goods usually reached him by water; and if he invested he probably invested in a business or trade that involved use of the seas. Moreover, the odds favored our hypothetical American having reached the New World by water. Maritime problems, in turn, would help drive that American to seek the uncertain security of independence.

It has been argued that the colonial policy of England throughout the century and a half before the Revolution was shaped by the exigencies of her conflicts with continental powers. In this view her restrictions on trade were efforts to strengthen her own commerce and deal a blow to that of the Dutch and French. This is a partial explanation since it overlooks the role of mercantilism in English thought. The mercantilists, especially in the eighteenth century, preached that colonies existed to provide raw materials and markets. It is quite evident from even a cursory study of the Navigation Acts, which controlled the trade of the British Empire that strengthening of the mother country's economy was the dominant element, with the channeling of the trade of the colonies into British-flag vessels a secondary object.

The earliest controls were those in 1621 forbidding the export of tobacco except to British ports. This was simply an effort to prevent Virginia tobacco from finding a market on the Continent without first passing through the hands of English processors and tax collectors. Twenty years later Parliament halted imports of whale products from the colonies in a clear effort to protect the ailing English whaling industry. The effect was small. Very few colonists caught whales except for local use until after repeal. In 1651 Parliament limited trade between the colonies or between the colonies and England to vessels whose owners, master, and a majority of the crew were English or colonial citizens. It also forbade entrance into England, Ireland, or the colonies of European goods on third-country vessels. This was the first Navigation Act to have a lasting effect, and that was positive. It preserved the colonial trades for English and colonial vessels.

The crew requirements increased to three-quarters English in 1660. The same legislation established an enumerated list of articles that could be sold only on the English market: sugar, tobacco, cotton, ginger, indigo, as well as fustic and other dye woods. While the regulation denied foreign markets to the producers of those products, it guaranteed them no foreign competition in England. Three years later Parliament added the proviso that with

Although most colonial trading vessels were small, an occasional large craft was built. The ship *Bethel* of Boston, shown here as a 14-gun letter of marque in 1748, is a good example of the latter. Courtesy of U.S. Naval Historical Center

certain exceptions goods bound for the colonies had to move on English- or colonial-built vessels. The exceptions are interesting and noteworthy: salt for drying fish; wine from the Azores and Madeira, which had a special market in America; as well as provisions, servants, and horses from Scotland and Ireland, whose shippers lacked the full benefit accorded their English competitors. Since enforcement of the new law rested in the hands of "naval officers" appointed by the colonial governors, local pressures ensured that interference with trade was minimal.

An 1673 law placing duties on intercolonial trade in enumerated goods had greater impact. As Governor Thomas Dongan of New York complained, the law kept his colony from serving as the collection point for tobacco grown in Delaware. It kept Boston, New York, and Philadelphia out of the Virginia tobacco trade as well as the West Indies-to-England sugar traffic. The lack of protest from the Americans, however, suggests that few vessels actually participated in those trades.

As the prohibitions took on greater importance, smuggling became a way of life for many American merchants. Much of Boston's trade between 1660 and 1675 was smuggling. This led to the famed struggle between the Massachusetts authorities and Edward Randolph, the Collector and Surveyor of Customs in New England. The colonists' flagrant obstruction of the royal official in his duties contributed directly to the annulling of the colony's charter in 1686.

Two years after the charter was lifted, HMS *Rose* appeared off Boston to stop illegal trade. She was so successful that the town suffered a recession. As soon as the man-of-war left, the Boston merchants returned to their old ways. So widespread was the evasion of the Navigation Acts that when the Earl of Bellamont reached the Bay Colony as governor in 1699 he reported that he could not enforce them. Since the Navigation Laws were seldom enforced they had only minimal influence on the colonists except to guarantee them a market for a limited number of products. Until about 1750 the Navigation Acts were probably advantageous to the Americans. Thereafter, British manufacturers increasingly dumped their surplus manufactured goods on the colonists while isolating themselves from colonial competition by heavy duties.

Most of the legislation enacted during the first half of the eighteenth century merely enlarged the number of enumerated articles. In 1705 rice, molasses, and naval stores joined the restricted list, followed in 1721 by beaver skins, furs, and copper. Only the fur trade provisions caused substantial changes in colonial trade patterns. Prior to the passage of the law 30–40 percent of New York's furs passed directly to the European market, yet the shift to the London fur market appears to have caused little hardship.

The approach began to veer in 1733 on the passage of the ill-conceived Molasses Act. It placed an uncollectable 9d. per gallon duty on rum and other spirits; 6d. per gallon on molasses; and 5s. per hundredweight on sugar imported into the colonies from the non-British Caribbean islands. The first provision was designed to protect the market of the West Indies distillers and the second was an attempt by the sugar planters to freeze their competition out of the North American trade. Yet their plantations did not have sufficient output to supply both the American and British markets. The utter foolhardiness of the law removed much of the taint of illegitimacy from its violation and gave smuggling a respectability in the rum-producing areas. Therefore, when revenue cutters began to appear in American waters in 1763 the opposition was nearly universal. In an attempt to overcome that resistance the British authorities in 1764 empowered Royal Navy officers to serve as customs officials, but the project foundered on naval opposition and lack of experience.

At the conclusion of the French and Indian War Britain sought new sources of revenue to support the large army that she, for the first time, had to maintain in America. The first of the new specifically revenue-raising laws to pass Parliament was the American Revenue or Sugar Act. It reduced the duty on foreign-refined molasses to 3d. per gallon but raised that on foreign sugar; and added iron, hides, whale fins, raw silk, potash, and pearl ash to the enumerated list. Despite stricter enforcement of the reduced tariff on molasses, the colonists continued their traditional trading patterns. Among the subterfuges commonly resorted to were "Anguilla clearances." That 36-square-mile island produced only about one cargo of molasses per year but its corrupt governor happily sold clearance papers certifying that the sugar or molasses covered came from the island. In practice the law was unenforceable, and the public's attention soon shifted to the Stamp Act.

The most effective opposition to the Stamp Act came not from Samuel Adams and the Boston mob or other harassment of the stamp sellers but from the merchants of Boston, New York, and Philadelphia who agreed not to import British goods after mid-1765. That threatened loss of trade, following a 13.6 percent drop between 1764 and 1765, furnished the fuel for the British exporters who secured repeal of the obnoxious act. When the British government turned from direct to indirect taxation, which seemed to be what the colonists wished, in the Townshend Duties of 1767, the Americans revived nonimportation. But they did so with less alacrity or pleasure than before. The Philadelphia traders, for instance, refused to participate until 1769. While exports to the colonies fell from £2,157,218 in 1768 to £1,336,122 the following year the development of new markets in Europe cushioned the effect in England. In America, however, the confrontation grew warmer in 1768, when Boston customs officials seized John Hancock's sloop *Liberty* for smuggling wine from Madeira among other derelictions. The Bostonians responded with such a wave of rioting that British troops had to be called down from Halifax to protect the customs officials.

Although some merchants sought the relaxation of the new restrictions on trade and played a leading role in the colonial resistance during the early stages of the events leading to the Revolution, they lost influence after 1769. When the radical wing gained control of the colonial protest movement that year, it cleaved the merchants into two groups. One segment allied itself with the radicals in an effort to moderate or soften the movement; others, especially after the first Continental Congress, moved towards Loyalism.

When the British government cut back the duties to a token one on tea in 1770, it broke the back of the nonimportation movement but did not drop the price of tea below that smuggled from Holland. This helped set the stage for the destruction of the tea brought to Boston in the Nantucket whaler *Dartmouth* three years later, which resulted in the closing of the port of Boston. The American response in 1774 was a revival of nonimportation and a boycott of British goods. In late 1775 they added an embargo on exports to Britain, Ireland, and the West Indies. That economic campaign was generally in effect throughout the colonies by the spring of 1775, but the extralegal political activities that this entailed divided the commercial community still further. It also set the stage for the initial maritime actions of the Revolution: the May 5 capture of the Royal sloop *Falcon* off New Bedford, Massachusetts, and the better-known June 12 seizure of the *Margaretta* by the lumberjacks of Machias, Maine.

It was altogether fitting that some of the earliest shots of the American Revolution occurred on water for the Americans of 1775 still lived in a water environment and were being pushed towards independence by pressures whose origins were in large part maritime. No single cause exists for the decision to break the bands that tied America to Britain, but the independence encouraged by life at sea, the restrictions of the Navigation Acts, and the self-confidence of Yankee seamen, shipbuilders, and traders played major roles.

Chapter Two

A NEW MARITIME POWER SETS SAIL

INDEPENDENCE CREATED NEW OPPORTUNITIES AND NEW PROBLEMS FOR maritime America. The limitations of the Navigation Acts no longer shackled the overseas traders; the slowly developing bonds between the states opened possibilities of ever greater trade; and the breaching of the Appalachian barrier called for new water-borne trade routes from the West. Yet the new nation still lacked the strength and the national acceptance to derive full benefits from these opportunities. It was too parochial to move smoothly into interstate trade and had yet to develop the technologies to flatten the Appalachian barrier.

Nevertheless, the new American republic arrived upon the political scene at a propitious moment. Despite its weaknesses and a faltering government prior to 1789 the United States faced only limited foreign political and economic threats. Britain and France were too exhausted or too concerned with domestic problems to offer more than theoretical danger to the new nation; Spain had a stronger and more active hostility, but her capabilities were too limited for her to pose a serious threat. After 1791 Europe's nearly quarter century of constant internal struggle precluded any serious effort to curtail the American experiment until the new nation grew strong enough to withstand it. Conversely, the political, economic, and intellectual climate into which the United States thrust her star-sprinkled flag served to hasten her growth. The industrial revolution marked its start with James Watt's 1776 steam engine just as the American Revolution freed the innovative talents of the new nation. The twenty-five years of war that disrupted the European economic system created great opportunities for the American deepwater merchant marine. It ensured the start of American industrialization and hastened the growth of the coastal trade. Moreover, the shipping boom of the wars of the French Revolution and of Napoleon laid the foundation for the maritime renaissance that would follow.

1. Maritime Influences on the Constitution

Along with independence the United States acquired massive problems. The Revolution had been fought under the cooperative, loosely woven Articles of Confederation, which placed the direction of national affairs in the national government and the power in the states. Lacking money, strength, or other means of persuasion, the central government exercised minimal influence on events. It could neither curb the destruction of its currency by inflation nor prevent the near ruination of the nation's economy by the dumping of British goods on the American market. Furthermore, Americans could not secure the restoration of their prewar trading rights in the British West Indies. Nor could the Continental Congress negotiate the removal of the Spanish restrictions on the utilization of the Mississippi River. Yet the untrammeled use of the waterway was critical to the development of the area beyond the Appalachians. Moreover, the Congress could not force Great Britain to withdraw her troops from those posts on American soil south of the Great Lakes that dominated the trade routes of the region. Moreover, in default of treaty arrangements American deepwater trade moved at the whim of local potentates, whether Barbary deys, British colonial governors, or Chinese mandarins.

As soon as peace arrived in 1783 American merchants dispatched vessels to foreign ports. The first vessel flying the Stars and Stripes to reach England ironically came from the war-devastated fleet of Nantucket. On February 6, 1783, the *Bedford* arrived at London. There her captain found, as those who followed him would, that while the British were glad to welcome him the lack of a commercial treaty left American goods at the mercy of British navigation acts and customs officials. This restricted the quantity of American goods flowing into English markets although the tobacco-growing states rapidly regained their trade. Virginia reached her prewar level of exports of 1786, a year in which Massachusetts could claim but 25 percent of hers. If this was not discouraging enough, British shippers sent large cargoes of consumer items to their former colonies. The long-missed goods and current geegaws absorbed the small supply of hard money and threw the whole American economy into near panic. The American minister in London, John Adams, sought to correct the trade imbalance through a commercial treaty but could not do so in part because the central government simply could not ensure its observance by the states.

The individual states demonstrated their independence by enacting tariffs that applied both to foreign goods and frequently to those from neighboring commonwealths. When Massachusetts and Rhode Island responded to the British dumping by placing prohibitive duties on goods arriving in British vessels and forbidding them export cargoes, Connecticut seized the opportunity to increase her overseas trade and admitted the goods duty free. Other states encouraged domestic industries and attempted to conserve coin by taxing goods originating in other states. New York sought to seize the trade of Connecticut and New Jersey by heavily taxing all non-New York vessels arriving from their ports. Delaware and New Jersey, on the other hand, attempted to entice trade away from Philadelphia by offering lower duties.

As early as 1784 the inability of the central government to regulate foreign trade was recognized as a major problem for the new nation, but it took three years for the states to agree to a convention to discuss the necessary changes. The immediate, direct cause for the calling of the Philadelphia Convention was a pair of meetings in 1785 and 1786. The first, at Alexandria and Mount Vernon, settled jurisdictional disputes between Virginia and Maryland over navigation on the Potomac. It issued a call for a general convention of all the states at Annapolis, Maryland, to study the whole question of interstate commercial relations. That second conference concluded that nothing could be solved by merely revising the Articles of Confederation.

The Constitution so carefully drafted at the Philadelphia Convention reflected both the experience of the country since independence and the strong commercial bias of its authors. The debilitating restrictions on trade vanished with the elimination of interstate barriers and the establishment of a single national set of port duties and tariffs. Not only did the new document give primacy to the central government in dealings with foreign powers, it made the agreements reached superior to the legislation of the states.

One of the events influencing the decisions at Philadelphia was tied directly to the question of western navigation rights on the Mississippi. During long negotiations in 1785–86 Secretary for Foreign Affairs John Jay could not secure Spanish agreement to open the Mississippi to American trade. By giving up that right he got Spain to open her homeland ports. The seven states without western lands were agreeable to the arrangement, but Jay could not gain the concurrence of the two-thirds required by the Articles of Confederation. The emotions raised by Jay's proposal played a major role in the decision at the Constitutional Convention to require a two-thirds majority to ratify a treaty.

2. Seeking New Markets

The earliest substantive legislation passed by the new government was the July 4, 1789, tariff. It instituted discriminating duties that reduced the tariff paid for goods arriving in American craft by 10 percent or more. The law required domestic construction for American ship registry. Within a month a second law established standard tonnage duties for vessels entering American ports. United States-built and -owned craft paid six cents per ton; American-built but foreign-owned craft paid five times that while foreign-owned vessels of foreign origin paid fifty cents per ton. Although foreign vessels were not excluded from the coastal trade until 1817, their participation was discouraged by the stipulation that domestic craft paid the tonnage duty annually while foreign vessels paid upon each entry.

As early as 1795 the combination of foreign complications and the American protective measures placed 92 percent of all imports and 86 percent of the exports on American-flag vessels. Another indication of the immediate impact on the maritime industry of the new conditions can be seen in the growth of the fleet hailing from Salem, Massachusetts. In 1791 the town residents owned 9,031 tons of vessels, which grew to 24,682 in 1800 and 43,570 in 1807. Before his death in 1799 the leading Salem shipowner, Elias Hasket Derby, owned in full or in part at least forty vessels and cleared as much as $100,000 on a single voyage. At his death his estate was valued at over $1 million, the largest in the country. A second major Salem trader, William Gray, owned at least 113 vessels before 1815 and was reputedly worth $3 million when he left Salem in 1809 for Boston. Salem was not unique.

The explosion of the American seaborne trade resulted only in small part from the reopening of the pre-Revolutionary routes. Most of the growth sprang from expansion into new regions. In 1784, for instance, both Derby and George Cabot of Beverly, Massachusetts, initiated exchanges with the Baltic ports. Although fifty New York and Massachusetts vessels visited Baltic ports in 1808 and Russia became nearly the sole source of America's hemp, a major trade never developed. The American inability to capture the Baltic trade reflected low Scandinavian shipbuilding costs, which offset the price advantage normally held by the Yankees over their European competitors.

An unlikely trade, centering on Mauritius, developed in the Indian Ocean. The French island served as a base for a hardy group of privateers who preyed upon British merchantmen plying between India and the exotic ports around the periphery of the Indian Ocean. During the three years between 1796 and 1798 an average of forty vessels from the United States called at the island. Usually they exchanged specie for coffee, sugar, spices, and tea. The trade reached its peak in 1806 and died in 1815, when the return of tranquility to the Indian Ocean eliminated prey for the island's privateers. Direct trade with India, although pioneered by the Philadelphia ship *United States* in 1784, was handicapped by the onset of the War of 1812.

More important in the long run was the China trade. Prior to the Revolution, American trade with China had been virtually impossible because of the monopoly held by the East India Company. The earliest effort to initiate an exchange with Canton, the sole Chinese port open to westerners, came in 1783. That year the 55-ton Hingham, Massachusetts, sloop *Harriet* sailed for the Orient with a cargo of ginseng. At the Cape of Good Hope the East India Company's agent persuaded her captain to exchange his cargo for tea.

The following year a group of Philadelphia and New York merchants fitted out the ship *Empress of China,* which returned from Canton in 1785 with a cargo that yielded a 25 percent profit. That demonstrated the potential of the trade, and other New Yorkers, Philadelphians, and Yankees followed. Philadelphia sent her first vessel in 1785. Elias Hasket Derby dispatched his *Grand Turk,* the first from Salem, the following year. She was the vanguard of a large contingent of Salem traders that moved into the trade. Of the fifteen American vessels reaching Canton in 1789 one-third hailed from Salem, not a bad showing for the sixth largest city in the country.

The Canton trade helped place American foreign trade on a paying basis and set the scene for the fabled China trade of the nineteenth century. The basic commodity that American traders brought back to the United States was tea. Porcelains, silks, and special cottons like nankeens had secondary importance. Finding trade goods attractive to the Chinese taxed the ingenuity of American merchants. Goods manufactured by the "Flowery Flag Devils," as the Americans were known, were too crude before 1812 to appeal to Oriental purchasers. Moreover, the United States produced few natural products that had a market in China. Almost alone was the ginseng root from which the Chinese made a tonic believed to improve potency. American merchants trading with China, therefore, either had to devise a profitable triangular trade or buy European goods for reexport.

Local differences soon developed. Boston shippers tended to send their vessels out by way of Cape Horn with stops in South America, the Pacific Northwest, or in the Pacific islands to trade for the seal, sea otter, and other skins or the sandalwood that commanded a premium on the Canton market. Salem vessels, on the other hand, generally sailed via Madeira, Mauritius, India, the East Indies, and the Philippines to trade for wines, cottons, opium, and spices. Since the voyage through the southern waters improved the flavor of the wine, most vessels stopping at Madeira also laid in a few pipes for home consumption. Most of the remaining Madeira went to Calcutta, where the Derbys developed a particularly profitable trade for cottons. It was from Calcutta, too, that Captain Jacob Crowninshield in 1796 imported the first elephant to reach the United Sates.

The Russians and Spanish had discovered that the sea otters of the Pacific Northwest commanded a premium on the Chinese market. Despite the efforts of John Ledyard, an American who had accompanied Captain James Cook on his last expedition, American merchants showed little interest until 1787. Then a group of Boston investors outfitted a pair of craft, the ship *Columbia* and the sloop *Lady Washington,* to trade for sea otter skins with the Indians of the Northwest. The *Columbia* under Captain Robert Gray carried the skins collected to Canton and returned home in 1790 to complete the first American circumnavigation of the globe. Although the enterprise proved less profitable than had been expected, it did demonstrate that the trade was feasible. Five other vessels followed the *Columbia*'s trace within a year of her return. On a second expedition in 1792 Gray in the *Columbia* discovered the river that bears her name and laid a strong American claim to the Northwest coast. The sea otter trade became such a Boston monopoly that the generic term for white men among the northwestern Indians was "Boston man."

The most serious challenge faced by the Bostonians in the years before the War of 1812 came from John Jacob Astor. About 1800 he made a $55,000 profit on an experimental fur shipment to Canton. That led him to devise a scheme to dominate both the fur trade in North America and its sales in China. He concluded that a shipping point on the West Coast, drawing its furs from the Rocky Mountains, would allow him to undersell the East India Company at Canton. Since the British monopoly had to buy its furs from the Hudson Bay Company, Astor reasoned that his cheap furs would gain him a monopoly of the Chinese market and force the Hudson Bay Company into bankruptcy. Then his American Fur Company could acquire its chief competitor at a bargain price.

As a first step in the campaign, Captain Jonathan Thorn in the *Tonquin* established a post at Astoria at the mouth of the Columbia River during 1811. Before it could be tested, Astor's great plan collapsed. The outbreak of the War of 1812 forced Astoria's sale to the Northwest Fur Company of Montreal. Astor continued active in the China trade after the war but with a new cargo, sandalwood. By the end of the eighteenth century the sandalwood forests of India, Java, Timor, and Malabar were badly depleted. This threatened cultural disaster throughout much of the Far East since Buddhists used sandalwood for incense and joss sticks; Hindus used it in the paste for caste marks; and sandalwood oil could be distilled from the shavings. In 1791 Captain John Kendrick discovered the trees growing on the island of Kauai. His report brought other Bostonians to Hawaii seeking supplies and cargoes of sandalwood. The latter they discovered could be secured cheaply since it had no special value to the Hawaiians. In 1812 Jonathan and Nathan Winship and William H. Davis secured a monopoly of the sandalwood trade from King Kamehameha I but lost it the next year. Following the War of 1812 control of the sandalwood forests passed from the king to local chieftains who rapidly denuded the island although demand declined after 1827 as the Canton market became glutted and new East Indian sources appeared.

Even more profitable was a trade dominated by Salem merchants. In 1793 Captain Jonathan Carnes discovered that wild pepper grew on the north coast of Sumatra. Four years later he brought the first bulk pepper cargo to the United States in the schooner *Rajah*. The voyage cleared a 700 percent profit. In 1802 imports reached 1 million pounds and three years later passed 7.5 million, which was over seven-eighths of the northern Sumatra crop. Although the volume of pepper imports declined after the War of 1812 the trade remained the backbone of Salem's commerce for fifty years.

Another of Salem's unique trades was that with Mocha on the Arabian coast. Captain Joseph Ropes in the *Recovery* first visited the port in 1798 to secure the initial shipment of coffee. Three years later he brought a full cargo of the bean back to Salem. By 1805 the trade reached 2 million pounds per year but declined after 1809 as Salem shippers faced growing competition from Brazilian coffee imported by Philadelphia and Baltimore traders.

In 1796 Derby's ship *Astrea* pioneered the Manila trade, but it grew slowly because of the resistance of ropemakers to using Philippine hemp. The following year Captain W. R. Stewart took the *Eliza* of New York into Nagasaki with a cargo of Dutch trade goods. In the next twelve years the Dutch chartered seven other American vessels for the run from Batavia to Nagasaki because they feared seizure of their own craft by British cruisers. A pair of American skippers also attempted to open trade on their own. Stewart returned to Nagasaki in the *Eliza* during 1803, but the Japanese would not deal with him or with Captain John Derby of Salem, who tried to open a new market for opium.

Boston took the lead in the California trade. Initially the scattered settlements there appealed to the East Coast traders only as stopping places enroute to the sea otter grounds of the Northwest Coast. As it became better known, the California coast was recognized as a source of sea otters and then developed into a major supplier of hides and tallow. The earliest American vessel to grace California waters, the *Otter,* visited Monterey in 1796. Seven years later the *Lelia Bird,* the initial otter hunter, put into San Diego. Even so, before 1812 the American portion of California's trade never matched the growing Russian presence.

On July 25, 1785, the Boston schooner *Maria* gained the dubious distinction of being the first American craft seized by Algerian warcraft in the Mediterranean. The threat from the Barbary States, long recognized by American leaders, was now a reality. Although that danger would not be erased until after the War of 1812, the maintenance of a naval squadron in the Mediterranean after 1801 eased the danger. The Napoleonic Wars inhibited trade, but some American merchants still gambled on voyages to the eastern Mediterranean as well as to French, Spanish, and Italian ports. The first American vessel visited Constantinople in 1786, and J. and T. H. Perkins of Boston established an office in Smyrna, Turkey, in 1795. It purchased opium for the Canton market, the leading cargo of American vessels in the eastern Mediterranean trade. Despite legal impediments raised by the Turks and competition from French merchants, American purchasers by 1828 were buying nearly the entire Turkish production.

Particularly notable is the youth of some of the eighteenth- and early nineteenth-century shipmasters. Nathaniel Silsbee of Salem went to sea at fourteen and commanded his first vessel at nineteen. On his first voyage as master he took the ship *Benjamin* to the East Indies with a pair of twenty-year-old mates. George Cabot also held his first command at twenty, and Stephen Higginson was but a year older when he assumed his first command. New England shipowners often sent their children to sea either before the mast or as ships clerks for a few years' seasoning before promoting them to masters or bringing them into the counting house. As a result, nearly all of the early New England merchants had a first-hand knowledge of the sea. That was less true in the ports to the southward although many, if not most, New York, Philadelphia, and Baltimore traders served an apprenticeship at sea. That training was less common in the new generation that came to dominate the shipping industry after the War of 1812.

In the years between the Revolution and the War of 1812 seafaring was a well-regarded profession that attracted respectable men both before the mast and onto the quarterdeck. Sailors commonly received three times the pay of comparable laborers ashore, although the situation varied somewhat from port to port. One reads little of labor strife in American ports before 1812. Whether that resulted from selective reporting or from labor peace is uncertain. Conditions of service depended upon the owner and master, since the Maritime Act of 1790 followed British practice, which made the latter the absolute ruler over a seaman once he signed the shipping articles. The United States, however, did concern itself about the well-being of sick and disabled sailors. In 1798 Congress imposed a twenty cents per month tax on all mariners to create a fund for their temporary relief. Although collections were haphazard, sufficient money had been raised by 1861 to build twenty-seven marine hospitals.

American vessels maintained a competitive advantage throughout the federal period. Until the mid-1790s American operating costs were lower than those of Europe largely because of the low price of American construction. American shipyard charges remained below European, except for Scandanavian-built craft, until about 1830 because of the proximity of the stands of shipbuilding timber and the paucity of orders for vessels above 400 tons or 100 feet in length. Below that size American builders could turn out inexpensive hulls carrying moderate sail plans that required small crews and kept operating costs low.

Despite their vaunted reputation as craftsmen, American builders could produce poor products if given the chance. The classic example was the large 600-ton trader *Massachusetts,* built at Quincy in 1789 for the China trade. Her builders, seeking to cut costs, used unseasoned white oak that soon deteriorated. In addition her owners shipped a cargo of masts and spars that were stowed while still wet. Once she sailed into the tropics this cargo rotted, as did several hundred barrels of beef. By the time the *Massachusetts* reached Canton she was so decayed that she had to be sold.

If the *Massachusetts* was an unusually striking example of a poorly built vessel, others had amazing careers. Stephen Girard's 1803 Baltic trader *Rousseau* lasted until 1893, spending her last years as a New Bedford whaler. The ship *Rebecca Sims,* an 1807 Kensington, Pennsylvania, product, made a hundred transatlantic voyages before starting a second career as a whaler. She circumnavigated the globe eleven times before depositing her bones on the approaches to Charleston, South Carolina, as one of the 1862 Stone Fleet.

Partially as a result of the experience with the *Massachusetts,* New England builders turned only reluctantly to large vessels. As late as 1830 many Massachusetts mariners believed that no vessel over 500 tons was safe. Practicality, not superstition, governed the Yankee shipowners, however. They purchased smaller craft because of the inability of many trades to support larger vessels and the limited capital to pay for them.

Navigation changed slowly. The first truly American contribution was the development of a reflecting quadrant by Philadelphian Thomas Godfrey in 1731 simultaneously with, but independently of, John Hadley in London. Over the next twenty-five years Godfrey's instrument evolved into the modern sextant, which gave the mariner his first practical means of taking accurate sights from the moving deck of his vessel. The development was an outgrowth of a new method of navigation that involved lunars, the distance between the moon and a known fixed star. It allowed a mariner, if he was skillful enough as a mathematician, to use the tables in the *Nautical Almanac* first published in 1767, to calculate his position. Few navigators were that good and most, therefore, relied on dead reckoning, which on long voyages could be disastrous. The *Massachusetts,* for instance, spent three weeks wandering about in the Indian Ocean when she missed Java Head on her 1790 voyage.

Although they were the only good way to determine longitude, chronometers appeared infrequently on board early nineteenth-century American merchant vessels. Scarce and expensive, the first one made in the United States did not appear until 1812. As late as 1823 the Boston firm of Bryant and Sturgis refused to reimburse their captains for the purchase of a chronometer, and not until three years later did the navy begin issuing them to warships.

Of a more immediate importance to American seamen was the publication in 1796 by Edmund M. Blunt of Captain L. Furlong's *American Coast Pilot,* which offered the first set of sailing directions for the entire east coast of North America as well as part of the southern continent. In 1799 Blunt published the *New Practical Navigator,* an improved version of a popular English work. The corrections were made by Nathaniel Bowditch, who three years later published a revised version as *The New American Practical Navigator.* "Bowditch" as it became universally and affectionately known by navigators, has remained their bible ever since. It remains the best-known, if not the most important, American contribution to safe navigation.

The 1790s also witnessed the start of improvements in the aids to navigation along the coast. Lighthouses had been built in colonial times, starting with the Boston Light in 1716, but only nine shown before the Revolution. In 1789 Congress created the Lighthouse Establishment and to it assigned responsibility for the aids to navigation. It assumed the existing state responsibility for lighthouses and in 1791 embarked on a program of new construction. From this modest beginning, and a faltering early history, the lighthouse service developed the aids of navigation into an integrated system of lighthouses, lightships, buoys, and marks that permitted safe navigation of coastal waters in all but the most treacherous of conditions. In 1939 its responsibilities were shifted to the Coast Guard, which already embraced the other federal maritime safety and enforcement agencies.

Boston Lighthouse as it appeared in 1789 at the time of its acquisition by the federal government. Note the small sloop in the foreground, which differed little from the smaller pinnaces of the era of exploration. Official U.S. Navy Photograph

3. The Neutral Carrier

The European wars of 1792–1815 offered unprecedented opportunities along with great uncertainties for American merchants, shipowners, and seamen. Although international agreements and domestic statutes like the British Rule of 1756 nominally controlled maritime warfare, the volatile conditions of the war at sea sometimes altered the rules radically and with little notice. A vessel could begin a voyage under one set of rules and find herself facing a differing group on her arrival in port. Two cases involving Massachusetts vessels illustrate this. In 1800 a British warship seized the ship *Polly* bound for Bilbao, Spain, with sugar from Havana and cocoa from Caracas under longstanding regulations excluding neutral vessels from trades in which they were banned during peacetime. In this instance it was a Spanish prohibition against foreign vessels carrying goods between Spain and her colonies. The British admiralty court freed the *Polly* on the grounds that the cargo had passed through American customs at Marblehead before starting the second leg of their journey to Spain. That made it in effect two separate trips, each of which was legal under prewar Spanish law. In 1805 the British courts reversed themselves in a case involving the ship *Essex*, ruling that the two legs of the trip were in reality only separate portions of a single continuous voyage, which made the goods and the ship that carried them legal prizes.

These restrictions conflicted with the established American doctrine on freedom of the seas, which had been officially enunciated as early as 1776: Neutral vessels have a right to carry noncontraband goods irrespective of their ownership between any ports not under blockade. In the parlance of the period this became "Free ships make free goods." Moreover, American practice defined contraband very narrowly as only munitions clearly consigned to a belligerent power. As might be expected from the dominant sea power and the nation that stood to gain most from the restrictions on neutral shipping, Britain adamantly refused to recognize the American doctrine. Neither would the United States when it controlled the seas during the Civil and later wars.

As far as many American shippers were concerned, the profits to be gained from neutral trade between 1790 and 1807 overshadowed the risks. Maritime and commercial investments so dominated the economic life of the nation that they absorbed most of the available risk capital in the country. As a result, before 1807 few investors placed money in such risky investments as manufacturing establishments. The few efforts towards industrialization that did occur were funded to a great degree with wealth created by maritime trade. For instance, when Samuel Slater arrived in

New York in 1789 to construct his cotton spinning mill he made contact with Moses Brown, the wealthy Providence, Rhode Island, shipper. Brown also provided the capital to build the mill at Pawtucket in 1791 from which sprang the American industrial revolution.

The agricultural impact proved to be nearly as great. The war boosted the demand for American wheat as England turned to the United States for her grain. This drove the price from $5.40 to $9.12 per barrel. The unheard-of prices triggered a sudden rush into the grain-growing regions of Pennsylvania and New York as well as into Ohio and the Lake Erie basin. But the westerners found that it cost them as much as $10 per ton per hundred miles to move the grain by wagon. Another result was that New England farmers abandoned high-cost grain farming in favor of garden and fruit growing, or, in the case of Massachusetts and Vermont, of sheep raising.

On purely civic matters the wealth of the maritime renaissance early demonstrated its vitality. Boston not only appropriated $1,600 for buoys to mark the path into the harbor but erected a magnificent new wharf designed by Charles Bulfinch. By 1800 local merchants built a semaphore telegraph line to Woods Hole that hastened reports of incoming vessels. New York City underwent a similar maritime boom, which caused the town to grow 129 percent between 1790 and 1805, from 33,000 to 75,000 people.

Despite great success of the neutral trade, it became a political issue when Thomas Jefferson attempted to employ the economic weapons that he perceived as having been successful against Britain during the Stamp Act crisis and under The Association of 1774. He believed that he could pry economic and political concessions from the warring powers by closing the American market to them. The Jeffersonian program culminated in the embargo of December 1807, which closed American ports to foreign trade and required coastal craft to post bonds guaranteeing that their cargoes remained in the United States. The opposition was strong and instantaneous: shipowners, who saw their livelihood eliminated; sailors, who found themselves unemployed; shipbuilders, who produced a product few wanted; and farmers, who suddenly discovered how much of their produce moved overseas.

The embargo caused massive dislocation. An estimated 55,000 seamen lost their livelihood, as did nearly twice that number in related industries. In New England ports sailors staged protest

The Newburyport, Massachusetts, schooner *Lidia* entering Marseilles harbor in 1807. She was an example of the larger schooners and brigs of the era that were used in both the deep-sea and the coastal trades. Courtesy of U.S. Naval Historical Center

marches. Perhaps the most colorful of these occurred in Portland, Maine, where demonstrators pulled a dilapidated, unpainted long-boat with unbent sails and loose, swinging rigging, called *O-Grab-Me* (embargo in reverse), through the streets stern first. It was followed by a band playing a funeral dirge. In some of the Maine seacoast towns as many as 60 percent of the inhabitants lost their jobs, and soup kettles appeared on the town greens. Wiscasset, for example, had sent sixty-seven vessels to sea in 1806, but in 1808 only two operated and thirty gently rocked on the Sheepscot River with empty holds, deteriorating gear, and "Jefferson's night caps" (inverted tar barrels) at their mastheads. When nine vessels belonging to William King, the leading owner at Bath, Maine, were caught in port it cost him over $5,500 per month in lost earnings. All of this fed the traditional American distaste for restrictions. Those shipowners who could arrange for their vessels to remain overseas out of reach of the regulation did so. Others, bolder in their defiance, openly flouted the regulations by trading with Canadian ports or even the West Indies.

Since the embargo brought no concessions, a Non-Intercourse Act replaced it in March 1809. It reopened trade with all nations except Britain and France, but this did little to quiet the calls for free trade. As a result of the continuing opposition, Macon's Bill No. 2 of 1810 temporarily reopened trade with the two powers. The impact was both immediate and great. American deep-sea tonnage jumped to 981,019 tons, the highest per capita figure it would report for another thirty-seven years.

Between 1807 and 1815 the United States had unimpeded foreign trade for only fifteen months, yet in 1807, the last year of normal trade, 60–70 percent of America's imported manufactured goods came from English factories. The loss of English goods coincided with the freeing of most of the capital that had been invested in shipping and the birth of the American industrial revolution. To say that it was the embargo and the British blockade of the War of 1812 that created the American industrial revolution is an oversimplification, but that development would have been greatly retarded without the economic and psychological impetus that they gave.

It has been estimated that in the first six months after the imposition of the embargo that $5 million in capital shifted from commerce to manufacturing. The initial movement of capital triggered development in the cotton textile industry, historically the cutting edge of industrialization. In 1808 the United States possessed only 15 cotton mills operating 8,000 spindles; a year later 102 mills contained 31,000 spindles. This was the start of the textile industry in the United States.

Impressment raised a secondary but highly emotional issue. The Royal Navy had the right to press, or forcibly enlist, seamen from British vessels on the high seas when that became necessary in order to fill out the complement of a man-of-war. Since the demands of the service and its lack of attractiveness limited volunteer enlistments, the Royal Navy during the Napoleonic Wars stopped non-British vessels at sea and impressed British subjects found among their crews. In the case of American vessels, on which perhaps 20,000 British seamen served, it was extremely difficult to determine nationality. The British refusal to recognize expatriation, and the great ease with which fraudulent American papers could be secured, further complicated matters. As a result the treatment accorded the crew of an American vessel visited by a press party depended upon the whim of the officer in charge. Figures on the total number of Americans pressed over the quarter of a century before 1815 are imprecise, but they numbered approximately 10,000 seamen.

4. Slave Trade

The status of slave trading during the early years of independence remains unclear. The trade resumed once the seas became safe after the Revolution, and as many as 15,000 slaves a year reportedly entered North Carolina alone in the late 1790s. Opposition also spread. Massachusetts attempted to prevent her vessels from participating in the trade, but other states were slow to follow her. By the time of the Constitutional Convention the antislavery feeling was strong, although southern influence delayed elimination of importation for ten years.

The impending halt to the trade hastened the departure from it of some of the larger Rhode Island houses. Aaron Lopez and Moses Brown had abandoned the business before the Revolution, leaving the mantle of leadership to the de Wolfs in Providence. They began shifting investments into distilleries and textile mills by the start of the nineteenth century. As a result the trade passed into the hands of small operators who could afford to secure only a cargo or two at a time in the West Indies, notably Cuba, and run them into southern ports.

With the closing of legal importation in 1808 the trade became clandestine. Yet the United States government expended little effort in attempting to stamp out the business. Amelia Island on the Georgia-Florida border was a notorious slave-landing point prior to the War of 1812 while in later years many came overland from Texas. While we know that a considerable number of slaves came ashore illegally, we have only limited estimates of their numbers. The import restriction, however, drove up prices. Prime field hands brought $500 in 1805; $1,500 in 1825; and up to $2,500 in 1860. Most slaves came from the upper South and many, if not the majority, moved to their new homes by water.

The prohibition on importation did not prevent American involvement in trade on the Middle Passage from Africa to the West Indies or to Brazil. Not until 1820 did Congress declare the transport of slaves to be a form of piracy. Even then, it was seldom enforced. Other nations took stronger steps. The British forbade participation by British subjects in 1807; Sweden prohibited the trade in 1813; while the Spanish and Portuguese agreed to abandon it north of the equator the following year. The French withdrew in 1816, and in 1818 the Dutch agreed to a mutual right of search of suspected slavers. The latter dovetailed with British efforts to create an international police force off Africa to interdict the trade. The plan foundered on American, French, and Spanish refusal to permit search of their vessels. In 1842 the United States did agree to maintain an antislavery patrol off West Africa although it seldom operated at the required strength.

Some Americans remained active in the trade until the Civil War, but their participation apparently declined as the century progressed. One of the diehards was the infamous Captain Nathaniel Gordon of Portland, Maine. He made two voyages to Cuba and one to Brazil before being caught with 967 slaves on board his 500-ton vessel. Tried and hanged in 1862, Gordon was the only American to pay the full penalty for trafficking in slaves.

Although a naval squadron attempted to drive American participants from the African slave trade, no concerted effort was made to intercept domestic slave smugglers. Only an occasional slaver was seized. Even so, some of the craft were colorful like the schooner *Wanderer,* which flew the flag of the New York Yacht Club, and the fast Portsmouth, New Hampshire-built clipper ship *Nightingale.* Part of the difficulty in stamping out the clandestine trade was a requirement in the 1819 law that a suspected smuggler be tried in the state from which the vessel hailed. This ensured in most cases trial before a southern jury, which usually showed scant interest in a conviction. Moreover, it was difficult in many cases to prove with legal certainty that the vessel was indeed smuggling slaves since interstate shipment was legal and forged or improper papers were easily obtainable.

5. The Yankee Harnesses Steam

The notion that steam could be used to propel a vessel through water occurred to many men throughout the ages. Hero in 180 B.C. described a hot-air engine. Blasco de Garay in 1543 may have attempted to move a vessel by steam-driven paddle wheels although most non-Spanish historians doubt the claim. Denis Papin in France in 1707 did build a paddle-wheel steamer, but it evoked little interest. Many Britons, Frenchmen, and Americans during the remainder of the century followed in Papin's wake, but none succeeded in harnessing steam power to maritime uses. Indeed, not until James Watt's development of the double-acting, condensing, engine in 1782 did a powerplant exist with a sufficiently high power-weight ratio to give hope of either cargo capacity or speed.

In the United States two pioneering names stand out: James Rumsey and John Fitch. Between 1784 and 1787 Rumsey, an innkeeper and man of the world, experimented with both pump- and pole-driven craft in the upper Potomac River around Shepardstown, [now West] Virginia. Despite the patronage of George Washington and other prominent people, Rumsey could not raise enough money either in the United States or Britain to build a successful full-sized example.

Rumsey's great competitor was the moody, eccentric craftsman John Fitch, who struggled between 1785 and 1798 to perfect his design. Fitch built a working two-man boat in 1786; one driven by six paddles the following year; and a third, 60 feet long, capable of carrying 66 passengers two years after that. In 1790 he ran a pair of boats on regular service between Philadelphia and Trenton, New Jersey. This must be considered the first commercial use of steamboats. Fitch's designs were imperfect and he, like Rumsey, could not raise the money necessary to continue his work either at home or abroad.

Although Patrick Miller, James Taylor, and William Symington developed a practical design in Britain in 1788–89, the opposition of the Watt interests slowed experiments. Not until 1802 did Symington produce the first British steamer. In the United States several men picked up where Fitch and Rumsey stopped. Between 1790 and 1797 Samuel Morey operated a series of experimental steamers on the Connecticut, Hudson, and Delaware rivers, but we know very little about them. Oliver Evans in Philadelphia not only built an amphibious steam-powered dredge in 1804 but two years earlier sold a high-pressure engine to a pair of New Orleans entrepreneurs, James McKeever and Louis Valcourt, who planned to install it in a steamer for use on the Mississippi River. Unfortunately for their place in history, the spring floods deposited their nearly completed craft in a field so far from the river that they abandoned the project and sold the engine to a sawmill. Other pioneers like Elijah Ormsbee and David Wilkinson in Rhode Island, Nicholas Roosevelt in New Jersey, and Nathan Reed in Massachusetts experimented with steam power.

At the same time Robert R. Livingston, patrician, politician, and gentleman inventor, became interested in the new source of

Robert Fulton's *Steam Boat* was the first commercially successful steamer. The replica shown here was built for the Hudson-Fulton Celebration of 1907. Official U.S. Navy Photograph

power. He secured a monopoly of the use of steam in New York waters, enlisted some of the best minds in the country including Morey, Roosevelt, and John Stevens, but could not develop the craft. Stevens, who was Livingston's brother-in-law, continued development on his own. In 1804 he built a steam-powered, screw-driven open boat. Her screws and boiler can be seen in the Smithsonian Institution's Museum of History and Technology. Because he believed that American shops then could not produce high-pressure machinery, which the screw design required, Stevens abandoned that approach, shifting to low-pressure engines and paddle wheels.

In 1803 Robert Fulton, who had gone to England to study painting, become fascinated by steamboats. In France he met Livingston, now an American minister, and agreed to build a working steamer. Livingston then renewed his New York State monopoly. After securing an engine from Boulton and Watt at an exorbitant price, Fulton returned to New York, where he had a hull

built to his design. On September 17–21, 1807, his *Steam Boat**
made her epic round-trip voyage to Albany. The steamboat had
arrived. Although no single part was Fulton's invention, he combined them so as to produce a workable and commercially viable
vessel.

In no small degree Fulton's success grew out of the nature of
the Hudson River valley. Sailing vessels heading upriver usually
had to fight unfavorable winds or disturbed air flowing over high
or wooded banks. Under optimum conditions the best that a fast
river sloop could hope for was a forty-eight-hour passage to Albany. Fulton's steamer made the run in thirty hours.

The impact was immediate despite the relatively high fare of
$7 charged between New York to Albany. But thanks to the mo-
nopoly granted by the legislature, Fulton had no competition.
Stevens's *Phoenix,* the second practical steamer, was not finished
until shortly after the *Steam Boat* and was, therefore, frozen out of
New York waters. In 1809 Stevens sent her to the Delaware River,
which necessitated the first open-water passage by a steamer. She
ran between Philadelphia and Bordentown, New Jersey, to connect
with the New York stage coach. In 1809 steamboats also appeared
on the St. Lawrence River and on Lake Champlain. The following
year the Paulus Hook–New York steam-ferry route acquired its first
vessel. In 1811 Nicholas Roosevelt, as the agent of the Fulton-
Livingston group, built the *New Orleans* at Pittsburgh. She successfully navigated the Ohio and the Mississippi to operate out of her
name city until wrecked in 1814.

By 1813 Fulton and his backers had developed plans for an
integrated system of steamboat and stage lines running from Can-
ada to Charleston, South Carolina, and from Pittsburgh to New
Orleans. They envisioned steamboats plying Lake Champlain; run-
ning between Albany and New York; from New York and New
Brunswick, New Jersey; between Trenton and Philadelphia; along
Chesapeake Bay to Baltimore; south from Washington to Norfolk;
Norfolk to Berne, North Carolina; Newport Inlet to Little River,
North Carolina; and Little River to Charleston. The intervening
overland segments would be covered by stage coaches running on

---

*Fulton's vessel bore the name *Steam Boat* until 1809, when she
became the *North River Steam Boat.* She never carried the name
Clermont, nor was she ever referred to as such while in service.
Clermont, however, was her port at various times.

schedules fitted to those of the steamers. In 1813 all parts of the network north of Philadelphia and between New Orleans and Natchez existed, but the hostilities killed the rest of the plan.

Although steamboats had operated successfully on lakes and rivers, steam power was just completing its experimental period at the end of the War of 1812. Ahead would be the appearance of the scheduled coastal runs, transatlantic service, and that fleet of steamers that would revolutionize the commerce of the Mississippi basin and make possible the settling of the region between the Appalachians and the Rocky Mountains. That movement, one of the great migrations in the world's history, would not have been possible without the steamboats that placed farms and plantations, villages and hamlets, and mines and factories in contact with supplies and markets.

6. Foreign Trade

The world into which American shippers ventured after 1815 differed greatly from that which had existed before 1812. Their role as the great neutral carriers for a world at war had ended. As emotionally satisfying as it might have been to the shipowners to have the United States emerge from the War of 1812 as an established and respected nation, that status did not guarantee new trade for vessels flying the Stars and Stripes.

But that did not bother a nation whose self-assurance verged on adolescent posturing and who held the conviction that the United States had developed the system of government that would save the world from autocracy. That the real world was not as Americans conceived of it is not important, for the United States was on the verge of her first great step towards world leadership. In the half century following the War of 1812 the United States passed from apprenticeship to majority. Maritime affairs played a major role in that development.

It is conventional to think of the period between the War of 1812 and the Civil War as foundation-building for the industrial surge of the last quarter of the nineteenth century. It was much more. It was a period of rapid physical expansion. The frontier pushed inexorably westward as the largely waterborne transportation web developed sufficiently to support the new settlers. It was a period of massive immigration, but since the new settlers were preponderantly Irish, German, and English the problems of their acculturation left little imprint on the consciousness of twentieth-century Americans. The years between 1815 and 1860 also saw the American merchant marine reach its zenith in terms of percentage of American trade carried. Only in the aftermath of the two World Wars would its world rank in total tonnage stand as high.

American shippers retained a price advantage over Old World competitors throughout nearly all but not the entire period. While it is extremely difficult to compare international building costs because of differences in definitions and contract terms, the relative advantage of cheap American wooden hulls began to decline after 1830 as local timber supplies were exhausted. Whether the increase in American building costs became critical before the Civil War is debatable since there are figures that suggest a price advantage in 1856–57 that was nearly as great as that in 1791. The increasing demand for larger vessels, those over 400 tons burden or 100 feet in length, which developed in the 1830s, intensified the increase in building costs. Previously, vessels could be built by small gangs of workers in improvised yards that could be set up nearly anywhere the necessary topography and depth of water coincided. But the larger craft coming into use after 1830 could not be built by such haphazard methods. Their construction demanded increasingly sophisticated machinery and techniques, available only in larger yards that by their very nature became permanent operations. The new yards demanded greater capital investment and higher managerial and design skills than the traditional plant. At the same time the escalation of material costs, since larger timbers had to be fetched from ever more distant timber stands, drove the price of new hulls higher.

Not only did shipowners turn to larger vessels as more efficient carriers but they shifted to specialized types: fast passenger and premium freight-carrying packets; large but slow bulk carriers, notably for cotton; fast medium-sized brigs and schooners, which hauled fruit and coffee; and large, swift deepwater freighters for the China trade, to mention only the most prominent.

The shifting economic currents hastened the decline of the small trading partnership that employed its vessels on numerous and diverse routes and its replacement by firms, increasingly operating as common carriers rather than merchant owners, concentrating on a single or limited group of trade routes. An incidental, but not to be overlooked, contribution to the exponential growth of the American foreign-trade merchant marine before 1849 was the British prohibition on the admission of foreign-built vessels to British registry. It came at a moment when shipbuilding costs there rose dramatically. As a result British shippers, as did their American counterparts a century and a half later, came to depend on trades sheltered by the Navigation Acts for their livelihood since the unprotected routes soon passed into American or Scandinavian hands.

The growth of common carriers, shippers who for a fee regularly transported goods owned by others, had far-reaching effects. It permitted a carrier to combine several small shipments into a single large one for greater efficiency. Even more important, it smashed the traditional unity of ship and cargo ownership or alternatively the chartering of a vessel by a single shipper to carry his goods alone. The change reflected the relative safety of transit that reduced the risks for the carrier; it marked the development of trade large enough to permit a division of labor; and it signaled the creation of capital to provide the necessary vessels. The change coincided with some significant alterations in the American economy. The prewar system served the needs of an agricultural or small factory economy that depended upon a collector to handle the large-scale marketing of its goods. As the economy of the nation expanded, it had less need for the old system since individual producers could now finance their own foreign trade.

The new conditions manifested themselves in the creation of packet lines, groups of vessels offering scheduled services sailing whether full or not. The concept was old. The British Post Office instituted scheduled transatlantic mail service in 1710, and in 1783 the French government established a similar service to New York. In 1805 a group of Boston merchants started a short-lived line to Liverpool. Regular traders who sailed between fixed ports, but only when a full cargo had been secured, had also existed since colonial times.

In 1810 a packet line appeared on the Hudson River and was followed in 1814–15 by lines from New York to Richmond, Virginia, Philadelphia, and Baltimore; Boston to Albany and Troy, New York; and Baltimore to New Orleans. The success of the coastal packets encouraged Jeremiah and Francis Thompson, Benjamin Marshall, Isaac Wright, and other textile importers to announce on October 24, 1817, a similar service across the Atlantic to Liverpool. The port on the Irish Sea was chosen because of its advantages over London and other east of England centers. Liverpool was 224 miles closer to New York than London and avoided the usually difficult passage up or down the English Channel. Moreover, Liverpool had good canal connections with the industrial areas of the Midlands, especially the Staffordshire potteries, which produced a major share of the exports to America. In addition it was a well-established embarkation point for emigrants.

The Black Ball Line, as the new service was called after its distinctive insignia, sailed from New York on the fifth and from Liverpool on the first of each month. The passenger accommodations were superior to any offered up to that time, at least for those sailing first-class. For 45, later 35, guineas a passenger received such amenities as fresh eggs from the hens living in a coop atop the midships longboat under which were sheltered the pigs and sheep that provided fresh meat. Fresh milk came from the cow quartered in her own house atop the main hatch. Steerage passengers, generally immigrants, furnished their own bedding, food, and utensils but paid only £5.

The first Black Baller, the *James Monroe* under Captain James Watkinson, sailed on January 5, 1818. She carried only 1,141 barrels of apples, 860 barrels of flour, 400 barrels of ashes, 71 bales of cotton, and smaller quantities of cranberries, hops, and wool. Nevertheless, the service soon attracted passengers and express cargo. The Panic of 1819 delayed the appearance of competition. Finally in 1822 Byrnes, Trimble, and Company inaugurated a line that sailed from New York on the twenty-fifth of the month and Liverpool on the twelfth. The Black Ball's operators responded by doubling their sailings—one each way on the first and the sixteenth. Later in the year the firms of Fish and Grinnell and Thaddeus Phelps and Company established a fourth line departing eastward on the eighth and westward on the twenty-fourth. None of the opposition lines offered as large or as well-fitted vessels as the two Black Ball services, but they still were profitable. The 1822 commercial treaty with France induced Francis Depau to establish a packet line between New York and Havre. Its success brought a second line the following year.

The success of the New York lines lay in their ability to find eastbound cargoes. Mixed cargoes with a heavy leavening of grain,

By the 1830s New York had reached her preeminent position as the nation's leading seaport. Her wharves bustled with vessels taking on and offloading cargo. Official U.S. Navy Photograph

flour, and cotton gave shippers paying freight that other ports lacked. Ports with moderate quantities of outbound freight did maintain small transatlantic lines. Most were short lived. Boston, for instance, started a packet line in 1822 that, in order to secure outbound cargo, detoured to Charleston for cotton. Since most passengers when enroute to Liverpool found little attraction in a visit to South Carolina, the lines failed. Boston, despite becoming the terminus of the Cunard Line steamers in 1840, could not generate enough business to support a permanent packet service until 1844. Philadelphia, which drew on western Pennsylvania for exports, fared better. It supported a line that regularly operated four or five packets from 1822 until after the Civil War. The cotton ports, on the other hand, did not crave enough imports to justify lines until 1851, when New Orleans hosted one sailing to Liverpool. Yet New York by the mid-1850s could claim sixteen lines to

Liverpool, three to London, three to Havre, two to Antwerp, and one each to Glasgow, Rotterdam, and Marseilles.

At a time in history when no passenger vessels, flying the United States or any other flag, regularly ply between North America and Europe, it is difficult for most people to realize how completely the American packets and combination vessels dominated the "North Atlantic Ferry" in the second quarter of the nineteenth century. While passengers who desired a speedy passage and first-class service chose steamers, those who wished a cheaper but slower crossing rode sailing packets. Few steamers flew the Stars and Stripes, but the loss of passengers was more than offset before 1857 by an increase in the number of steerage passengers. As late as 1856 only 3.6 percent of the travelers reaching New York came on steamers while not until 1847 did European-flag sailing packets offer significant competition. Although the strikingly beautiful clipper with her sleek lines and towering masts caught the fancy of successive generations of Americans, it was the equally beautiful packet with her more moderate lines and sail plan that brought the American sailing fleet its economic power.

Part of the success of the packets derived from their stress on speed. The best could reach 12–14 knots. The *James Monroe*'s initial eastbound passage time of 28 days was soon bested by other packets. The record was dropped to 15 days 16 hours by the *New York* in 1824. The *Yorkshire* reduced the time to 14 days in 1846. Eight years later the fastest of all the transatlantic packets, the *Dreadnaught* of the St. George's Line, cut the record to 13 days 11 hours, which she shaved by three hours in 1859. Westward crossings were consistently slower because of the adverse winds, the record being 15 days 12 hours from Belfast by the *Josephine* in 1830 and matched sixteen years later by the *Yorkshire* from Liverpool. Most crossings took considerably longer. In 1839 the average crossing to Liverpool lasted 22 days 1 hour and the return 34 days.

The packets were driven as no vessels had been driven before them. Speed was both the essence and the appeal of the service, so owners paid handsome bonuses to masters and crews who made good times. In part reflecting the harshness of the demands on them but even more attesting to the American's turning of his face to the soil and his back to the sea, the packets increasingly relied for crews on the tough, wild, and nearly unmanagable scum of the Liverpool saloons and boardinghouses. When led by a strong captain and hardnosed "bucko" mates whose doctrine insisted that

The Boston-Liverpool packet *Clara Wheeler,* built at Medford, Massachusetts, in 1849. She was an example of the North Atlantic packet at its peak. Courtesy of the U.S. Naval Historical Center

only violence could control them, the "packet rats" were superior to any other crew, able to endure nearly any hardship afloat even to climbing aloft in a blinding snow squall to handle frozen sails and ice-coated lines.

In 1822 a group of Boston merchants formed a line to Liverpool, but it lasted only four years because of the New England port's long-term problem of a shortage of eastbound cargo. A second Boston and Liverpool line operated in 1827–30 but proved no more successful. Finally in 1844 Enoch Train launched his version, which offered irregular sailings down to 1855, when it passed into new hands and continued scheduled sailings until 1858. Philadelphia, which had good trade routes west, was more successful. Thomas P. Cope and Son started a service in 1822 that lasted until 1868 offering monthly departures. Two other Philadelphia firms operated lines that lasted better than a decade each: Spackman and Wilson's New Line (1824–37) and Richardson, Watson and Company's Black Diamond Line (1846–57). Baltimore's Corner Line also sent monthly sailings to Liverpool between 1846 and the Civil War. Alone among the cotton ports, New Orleans housed a series of packet lines. Three of them (Crescent City Line, White Star Line, and English and Brandon's Regular Line) operated, with little overlap, from 1851 to the Civil War. The port also had a line running to Hamburg, Germany, in 1852–60.

The New York packet lines lost most of their express trade to steamers during the 1830s and came to rely on cotton for the bulk of their eastbound cargoes. The Philadelphia and Baltimore lines faced no comparable competition, but like their Boston counterparts they had difficulties making up eastbound shipments. Few of the lines survived the trade dislocations of the Civil War.

An often overlooked counterpoint to the packets were the immigrant lines, which hauled almost 5 million Europeans, chiefly Irish, Germans, and English, to the New World between 1815 and 1860. The packets themselves each carried several hundred men, women, and children in steerage on their westward passages, but infinitely more traveled in immigrant liners that sailed from Liverpool, Greenock, Hamburg, Antwerp, and lesser collection points. Many of the immigrant craft found return cargo at one of the cotton ports. The earliest lines catering to immigrants began operations to New York and Philadelphia in 1824. The best-known and the largest of the lines was the Black Star, which in 1847 dispatched a vessel every sixth day from Liverpool to New York.

Conditions on many of the immigrant vessels were atrocious. For their passage money the travelers received a place to sleep, drinking water, and access to a stove to cook the food that they had to provide. The mixed odor of massed human bodies, stale food, slop barrels, and vomit was a stench whose memory remained with many immigrants throughout their lives. As early as 1819 the United States placed limits on the number of persons who could be crowded on board and in 1847 required that each passenger be provided with at least fourteen square feet of deck space. These efforts eliminated the worst of the conditions, but at no time was the passage an easy one for the immigrants. The crowded and verminous conditions helped spread contagious diseases, especially typhus or ships fever as it was then commonly called. In order to encourage better health practices, during 1855 the United States enlarged the space per passenger to sixteen square feet and reduced the number carried to one passenger for each two tons of the vessel. The law also fined the individual master $10 for each passenger dying during the crossing. Nevertheless, the number of lives lost in wrecks or from illness during the passage was relatively small considering the conditions that prevailed. If it were not so, a great many of us would not be here.

Because of their lower operating costs, sailing vessels carried the bulk of immigrants before the Civil War. In 1856, 136,459 people reached New York on sailing craft but only 5,685 on steamers. However, by 1862 the figures had shifted to 55,615 and 26,171, respectively. Since the European agents who operated nearly all the immigrant lines after the Civil War employed steamships almost exclusively, the proportion carried by sail dwindled rapidly.

Cotton rivaled the immigrant trade as a spur to the growth of the American merchant marine during the first half of the nineteenth century. Cotton constituted at least a quarter of the country's exports in 1817 while after 1830 it generally fluctuated between 40 and 50 percent. Table 2–1 gives the volume of cotton exports. Less easily determined is the division of the crop between American factories, direct shipments to Liverpool or other foreign ports, and transshipments via New York, Boston, Philadelphia, or Baltimore. The best estimates indicate that before the Civil War about one-third of the crop fed American mills and a third moved directly to foreign ports. Irrespective of its destination, the cotton traveled in American vessels. Even at Liverpool as much as two-thirds of the cotton arrived in American vessels.

The reasons for the American dominance are not difficult to understand. Since the northeastern ports lacked voluminous car-

Table 2–1. *Cotton Exports*

Year	Quantity (million pounds)	Value ($1,000)
1815	83	17,529
1820	128	22,309
1825	176	36,847
1830	298	29,675
1835	387	64,961
1840	744	63,870
1845	873	51,740
1850	635	71,985
1855	1,008	88,144
1860	1,768	191,807

Source: Bureau of the Census, Historical Statistics Colonial Times to 1970 *(Washington, 1975), II, 899.*

goes to counterbalance their imports and the cotton centers lacked the import demand to offset their cotton shipments, a triangular trade developed. American vessels, usually owned in the Northeast, carried goods for the southern market or sailed in ballast to a cotton port. There they loaded cotton or occasionally naval stores or timber for Europe. From Europe the freighters returned with manufactured goods, coal, raw materials, and occasionally immigrants. Less frequently, traders moved clockwise from the cotton ports to Europe with a northern stop to top off the cargo. Since the triangular trade involved a coastal leg, foreign vessels, except for a few English ones that could substitute a Canadian stop for a northeastern port, were excluded.

The development by 1840 of specially designed cotton carriers, commonly called "kettle bottoms" because of their shape, demonstrated Yankee ingenuity. Being very light, 100 cubic feet to a ton before the introduction of cotton presses and 60 cubic feet afterwards, cotton required large vessels. Since port charges depended on the tonnage of the vessel and tonnage was a function of the beam at deck level, they were built with great tumble home, i.e., sides bulging outward below deck level, but very deep, and with large open poops and forecastle decks on which cotton bales could be stowed but which did not figure in the tonnage calculations. In order to maximize their cargo capacity the kettle bottoms had bluff bows and square sterns. This made them efficient freighters but scarcely handsome vessels. Because the cargo could be handled easily without heavy tackle, enterprising captains stowed it in every vacant space on board. There are even stories of captains using a bale or two as a mess table.

The Maine yards, notably those along the Kennebec River, produced a large proportion of the cotton freighters. They turned out 139 in the years 1830–32 alone. The Bath-built 1,133-ton ship *Rappahannock* of 1841 was so capacious that New Orleans freight rates supposedly dropped 1/8 cent per pound whenever she appeared in the Mississippi.

7. Transatlantic Steam

Captain Moses Rogers was a pioneer steamship master. He had charge of John Stevens's *Phoenix* on her epic trip to the Delaware River; had commanded the *Fulton* on the Hudson River; and in 1815 operated the *Eagle* on the run between New York and Baltimore. In 1817 he took over the *Charleston* in service to her name city. He next promoted the Savannah Steam Ship Company to operate a vessel to New York.

Rogers bought the unfinished hull of a packet and redesigned her to carry a pair of collapsible paddle wheels powered by a small steam engine. The questionable design and the panic of 1819 so frightened Rogers's backers that they decided to sell the vessel. Since the Russian government had expressed interest in operating a steamer in the Baltic, the Americans decided to try to sell their craft, now called *Savannah,* at St. Petersburg. She left Savannah on May 24, 1819, and reached Liverpool June 20, having used her engines for about three and half days during the crossing. Nevertheless, that qualified her to be considered the first steamer to cross the Atlantic although it was scarcely a steam-powered crossing. Unable to sell her, Rogers brought the *Savannah* back to the United States under sail. With her engines removed she operated as a coastal packet until wrecked near Moriches, Long Island, in November 1821.

Despite the pioneer crossing and the initial lead of the United States in steam navigation only one serious American attempt to establish a transatlantic line followed the *Savannah*'s trip. The Ocean Steam Ship Company had the *Robert Fulton* built in 1820 but never placed her in service because Congress refused to grant tariff drawbacks on foreign coal and stores, without which the service was uneconomical. As a result, the handful of steamers that did cross the Atlantic in the twenty years following the *Savannah*'s trip all flew European flags.

In 1838 three different British groups began transatlantic steam service, but none lasted more than a handful of years. The first long-lived concern appeared two years later when Samuel Cunard's British and North American Royal Mail Steam Packet Company secured a $425,000 subsidy for service between Liverpool, Halifax, and Boston. In 1847 Cunard added New York as a port of call.

The steamers attracted cabin and saloon passengers along with the express freight, which heretofore had moved on sailing packets. The immigrant trade remained in the hands of the sailing craft, as we have seen. By 1860 steamers dominated the eastbound passenger traffic from New York since it consisted almost entirely of travelers able to pay the additional cost. On the other hand, the relative inefficiency of single-cylinder engines ensured that sailing vessels would remain the most efficient carriers for bulk cargoes until well after the Civil War. In some bulk trades, notably timber, coal, nitrate, and grain, where the speed of delivery was a secondary consideration, the sailing freighter held her own into the twentieth century.

As early as 1841 Senator Thomas Butler King of Georgia argued for nationally subsidized American-flag steamship lines. His appeals fell on deaf ears until 1845 when complaints about poor transatlantic mail service caused Congress to authorize the postmaster general to arrange with American shippers to carry foreign mail. The initial contract went to the Ocean Steam Navigation Company in 1846 for semimonthly service to Havre and Bremen via Southampton at a rate of $350,000 per year. The line could not raise the capital required and sold off the Havre portion of its service. The Bremen line, maintained by a pair of steamers, operated until 1857, when the suspension of subsidies and the formation of the North German Lloyd combined to kill it. The Havre line of the New York and Havre Steam Navigation Company, although beset with numerous problems, lasted until 1861, when its owners found they could generate a greater profit by chartering their vessels to the federal government for war service.

The major American transatlantic steamship line was the New York and Liverpool United States Mail Steam Ship Company organized in 1848 by the former packet operator Edward K. Collins. Since Collins's line ran in competition with the Cunard Line, Congress granted a subsidy of $385,000. Four years later the payment rose to $850,000. Collins ordered four magnificent vessels, the finest craft of their day. The *Atlantic, Arctic, Baltic,* and *Pacific* were near sisters of 2,850-tons burden, 282 feet long, with massive slow-speed, side-lever engines driving paddle wheels. Their heavily built wooden hulls came from the leading yards in New York. Driven hard, commonly operating at 13 knots, the Collins steamers set a series of transatlantic eastward records:

1850	*Pacific*	10 days 4 hours
1851	*Pacific*	9 days 20 hours 26 minutes
1852	*Arctic*	9 days 17 hours 12 minutes

The *Baltic* set a westward record of 9 days 18 hours in 1851. Finely fitted as well as speedy, they offered steam-heated cabins, a smoking room, bathroom, and a barbershop. Collins took the cream of the transatlantic passenger traffic away from Cunard, carrying 40 percent more passengers than the British concern.

The Collins liners were magnificent failures. They cost considerably more to build than their British competitors and lost an average of $16,928.74 per voyage in the first year alone. Moreover, the wooden hulls could not withstand the pounding of their powerful machinery and required frequent and costly repairs that consumed much of the line's revenue. The loss of the *Arctic* in 1854 after a collision off Cape Race, Newfoundland, from which only 87 of the 365 people on board survived, further complicated Collins's problems. Two years later the *Pacific* disappeared on a westward passage with 45 passengers and a crew of 141.

Although the *Adriatic* replaced the *Arctic* in 1857 the firm never recovered from the loss of the *Pacific*. In 1857 Congress dropped the subsidy to $385,000 and eliminated it completely the following year. Without federal assistance Collins could not operate. He was the victim of a combination of circumstances: the rampant sectionalism that was then driving the nation inexorably towards Civil War, congressional unwillingness to provide sufficient subsidy to permit competition with Cunard, reliance on the expensive wooden hulls and side wheels, bad luck, and the panic of 1857.

Although the demise of the Collins Line left Cunard the dominant force on the Atlantic crossing, other lines, including a few American ones, rose as challengers. Some were successful but most, like all the American efforts, were not. Part of Cunard's success resulted from his adoption of iron hulls in 1856. Iron hulls were stronger than wooden ones and better able to support the larger engines that allowed Cunard to reclaim the Atlantic blue ribbon lost to Collins. They were also lighter, which enabled the vessels to carry more paying passengers and cargo. Nevertheless, not until 1862 did a steamer appear that was large enough to carry a significant number of steerage passengers.

The main American opposition came from Cornelius Vanderbilt, who saw in the North Atlantic new opportunities for conquests. When the British government requisitioned many of the Cunard vessels for Crimean War service, the line had to suspend sailings to Boston and for a short time even to New York. Vanderbilt sensed the opportunity and proposed to Congress in 1855 that he carry the mails for less than half the subsidy on which Collins was losing money. Collins beat off the assault but, as we have seen, lost his own subsidy three years later. Despite his failure to secure governmental support, Vanderbilt placed two steamers on the New York-Cowes-Havre route in 1855. Although his vessels lost money,

The *Fulton* of the New York and Havre Steam Navigation Company taking on coal. She is a good example of the paddle-wheel steamers that served transatlantic routes before the Civil War. Signal Corps Photograph Courtesy of the National Archives

he decided that a larger vessel might succeed even without a mail contract. Therefore in 1857 be built a huge 3,550-ton, 331-foot-long, wooden paddle steamer named *Vanderbilt*. She served until the Civil War, when she went into uniform, spending most of her time as an auxiliary cruiser.

8. Distant Trades

The cotton trade was the singular exception to the persistent problem that faced the United States economy during the early nineteenth century. It was the identification of exports for which there was a market in Europe. The prime demand was for agricultural products, like cotton. Tobacco was the second largest export. Grain exports increased after the repeal of the English Corn Laws in 1846 caused wheat to flow eastward in an ever increasing stream to feed the workers in the Midlands textile mills. At the same time America came to rely less on imported wares to supply her domestic needs. Luxury imports like laces, wallpaper, cutlery, and wines as well as specialized products like heavy castings, rails, and chemicals still flowed into American ports in quantity although the nation increasingly relied on her own factories to fill her basic needs. Manufactured goods, notably watches, guns, machine tools, locomotives, and shoes, in limited but ever increasing quantities, passed outward. Some even found markets in Britain and France.

A different pattern developed in the Mediterranean. Trade with the Middle East and southern Europe grew substantially after the 1815 naval expedition that forced the Barbary Powers to abandon harassment of American shipping. That encouraged shippers to evolve two trading patterns in the region. One group of traders developed a trade in the Middle East for opium, which could be sold in China. The other carried fish to Spain, the Riviera, and Italy for exchange for wines, fruits, and other local products.

Another area, previously little exploited, that beckoned to United States traders and shipowners in the euphoria which followed the Treaty of Ghent was Latin America. The markets there had been closed by Spanish and Portuguese navigation acts prior to the independence of the newly formed republics and empires. Logically, since most of the new nations had copied United States political institutions, they should look to it for those goods that they could not produce at home. While the commercial interests were clearly secondary to the political ones, the maintenance of open trade with Latin America had a major role in the formulation of the Monroe Doctrine. Commerce played an equally great part in the British decision to support the new nations and the Doctrine.

The *John* of Philadelphia in 1799 scouted business possibilities in the Rio de la Plata. Her success brought imitators, 44 craft calling at Buenos Aires in 1801–02 alone. Philadelphia led the way, but Boston was not far behind. In 1804 William P. White of Boston established a mercantile agency in Buenos Aires, but the trade proved not to be as large as expected. Baltimore's shippers found that the locally milled flour made from Virginia and Maryland wheat had exceptional keeping qualities and developed a loyal Latin American market. Although initially importing primarily sugar and coffee, Baltimore after 1825 added hides from the La Plata and Brazil. The perishable nature of so much of Baltimore's trade caused her shipbuilders to develop a class of medium-sized fast freighters generally called Baltimore Clippers. By the middle

The ship *Glide* was one of the Salem vessels that tested distant waters. She is shown here in the Mediterranean after the War of 1812. Courtesy of U.S. Naval Historical Center

of the next decade the port's trade had shifted nearly exclusively to coffee, although most of the beverage was consumed in the West and increasingly entered the country through New Orleans. A similar decline developed before the Civil War in grain exports to Chile as the South American nation developed her own production. After 1850, primacy in Baltimore's import trade shifted to guano, with copper forming a distant second.

After the War of 1812 American merchants attempted to restore their prewar China trade. Between June 1816 and May 1817 some thirty-nine American craft entered Canton. They included eleven from Boston, nine from Philadelphia, seven from New York, five from Salem, four from Baltimore, and three from Providence. In the conditions that then existed American traders faced difficult times. United States cotton mills had yet to produce goods that commanded a premium on the China market while the traditional sea otter and sandalwood trades declined. Some of the American houses, like John Murray Forbes and Russell and Company, turned to opium importing although apparently a split existed among the American merchants over the ethics of the trade. Since opium had to be smuggled into China, no reliable figures exist as to the size of the American participation. The best estimates are that it accounted for about 10 percent of all American trade with the Chinese. In the early 1840s the efforts of the opium smuggling houses to secure fast vessels brought about the construction of a group of speedy schooners and brigs that contributed to the development of the clipper hull.

The zenith of profits for the China trade came in the early 1850s. A fast vessel could earn $80,000 on a voyage from New York to California and an additional $50,000 by carrying teas from Hong Kong to London, or twice the initial cost of a clipper. Other aspects of the trade, especially the laxity in collection of import duties in the United States, added to the profit.

The relaxed customs payment arrangements had been in effect for a long time. The following is a hypothetical but not unusual direct trade arrangement. A merchant loaded a vessel with $30,000 in ginseng, lead, zinc, iron, or other goods having a market in Canton, along with $170,000 in Spanish silver dollars. He exchanged the cargo for tea on which the duty was $400,000 but which could be sold in New York for $700,000, giving him a profit of 50 percent or $100,000 on his investment. Commonly the importer sold the tea to wholesale grocers who paid for it in four- to six-month notes. This presented little difficulty for the importer since he could pay the duty in longer, nine- to eighteen-month notes. Moreover, the importer could convert his $700,000 into sufficient cash to send out and fetch back two shipments before the customs notes became due. John Jacob Astor worked this arrangement so well that for about twenty years he had in effect an interest-free loan of $5 million from the United States government. Moreover, the risks of the trade were borne by the United States. When Thomas H. Smith and Sons, one of the larger New York houses, failed, they owed the Treasury $3 million.

Although a few American vessels participated in the clandestine African slave trade a handful of others developed a small but significant legitimate trade. In 1822 the French opened the island of Gorée off Senegal as an entrepôt for foreign traders. Two years later the British permitted American craft to trade with Gambia and in 1828 with the Gold Coast. While that trade constituted a minute fraction (0.6 percent in 1840, 0.7 percent in 1850, and 1.0 percent in 1860) of the overall United States foreign trade, it constituted as much as 41 percent of the trade of the Gold Coast in 1860. The American traders exchanged tobacco, rum, lumber, kerosene, flour, and manufactured goods for African hides, peanuts, palm oil, gold, ivory, dye woods, and tropical products. The West African trade flourished until about 1880, when the European powers began to restrict trade in the regions under their dominance.

Simultaneously, other Americans developed a significant trade with Zanzibar, exchanging textiles for cloves. That exchange was so large that the island's first commercial treaty in 1833 was with the United States. The Zanzibar Arabs merchandized the American textiles throughout East Africa so successfully that *merikani* became the generic East African term for cotton goods and blankets.

The first American vessel to touch at a California port did so in 1799. By 1816 much of the trade of the area rested in American hands. The local authorities, Spanish or Mexican, could not enforce the prohibition against visits by foreign craft or themselves provide the goods that the traders brought. In 1821 Mexican authorities opened California ports and five years later 58 percent of the vessels entering her ports flew the Stars and Stripes. Between 1822 and 1827 American traders eliminated their British competition and within another three years the Boston firm of Bryant and Sturgis held a near monopoly. In the decade of the 1830s their vessels brought 500,000 cattle hides east to the tanneries of Boston and New York. One of the craft was the *Dolphin,* in which Richard Henry Dana sailed. They were not the only Americans on the California coast. Many of the whalers that cruised the Pacific also put into Monterey, San Francisco, San Diego, and lesser ports to trade, make repairs, or refresh their crews.

The naval forces of Commodores John D. Sloat and Robert F. Stockton seized California in 1846–47. A year later James W. Marshall discovered gold in the race of John Sutter's mill on the American River. No sooner did the news reach the East Coast than vessels prepared to sail. The first, the bark *J. W. Coffin,* departed Boston on December 7, 1848. Within a year 774 others followed in her wake. When the gold fever reached its peak, any vessel that could float, regardless of seaworthiness or size, seemed to embark its party of gold seekers. So many craft were abandoned by their gold-hungry crews at San Francisco that their masts made the anchorage look like a forest. One observer in 1850 counted 300 abandoned craft. During 1849, 233 vessels brought 25,000–30,000 people, about 70 percent of them Americans, to California. Another 50,000 to 58,000 had embarked on 465 vessels still enroute. Nearly all landed at San Francisco. Despite the dangers of the Cape Horn passage and the Central American crossing, half of the gold seekers arrived by water.

The gold seekers drove prices in San Francisco to levels scarcely reached even in today's inflated world. Flour sold for 50 cents a pound; lumber fetched $400 per thousand board feet; brandy sold for 25 cents a glass; whiskey for $40 a quart; and eggs went for $1 apiece. A shave cost $4 and stevedores demanded $20–30 per day. With prices so high, cargoes destined for California could afford premium rates for quick delivery. The fat cargo rated in turn spurred East Coast shippers to order the sharp-lined, oversparred, heavily crewed beauties we call the clipper ship.

9. Clippers

America's most colorful sailing craft were undoubtedly the clipper ships. With their billowing sails reaching towards the sun, sleek, flush-decked hulls, easy passage through the sea, and their brilliant speed records the clipper ships represent the height of the nation's maritime development to most Americans. That they were often not ship-rigged, frequently disfigured by their conflicts with the unforgiving sea, were poor cargo carriers, and often equaled in speed by the "Downeasters" of a quarter century later has not dimmed their reputation.

The term *clipper* properly describes a hull form having a sharp entry, i.e., an underwater form that cuts through rather than pushes aside the water by widening gradually for as much as 40 percent of the vessel's length rather than having the rapid flaring or bluff bow of the conventional freighter. The clipper carried a mass of sail and was rigged strongly enough to permit nearly all of it to be carried in heavy weather.

The clipper concept did not spring full blown from the brilliant mind of a single designer, or group of designers. Its origins can be traced back through a development that encompassed the swift-sailing privateers of the War of 1812, slavers, opium runners, pilot boats, and fruit carriers, to say nothing of the big transatlantic packets and fast warships. They evolved so slowly that maritime historians can not even agree which vessel should be considered the "first clipper." Some would accord the honor to Baltimore's *Ann McKim* of 1832, a fast vessel stemming from the earlier "Baltimore clipper" brigs and schooners. Others give the prize to John W. Griffith's *Rainbow* design of 1843, which introduced the hollow bow line, long hull, and sharp rise of floor that came to characterize the clipper.

Despite their speed and beauty the clippers were poorly designed as cargo carriers. Their narrow hulls and hollow lines constricted capacity; their towering suits of sails could be handled only by oversized crews; and their constant driving by masters responding to the demand for speed rapidly wore out their wooden hulls. The life of clippers as fast cargo craft rarely exceeded ten years; most lived shorter periods.

The best-known of the clipper builders was the Nova Scotian Donald McKay, from whose East Boston yard flowed a series of unbeatable vessels for the California and China trades, including *Flying Cloud, Stag Hound,* and *Sovereign of the Seas.* They culminated in the *Great Republic* of 1853. The largest and most innovative vessel yet built in the United States, she sported double topsails, four masts, and a steam engine to aid in handling her anchors. Unfortunately, she caught fire before her first trip and was rebuilt with a diminished rig, so we do not know how she would have performed. Among the other great clipper designers were William H. Webb, who built more than any other builder; Samuel H. Pook, whose designs were particularly well regarded by modern naval architects; Griffiths; and George Raynes in Portsmouth, New Hampshire.

The clipper as developed in 1848–57 was highly specialized and suitable only for the few routes where speed commanded a premium. Speed they had. In 1854 the *Flying Cloud* ran from New York to San Francisco in a record 89 days 8 hours; the *Messenger* that same year dashed from San Francisco to Philadelphia in 82 days, while the *Northern Light* reached Boston in 76 days 6 hours. The *Comet* flew from San Francisco to New York in 76 days. The *Mary Whitridge* crossed the Atlantic from Baltimore in 12 days; the *Red Jacket* ran from New York to Liverpool in 13 days. Westward, the best passage from Liverpool to New York was 15 days by the *Andrew Jackson* The transpacific record went to the *Memnon,* which crossed from San Francisco to Whampoa in 36 days, the same time it took the *Golden City* to reach Woonsung. In 1854

The largest of the clippers, Donald McKay's *Great Republic,* shown here in her original four-masted rig. Courtesy of The Peabody Museum of Salem

the *Flying Cloud* ran from New York to Canton, via California, in 126 sailing days; her round trip that year took a record 6 months 16 days.

The clippers's speed resulted from more than fast lines. The crews were largely English and Scandinavian since American seamen, attracted by California gold and shore occupations, had become scarce. They were driven by some of the toughest sea captains ever to pace a quarterdeck. Successful clipper-ship masters were nerveless. They could drive their vessels through fearsome storms with full suits of sails until the last moment of safety before sending their large crews into the rigging to reef and shake.

They found the best winds by studying the newly published wind and current charts prepared by the Naval Observatory in Washington under the leadership of Lieutenant Matthew Fontaine Maury. The charts cut days off their passages by indicating where the best winds were likely to be found. In one of the first massive collections of statistics Maury and his colleagues consulted millions of entries in navy and civilian logbooks in order to determine the direction and frequency of the wind in each 10° square for each month. Using Maury's wind charts a navigator could easily lay out a course that would give him the best chance of finding favorable winds.

At their peak the California freight rates generally exceeded $25 per ton and in special instances went as high as $60. That brought such a rapid construction of craft for the trade that the market was oversupplied with shipping and glutted with goods. Not only did massive numbers of sailing craft pass Cape Horn, but the twelve steamers plying between San Francisco and Panama exceeded the number running between New York and Europe. That drove down the freight rate so rapidly that it was $12.75 per ton in 1856. A year later the rate fell to $11, well below the $15 needed to operate a clipper profitably.

Another nail in the coffin of the wooden clipper was the British shift to composite craft having iron frames and wooden planking. This produced a stronger vessel for less money. After 1857 American wooden vessels found it increasingly difficult to compete in the tea trade from Canton to London, to which many had migrated after the collapse of the California boom. Some clippers found temporary haven in the Britain-Australia trade after the discovery of gold in Victoria in 1851. Others survived in general trade during the Crimean War-induced shipping shortage. Still others turned to less colorful and less remunerative work such as carrying Chinese coolies to work the guano mines of the Chincha Islands of Peru.

By 1860 the California trade pattern had shifted. It moved from the importation of consumer items to the export of wool and grain. Nearly three million pounds of wool departed for New York in 1860, a year that also saw the beginnings of the great wheat trade that would dominate the intercoastal traffic and the deepwater route to Europe in the last quarter of the century.

10. The California Steamers

In 1845, at the height of the dispute with Britain over Oregon, Congress authorized mail service from New York to the Columbia River settlements. The plan envisioned steamers carrying the mail from New York to Chagres in Panama for transfer across the isthmus by canoe and muleback and then cartage to Oregon by a second group of steamers. The inadequate subsidy offered, however, attracted no operators.

The proponents of the Oregon route persevered and two years later secured the inclusion of both a construction and an operating subsidy in a Naval Appropriation Act. The resultant $290,000-per-year contract for the Atlantic section, including way stops at Havana and New Orleans, passed into the hands of the United States Mail Steamship Company. In order to maintain biweekly services the firm built five steamers. A similar contract for the Pacific leg went to the Pacific Mail Steamship Company headed by William H. Aspinwall. Service began December 1, 1848, when U.S. Mail's steamer *Ohio* departed New York. The Pacific Mail's *California* completed the initial trip at San Francisco on February 28, 1849, at the peak of the gold frenzy. Her whole crew, except for the captain and the third engineer, departed for the mines, and the *California* swung at anchor for four and a half months before enough men could be signed on to take her to sea again.

Until the completion of the Panama Railroad in 1855 the passage of the isthmus was difficult, dangerous, and slow. Although the danger of yellow fever remained, the railroad offered passengers and freight a quick and scenic trip from one ocean to the other. So much traffic passed over the route that it made a profit of $6 million in 1856 and consistently paid 12 percent dividends until the completion of the transcontinental railroad in 1869. Although losing a portion of its business to the new competitor, the Panama Railroad continued to show a profit until its acquisition by the French Panama Canal interests in 1880.

Despite the obvious advantages of cooperation, the U.S. Mail and Pacific Mail companies fought each other as well as Cornelius Vanderbilt, Charles Morgan, and others for the lucrative California trade. In 1851 the two companies agreed on spheres of operation, but intermittent struggles continued throughout the decade among the two lines and their competitors for domination of the route. Since Pacific Mail paid dividends of 50 percent in 1851, 20 percent from 1851 to 1853, and 10 to 30 percent in the decade between 1857 and 1867, the arrangement was worth preserving.

11. Shipbuilding

The vessels constructed in the years before the War of 1812 were generally under 400 tons capacity, a size that could be built at many locations along the coast by ship carpenters who required only a minimum of capital to outfit their yards. Although yards existed at many points from the Carolinas northward, the most were in the Northeast, primarily in Massachusetts and Maine. Between the War of 1812 and the Civil War the industry concentrated there even more tightly. Maine built the greatest number of vessels, although the largest craft usually went down ways into Massachusetts or New York waters. Builders in the Pine Tree State relied on native timbers until about 1840, although some experimented with southern pitch pine for planking as early as 1812. Even in Maine the trend towards construction of larger craft caused the yards to concentrate at a handful of towns mostly east of Portland. Other localities ceased building or produced only small craft as they exhausted the local supplies of large timbers.

Maine dominated small freighter building because wood in the sizes they needed could still be cut close to the yard and because the workers were subsistence farmers who labored for lower wages than their counterparts elsewhere in the nation. As a result, Down East vessels cost $5–15 per ton less than the products of other United States yards. On the other hand, they tended to be plainer than vessels from Boston or New York. Since Maine builders often built on speculation, they did well into the 1850s. When the California clipper bubble burst, prices even on smaller freighters fell to well below costs. This killed many of the smaller yards.

Boston continued as a major building center because of its ability to draw upon the New Hampshire forests via the Merrimack River and the Middlesex Canal. In 1834 an enterprising group of Boston merchants formed the East Boston Timber Company to attract shipbuilders to that Boston suburb. They purchased Grand Island in the Niagara River just above the falls, where they erected one of the largest sawmills in the world. In 1836 the mill began shipping prefabricated frames, but within four years exhausted its supply of white oak trees and closed. Nevertheless, the forward-thinking Boston timber merchants by then had secured other supplies. As a result they remained among the most successful in the country down to the close of the clipper era. From the yards of Donald McKay, Samuel Hall, Paul Curtis, and others in the Boston area came a series of exceptionally successful clippers and other large sailing craft.

New York relied upon the Hudson River basin and the timbers brought east over the Erie Canal to surge into importance as a building center after 1800. A group of highly successful yards stretched along the East River, including William H. Webb, Smith and Dimon, William H. Brown, Brown and Bell, and Jacob Westervelt, which produced a constant flow of successful large, wooden-hulled steamers and sailing craft. The East River yards provided most of the transatlantic packets, a large proportion of the clippers, and a majority of the nation's deepwater steamers. New York's importance as a building center dwindled after the Civil War because of the inability of its yards to switch to iron and steel construction.

Philadelphia drew upon the upper Delaware River forests for wood until they became exhausted, but after 1835 her builders turned increasingly to iron construction. By the time of the Civil War nearly all the yards in the nation regularly building iron hulls were clustered along a twenty-five-mile stretch of the Delaware River. Even though Baltimore and Norfolk both retained small shipbuilding industries neither port threatened the northern ports in quantity of output. No other significant building centers existed along the remainder of the East Coast or on the West Coast prior to the Civil War although San Francisco Bay began to emerge as a center in the late 1850s. Yards there could draw on the northern California forests and, after the Civil War, on the firs of the Puget Sound.

Until the Civil War, shipbuilding continued to be a highly competitive industry since it remained essentially a handicraft, one demanding only limited capital to enter. Since entry into the business was easy, most of the yards were small. Many were operated by a master carpenter who designed the vessels, usually relying on the elaborate rules of the classification societies, selected the timbers, supervised the construction, and handled the financial matters. Others, supervised by men less widely skilled, divided the responsibilities between an operator who handled the financial and non-structural aspects and a master carpenter who designed and constructed the hull. A vessel could be built by a group of 3 to 25 men and normally much of the work would be subcontracted to specialized gangs of ship carpenters, calkers, riggers, sailmakers, and the like since few yards maintained a sufficient level of activity to warrant a permanent work force. Although the numbers decreased as larger vessels became common after 1840, about 10–20 percent of the vessels came from yards that operated only intermittently. In 1850, for example, roughly 1,000 yards contributed to the year's production of 1,126 sailing craft.

When they could do so, most master builders selected white

oak for frames. The renowned live oak frames were so expensive that they were used only for warships and special commercial craft. Cedar and locust were alternatives but better for top timbers. Planking was of white oak until it became too expensive and was replaced by southern hard pine. Decks and joiner work were commonly of white pine or spruce although beech, maple, birch, black and yellow oak, chestnut, hackmatack, ash, hickory, and juniper, were sometimes used. Spars and masts were normally made of white pine since it was the best mast material in the world.

Great care had to be taken by the loggers in cutting and preparing the wood. The best timbers came from well-dried trees cut during the winter when the sap was down. Here the economics of the industry entered the scene because the premium required to secure well-seasoned, top-quality timber for a vessel increased her finished cost. As a result, many of the smaller craft built for economy-minded owners were constructed of poorly seasoned wood that soon rotted. Since colonial times the low quality of some vessels had provided fuel for the dispute between their owners and the British insurance companies, which downgraded American woods in comparison to English oak. This, in turn, led to the formation of American classification societies, starting with the New York Maritime Register in 1857.

Iron hulls would have corrected the insurance problem, but American builders seldom could produce one sufficiently inexpensive to attract a buyer. As might be expected, iron-hulled vessels first appeared in Britain, where a small 12-foot, sheet-iron pleasure craft took the water in 1777. Iron hulls were not practical until plates appeared in 1783–84. Even then no practical iron-hulled steamer appeared in Britain before the *Aaron Mahby* of 1822.

In 1825 the pioneer American iron hull, the *Codorus,* appeared on the Susquehanna River. Four years later Jesse W. Starr, a Philadelphia boilermaker, fabricated an iron barge for use on the Lehigh River, the first of over a hundred similar craft to ply American canals and rivers before 1840. Yet the introduction of iron hulls in the United States was slow both because of its cost, which was 40–100 percent greater than in Britain, the infancy of the American iron industry, and the resistance of many shipowners who believed that the metal was too brittle to withstand groundings and collisions. Only when the English iron-hulled, transatlantic steamer *Great Britain* survived pounding by winter storms while ashore on the Irish coast in 1846–47 did opinion change.

Some idea of her strength can be gained from her later history. She served as an active ocean carrier until 1886 and as a storage hulk in the Falkland Islands for another fifty years. She is now preserved as a museum ship at Bristol, England.

Meanwhile, experimental iron construction continued. In 1834 John Cant of Savannah purchased the prefabricated steamer *John Randolph* in Britain and put her to work on the Savannah River. Four similar craft followed. In 1839 Captain Robert F. Stockton of the Navy had a 70-foot steamer built in England to demonstrate John Ericsson's screw propeller. She subsequently crossed the Atlantic and entered service on the Delaware and Raritan Canal, the first commercial vessel powered by Ericsson's screw. That year also saw the first iron-hulled craft on western waters, a 220-ton steamer put together in Pittsburgh. The most interesting of the Pittsburgh-built iron hulls undoubtedly was the navy gunboat *Michigan* erected in 1842, knocked down, and carted to the shores of Lake Erie for reassembly. She survived until 1942, when her plates contributed to the first of World War II's scrap drives.

Occasional iron-hulled craft challenged the hold of wooden craft on the American carrying trade. Many of the early experiments, like the small, canal-sized *Ashland* and *Ocean* built in 1844 for the Philadelphia-Troy, New York, coal trade and the pioneer twin-screw steamer *Bangor,* were not repeated. Not until Harlan and Hollingsworth built the *Champion* in 1859 did an American yard produce a truly first-class, sea-going, iron-hulled steamer.

The rapid decline of construction for foreign trade in the half decade before the Civil War can be explained partly by the inability of American yards to produce competitively priced iron hulls. Although wooden vessels reached their practical limits in the late 1850s, few American owners shifted to iron. Most, faced with high domestic construction costs and strong foreign competition, brought their investments ashore. Only on the banks of the Delaware River between Wilmington and Philadelphia could there be said to have been an iron shipbuilding industry. In the twelve years between 1845 and 1857 the yards along "the American Clyde" launched forty-nine of the sixty iron hulls built in the United States.

Despite the relative backwardness of the iron industry American engineers developed several distinctive steam engine designs.

In its original form, as devised by James Watt, the engine used a vibrating connecting-rod from the cylinder to drive the crankshaft. A simple box boiler produced steam at atmospheric pressure. Fitch, Stevens, and Fulton modified the Watt engine into the steeple or crosshead type in which the piston rod drove a crosshead, set between guides, that had connecting rods to the crankshaft. The next American development, appearing in 1822, was the walking beam. In that arrangement the piston rod drove a crossbeam pivoted at the center, which in turn was connected to the crankshaft. The British, whose vessels operated in rougher waters than most American craft, modified the beam engine in the 1830s by placing the crossbeam close to the vessel's keel for greater stability. This design became known as the side-lever engine.

The walking beam engine had several advantages for American operators. It worked well in the shallow-draft craft employed on river and coastal runs. It took considerable misalignment without complaint and required a lighter foundation than the side-lever design. Not only were the walking beam engine's foundation plates lighter and cheaper to fabricate, but the engines required smaller castings that were well within the capabilities of American foundries.

In 1802 Oliver Evans introduced his "Columbian Engine," which most contemporaries called a Grasshopper from its motion. More accurately it should be described as a half-beam engine since the vertical piston rod was connected to a beam that in turn was attached by a bridle on either side to the framing of the cylinder, which permitted a straight-line motion while the other end pivoted on long rocking links that moved back and forth to give the engine its descriptive name.

The idea of using the expansion of steam successively in a pair of cylinders had been envisioned by Watt and patented by Jonathan Hornblower in 1781, but the early engines were not tight enough to permit the idea to work successfully. In 1804 Arthur Woolf improved Hornblower's design into what later came to be known as the compound type. The earliest Woolf-type engines used in the United States appeared on the Hudson in the 1820s. They failed because the boiler pressures then possible were too low.

The screw propeller is frequently acclaimed as an American invention, but it is not exclusively so. The earliest actual use of one was by the American David Bushnell in his hand-propelled submarine *Turtle* in 1775. John Fitch probably operated a small screw steamer on Collect Pond on Manhattan in 1796 while, as we have noted earlier, John Stevens installed a pair on his little *Juanita* in 1802. The next development came in Britain, where Francis P. Smith constructed a screw propeller vessel in 1836 and in Sweden, where John Ericsson did likewise.

Ericsson moved to the United States in 1839 and soon received a commission from the Boston merchant Robert Bennet Forbes to design the twin-screw 148-ton auxiliary bark *Midas*. The larger *Edith* followed in 1843, but she proved unsuited for her intended role in the Chinese coastal trade. Nevertheless, Forbes ordered a third Ericsson-designed craft, the *Massachusetts,* which for a short time ran unsuccessfully against the Cunard steamers on the Atlantic. Meanwhile, in 1841 the first Ericsson screw went into service in the Great Lakes on board the *Vandalia*. The following year Stockton used his considerable political connections to secure the construction by the Navy of the screw sloop of war *Princeton* using Ericsson's designs. With her screw propeller, anthracite-burning furnaces, and heavy shell guns she was one of the most revolutionary warships of her age.

Ericsson's leading competitor in the United States was Philadelphia engineer Robert F. Loper. Less flamboyant than the Swede, he was more consistently successful in his designs. Loper's propellers were simpler, and his engines more carefully designed. Moreover, Loper carefully coordinated the design of the screw, engine, and hull to produce a series of successful vessels during the 1850s. His residence in Philadelphia, along with the young iron shipbuilding industry there, played a major role in the antebellum importance of the Delaware River yards.

Boilers were a further area of intense interest to American engineers. Initially all boilers consisted of copper plates bolted together to form a rectangular box. Because it was nearly impossible to make the seams watertight, early boilers leaked and could not operate at high pressures. Moreover, being built of copper they often had a salvage value greater than the rest of the vessel combined. Not until 1819 could iron plates be rolled in sizes suitable for use in boilers. As technology improved, so did the pressures. Most early eastern engines operated at about 10–12 pounds per square inch (psi) while the high-pressure ones favored in the West reached 30–40 psi. Occasional vessels had engines employing much higher pressures, such as the 1840 Ohio River steamer *Messenger*, whose machinery operated at the unheard of 200 psi.

Initially boilers followed the water tube design patented by Nathan Reed in 1791. In them the water passes through the fire in tubes. Despite considerable experimentation with boiler designs, especially by the Navy, water tube boilers remained standard until the 1850s. Then fire tube designs in which the fire passed through the water in tubes began to enter marine service. They had been used on locomotives for twenty years.

Low boiler pressures retarded the introduction of screw propulsion. Low-pressure engines operate at slower speeds than higher-pressure ones while screws need to revolve at relatively high speeds for the maximum thrust. Therefore, most of the early screw installations had to use bulky gearing to achieve the necessary propeller speed. But gears not only took up cargo space; they added considerably to the expense of the power plant. In the mid-1850s conditions changed as boiler pressures rose, permitting more compact machinery and higher speed engines that could be coupled directly to the propeller shaft.

Because of its availability and the simple fireboxes fitted to the early boilers, all steamers burned wood until 1816. That year both the *Car of Neptune* and *Chancellor Livingston* on the Hudson River experimented with bituminous coal, but its relative expense and difficulty in handling slowed adoption. Not until Robert L. Stevens introduced forced draft on the boilers of his *North America* in 1827 did coal become a useful fuel.

One of the earliest development contracts let in the United States was granted to President Eliphalet Nott of Union College by several anthracite coal mine operators to develop a grate that would permit use of their coal in boilers. In 1830 he installed his newly perfected grate in combination with forced draft on the amazingly successful *Novelty*. The twenty tons of coal she consumed on the trip from New York to Albany occupied only 20 percent of the space needed for the 40 cords of wood normally burned by other boats on the run. Equally important, the coal cost only $100 as opposed to $240 for the wood. There was one drawback. The high temperature at which the coal burned made the *Novelty*'s cabin so uncomfortable that anthracite's adoption had to await the development of better insulation.

Explosions were common in the early years of steamboat operation because of the recklessness of the engineers and their ignorance of the limits of strength of boilers. Despite long-standing public concern over the accidents, legal steps to prevent them came slowly because of the traditional American horror of restrictive legislation. The boiler explosion on the Hudson River steamer *Aetna* in 1824 started efforts to secure a federal steamboat-licensing law. The initial efforts were unavailing, but the continued rash of explosions caused one of the federal government's earliest efforts at direct support of outside scientists. During 1831–36 the government financed an investigation of the problem by the Franklin Institute of Philadelphia. Its report and the loss of over 400 lives to boiler explosions in 1838 alone caused Congress to enact regulations governing vessels carrying passengers. These required periodic inspections of the hull and boilers as well as the employment of qualified engineers. Although slackly enforced, the law represented a philosophical springboard for later regulations. Its 1852 revision tightened some of the rules and instituted licensing of engineers. The new law had an immediate effect as accidents fell 65 percent following its enactment. As a result of the horrible *Sultana* fire in 1865, during which about 1,500 lives were lost, the inspection procedures were further tightened, and in 1873 licensing examinations became mandatory for steamer captains and mates.

The distinctive steam whistle that added so much personality to individual steamers as they churned along the reaches of the great rivers or slid into the bustling ports and quiet landing of the coasts first appeared in 1837 on the Fall River-Providence steamer *King Philip.* Her owner, it is claimed, had seen one on a locomotive and decided that his pride and joy should sport one also. About seven years later a similar instrument appeared on the Pittsburgh packet *Revenue,* whose captain allegedly gained his inspiration from a factory whistle. In 1855, soon after he invented the steam calliope, Joshua C. Stoddard installed one temporarily on a New York harbor tugboat. In 1858 he placed a 34-whistle unit on the Hudson River steamer *Armenia,* but it required so much steam that the engines slowed noticeably whenever she greeted the surrounding countryside with her melodic snorting. In 1857 the St. Louis steamer *Amazon* became the first of many western boats to sport a calliope. As long as steam power persisted on the western waters the calliope survived as an important adjunct to showboats and excursion vessels, as it does today in the *Delta Queen*.

12. The Impact of Industrialization

As the country moved towards its seventy-fifth birthday the impact of overseas trade on the average American diminished. Increasingly American factories drawing upon American raw materials and technological skills reduced the variety of goods that the nation sought abroad. Since the United States still produced few manufactured goods for export, American workers did not see foreign trade as a significant ingredient in their job security. Even the cotton, tobacco, and grain farmers who did depend for a large portion of their livelihood on foreign sales found their major market at home. It is no surprise, therefore, that the American deepwater marine found few champions among politicians, publicists, or proletariat.

For rather obvious reasons the shipping community supported free trade. Once maritime-produced wealth came ashore, however, it usually embraced protection. Francis Cabot Lowell and Patrick T. Jackson of Boston were good examples. Both were scions of noted shipping families who became leading manufacturers after forming the Waltham Company to manufacture cotton textiles on the new power looms developed by Lowell. In 1816 they were instrumental in securing passage of a strongly protective tariff. Within a generation the great textile centers of Lowell, Lawrence, Chicopee, and Manchester sprang into being with the aid of shipping-derived capital. Patterson, New Jersey, and Cohoes, New York, were not far behind. By 1840 Massachusetts had passed from a commercial to a manufacturing state, soon to be followed by New Jersey, Connecticut, and New York.

Just as the protective tariff presumably aided the youthful American factories, the 1816 tariff law introduced a conciliatory note with a scorpion's stinger in its tail. It placed treatment on a reciprocal basis. For those nations that dropped charges above the normal tariff and port fees against American goods and vessels, the United States would withdraw its extra charges. Particularly important was the inclusion of a reciprocity provision in the 1815 commercial treaty with Great Britain, which lifted all discriminatory fees on vessels and products of the two countries. In 1817 the United States heightened the campaign for nondiscrimination by imposing a $2 per ton tax on foreign vessels arriving from ports closed to American vessels and banning vessels trying to evade that regulation by stopping at an open intermediate port. This was an attempt to pry open the British West Indies by halting indirect trade via Canada. It did not work. Yet by reducing the costs of shipping on foreign-flag vessels the reciprocity laws cut the price advantage of American carriers and helped set in motion the forces that would ultimately place most of our foreign commerce under foreign flags. Reciprocity remained the guiding doctrine of American shipping policy until 1873.

There were efforts to change the policy, none having a long life. The 1845 and 1847 Mail Subsidy Acts provided for government subsidy of selected steamship lines. This greatly irritated southern politicians, who saw their tax money going to support New York-owned steamship lines; western legislators, who viewed it as a money grab by eastern capitalists; and sailing line operators. Together they killed the subsidies. Nevertheless, the federal largess paid for the construction of the magnificent Collins liners in the transatlantic trade and helped establish the intercoastal run via Panama.

The American merchant marine boomed for a number of reasons—relatively low construction costs for wooden sailing vessels, the immigrant and California trades, and a general expansion of world shipping in the 1850s, to mention a few. It reached 4,212,000 tons in 1855 but then leveled off. Salt-water construction fell from 427,000 tons that year to 125,000 in 1860. Even more striking was the decline in the proportion of foreign trade carried by American vessels. It fell from 73.7 percent in 1858 to 66.9 percent in 1859 and accelerated by the pressures of the Civil War to a mere 25 percent in 1866.

Although she could not ignore her freshwater trade arteries, America had firmly planted both feet on dry land, turned her back to the salt air, and embraced the mother earth. Never again, except under the pressures of wartime survival, would she challenge for commercial supremacy on the high seas.

Chapter Three

THE COASTAL TRADE BLOOMS

T HE THIRD LAW ENACTED BY CONGRESS AFTER THE ESTABLISHMENT OF the new government under the Constitution was the Tonnage Act of July 20, 1789. It required all craft over twenty tons built in the United States or imported before the preceding May 16 to be "enrolled" or licensed for coastal trade before engaging in commerce between customs districts. The law provided that foreign-built and -owned vessels must pay fifty cents per ton on entering an American port; that foreign-owned but United States-built craft would be assessed thirty cents per ton; while American-built and -owned traders paid only six cents per ton per year. This effectively froze foreign traders from the coastal trade. The law was a conscious effort to encourage the development of the merchant marine. Similar regulations, such as the British Navigation Acts, existed in most maritime nations. The absolute closing of the coastal trade to foreign vessels did not occur until 1817.

For American shipowners, exclusion of foreign competition from the coastal trade was more than a perfunctory exercise of a sovereign right. The intercolonial trade had been the second largest portion of the pre-Revolutionary War maritime commerce, so it was not surprising that the shipping community looked to it as the foundation of their prosperity. In their view, recovery was impossible if foreign competitors were allowed to take away business.

104

1. Establishing the Trade

The tonnage of shipping engaged in coastal trade during the Federal and Jeffersonian periods amounted to roughly 25–30 percent of the total merchant marine tonnage or about 40 percent of that sailing overseas. Even so, coastal shipping doubled every decade between 1790 and 1810, when it reached 405,000 tons. The growth resulted from the general economic health of the country rather than from any single factor. The population nearly doubled in those years, from 3.9 to 6.3 million, but the country remained largely a nation of subsistence farmers although regional specialization was beginning to make itself felt. The New England farmers began the shift to sheep, horse and cattle raising, and truck farming; the middle states increased their dominance of wheat and other grain production, while the southern continued to be the source of tobacco, although cotton was fast displacing it as the section's prime product. The rapid rise in cotton crop after Eli Whitney's invention of the cotton gin in 1793 helps account for a part of the sharp increase in the tonnage of vessels engaged in coastal trade during 1797–1807.

Other bulk commodities, especially grain and lumber, contributed to the growth of the domestic merchant marine. The great forests of Maine supplied most of the wood used in New England while the Middle States drew on those of the Delaware and Hudson River watersheds. Until about 1815 Wiscasset was the chief lumber shipping port in Maine, owning some 20,000 tons of timber carriers herself. Her merchants readily acknowledged their debt to the sea. When they formed the Lincoln and Kennebec Bank in 1802 they indicated the value of their notes by the rigs of the vessels shown on them. In spite of the bank, Wiscasset lacked the capital to develop her operations further. The Sheepscot, Wiscasset's river, tapped only a limited hinterland, so the industry migrated eastward to lands controlled by others.

The War of 1812 restricted but did not eliminate coastal shipping. Since coastal traders offered the only means of moving goods in quantity between the North and South prior to the completion of the intersectional railroad systems shortly before the Civil War, the effect of peace was immediate. Between 1815 and 1817 an average of 1,282 vessels, most of them coastal, annually left the ways of American shipyards. By 1817 so large a surplus of ship-

No. 5. BRIG (Bg.).

A brig of the type that carried much of the coastal trade of the United States before the Civil War. From *Merchant Vessels of the United States, 1892*

ping existed that it served as one of the catalysts for the recession that came two years later. In 1821 good times returned. Cotton prices doubled, and the Rhode Island mills alone consumed 31,000 bales that year. At Baltimore, then the flour-milling center of the country, prices rose from the postwar low of $3.37 to $10 per barrel. Already it was clear that growing industrialization would cause the coastal trade to supplant foreign trade as the major activity of the merchant marine. The shift gained impetus when the legislation formally closing the coastwide trade to foreign vessels took effect in 1817. The postwar revival brought a rapid growth in coastal packet lines. A dozen New York merchant houses operated lines by 1822, as did half that number of Boston firms.

Coastal steamers appeared during the war. In 1813 five steamers plied the protected waters of the Delaware River and Chesapeake Bay, offering service in conjunction with stage lines that cut the time of travel under optimum conditions between New York and Baltimore to two days. Steamer lines developed slowly because of the monopolies granted by individual states to local entrepreneurs. Most noted, and important, was that given to the Livingston-Fulton interests, "the Monopoly," by New York State, which froze all competitors from the waters off Manhattan. It inhibited the development of steamboat lines until after the Supreme Court's landmark decision in the 1824 *Gibbons* v. *Ogden* case overturned the state grants as invasions of the federal power to regulate interstate commerce. The freeing of steamboat operations from the anaconda grasp of the Monopoly coincided with a surge of investor willingness to advance the large sums needed to develop coastal steamship lines. By 1840 steamer lines connected all major East Coast ports.

2. New England

In 1815 Boston resumed her primacy among the New England ports. Her coastal shipping faced little competition until steamers began braving the swells of Long Island Sound to connect with the railroads radiating from the Hub.

The *Chief Justice Marshall,* a Hudson River steamer named in honor of the author of the *Gibbons* v. *Ogden* decision. Official U.S. Navy Photograph

Although a handful of small, underpowered steamers ventured north immediately after the War of 1812 they quickly demonstrated their inability to withstand the rough waters off the New England coast. Their failure caused few problems since the prevailing westerly winds north of Boston gave fast, frequent, and dependable sailing communications, while the limited population in the region could not generate enough trade to support the relatively expensive steamers. In addition, many of the cargoes originating in Maine, like lumber, lime, granite, and fish, traveled easily and cheaply by sailing craft.

Maine firewood dominated the Boston heating market. In 1829 the Down East forests provided 83 percent of the 120,000 cords consumed. Nearly all of it arrived by water. Coal began a steady inroad into the heating market after the arrival of the first shipments from Cape Breton in the early 1820s and those from Pennsylvania in the following decade. Nevertheless, Boston's coal trade did not become substantial until after the Civil War.

Captain Seward Porter established an abortive steamer line between Boston and Portland, Maine, in 1823 and a successful one seven years later. Portland developed into a regional hub. Secondary lines soon fanned out from her wharves to the Kennebec River, Penobscot Bay, Eastport, and St. John in New Brunswick. The Cumberland and Oxford Canal from Lake Sebago reached Portland in 1830. Although originally intended as a mechanism for settling a potentially prosperous agricultural area, the canal proved most valuable as a lumber carrier.

Portland achieved a rail tie to Boston in 1842. The new route reduced freight traffic on the steamship lines, but it could not match either the comfort or ease of the sea voyage, which attracted a major portion of the passenger traffic until World War I. Because of its inability to bridge the Kennebec River the railroad carried few passengers to coastal points beyond Bath before 1927. Their travelers instead rode the small steamers that served the routes radiating from Portland, Rockland, and Bangor, much as the Puget Sound ports later in the century relied upon feeder lines to Seattle. In Maine, as elsewhere along the coasts, heavier freight moved by sailing craft, leaving only express and passengers to the steamers.

After the opening of the Grand Trunk Railroad to Quebec in 1853 Portland became the winter port for much of eastern Canada. Six years later the port even built a special wharf to accommodate

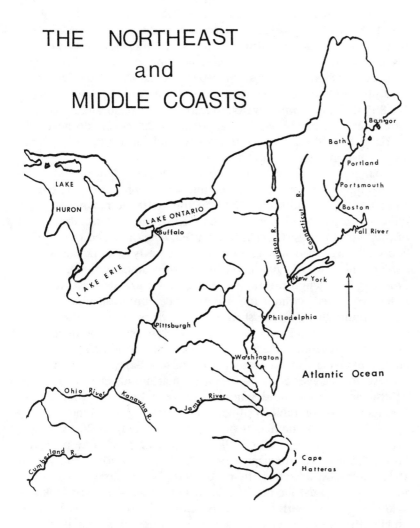

THE NORTHEAST
and
MIDDLE COASTS

Bangor

Bath

Portland

Portsmouth

LAKE

HURON

Boston

LAKE ONTARIO

Buffalo

Fall River

Hudson R.

Connecticut R.

LAKE ERIE

New York

Philadelphia

Pittsburgh

Washington

Atlantic Ocean

Ohio River

Kanawha R.

James River

Cumberland R.

Cape
Hatteras

the *Great Eastern,* but the great iron ship never appeared. Nevertheless, the Portlanders continued to hope, in vain as history would demonstrate, that they could tap the great cascade of wheat that flowed through the St. Lawrence River ports to Britain.

If Portland's grain trade never developed, an important connection with Havana matured after the War of 1812. By the mid-1820s Portland traders handled about 10 percent of the traffic flowing through the Cuban port. The volume grew in the 1840s and 1850s as Maine became nearly the sole source of the boxes, hogsheads, and tierces within which sugar and molasses reached market. During the half decade preceding the Civil War over 98 percent of export cargos of lumber leaving Maine ports cleared for Cuba. Following the construction of the Portland Sugar House in 1855 the Maine port developed into a major sugar and molasses consumer. During the latter years of the century the distance of Portland from the major sugar markets and the formation of the sugar trust brought a contraction of the industry.

Bangor, the center of the lumbering industry after 1820 and fast becoming the world's leading lumber-shipping port, started a steamship line to Boston in 1833. In the 1840s dominance of the Bangor run passed to Menemon Sanford's Independent Line. One of the line's masters, Captain William Flowers, invented the "time courses" method of navigation, which quickly became the standard method in coastal waters. By steering predetermined directions for fixed lengths of time a pilot could bring his vessel to any point he wished without the use of navigation aids, which were scarce along the Maine coast in the early years of the century.

Bangor's lumber trade offers a good example of the interrelationship of maritime affairs with the general development of a region. It explains why the waters of Penobscot Bay were among the earliest to receive extensive sets of marine navigation aids—lighthouses, buoys, and day marks. Between 1832 and 1888 Bangor shipped 8.7 billion feet of lumber, 242 million in the peak year of 1872 alone. At the height of the trade as many as 250 vessels loaded at one time. Not only did Bangor and its satellite port of Brewer draw on the drainage area of the Penobscot River but, after 1832, railroads stretched their iron tendrils out into less favorably located lands. Despite her local rail network Bangor lacked land connections with her markets until well after the Civil War; timber, therefore, moved to market by water in fleets of large schooners.

Although they maintained frequent sailing packet service with the ports in her immediate vicinity, Boston shipowners approached steamships with the wariness of a navigator on an unfamiliar coast. Regular service to Salem on the North Shore waited until 1820, and another nine years passed before a steamer regularly ran to Hingham on the South Shore. Most of the North Shore commuter lines died following the opening of the Eastern Railroad to Salem in 1838 although a few to places without rail connections, like Nahant, continued healthy.

In 1852 the Boston and Philadelphia Steamship Company inaugurated service, as did the Merchants and Miners' Transportation Company running to Baltimore. The two firms represented Boston's earliest ventures in long-distance coastal steamship operations. Both proved successful and long lasting. In the years immediately before the Civil War Boston promoters, including the clipper-ship builder Donald McKay, initiated service to New Orleans and to Savannah in hopes of tapping the cotton market. Although the lines operated until the outbreak of hostilities, they were not resumed after the war.

Despite their close business ties, Boston did not establish scheduled all-water steamship service to New York until 1864 because of the distance and the danger inherent in rounding Cape Cod. Until then trade either moved by sailing freighter or by steamer on Long Island Sound after passage by rail to one of the terminal points of the railroads radiating from Boston. In part the delay in the development of steamer connections reflected the nature of the textile industry. Before the Civil War, New York City served as the chief distribution center for imported textiles but played a very limited role in the movement of the domestic product. As the center of the American textile-producing area, Boston handled domestic shipments through her own commercial houses just as her merchants brought raw cotton directly to their wharfs from southern ports. Indeed, except for local consumption, there is little evidence of a New York role in the distribution of any manufactured goods from upper New England.

The impact of the cotton trade on the northern ports becomes clear from the shifts in their relative standing. Boston's foreign trade increased from $17 million in 1821 to $58 million in 1860, but that growth was not as great as that of the cotton arriving to feed the ever growing number of the New England textile mills. Before the Civil War, Boston handled about half of all cotton consumed domestically. In 1830 46,203 bales crossed her docks, while nineteen years later that figure had risen to 270,593. Almost as effective a gauge of the growing industrialization of New England was the simultaneous surge in flour imports. In the same nineteen years they rose from 309,997 to 987,988 barrels.

3. Long Island Sound

New York served as the distribution center for goods produced by the factories of Connecticut and western Massachusetts. They flowed to market by way of the Long Island Sound ports. Most of the Connecticut shore towns, especially those west of the Thames River, had historically been closely tied commercially to New York while Connecticut River farms and factories shipped half of their produce there. Sailing vessels regularly ran between New Haven and New York as early as 1789. In 1819, for instance, Norwich shippers could use any of six packets sailing to New York while another six or seven operated out of New Haven.

The trade attracted the Fulton-Livingston steamboat monopoly. In 1813 they built the *Fulton*, their first non-Hudson River steamer, to operate between New York and New Haven. The War of 1812 prevented her use until 1815. She and the *Connecticut,* which began plowing her way to New London the following year, waged a rate war with locally owned steamers that culminated in their being legislated off Connecticut waters and Connecticut craft being forbidden to operate in New York. The *Gibbons* v. *Ogden* decision in 1824, by opening state waters to all craft, ended the comic opera episode. During that struggle one useful innovation appeared. One of the antimonopoly steamers, the *United States,* introduced simple cardboard tickets. Heretofore, passengers had been waybilled like bundles of freight. The simplicity and ease of the new arrangement brought its universal adoption.

During the 1830s the construction of railroads radically changed the transportation systems of southern New England. The early railroads in the area nearly all ran north and south along the river valleys and relied on the steamboat lines to furnish connections to New York. Because of the difficulties in bridging the larger streams, east-west rail lines had only a very limited effect on the passenger trade of the Sound steamers until the addition of sleeping cars after the Civil War. The new rail service killed several of the weaker lines whose vessels could not compete in the luxury of their accommodations.

Providence gained steamboat connection with New York in 1822. Since the Rhode Island capital had good stage lines and only a forty-mile trip to Boston the service proved to be an immediate success. The $10 fare from Providence to New York was less than the cost of the stage, and lodgings on an overland trip and matched that charged by the sailing packets. Providence's freight trade increased substantially after the construction in 1824–28 of the Blackstone Canal to Worcester in east central Massachusetts. It served as the outlet for the farmers of central Massachusetts until the opening of the Boston and Worcester Railroad in 1835 and the Providence and Worcester in 1847 drained away traffic. Coincidentally, the canal suffered from ever increasing diversions of the Blackstone River to power the mills that sprang up along its banks.

As the steamboat company prospered it attracted competitors. The most notable of those was Cornelius Vanderbilt, who in 1835 ran his new, fast steamer *Lexington* to Providence. Since the *Lexington* could make the 210-mile trip from New York in less than twelve and a half hours, and Vanderbilt had cut his fares to as little as $1.00, he quickly acquired a large following. He gathered more passengers by innovative marketing like the earliest recorded sale of excursion tickets. This first effort of Vanderbilt outside the waters of the Hudson River not only heralded a new phase in the career of the most successful of the cutthroat operators but awakened the established lines to the threat of an inspired and unscrupulous competitor.

In 1835 the Boston and Providence Railroad started operations. The following year it joined with a pair of the Providence-New York steamer lines to form the Boston and New York Transport Company which offered through-tickets and bills of lading as well as faster service and better accommodations than the stage lines. Within two years, however, the bulk of the passenger traffic shifted to Stonington, Connecticut. The building of the Providence and Stonington Railroad allowed travelers to eliminate the rough-water passage around Point Judith and permitted use of larger vessels than could enter the shallow Providence harbor. The Stonington Line dominated the New England-New York route until the formation of the Fall River Line in 1847.

The new line grew out of the completion of the Fall River Railroad from Boston. That prompted Colonel Thomas Borden and other local investors to form a Fall River-New York Steamboat Line. Because the new route offered the fastest service between the two major northeastern cities it prospered. As a result it consistently attracted more able managers than its competitors and commanded sufficient financial resources to remain the leading Long

Island service and the main New York-Boston line well into the twentieth century. The financial strength of the line allowed it to construct larger and more attractive vessels than its competitors during the post-Civil War boom era.

A few competing routes held the attention of shippers and travelers for short periods, but none had the staying capacity of the Fall River Line. While the New London and Norwich Steamboat Company put the 346-ton steamer *Norwich* into service in 1836, the line's importance awaited the Norwich and Worcester Railroad's opening four years later. Not only did the railroad create a new outlet for the Worcester factories but, by connecting with the Western Railroad, it opened an alternative route to Boston that lasted into the 1890s.

Hartford, Springfield, and the other upper Connecticut River towns faced great difficulties connecting their wharves to salt water. Above Middletown the river had only a 5^1/$_2$-foot-depth while falls at Enfield, Connecticut, and South Hadley and Turners Falls, Massachusetts, broke the river into three pools. Between 1795 and 1829 local entrepreneurs built small bypass canals around the falls to permit limited trade between Hartford and the upriver communities. In 1800 a further step occurred with the formation of the Union Company to dig a 7^1/$_2$-foot-deep channel between Middletown and Hartford. That helped Hartford increase her West Indies trade in beef, flour, horses, and lumber and in 1818 led to the formation of the Connecticut Steam Boat Company to operate to New London and New York. Although six years later the service passed to an enlarged Connecticut River Steamboat Company, upriver farmers still lacked a cheap and reliable contact with their markets. That appeared in 1828 when the first steamers churned north from Springfield. Unfortunately, their small size restricted their usefulness, and they easily succumbed to the competition of the railroads. The downriver steamer lines, however, could offer the railroads stronger competition and continued until after their absorption by the New York, New Haven, and Hartford Railroad in 1895.

The lack of navigable feeder streams into New Haven harbor limited exploitation of one of the better sites on Long Island Sound. During the 1820s New Haven investors attempted to reduce their handicap by building a canal to Farmington, west of Hartford. Unfortunately, before completion the project became enmeshed in a pipedream of a waterway to the St. Lawrence. Work on the southern end of the canal began in 1825. It reached Farmington four years later but was stopped in the late 1830s at Northampton on the Connecticut River after the expenditure of $2 million. In service, the New Haven and Northampton Canal proved to be poorly built, undercapitalized, and lacked traffic. It breathed its last in 1847 and suffered the consumate indignity of having its right of way converted into a rail line.

Although closer to New York, Bridgeport, Connecticut, gained a short-lived significance as a rail transshipment point in the late 1840s. The Housatonic Railroad ran from there north to a junction with the Western at Pittsfield, Massachusetts. That meant that shippers could move goods by steamer to Bridgeport and then by rail to Albany and the West. The route was especially important during the winter months when ice closed the Hudson. However, Bridgeport lost her advantage with the completion of the Hudson River Railroad's direct link to Albany in 1851. Although Bridgeport's coastal service declined rapidly after the demise of the western shipments, it continues to the present as a terminus of a trans-Long Island Sound ferry service to Port Jefferson, Long Island.

Most of the commuter and local shipping lines along the Long Island north shore proved to be short-lived because of the Long Island Railroad, which reached Greenport, Long Island, in 1844. Planned as a means to achieve one-day travel between New York and Boston, the railroad offered a "Boston train" that left Brooklyn in the morning and ran to Greenport. There the passengers transferred to a steamer for one of the Connecticut ports, usually Norwich. From there a second train hustled the travelers into Boston that evening. The Long Island's rail-steamer-rail combination carried 15,000 passengers in 1844 along with a large percentage of the New York-Boston mails. The Long Island's domination was demolished by the opening of the more convenient New Haven and Hartford Railroad in 1846 and the start of the even faster Fall River Line steamship service the next year. The Long Island abandoned its integrated route during 1847 and shortly passed into receivership. Nevertheless, it had acquired, and would retain control, of the commuter and market traffic on Long Island.

Once again experience demonstrated that a successful steamship line had to offer either service or speed that could not be matched by a railroad. The railroads with their more flexible schedules and ability to move goods directly from factory to store offered a convenience that the steamer could not match. Conversely, the steamer offered passengers better accommodations, especially on overnight trips, frequently faster times, and did not require bridges and tunnels, which demanded technologies often yet to be developed.

4. New York

New York passed from the dark days of the War of 1812 into the brilliant sun of her commercial dominance in the decade and a half after the Treaty of Ghent. Drawing on the upstate region drained by the Hudson River, northeastern New Jersey, and most of Connecticut, the Empire City dominated an area that in 1820 contained approximately 14 percent of the nation's population and between a quarter and a third of its economic activity. Her economic hinterland increased drastically after the completion of the Erie Canal in 1824 tapped the western grain area and opened the way west for tens of thousands of New Englanders and immigrants who in turn created a massive new market for goods passing through New York. It is an oversimplification to say that the Erie Canal caused the growth of the port of New York since other factors played major roles in that development, but there is no question that "Clinton's Ditch" was a significant element. It ensured New York a wider market area and a better balance of import and export trade than any other port north or south.

The postwar rise of New York also coincided with the growth of cotton production in the South. As the new cotton lands of Mississippi and Alabama came into production the crop rose phenomenally: 146,000 bales in 1814, 335,000 in 1820, and 732,000 in 1830. By 1825 the receipts at New York passed 150,000 bales and were well over twice that in 1846. In 1850 New York handled more cotton than any other port in the nation except New Orleans and Mobile. It exported more than any port except those two and Charleston. While New York fleshed out its southern trade with shipments of coal, sugar, molasses, rice, and manufactured goods, cotton was king.

As might be expected, the rise in cotton shipments coincided with a rapid growth in coastal shipping. In 1831 the coastal fleet for the first time exceeded the tonnage of the high-seas craft.*

---

*The official 1821 figures also show a larger coastal fleet because of a purging of 200,000 tons of foreign-trade vessels believed no longer in existence. A similar cleansing of coastal vessels did not occur until 1829.

New York's shipyards sent hundreds of packets, clippers, and more prosaic craft to sea during the maritime golden age. One of the best-known was the Smith and Dimon yard, seen here in 1833. Courtesy of the New York State Historical Association, Cooperstown Association, Cooperstown

During the next twenty years domestic shipping, coastal, lake, and river, more than tripled to 1,798,000 tons while that engaged in foreign trade rose only two and a half times to 1,440,000. After 1850, however, the spreading network of inter- and intrasectional rail lines slowed the growth of coastal trade.

Since New York was the major entrepot for European goods destined for the American market, it followed naturally that she would develop a distribution network for those imports and a collection system for the return cargos. In 1815–16 coastwise packet lines began sailing to Richmond, Virginia, Philadelphia, and Boston. Their growth was stunted by the panic of 1819. In 1820 the return of better times permitted the start of steam service to Charleston and New Orleans. The *Robert Fulton*, which pioneered the route, proved a failure because she carried no freight, without which she could not pay her way. Not until after the Civil War could a steamer in the coastal service make a profit on passenger service alone.

Although the coastal steamers of the 1820s and 1830s were still fragile craft, their acceptance spread rapidly because their relative certainty of schedule attracted both passengers and express freight. The boom, especially to the southward, proved short lived. In 1837 and 1838 the southern service received devastating twin blows from the foundering of the New York-Charleston packet *Home* and a boiler explosion on the Baltimore-Savannah steamer *Pulaski.* The two accidents killed 236 people; with them perished public confidence for much of the next decade. The southern lines, helped immeasurably by new, high-quality vessels, began their recovery in the late 1840s.

The cross-New York Bay routes to the New Jersey suburbs and the termini of the stage lines from the Delaware River carried the greatest volume of traffic. In 1809 Fulton patented the steam-powered, double-ended ferry. That year he also set his second steamer, the *Raritan,* to churning from Manhattan to Elizabethtown, New Brunswick, and Amboy. From New Brunswick stage coaches hurried her passengers across New Jersey to Trenton, where they boarded John Stevens's *Phoenix* for the remainder of the trip to Philadelphia. It was on the New York harbor waters that later occurred the confrontation that led to the Supreme Court decision killing the steamboat monopoly. Aaron Ogden held a license from the Fulton-Livingston interests for the New York-Elizabethport ferry but found himself beset by competition from Thomas Gibbons and his captain Cornelius Vanderbilt. Ogden sued to oust Gibbons from the route but lost the case in the Supreme Court, which ruled the monopoly to be an unconstitutional invasion of the federal right to control interstate commerce.

The opening of the lucrative New York harbor trade to all operators brought on a series of rate wars in which Cornelius Vanderbilt, who took over the Gibbons interests in 1829, played a major role until he sold out to the Stevenses. The latter, along with a number of other New Jersey promoters, then created an effective monopoly of the transportation across the state that in 1832 formed the Camden and Amboy Railroad.

The Hudson River served as the major north-south artery in the Northeast. The stream tied the merchants of New York with their traditional upriver trading partners and with the rapidly growing settlements between the head of navigation and Lake Champlain as well as those extending westward along the Mohawk. River transport was in the hands of the majestic and striking river sloops. They were 65–75 feet long with masts that stretched skyward for as much as 110 feet and moved under mainsails attached to a 75–85 foot boom. A smartly handled craft might carry as much as 3,500 square yards of sail when conditions were right. Yet the Hudson River sloop was a handy craft commonly sailed with a crew of only five, including the cook. The sloops originally served as local packets or as market vessels that stopped on signal to embark cargo and passengers. Not until the early nineteenth century did long-distance packets appear, sailing on regular schedules between fixed points. In part the regularization of service reflected the growing specialization of areas along the river. The Highlands produced the bluestone that New Yorkers used for sidewalks; Haverstraw and Kingston made the bricks for the houses of the new metropolis; plaster from Newburgh or Poughkeepsie coated their interiors; and Albany provided the lumber.

Few cities in history could boast the combination of favorable factors that New York possessed during the first half of the nineteenth century. Her economic hinterland had such size and diversity that it fed a stable flow of goods onto her docks. Her rapidly expanding industrial activity absorbed a seemingly endless flow of immigrants. Her rise to banking dominance during the second quarter of the century combined with her magnificent harbor and her driving, innovative shipping leadership to make her the great port of the United States.

5. Philadelphia

Philadelphia owes much of her maritime importance to her location at the junction of the Schuylkill and Delaware rivers. The former gave access to the granary and coal fields of eastern Pennsylvania while the latter drew foodstuff, timber, and coal from an area that extended as far as central New York State. Although Philadelphia was the nation's leading industrial city in 1830, her coastal trade increasingly concentrated thereafter on coal as industrialization gained elsewhere, grain production shifted to the South and West, and the efforts to win the Susquehanna River traffic away from Baltimore failed.

The slow development of Philadelphia as a coal port resulted from the characteristics of the anthracite coal mined nearby. Unlike the softer bituminous variety, anthracite is very difficult to ignite and keep burning although it is an immensely cleaner and more efficient fuel. The first Mauch Chunk anthracite reached Philadelphia in 1806 but could not be used until the invention in 1814 of a grate on which to burn it. Anthracite's superior qualities as a heating fuel not only brought it dominance of the Philadelphia market but that of the New York City as well. As a result shipments of anthracite rose from 200 tons in 1822 to 63,000 in 1830, and 1,075,000 in 1850.

In the latter year the tonnage of colliers exceeded that of any other group of vessels engaged in the movement of a single domestic product. Initially the coal moved to the New York market over the protected waters of the Delaware and Raritan Canal, and only a limited quantity traveled the coastal seas. In 1836 the Lehigh Coal Company and the Philadelphia Steam Towboat Company began using tugs to pull barges and canal boats through the canals. The need for tugs able to negotiate the narrow locks of the coal canal caused Philadelphia operators to develop interest in screw propulsion. Their demand helped the Delaware River shipyards under the guidance of Captain Richard F. Loper take the lead in the application of that propulsion system.

Although unable to compete with the canalboats for New York-bound business, ocean-going colliers had the New England trade to themselves. Most coal moved northward in small and medium-sized brigs that after 1828 found a good return cargo in ice. In 1847 the anthracite shipments to New England passed 80,000 tons per year. Six years later the Reading Railroad, which owned extensive coal lands, launched an energetic sales program in New England. To carry its coal the Reading built a fleet of steam colliers. They proved to be too expensive to operate and found their way into the navy, which needed medium-sized vessels in 1858 for an impending punative expedition to Paraguay.

In 1802 merchants in the Delaware River valley and in the Chesapeake Bay ports revived a pre-Revolutionary War proposal for a canal connecting the two bodies of water. It would serve a dual purpose. Primarily, they argued, it would make possible all water, or nearly all water, transportation among the ports between New York and Norfolk. Many of the Philadelphia promoters had another but more immediate objective: to tap the trade of the Susquehanna River valley. Although some work was done in 1802–1804, the project lay dormant until 1822. Construction resumed that year and the full 13.6-mile-long Chesapeake and Delaware Canal opened in 1829. Initially the canal drew timber and grain from the Susquehanna Valley, but coal replaced them in importance after 1840 as the bituminous fuel from the Cumberland fields flowed northward. By 1870 coal composed half of the cargoes transiting the canal. Yet it was not a financial success, and the Baltimore interests who controlled the coal trade lobbied for federal operation in order to secure the money to enlarge the waterway. Finally in 1919, after intense political maneuvering, the canal became federal property.

Closely connected to the Chesapeake and Delaware was the Susquehanna and Tidewater Canal. Its origins lay in an abortive effort by Baltimore in 1783–1817 to tap the central New York lake region with its rich lumber and grain trade. The promoters of the canal also envisioned the Susquehanna River as a major segment in a passageway between the Atlantic and both the Ohio River and the Great Lakes. Greater acquaintance showed the upper reaches of the shoal and rock-strewn Susquehanna to be poorly adapted to navigation and usable only during the few weeks of high water. Before the upriver navigation dream collapsed, John Elgar in 1825 built the first iron-hulled steamer in the United States, the *Cordorus* at York Haven, below Harrisburg. Although she reached Binghamton, New York, on her maiden trip, she spent four months returning. Subsequent attempts to introduce steamboating on the upper Susquehanna fared no better. What traffic remained was restricted to flatboats and rafts.

The western branch of the Susquehanna, less treacherous than its northern one, did support a considerable flatboat traffic in goods moving east from Pittsburgh. In 1835–40 Baltimore investors built a canal along the Susquehanna from Havre de Grace, Maryland, to Wrightsville, Pennsylvania, to snare the traffic for the Maryland seaport. It succeeded, and by 1844 the canal carried roughly half of the Pittsburgh-Baltimore traffic and roughly a third of all the goods flowing in the opposite direction. Between 1840 and 1860 the Susquehanna and Tidewater fed about a quarter of the traffic carried by the Chesapeake and Delaware. Notably innovative, the Susquehanna's operators in 1861 proposed using double or tandem canal boats that could move twice the tonnage of a single boat at only a slight increase in cost. Despite its originality the canal lost most of its business to the railroads in the two decades after the Civil War and ceased operations in 1895.

6. The Coal Canals

The now largely forgotten canals in northeastern Pennsylvania, southern New York, and northern New Jersey played a significant role in the development of the eastern megalopolis. Across them passed the cargoes of coal that provided New York, Philadelphia, Boston, and intervening points with the fuels for their heating and industrial plants. The availability of plentiful supplies of clean-burning anthracite coal made possible the industrialization that supported their growing populations. Wood was too dear and too inefficient to power a major city and bituminous coal too dirty. Moreover, not until after the Civil War would soft-coal prices fall enough to overcome the resistance to the dirty fuel.

In 1793 a group of Philadelphia businessmen formed the Lehigh Coal Mine Company to exploit 10,000 acres in the rugged Mauch Chunk region near the Lehigh River. Their initial efforts collapsed when the state failed to make the stream navigable and their anthracite found little market. In 1817 Josiah White and Erskine Hazard leased the lands and began improving the river. White designed an inverted V-shaped dam with a "bear trap" or sluice gate at the apex that could be raised and lowered to create a freshet which could carry barges safely over the rapids below. Coal began to move down river in 1819.

Between 1825 and 1829 a 56-mile-long canal between Mauch Chunk (now Jim Thorpe) and Easton, designed by Canvass White, replaced the dams. Canal traffic swelled as Lehigh anthracite developed a large market in Philadelphia and moved into the coastal trade. In the peak year of 1860, 1,338,875 tons traveled through the canal. Two years later a devastating flood destroyed a large portion of White's canal. While some parts quickly returned to service, the cost of repairs and the growing competition of the railroads destroyed the vitality of the operation. By the end of the century the waterway had become uneconomical although it staggered along until 1931.

Maurice and William Wurts, owners of a large coal-rich area around Carbondale, 50 miles north of Mauch Chunk, decided to tap the New York market. In 1823 they had Benjamin Wright, the chief engineer of the Erie Canal, lay out a route that followed the Delaware and Lackawanna rivers and a canal across New York from Port Jervis to Kingston on the Hudson. The plan encountered such strong opposition from lumbermen, who needed a river clear of dams in order to float their timber rafts to market, that the Wurts shifted to an all-canal route running from Honesdale on the Lackawaxen River to Rondout on the Hudson. The final design came from the pen of John B. Jervis, one of the most distinguished of the junior engineers produced by the Erie Canal. Between July 1825 and October 1828 Jervis directed the building of the Delaware and Hudson Canal, 108 miles long with 109 locks, 36 feet wide and 4 feet deep, adequate to float 30-ton barges. As the traffic increased the canal expanded to a 5-foot depth in 1842–44, 5½-feet in 1845, and 6 feet in 1847–50. By the mid-1850s over a million tons of coal a year moved along the canal from the fields around Scranton and Wilkes-Barre. After 1860 the company increasingly shifted to rail shipments although barge traffic persisted until 1898.

The second coal canal that introduced anthracite into New York was the Morris Canal and Banking Company's route from Phillipsburg on the Delaware River across northern New Jersey to Newark Bay. Built between 1824 and 1832 according to a plan developed by James Renwick, it combined a canal and inclined planes. It had 23 locks and 23 inclined planes, and was considered one of the great engineering works in the nation. Twice enlarged, it operated successfully for about two decades. Thereafter it lost traffic to the railroads and closed in 1924.

The route across New Jersey, tying New York City to Philadelphia as it did, became perhaps the most sought-after prize in the first quarter of the nineteenth century. Yet no canal was dug during the first three decades of the nineteenth century. Finally in 1830 both canal and railroad promoters applied to the New Jersey legislature for charters, and the legislators with great magnanimity authorized both. The Delaware and Raritan Canal ran from New Brunswick to Bordentown on the Delaware River, a route closely paralleled by the Camden and Amboy Railroad. The waterway, designed by Canvass White, was 80 feet wide and 8 feet deep. It served primarily as a coal route, especially after it gained a connection with the Lehigh and Schuylkill canals in 1854. The canal fell under the control of the Camden and Amboy interests, and from them in 1871 it passed to that of the Pennsylvania Railroad. When the new owners refused to handle coal from routes controlled by the Reading Railroad, shipments fell by a million tons per year and continued to decline until the railroad could justify its abandonment. The story of the Delaware and Raritan demonstrates both the ability of waterways to compete against railroads for bulk cargoes and the danger to maritime operations from railroad domination, whether it be direct as in this case or indirect as freight shippers to Boston discovered.

7. Baltimore

Philadelphia's great natural rival was Baltimore. The Maryland port not only stood near the head of the Chesapeake Bay but its proximity to the mouth of the Susquehanna and the Susquehanna and Tidewater Canal offered a natural route into middle Pennsylvania while the port's own hinterland included the grain and coal lands of western Maryland and the tobacco and fishing area of the Eastern Shore. Since colonial times Baltimore had maintained close commercial ties with the towns and villages of the upper Chesapeake Bay. Most bordered the numerous rivers that drain the area. A fleet of small, shallow draft sloops and schooners unique to the Chesapeake—bugeyes, skipjacks, and rams—carried the commerce of the region while a second fleet of similar craft sought the wealth that lived in its waters.

The protected waters of the bay attracted a number of pioneer steamship operators. In the year immediately following the War of 1812, Chesapeake Bay offered steamer service that was rivaled only by that on the Hudson River. Except for the width of the bay, which can make for extremely nasty seas during a storm, it offered the sheltered waters that early steamers required. Service to Elkton, at the head of the bay, as well as to Norfolk, at the foot, began in 1817. In 1832 the Peoples Steam Navigation Company instituted a passenger and freight barge service to Philadelphia through the Chesapeake and Delaware Canal. In 1843 the line ordered the screw-steamer *Ericsson* designed to pass through the canal. The new arrangement was so successful that the line took on the name of the steamer and shifted to all screw-propelled vessels.

In 1839 the Baltimore Steam Packet Line, more familiarly called the Old Bay Line, began runs to Norfolk. The line later extended service to Richmond and Washington. Despite the disruptions of the Civil War, it prospered until the appearance of the automobile, which diverted many of its passengers and nearly all of its express shipments onto the highways that began to traverse the area in the 1920s. Nevertheless, the doughty line bested war and depression to continue service until 1962, the last of the nation's coastal steamboat companies.

As their Latin American business declined, many Baltimore merchants turned to coal. Yet the port's location, 170 miles up the bay, kept it from wrestling the anthracite coal trade from Philadelphia or the bituminous trade from Newport News. The Baltimorians fought hard, especially after important Georges Creek coal mines opened in 1842. But effort alone was not enough. Baltimore retained a portion of the coal trade but could not compete with the Hampton Roads ports.

The Chesapeake is the natural outlet for the produce of lowland and Piedmont Virginia, where the shipping problems centered on moving the products to the navigable streams from which they could flow to the collection points at Alexandria, Baltimore, or Norfolk. Volume expanded after the opening of the Dismal Swamp and Chesapeake and Albemarle Canals added produce from the Albemarle district of North Carolina. Even so, Norfolk never developed the trade her location should have generated. Too many of her potential cargoes, especially tobacco, were shipped from intermediate ports like Richmond. Tobacco remained the chief product of the area in antebellum days although the Piedmont continued, as it had before the Revolution, to ship great quantities of grain. Most of both products entered foreign trade directly rather than moving coastwise to northern entrepots. Very little except slaves moved southward from the region, and most of the human chattels probably moved by land. Not until the post-Civil War coal boom did the Hampton Roads ports approach their potential.

8. The Cotton Ports

Below the Albemarle a multitude of shallow waterways threaded the lowlands of the Carolinas and Georgia, but only a handful of deepwater ports such as Wilmington, North Carolina, Charleston and Beaufort, South Carolina, and Savannah and Brunswick, Georgia, served the region. North Carolina faced particularly grave problems. During the early nineteenth century the only good passages through her outer islands were the Cape Fear and Ocracoke entrances. The latter was so dangerous that two thirds of the state's trade headed for Wilmington through the Cape Fear passage.

The trading center of the area was Charleston, through which passed the cotton, tobacco, rice, and other products of the region. Her local water-transportation network remained primitive since it relied on slave labor, which was believed capable of doing only the most simple tasks. The cargo carriers, therefore, tended to be rudimentary pole-driven or sailing craft of limited dimensions.

South Carolina expended $720,000 in 1792–1800 to dig the 22-mile-long Santee and Cooper Canal in order to tap the central upland area of the state. Although too small to be truly effective, it remained in service until 1860. Since most of the small craft that brought cotton to Charleston used the coastal rivers, the state between 1819 and 1838 spent about $2 million to improve the Pee Dee, Santee, Wateree, Catawba, Broad, and Saluda. Most of the work involved removal of obstructions and building of canals around falls. Like the Santee and Cooper Canal the program was too small in scale and the rivers themselves too limited in capacity to make the project a success.

Similar activities in Georgia between 1817 and 1831 produced equally unsatisfactory results. Starting in 1816 the Steam Boat Company of Georgia operated the earliest towboats in America to bring clusters of small craft down the Savannah River. The experiment proved uneconomical because of the small capacity of the tows. Their use declined after the 1820s, although shallow-draft "Cotton Boxes" and pole boats persisted until run off the river by railroad competition. The inadequacies of their waterborne routes explain in large part the early interest of Charleston entrepreneurs in railroads and the building of the Hamburg Railway.

As a result of her inability to broaden her economic hinterland through these and other efforts, Charleston lost her position as a foreign-trade port after 1815. Although only about 16 percent of her cotton shipments moved coastwise in 1825, by 1859 New York alone took 45 percent of these shipments. It is no wonder then that the South Carolina planters and merchants felt themselves ill served by the politicoeconomic system that developed in the decade and a half before the Civil War. Nor is it surprising that the Charleston hotheads of 1861 believed that the New York merchants would oppose any actions that would interrupt the flow of cotton.

During the French and Spanish periods of domination of the north shore of the Gulf of Mexico the only ports of importance were New Orleans and Pensacola, with the latter a poor second. After the American occupation of the territory between the Pearl and Perdido rivers, Mobile rose in importance, especially as a lumber port. Logs cut in the great pine forests of central Alabama were floated down the Alabama and Tombigbee rivers to Mobile Bay. There as many as twenty waterpowered mills reduced them to lumber. The industry reached its peak in the mid-1850s; 17.5 million feet being shipped in 1854–55, most of it to Cuban and Caribbean ports. Like the similar lumber produced in northern Florida and southern Georgia in the later years of the century, very little of it entered northern markets more easily supplied from Carolina and Georgia ports.

Coincident with the growth of the lumber business at Mobile came its rise as a cotton port. Only 500 bales passed through the port in 1817, but the following year steamers began hauling cotton from upriver plantations. By 1831 the port could claim shipments of 54,000 bales. Initially most of the cotton moved down the coast to New Orleans, whence it made its way to the mills of the English midlands and New England. During the mid-1830s, however, direct packet lines to Boston, New York, and Philadelphia started. They played a major role in increasing Mobile's shipments to 129,000 bales in 1850.

Texas was a maritime appendage of New Orleans during the Mexican period and continued so after independence in 1836. Although New York firms entered the Texas trade in the 1840s, another decade would pass before Texas reached its potential as the cotton center of the country. Five New York sailing lines began service to either Galveston or Matagorda between 1851 and 1856, but most of the cotton moved through New Orleans because the shallow water at the entrances of the Texas ports prevented entry of deep draft vessels. Only in the half decade before the Civil War did deepening of the approaches start; very little had been accomplished before hostilities began. Nevertheless, nearly all Texas cotton moved by water since no railroads yet connected it with New Orleans.

New Orleans was the magnet that drew much of the cotton grown in the United States. In 1858 it handled half of the cotton shipped in the country. The Mississippi River and its tributaries tapped the plantations of the upper South, west of the Appalachians, while coastal traders brought in the bales from Alabama and Texas. In the decade of the 1830s New Orleans grew faster in both wealth and trade than any other city in the country, but thereafter it was surpassed by New York because the northern metropolis increasingly attracted the trade of the region above the Ohio while the rail networks of Charleston and Savannah began to syphon cotton eastward. Despite the slowing of its growth, New Orleans expanded from 46,310 people in 1830 to 168,175 in 1860. In the same period the value of goods arriving from upriver points rose from $22 to $185 million, doubling every decade. Most of the increase came in cotton shipments, which by 1860 accounted for 60 percent of the movement. Western agricultural products, chiefly flour, pork, corn, wheat, whiskey, and tobacco, declined during the same period from 58 percent to 23 percent of the total trade of the port. Probably no other city, including New York, so fully demonstrates the impact of maritime activities on its economic health and growth.

The leading figure in the Texas trade, and a major one in that of New Orleans, was the New York shipowner Charles Morgan. After a brief fling with packets and steamers on the Charleston and Savannah runs he began a New York-New Orleans line in 1837 and quickly added a feeder service from Galveston. Morgan's craft carried passengers, provisions, and light merchandise to the Lone Star Republic and returned with cotton and hides. He had a sure sense for profit and made $4,000,000 by chartering his vessels to the government during the Mexican War. With the return of peace he instituted a New York-New Orleans steamship line but wandered afield to fight Cornelius Vanderbilt unsuccessfully for a share of the Panama steamship route. Learning his lesson, Morgan concentrated on his lines between New York, New Orleans, and Texas. By 1860 he operated six different routes out of New Orleans and Brashear (now Morgan City), Louisiana.

9. Pacific Coast

Coastal trade along the Pacific shore did not develop significantly until after the annexation of California. Following the Gold Rush, San Francisco became the gateway for manufactured goods arriving from Europe and the East. They were commonly exchanged for lumber and grain. In 1847 a pair of craft opened tenuous communication with the pioneer settlements in Oregon, but the prevailing northwesterly winds and the southerly setting California Current limited contact under sail.

Initially, lumber dominated the Pacific coastal trade. In 1828 the Hudson Bay Company began shipping it from a saw mill at Fort Vancouver on the Columbia River to Hawaii. Before the American occupation of California some timber had also flowed south from Bodega on the coast north of San Francisco. Neither trade was large. The demands of Gold Rush San Francisco, and of the mines themselves, changed that. In an effort to exploit the insatiable demand Captain William Talbot, his brother Fred, and Andrew Pope formed a partnership during 1849 to bring lumber from the great fir forests of Puget Sound to the gold fields. Three years later a sawmill opened at Mendocino City in the heart of California redwood country. Others followed. In the year 1860, 300 mills operated in California, and the Mendocino and Humboldt County redwood forests produced 65 million feet of timber. Nearly all the wood moved to market by water.

San Francisco not only surpassed all other California ports in volume of cargo handled during the Gold Rush but its harbor was clogged with vessels abandoned when their crews left for the gold fields. This photograph shows only a small fraction of that fleet anchored in the shadow of Telegraph Hill. Most of the vessels returned to sea, manned by disappointed gold seekers. Official U.S. Navy Photograph

Despite the provisions of its contract and the obvious advantage of steamers there, Pacific Mail ignored the coastal trade. It even dropped its Oregon service in 1860. Others recognized the opportunity. That year Charles Goodall and Chris Nelson formed a partnership that after the Civil War developed into the dominant Pacific Coast Steamship Company, which traversed the whole length of the coast from Alaska to San Diego.

In 1853 the coal mines at Bellingham Bay, north of Seattle, Washington, began shipping cargoes to San Francisco, but the bulk of the western Washington traffic remained local. The small logging and agricultural settlements that sprang up along the shores of Puget Sound and the other waterways of the area communicated almost exclusively by water. Except for the Hudson Bay Company's side-wheeler *Beaver,* which arrived in 1836, the first local craft were canoes, sloops, and schooners. Steam freight vessels appeared in 1851 or 1852. In 1854 James M. Hunt and John H. Scranton began a steam-powered line that served the Puget Sound communities for nearly a century. The network of steamers threading the intricate channels between Puget Sound's myriad of islands became the most extensive in the nation. It persists to the present in an abbreviated form in the Washington State Ferry System. Nevertheless, the Puget Sound connection with the Columbia River settlements and with San Francisco remained rudimentary until after the Civil War.

San Francisco quickly became the maritime center of California since it had the best port facilities on the coast and perched alongside one of the great anchorages of the globe. Equally important initially was its proximity to the gold fields. San Francisco served both as entrepot for the gold seekers and the terminus of extensive steamer service up the Sacramento River. In the long run, however, the grain fields of central California ensured the port's primacy.

The central coast relied on small ports like Monterey, Santa Cruz, and San Simeon, which served only their immediate hinterland and were wholly adequate to the limited needs of the region. Farther south the trade flowed through San Diego despite its difficult and shallow harbor entrance. The opening of steamship service to San Francisco in 1852 solidified her dominance. Despite the prominence of Los Angeles as the economic center of southern California her immediate ports could not settle their political feuds or rise from their mud flats and overcome their shifting harbor channels until the last years of the century. Then they began the growth that would establish them as second only to the San Francisco Bay ports as the state's maritime centers.

In some respects the history of the trade with the Hawaiian Islands parallels that with the mainland West Coast. It originated in a search for goods commanding a premium on the China market, in this instance, sandalwood. As the sandalwood forests fell before the woodsmen's axes the whalers appeared to make the islands a favorite resupply point as they pursued cachalot in the mid-Pacific grounds. After 1848 American whalers abandoned California as a refitting stop, shifting to Hawaii. This created a burst of activity in servicing whaleships as well as in transshipping eastward their cargoes of whale oil. During the Gold Rush period Hawaiian farmers supplied California with potatoes and fresh vegetables although that trade died off once the mainland farmers deserted the mines and discovered the true wealth in the California soil.

Until 1860 interisland trade went entirely by sailing vessel. Even then, the expense of coal, which had to be imported, delayed the demise of the interisland sailing traders. The first transpacific steamer to touch at Honolulu appeared in 1853 enroute from San Francisco to Sydney, Australia. Others appeared infrequently until regular transpacific steam service began in 1867.

In 1861, as the nation was about to tumble into the Civil War, the coastal marine totaled 2,705,000 tons. That was a figure that it would not significantly exceed, except in wartime, until 1890. Although the coastal freight and passenger lines had begun to feel the impact of rail competition, they still carried the bulk of the cargoes moving north and south on both coasts. Except in a handful of local instances the railroad still served as an adjunct to the maritime shippers by funneling produce and goods from the West or its hinterland to a port for movement by water. Over the next quarter century that relationship would change.

Chapter Four
CANALS

P ERHAPS THE MOST SIGNIFICANT POLITICAL MOVEMENT OF THE FIRST
half of the nineteenth century in America was the shift of the western states from alliance with the South to alliance with the Northeast. Like all major political shifts, the participating factors were many. Nevertheless, one looms very large: The replacing of the economic lifeline to New Orleans via the Mississippi with a web of transportation to East Coast ports. In that shift canals and rivers played an early and major role.

1. Early Canals

Man-made waterways are nearly as old as civilization. Egyptian and Babylonian engineers constructed canals as early as 5000 B.C. About 1380 B.C. the Egyptians tied the Nile and the Red Sea together with a ditch that lasted until 1859. Early explorers in Central America considered the possibility of connecting the Caribbean with the Pacific by a canal, but the technology did not yet exist to accomplish it. In the seventeenth century Louis Joliet proposed a canal between Lake Michigan and the Illinois River (essentially the route to be followed in 1827 by the Illinois and Michigan Canal) while in Massachusetts suggestions appeared for a canal across Cape Cod as early as 1676.

Although colonial America was dependent almost entirely on water for any extensive or long-distance movement of goods, most of the settled areas could be served without canals. Only a handful of small canals were dug, most to divert water to mill sites, but none had a long or important life.

Conditions changed shortly after independence. In an effort to permit through passage from the Piedmont, in 1785 the state of Virginia chartered the James River Canal Company. It built a 7-mile-long canal around the falls at Richmond that opened the upper James River to traffic and became the foundation for the later James River and Kanawha Canal, which sought unsuccessfully to reach the Ohio via the James and western Virginia's Kanawha River. Although the James would be improved to Lexington by 1858, shortages of money and immense technological problems stopped it there. The route looked attractive on a map but was equally as impractical as a water route as it had been as a land one. It remains to the present a difficult trek across the mountain spines

Canal boats on the James River and Kanawha Canal at Richmond. This 1864 photograph shows refugees crowd boats floating in the shadow of burned-out buildings. Official U.S. Navy Photograph

and through the narrow gorges of West Virginia. Despite the impossibility of completing the project, the failure to finish the canal so inflamed public opinion in the western part of the state that it contributed significantly to the movement for a separate West Virginia.

Another 1785 organization was the Potomac Company, established jointly by Maryland and Virginia, to build a road from the headwaters of the Potomac to the Cheat or Monongahela rivers. George Washington served as president and James Rumsey as general manager. The company planned to dig canals around the chief impediments to navigation of the Potomac—Great Falls, Seneca Falls, and Shenandoah Falls—to allow watercraft to reach the road head. Unfortunately for its promoters and for a generation of settlers headed west, the company ran out of money before it had much to show for its efforts.

More successful was the Dismal Swamp Canal, which tied the North Carolina sounds to Norfolk. Chartered by Virginia in 1787 in the hopes of fastening the trade of coastal North Carolina to Norfolk, its small capacity prevented it living up to the expectations of its promoters. Nevertheless, when opened in 1805 the canal brought lumber and some of the tobacco of the region to Norfolk markets as well as providing a vacation area for the Virginians. It remained the chief highway of the region until the opening of the larger Albemarle and Chesapeake Canal in 1859.

In 1793 Massachusetts authorized the proprietors of the Middlesex Canal to construct a waterway from the Medford River at Charlestown to the Merrimack. Completed in 1803, it was the earliest major canal in the United States. The waterway was designed by Loammi Baldwin, Sr., as a 30-mile-long-channel 30 feet wide and 3 feet deep. It passed through twenty locks. Although the engineering problems Baldwin faced were generally minimal, the project cost over a half million dollars.

In the minds of some New Englanders the Middlesex Canal was but the first step in a larger series of channels that would carry craft from Boston through the canal to the Merrimack River; up that stream and across New Hampshire to the Connecticut; up the Connecticut and from its upper reaches across the wilderness to the St. Lawrence near Quebec. In keeping with the tendency of many of the canal proposals of the early nineteenth century to ignore obstacles, the plans conveniently overlooked the White and Green mountains. A later but no more carefully thought-through

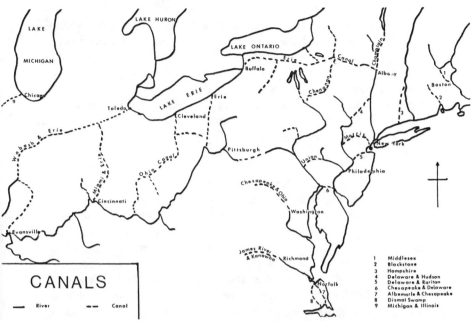

CANALS

— River   -- Canal

1	Middlesex
2	Blackstone
3	Hampshire
4	Delaware & Hudson
5	Delaware & Raritan
6	Chesapeake & Delaware
7	Albemarle & Chesapeake
8	Dismal Swamp
9	Michigan & Illinois

proposal called for a route across northern Massachusetts that followed the Millers and Deerfield rivers before bypassing the Hoosac Range of the Berkshires via a canal employing a mere 220 locks to connect with a tributary of the Hudson near Williamstown, Massachusetts. Not surprisingly neither proceeded beyond dreams once the engineers prepared cost estimates. The failure of the Middlesex Canal to pay a dividend before 1819 further reduced the attractiveness of other New England long-distance canal proposals.

Nevertheless, the Middlesex Canal and some limited channel improvements on the Merrimack did bring cheap timber from New Hampshire to the Boston market, especially to the shipyards. It also created the necessary route to market for the products of the massive Amoskeag mill complex at Manchester, New Hampshire. The canal captured the trade of the Merrimack Valley so completely that Newburyport, its traditional outlet, withered, never to recover until its invasion by shoe factories soon after the Middlesex succumbed to railroad competition in 1852.

Pennsylvania has the best river system of any of the coastal states. The Delaware runs along her eastern border and the Susquehanna, Juniata, and Schuylkill traverse her interior. The Pennsylvanians attempted to capitalize on their natural blessings soon after the establishment of the new government. Their projects, however, suffered from a shortage of capital and the limited market within areas yet to see extensive settlement. Even so, in 1791 work began on a route that had been surveyed as early as 1762, the Union Canal connecting Reading on the Schuylkill with Middletown on the Susquehanna. The promoters soon met overwhelming financial difficulties and suspended work after completing only four miles. Not until 1821 did construction resume.

2. The Erie Canal

Despite the inauspicious beginnings of the Potomac and the Pennsylvania canals, Elkanah Watson, a New Yorker of great persuasion, not only convinced his state legislature in 1792 to charter the Western Inland Lock Navigation Company but also secured a state subscription for $12,500 in stock, half the total. Watson planned to connect the Hudson River with Lake Ontario by constructing canals around the Cohoes Falls at the mouth of the Mohawk River; Little Falls farther west on the Mohawk; between the Mohawk and Wood Creek at Rome; and finally a bypass around Oswego Falls at Rochester. Despite its undercapitalization the company built the Little Falls canal in 1793–95 and generally improved the section between there and Lake Oneida. After 1798 the company even paid modest dividends. Nevertheless, because of its small capacity the Western Canal proved less than an outstanding success. Neither did it conquer its physical obstacles. By 1813 boats could proceed to within 12 miles of Oswego, but many shoals had yet to be removed, and the Cohoes Falls remained unconquered. Since the canal was barely 24-feet wide at the bottom and 2 feet deep it offered passage only to boats under 10 tons, scarcely enough to satisfy the needs of the growing region in central New York.

Particularly damning in the eyes of the farmers and merchants of the region were its high tolls. In 1818 shippers paid $5.20 per ton to send goods over the 100 miles of canal then functioning. In 1792 the Northern Inland Lock Navigation Company won permission to build a second canal from the Hudson to Lake Champlain.

The experience of the War of 1812, when the state and nation had to organize a series of military campaigns on the Niagara frontier, Lake Ontario, and Lake Champlain, gave strength to a mixture of land speculators, commercial promoters, shipping operators, and nationalists who championed the construction of an improved and lengthened canal. When Governor Daniel Tompkins in 1817 proposed improving the roads between the Hudson and Lake Erie the legislature under the leadership of DeWitt Clinton converted it into a call for a new canal. A five-man commission headed by Clinton investigated the route. They reported that a canal was feasible although no federal assistance would be available because of President James Madison's constitutional scruples. The proposal faced intense opposition from New York City, whose representatives thought that spending $6 per man, woman, and child in the state to benefit a handful of frontier villages upstate was stupid; as well as from Hudson valley farmers who feared western competition and from lower Hudson ports, which feared the advantage that the canal would give to Albany and Troy. Intense political lobbying by Clinton and his supporters finally won. On April 15, 1817, the governor signed a law directing the construction of both the Western or Erie and the Northern or Champlain canals.

The canal commissioners led by Clinton sagaciously decided to start construction near Rome because it was the easiest section and would give them the maximum publicity. Work on the Erie Canal started July 4, 1817. It soon became clear that the commissioners had chosen their engineers wisely. The chief engineer was a lawyer turned surveyor, Benjamin Wright, who had laid out the section between the Seneca River and Rome. His chief assistants were James Geddes, who surveyed the Lake Erie—Seneca River

Canal boats crowding the Coenties Slip in New York. It served as the major offloading point for cargoes arriving from the Erie Canal. Note the tow of canal boats and the Long Island Sound steamer in the stream. Courtesy of the Seamen's Church Institute

route, David S. Bates, who built the Genesee aqueduct, and Canvass White, who developed a good hydraulic cement using the meager lime found at Chittenango. The commissioners followed the practice of letting local contracts for short sections of the canal. This had several benefits: it guaranteed a political faction with a vested interest in the canal; embraced local pride; and gained the ingenuity of many bright minds at a very low cost. The canal was built to standard dimensions with a 40-foot width at top, 28 at the bottom, and a 4-foot depth. The commissioners opened each section to local traffic as soon as it was completed. The first, Utica to Rome, began operating in 1819. It was extended to Little Falls in 1821 and to Schenectady on the east and Rochester on the west the following year. In 1823 the Schenectady-Albany and Rochester-Brockport portions were added. The final two western sections, Brockport to Lockport and Lockport to Buffalo, opened over the following two years. Although the completed canal stretched 360 miles it passed through relatively level terrain for most of that distance and rose only 568 feet while crossing the state. The most difficult engineering problem was the double set of 5 locks that carried the canal over the 62-foot escarpment at Lockport. Less dramatic were the set of 27 locks bypassing Cohoes Falls on the east end, the 1,199-foot aqueduct over the mouth of the Mohawk River, and the 802-foot aqueduct that carried the canal across the Genessee River at Rochester.

Although 2,000 boats were already using the completed portions of the canal, Clinton staged a colorful ceremony to mark the official completion of the entire structure. He led a column of boats from Buffalo in the specially built *Seneca Chief* on October 26, 1825. Their departure was announced by the firing of cannon stationed at 8–12-mile intervals along the canal and down the Hudson to New York City. It took 55 minutes to pass the message. The flotilla reached New York on November 4, and Clinton ceremoniously emptied a barrel of Lake Erie water into New York harbor. Many in the crowd simply emptied the contents of other barrels into themselves.

The impact of the canal was almost instantaneous. The freight rate between Albany and Buffalo fell from $100 per ton to $10. It was now cheaper to ship goods from Philadelphia to Pittsburgh via the Hudson River and the Canal than sending them overland through Pennsylvania. In the first year 19,000 canal craft and rafts passed Troy, while up to 40 a day entered the canal at Albany. In 1826 tolls passed $750,000 and five years later exceeded $1 million. The impact on villages along the route was as marked. Rochester in 1816 had 331 settlers. In 1822, the year the canal arrived, the town could claim 2,700 inhabitants and shipped its first cargoes of flour. In 1825, after the canal was open to the Hudson, the number climbed to 4,274 and three years later reached 11,000 by which time it had already become the milling center of the world. By 1838 Buffalo, the western terminus of the canal, shipped more grain than New Orleans and seven years later had a greater volume of trade in grain, flour, and livestock than any other city in the United States. Buffalo's experience offers a good example of what a few strong, dedicated men could do for a small struggling village. Her selection as western terminus of the Erie Canal grew out of Samuel Wilkeson's construction of a breakwater, following the War of 1812, that created a port where none had previously existed. Buffalo's position as a grain center derived from the steam-powered grain elevator opened by Joseph Dart in 1843.

The growth of Chicago was an indirect result of the canal. Between 1836 and 1853 the value of goods shipped west over the canal rose 940 percent, much of it continuing on Lake freighters to Chicago, which became an increasingly important shipping and receiving point for goods from New York City. Goods arriving via the canal and the lakes could be shipped westward from Chicago at a cost well below that through New Orleans and St. Louis, even when destined for upper Mississippi River ports. In the 1850s Chicago firmly replaced St. Louis as the wholesale center for the upper Mississippi River valley. Equally impressive was the effect upon Cleveland. Here the benefit flowed both from the Erie and from the Ohio canals. As early as 1842 the value of produce shipped from Cleveland nearly equaled that from New Orleans.

As important as was merchandise, it was in passenger travel that the greatest impact was felt. The first boatload of immigrants reached Buffalo only three days after the opening of the canal. In 1826 as many as 1,200 people arrived there in a single day. Even the towns not entirely dependent on the canal, like Albany, had a phenomenal growth. Between 1824 and 1850 the New York State capital grew 400 percent to 50,000 people. Environmental effects of the canal appeared almost immediately. In July 1825 the *Troy Sentinel* noted the appearance of Oswego bass, heretofore restricted to Lake Ontario, in the Hudson.

One not unexpected problem generated by the success of the Erie Canal was the press of localities distant from the waterway that wished the state to finance a canal joining them to the golden trough. The earliest to get a nod of approval from the legislature was a spur to Geneva on Lake Seneca constructed in 1826–28 and rebuilt the following year. For the next forty years the settlers at either end of the lake argued over the proper water level since the height that allowed easy navigation on the canal flooded farm land at the south end. In 1829 the Erie Canal commissioners completed the canal to Oswego Lake that had been begun by the Western Canal Company, but it produced little traffic. Between 1829 and 1833 the Chemung Canal was constructed from Seneca Lake to Elmira. It was later extended to connect with the Pennsylvania system, but it neither developed the trade that its promoters expected nor syphoned goods off to Philadelphia and Baltimore as its detractors feared. Potentially the most valuable feeder line was the Black River Canal running from Rome to Port Leyden on the west side of the Adirondacks. Unfortunately, a poorly chosen route and late construction (1840–50) negated its significance as a lumber and iron carrier. Another local waterway looked upon by many as having great potential was the Genesee Valley Canal, which it was hoped would tap the Pittsburgh and western Pennsylvania coal trade but never extended far enough to do so. The Chenango Canal opened to Binghamton in 1837 was perhaps the most successful of the spur lines, although that is faint praise.

In 1854 83 percent of the nation's entire shipment of grain moved over the Erie Canal. Thereafter railroads captured such an increasing amount of grain shipments that in 1868 the canal's portion dropped to 45 percent. By 1871 it was down to 30 percent. Even so, the volume was substantial. In 1871–72 the rebuilt Erie Canal carried eastward 3,087,212 tons of cargo, which was a quarter of all the tonnage carried between the West and the East coasts that fiscal year. The cargo moved on 7,140 canal boats employing 28,000 persons. The chief cargo remained grain although its percentage of the canal's traffic continued to drop as did the portion of shipments headed for New York City.

Despite its declining use, New York State between 1914 and 1921 replaced the obsolescent canal with a new one. The New York State Barge Canal was designed for large barges and high-powered towboats. It cost $200 million. Construction involved 39 dams, 57 locks and replacement of two-thirds of the old canal. As a result, today no segment of the original Erie Canal is in use and most portions have completely disappeared. The St. Lawrence Seaway absorbed much of the canal's remaining trade with the result that by the 1980s commercial traffic had shrunk to levels that raised questions about its viability, except on the Lake Champlain section. It was, however, still heavily patronized by pleasure craft.

3. The Eastern Response to the Erie Canal

The success of the Erie Canal caused a redoubling of efforts by New York's competitors to build ties to the West. After discovering the impossibility of waterways to the St. Lawrence and the Hudson, Boston turned to the railroad as the best solution to her problems.

Philadelphia, as we have already seen, had a long history of attempts at driving canals into the central Pennsylvania and central New York farming areas as well as the northeastern Pennsylvania coal fields. In 1762 colonial surveyors laid out a route from Reading on the Schuylkill to Middletown on the Susquehanna, but Pontiac's Rebellion prevented construction. After the Potomac Company's organization in Virginia and Maryland, a group of Pennsylvania promoters formed the Society for the Promoting of the Improvement of Roads and Inland Navigation in hopes of capturing the trade with the Great Lakes. The society's lobbying secured an appropriation in 1791 to build a waterway to Lakes Ontario and Otsego in New York by way of the Delaware River along with eight other canals radiating north, northwest, and west from the Susquehanna River. Work on a Reading-Middletown canal was actually started, but only 15 miles had been dug by 1794, when the state's efforts shifted to road building. Reorganized in 1811 as the Union Canal Company, the concern had to delay construction once again until after the War of 1812. Under Loammi Baldwin, Jr., and Canvass White as successive chief engineers, it finished the 82-mile work in 1827. Unfortunately, the canal design was faulty. It was so narrow (only 17 feet wide at the locks) that it attracted very little business until the anthracite fields opened along the headwaters of the Susquehanna.

In 1814 three routes to the Lakes were studied:

1. The Delaware River to Trenton Falls; then by canal to northeast branch of the Susquehanna; and finally a second canal to Lake Otsego
2. The Lake Otsego route to the Chemung River; a canal from Elmira to Newtown Creek and Lake Seneca; and

then by canal to the Onondaga River and Oswego on
Lake Ontario

3. Up the Schuylkill to the limits of navigation; then by
canal to the Susquehanna; up the Susquehanna and Juniata
rivers to Poplar Run; a portage to Conemaugh; and then
up Stony Creek to the Allegheny River and down it to
Pittsburgh.

If the Allegheny could be improved from Stony Creek to
Le Beouf on French Creek, a short canal would also carry boats to
Lake Erie. The Pennsylvanians cannot be accused of thinking
small! The third route, the darling of those in the western part of
the state, tantalized with the prospect of trade with Quebec, Pittsburgh, and New Orleans as well as the central New York salt fields
and the copper country of Lake Superior.

Many in Philadelphia had other objectives. They feared the
encroachment of Baltimore on the Susquehanna trade as much, if
not more, than the loss of business to New York. In 1824, therefore, Philadelphia promoters revived the proposal for a trans-
Pennsylvania route, securing state support for a survey. The plan,
presented in 1825, recommended a route from Philadelphia to the
Susquehanna above Harrisburg; along the east bank of the Susquehanna to the upper forks of the Frankstown Branch of the Juniata
near Hollidaysburg; a 4-mile tunnel to the Little Conemaugh; and
thence to Pittsburgh. The following year the route received formal
state sanction and support. Work began immediately. The eastern-
most 172 miles to Hollidaysburg opened in 1832. That section
required 108 locks. The next 26 miles, across the spine of the
Allegheny Mountains, were handled by a series of inclined planes
over which the canal boats traveled on special cars. At Johnstown
the boats returned to their natural element for the remaining 104
miles and 66 locks to Pittsburgh. The Main Line Canal, as it came
to be called, opened along its full length in March 1834. The Main
Line canal boats were notably colorful. The *Pittsburgh,* the first
passenger packet to make a full westbound passage, had a red and
black hull with a white superstructure broken by twenty green
shuttered windows along the side of the cabin. A crew of nine
maneuvered the 75-foot-long vessel and attended to the needs of
150 passengers.

Nevertheless, the effect of the Pennsylvania canal system on
the West was almost as dramatic as that of the Erie. Wheat prices in
Cincinnati rose from $4 per barrel in 1826 to $8 in 1835; flour
climbed from 25 cents to $1.00 a bushel; and whiskey jumped

from 18 cents to $1.50 per gallon. In 1846 over half of the manu-
factured goods imported into the Ohio River basin came through
Pennsylvania. Yet the combination canal-inclined plane system was
too expensive to operate economically even at its relatively high
volume of traffic. Therefore, in 1857 the state sold the Maine Line
Canal to the Pennsylvania Railroad, which promptly converted it
into a wholly rail route. Local political pressure also forced Pennsylvania to construct a series of subsidiary lines including one up
the Susquehanna to Wilkes Barre and a connection with the New
York system, another to Williamsport, and a third line tying the
Allegheny to Lake Erie. None developed large traffic, and all were
sold by the state in 1843.

Baltimore's efforts to tap western trade came in two forms.
Both began construction July 4, 1828. One was the Baltimore and
Ohio Railroad, intended to tie the port with the Ohio River at
Wheeling, using horse cars and later steam trains. Less visionary
was the Chesapeake and Ohio Canal Company. Its founders
planned to follow the Potomac River before crossing the Appalachians to the Ohio River watershed. Enroute the waterway would
have to scale 2,754 feet, but that scarcely worried its promoters
since their initial objective was the rich Cumberland coal fields.
The canal began with great hopes. The first section, 20 miles from
the Little Falls of the Potomac to Seneca, Maryland, opened in
1830, but the remainder languished as a result of a long court fight
with the Baltimore and Ohio over the right to build along the
north bank of the Potomac around Harper's Ferry and the decline
of government support. Not until 1 October 1850 did the final 164
miles necessary to reach Cumberland open. The canal went no
further, abandoning the role of connector to the west to its rail-
mounted adversary. Nevertheless, the canal competed successfully
with the railroad for the western Maryland coal trade, carrying a
peak load of 973,805 tons in 1875. Thereafter traffic fell rapidly
and, following the great flood of 1889, which destroyed large sections of the waterway, it ceased operations. Today only a few sections remain to offer both pleasant walking and bicycling on their
tow paths and a nostalgic trip on a replica canal boat.

4. The Western Response to the Erie Canal

In 1816 the War Department ordered Major Stephen H. Long to
reconnoiter the land between the Ohio and Mississippi rivers and
Lake Michigan. He reported that the Ohio, Mississippi, Illinois,

and Chicago rivers were natural communications routes but recommended construction of several canals. These included a route between the Illinois River and Lake Michigan via the Des Plains River; one connecting the Illinois, Wabash, St. Joseph, and Maumee rivers; and another across southern Illinois to tie the Mississippi and the Ohio above the bad water north of Cairo. But the estimated costs were prohibitive, and federal attention shifted elsewhere.

The western response to the opening of the Erie Canal can best be described as "duplication." Leaders of the western states promptly recognized in the Erie Canal and later in the Pennsylvania Main Line a very practical solution to one of the most difficult economic problems facing their citizens—where to find a satisfactory alternative to New Orleans as the market point for their produce. New York and Philadelphia obviously were such locations. Moreover, if the canals could be dug connecting the Ohio River with the eastward-flowing systems, the central portions of Ohio, Indiana, Illinois, and Michigan, which had neither navigable streams nor significant population, could prosper.

A further incentive to canal construction was their relatively low transport charges. In 1839 the distinguished engineer Charles Ellet, Jr., estimated that the cost per ton/mile (in cents) by various methods was:

Canals (excluding tolls)	$1^{1}/_{2}$
Railroads	$2^{1}/_{2}$
Macadam Roads	10–15
Common Turnpikes	15–20
Lake Steamers	2–4
Ohio & Mississippi river steamers	$^{1}/_{2}$–$1^{1}/_{2}$

Ohio considered state-financed canals before the War of 1812 but dropped all thoughts for the duration. Governor Allen Brown revived the idea in 1818. Four years later the state legislature authorized engineering studies of a route connecting Lake Erie and the Ohio River. In 1825 it voted to build canals from Cleveland to Portsmouth on the Ohio and from Cincinnati to Dayton with a possible extension to Toledo.

Construction of both started immediately. The Ohio and Erie, or "Ohio Canal" as it was more commonly called, which needed only 152 locks to scale a 94-foot rise in its 307-mile-course, opened in 1832. That was a year after Canada opened her ports to American wheat in transit, which permitted the Ohio grain growers to develop an export trade via the Welland Canal. Although the Ohio Canal achieved less traffic than its promoters anticipated, it played a significant role in developing the inland trading centers of Akron, Massilon, Newark, and Chillicothe. Its days of glory were few. Within five years it began to feel the first tremors of the assault by the railroads.

The second, or Miami, canal reached Dayton in 1828. Five years later, using the proceeds from the sale of lands donated by the federal government, it began inching northward to Toledo. The canal finally reached the lake port in 1845, but it was then too late to attract sufficient traffic to survive. Nevertheless, the canals played a significant role in establishing Ohio's five economic regions:

1. The Western Reserve around Cleveland, a grazing, dairying, poultry-raising area that sent its produce to market via the Great Lakes. Philadelphia traders tapped the market in the 1830s through a connector canal from the Pennsylvania system.
2. The southeast coal mining region, about sixty miles deep, which paralleled the Ohio River from the Scioto River to the Pennsylvania line. Its development benefited from a canal through the Hocking River valley to the Ohio.
3. The Central Region stretching across the middle of the state from the Pennsylvania boundary to the Great Miami River, a grain-growing region that, at least in theory, benefited from the market option made possible by the opening of the north-south canals.
4. The northwest cattle-producing region that looked to the Miami Canal for its route to market
5. The southwest corn and pork region, along the Ohio and west of the Scioto, which fed Cincinnati's packing houses and used the great river as its means of transportation

In 1836 the Ohio legislature yielded to the pressure of promoters and the areas not traversed by the two canals and passed the well-named "Plunder Act." It opened the state's coffers to all manner of canal and turnpike proposals through a state guarantee of their bonds. One project was the Pennsylvania and Ohio Canal, intended to tie the Ohio Canal at Akron to the Pennsylvania system. It would have been a successful undertaking had Pennsylvania ever built her portion of the connector. A somewhat similar failure was the Cincinnati and Whitewater, which connected the Ohio River port to the unsuccessful Whitewater Canal in southeastern Indiana. More satisfactory was the improvement of the Muskingum River to Zanesville. It continued in service until the 1890s.

A similar speculative binge fueled the visionary Indiana scheme to build the Wabash and Erie Canal from Toledo, Ohio, across northern Indiana to the Wabash and then southward to Evansville on the Ohio. In 1827 Congress contributed over half a million acres along the projected right of way of the canal, but construction funds were so slow to appear that work did not begin until 1832. Hampered by a continual shortage of money, the canal progressed fitfully for the next four years. In 1836 the state legislature came to the canal's aid with the Mammoth Internal Improvement Act, which authorized the issuance of $10 million in state bonds to finance internal improvements. These were primarily the Wabash and Erie, the Central Canal from Logansport to Evansville via Indianapolis, the Whitewater Canal in the southeast corner of the state, and improvement of the Wabash River.

Not only was the $500,000 interest on the loan ten times the total tax revenue of the state, but the bond sales were mishandled, if not worse, by the canal commissioners, who lost nearly $4 million through the collapse of several of their agents. By 1839 the state of Indiana was effectively bankrupt although it continued construction of the Wabash and Erie. In 1843 service began between Lafayette on the Wabash and Toledo. For the next fifteen years the canal served as the main communication link in northern Indiana, yet the cost of maintaining the canal nearly equaled its revenues. In 1853 the last section, between the Wabash and Evansville, opened to make the canal at 458 miles the longest ever dug in the United States. Almost immediately the southern section came under physical attack from local farmers, who drained several of the reservoirs supplying that section and destroyed one of the aqueducts. Since cost of repairs more than ate up the revenues, and as the canal increasingly lost traffic to the railroads, the Evansville section closed in 1860. The rest of the route struggled on until 1872. (See Table 4–1.)

Table 4-1. *Canal Mileage in Operation*

State	1830	1840	1850
Maine	21	240	29
New Hampshire	0	11	0
Vermont	0	1	1
Massachusetts	74	89	89
Rhode Island	11	11	11
Connecticut	34	36	36
New York	546	640	803
Pennsylvania	230	954	954
New Jersey	20	142	142
Delaware	14	14	14
Maryland	10	136	136
Virginia	0	216	216
North Carolina	0	13	13
South Carolina	52	52	52
Georgia	16	28	28
Kentucky	2	2	2
Alabama	0	52	52
Ohio	245	744	792
Indiana	0	150	214
Illinois	0	0	100
Louisiana	0	14	14

Source: Baltbasar H. Meyer (ed.), Transportation in the U.S. Before 1860 *(Washington, 1917), 573.*

The grandiose plans that prompted the 1836 acts fed on the wave of speculation then sweeping the West, which infected even the staid money market of London. Between 1832 and 1836 the volume of money in circulation in the United States jumped from $59 million to $140 million while English investments in the United States rose $108 million in 1835–37. Much of the money hurried into land speculation. Land sales that had averaged less than 400,000 acres per year in the 1820s spurted to 38 million in 1835–37. In that heady atmosphere state bonds were readily marketable through New York and London banks to investors scarcely aware of the location of the state, let alone cognizant of the flimsy credit structure underlying the bonds or of the danger of repudiation.

In the fall of 1836 Andrew Jackson, concerned over the accumulation of worthless money issued by dead or insolvent state banks, directed that only specie be accepted for land sales. The Specie Circular burst the balloon of speculation. By the spring of 1837 the country was in a depression. Business establishments and banks foundered, the economy slowed, and the western states were saddled with enormous quantities of bonds sold to finance canals and railroads that were staggering along unable to pay even the state-guaranteed interest on their debts. Many had ceased construction altogether. Ohio owed $15,570,000, Indiana nearly $15 million, Illinois almost as much, and Michigan $5 million. Such sums were beyond the taxing capabilities of the thinly settled western states. Moreover, repayment of money to wealthy eastern or European investors was politically unpopular. In 1841 and 1842 nine states halted interest payments while Michigan and Indiana actually repudiated portions of their debt. It is the experience of the panic of 1837 that caused Indiana and Wisconsin to forbid state indebtedness in the constitutions that they wrote in the 1840s. These precautions were too late to protect the British investors, who are estimated to have lost $100 million as a result of their speculations.

The impact of the canals was significant. Farmers within easy carting distance of them could sell their produce for twice or two and a half times the old price and purchase goods for half as much. The new prosperity attracted a wave of immigration. The population in the counties adjacent to the Indiana canals rose 500 percent in 1835–40 and those near the Illinois and Michigan increased eight times that fast. Instead of opening alternative routes of shipment as their proponents had expected, however, the canals tended to divide the West into two trading regions. The older section drained by the Ohio and its tributaries remained largely a corn growing area that shipped via New Orleans until the arrival of the railroads while the newer, heavily wheat-producing region in the northern and central portions of Ohio, Indiana, and Illinois sent its produce to market via the Great Lakes and the Erie Canal. The division represented both the agricultural geography of the region and established trading patterns. The most noticeable effect of canals on the farmers of the Old Northwest was to raise the price of goods sold south rather than suddenly to shift their markets eastward. Not until the construction of the railroad trunk lines in the 1850s did Cincinnati, for instance, find her chief market in the East rather than the South.

As the country began to emerge from the panic in the early and mid-1840s the chastened westerners hesitated to return to canal-building. They had learned the hard way that canals had to be backed with the granite of reality, not the ooze of rhetoric. Canals, they realized, were expensive holes that consumed greater quantities of money than was available while the newly developed railroad could be built cheaper than canals; could go places a canal could not; disturbed the landscape less; could be built faster; and could ship goods nearly as cheaply (about $2^1/_2$ cents per ton/mile as opposed to the canal's $1^1/_2$ cents). The westerners, therefore, turned to the railroad as their internal communication system. To be sure, a handful of the canals begun earlier were completed, but none played a significant role in the economic life of the region except possibly the Illinois and Michigan Canal, which tied Chicago to the Mississippi River. Although the waterway nearly bankrupted the state of Illinois when constructed between 1836 and 1848, it helped Chicago replace New Orleans as the forwarding point for goods from the East bound for St. Louis. In 1857 it helped western farmers to ship 20 million bushels of wheat and corn to market through the Windy City. In the 1840s and 1850s, before the completion of a through railroad to the East, a consistent pattern of rail lines radiating from the leading ports and canal centers like Chicago, Detroit, and Cleveland joined the canals in funneling produce and raw materials for transshipment eastward by water.

On a broader scale the canals began one of the most significant political developments in nineteenth-century America. To the northeastern farmer forced off his farm by the shifts in agricultural demand; to the factory worker seeking his own opportunity; to the sailor hoping for a plot of his own land; and to thousands of others seeking their fortune in the West the Erie Canal offered the first cheap and safe route to the land of opportunity. As a direct result the lands of the Great Lakes basin and those serviced by the western canal lines were populated by northeasterners whose political, social, and economic attitudes conflicted with those of the southern-oriented earlier settlers in the Ohio Valley. By 1840 control of the states of the "Old Northwest" passed into the hands of the northeastern-oriented politicians, and this combined with the increasing importance of the eastward trade to draw the Old West into an ever closer alliance with the Northeast. That alliance, when added to the loss of the southern congressional veto in the Compromise of 1850, led to the sense of political isolation and feebleness that culminated in the secession of 1860–61.

The great canal period had passed by 1845. Its time upon the center stage was but two decades. The abandonment of canals was nearly as rapid as their flimsy construction had been during the heyday of rush building. Only the Erie Canal remained profitable. It alone connected the grain-growing West with the markets of the East and passed through the mixed agricultural and industrial area of central New York. Gradually the other long canals succumbed to railroad competition, declining traffic, and high maintenance costs. Between 1860 and 1900 almost 1,700 miles of canals ceased operation. The loss of traffic to railroads was precipitous. In 1868 canals transported 96.1 percent of the western grain shipments. It was half that in 1880 and a mere 12 percent in 1898. Almost as soon as they appeared the railroads swept up passenger service, except for that of the Erie Canal, whose cheaper fares continued to attract impecunious travelers. Not only did railroads go where most travelers wished, but they did so more rapidly than the canal boats.

Chapter Five

WESTERN RIVERS

A S IMPORTANT AS THE CANALS WERE IN THE DEMOGRAPHIC AND POLI-
tical shifts within the United States prior to the Civil War, their
significance in the creation of the economic foundation for the
region between the Appalachians and the Rocky Mountains was far
surpassed by the streams of the Mississippi River basin and those
draining the cotton belt of the Southeast. It was the ability to move
people and produce by inexpensive water shipment that created
the conditions that permitted the settlement of the vast central
region of the nation during the nineteenth century. Without river
traffic there would have been no Pittsburgh, Cincinnati, St. Louis,
Minneapolis, Memphis, or Bismarck.

1. Routes West

The movement westward beyond the Applachians began in the
final decades of the eighteenth century. At midcentury, French
traders and soldiers with both strategic and commercial motives
arrived in the Ohio River valley. Their presence served to pen the
British colonists east of the mountains and to establish French control of the hitherto largely ignored Ohio River waterway. In addition, by opening a route via Lake Erie, French Creek, the Allegheny
River, and the Ohio, the French acquired an alternative to the dangerous passage through Georgian Bay, and Lakes Huron and Michigan to the Illinois country and the Mississippi River. It was the

construction of the keystone post, Fort Duquesne at the junction of the Allegheny and Monongahela rivers, that ignited to the French and Indian War. The Peace of Paris in 1763 shifted all the land east of the Mississippi, except that around its mouth, to English control while that farther westward passed from French to Spanish domain.

Three fingers of English settlement thrust into the trans-Appalachian lands between the French and Revolutionary Wars. The occupation of the eastern regions of what is today Kentucky and Tennessee had started in 1748 with Stephen Holston's settlement on the river that took his name. Few other settlers moved westward for another twenty years. Then a handful of new settlements sprang up around the headwaters of nearby tributaries of the Tennessee River. In 1774 James Harrod founded Harrodsburg in Kentucky, but Indian hostility retarded the Kentucky settlements until the end of the Revolution. The Tennessee settlements, on the other hand, benefited from a peaceful Indian frontier and grew rapidly.

The rivers began to play a greater role as transportation routes once settlement reached the relatively free flowing reaches of the westward moving streams. One of the most colorful episodes of this period was Colonel John Donelson's movement of nearly 150 settlers from Fort Patrick Henry (modern Kingsport, Tennessee), on a flotilla of 30 flatboats down the Holston, Tennessee, and Ohio rivers and up the Cumberland to Nashville, a voyage of 986 miles.

The earliest Ohio River settlements, naturally, were at Fort Pitt (the English name for Fort Duquesne) and its vicinity. They quickly developed a maritime atmosphere. Boat building began at Fort Pitt in 1764 and at Elizabeth on the Monongahela in 1783. Although the Revolution slowed settlement, some Americans did move into the Ohio Valley. Louisville, at the Falls of the Ohio, for instance, was settled in 1778. Four years later it dispatched shipment of flour to New Orleans while in 1783 a store advertised goods shipped from Philadelphia via the Mississippi. Nevertheless, American shippers met with scowls from the Spanish officials. They promptly closed the Mississippi River to foreign navigators. The Spanish policy grew out of the realization that the free use of the Mississippi system would both strengthen the American western settlements and attract other settlers into the area, thus increasing the threat to Spain's hold on Louisiana.

Following the Revolution a few settlers moved north of the Ohio. In 1789 Colonel Ebenezer Zane opened a ferry across the river at Wheeling, Virginia, and counterparts shortly followed elsewhere along the river. Nevertheless, several factors inhibited settlement north of the Ohio River. Although obliged to do so by the Treaty of Paris, the British refused to surrender the posts along the southern shores of the Great Lakes and supported the Indians who

harassed settlements north of the river. A second limitation was the inability to ship produce to market. The cost of moving most goods overland to the eastern markets was prohibitive, so that without an outlet at New Orleans the westerners could not develop a viable economy. Yet the Spanish at New Orleans only occasionally granted export licenses and then only when it appeared politically useful to do so. Such an arrangement allowed General James Wilkinson to bring two flatboats loaded with tobacco, butter, lard, hams, flour, tallow, beef, and pork downriver in 1788. The Spanish authorities hoped thereby to seduce Wilkinson into leading a separatist movement in Kentucky. Fortunately, the creation of a new national government in 1789 and the rapid admission of the western areas into the Union killed that project, as it did the similar British one in Vermont. Despite Spanish restrictions, some goods did flow downriver. In 1790 at least 60 flatboats reached Natchez, and in 1801 over a million dollars worth of goods passed through her customs house. Flour was the staple of the trade, New Orleans receiving 8,600 barrels in 1797 and 14,500 in 1803.

Meanwhile, a small eager pool of migrants built up south of the Ohio waiting for the lands to the north of it to be freed of danger. That happened in 1794–95. In 1795 John Jay negotiated a commercial treaty with Britain that among its few welcome provisions provided for the Redcoats's withdrawal to the Canadian side of the lakes. That same year General Anthony Wayne defeated the Maumee Indians in the Battle of Fallen Timbers and the following spring extracted from them the Treaty of Greenville by which they surrendered southern Ohio and southeastern Indiana. In 1795 Thomas Pinckney, the American minister in Madrid, followed with a very favorable treaty that granted to Americans duty-free transshipment through New Orleans for three years and the right thereafter to maintain a port of deposit for goods coming down the river. These three treaties broke the log jam. The north bank of the Ohio was now free for settlement, and the settlers had an open river to send their produce to market. (See table 5–1.)

Three routes brought settlers to Pittsburgh (the town around Fort Pitt) from which they could move downriver to their new homes. One ran from Philadelphia across to the Susquehanna River and up its west branch. It then followed a forty-mile portage to Toby Creek, which was a tributary of the Allegheny. The second also headed west from Philadelphia but followed the Juniata River

Table 5–1. Population Growth* of Trans-Appalachian West

State	1790	1800	1810	1820	1830	1840	1850	1860
Kentucky	73.7	221.0	406.5	564.1	687.9	779.8	982.4	1,155.7
Tennessee	35.7	105.7	261.7	422.8	681.9	829.2	1,002.7	1,109.8
Ohio		45.4	230.8	581.3	937.9	1,519.3	1,980.3	2,339.5
Indiana		5.6	24.5	147.2	343.0	685.9	988.4	1,350.4
Louisiana			76.6	152.9	215.7	352.4	517.8	708.0
Illinois			12.3	55.2	157.4	476.2	851.5	1,712.0
Mississippi		7.6	40.4	75.4	136.6	375.7	606.5	791.3
Michigan			4.8	8.8	31.6	212.3	397.7	749.1
Missouri			20.8	66.6	140.5	383.7	682.0	1,182.0
Arkansas				14.3	30.4	97.6	209.0	435.5
Wisconsin						30.9	305.4	775.9
Iowa						43.1	192.2	674.9
Trans-Appalachian West	109.4	385.3	1,078.3	2,088.6	3,362.9	5,786.6	8,716.8	12,984.1

*In 1,000.

Source: *Bureau of the Census*, Historical Statistics of the United States Colonial Times to 1957 *(Washington, 1960)*, 13.

or the Forbes Road to Fort Ligonier, from which a portage brought the traveler to the Loyalhanna River, another tributary of the Allegheny. The third path ran from Alexandria and Baltimore up the Potomac River to Fort Cumberland and then traversed Braddock's Road to Youghiogheny or Redstone on the Monongahela.

Once the settler reached the Ohio he had several choices of vessel to carry him and his family to their new homestead. The most popular was the flatboat, a flat-bottomed box usually 20–60 feet long with sides two to three feet high that moved with the current, assisted by sweeps and long steering oars fore and aft. Because of their cheapness, flatboats continued to be used as cargo carriers down to the Civil War. For those who had sufficient money ($100) for more luxurious accommodations, the ark was popular. Built of heavy timbers with a broad V-shaped bow and stern and nominally steered by a giant sweep plied by two men, it was a very unwieldy craft. On the western waters arks usually had a house erected to shelter the family at one end and a cattle enclosure at the other. Like the flatboats the arks were normally taken apart at the end of the voyage, with the timbers frequently going into the owner's new home.

Less commonly used were the keel boats, 30 to 75 feet long, relatively narrow craft capable of carrying 15–40 tons of cargo. They were fitted with a walking board on each side so that their crew could propel them by setting poles. The boatmen, usually French Canadian voyageurs, often scrambled ashore to haul the craft along with long ropes called cordelles. Less frequently, sailing barges and pulling boats competed for business of the rivers. On all of the waterways canoes remained a common sight until the end of the fur-trading era.

Because of the near impossibility of making headway against the current, less than a tenth of the traffic on the Ohio and Mississippi flowed upstream. In 1794 service started between Cincinnati and Pittsburgh in four light but strongly built and well-defended keelboats similar to whaleboats. Although primarily intended to carry mail, they had passenger accommodations and could make the trip in twelve days. By 1815 keelboats ran regularly between New Orleans and Pittsburgh. Two years later about 20 passenger barges and 150 keelboats plied the Ohio on reasonably regular schedules. Most came from the boatyards at Brownsville, Pennsylvania, Pittsburgh, Cincinnati, and Marietta, Ohio. The greatest problem faced by sailors on the Ohio and Mississippi aside from the snags, rocks, and unexpected shoals was the perverseness of water levels, particularly in the heavily traversed Pittsburgh-Cincinnati stretch. The rivers could be navigated easily only in February-June and October-December. Safety began to improve in 1801 when the *Navigator,* the first of a long series of handbooks on the Ohio, appeared to guide craft to the best route.

The western river boatman is one of the great folk figures in American history. He reveled in the title of "Alligator-horse," with its suggestion of amphibious strength. Tall, thin, sinewy, with a face darkened by wind and sun, he was capable of tumultuous action but normally appeared ensheathed in a cocoon of listless lethargy. His near uniform of red flannel shirt, short, loose blue coat, coarse brown linsey-woolsey trousers, fur cap, and moccasins presented a spectacle seldom forgotten by those who saw him. Equally spectacular was his vocabulary of careless metaphors, similes, and comparisons that balanced his accuracy as a tobacco spitter. He was a prodigious fighter of the no-holds-barred school and like his folk-hero Mike Fink loved a fight.

The demand for transportation both of people and produce created a shipbuilding industry. Boatbuilders, as we have seen, wielded their saws, adzes, and hammers as soon as traders began to move about on the western rivers. Despite the nearby stands of white oak, larger craft had to wait. The earliest-known large vessel, the sloop *Western Experiment,* took the water at Pittsburgh in 1789 while a schooner reportedly took shape on the bank of the Monongahela four years later. The real start of shipbuilding came during the last year of the new century. The year 1800 saw carpenters at Elizabeth, Pennsylvania, at work on the 250-ton schooner *Monongehela Farmer* and the transplanted Yankees at Marietta framing the 100-ton brig *St. Clair.* Both made their way down the Ohio and Mississippi to New Orleans, where they entered ocean service. At least 34 other ocean-going craft of over 100 tons sailed from Ohio River yards in the next decade.

Traffic on the western rivers remained essentially one way until an inexpensive means of upriver movement could be found. In 1802 a pair of New Orleans merchants conceived of a steamboat and purchased a steam engine from Oliver Evans in Philadelphia. They had a hull constructed locally and had nearly completed fitting the engine into it when the spring flood of 1803 deposited the contraption in a cornfield a half mile from the river. Unable to drag the steamer back to its natural element, the owners removed the engine and used it to power a sawmill. A second imaginative group in New Orleans in 1807 built a horse-powered boat to run between New Orleans and Louisville but abandoned the project after the vessel wore out more than a dozen horses getting to Natchez.

Two years later the Fulton-Livingston interests, capitalizing on the success of the *Steam Boat* and the political connections of Chancellor Livingston, secured a monopoly on the waters of the Louisiana Territory for their Mississippi Steam Boat Company. Nicholas J. Roosevelt came west to build the Monopoly's first steamer, the blue-hulled *New Orleans,* at Pittsburgh. We know many things about her but not whether she was propelled by stern or side wheels. In 1811 she steamed to New Orleans with her builder and his family as passengers and went into service between there and Natchez. The *New Orleans* proved the utility of steamers on the Mississippi although her deep draft restricted her to the lower section of the river. Two of the steamers that followed the *New Orleans* played minor roles in the War of 1812, transporting supplies from Memphis to New Orleans for General Andrew Jackson's defense of the seaport.

Most historians, however, date the real start of steamboat service on the western waters from the 1817 New Orleans to Louisville round trip of the *Washington.* With her double-deck construction, she pointed the way to the uniquely designed western river steamer. She also played a role in the destruction of the Monopoly in 1818, when the Courts ruled that she could not be kept out of Louisiana waters. That decision opened the western rivers to a rapid growth of steam service. The charges for passage between New Orleans and Louisville soon settled at $125 upstream and $75 downstream, prices acceptable to those who could afford them since the steamers dropped the round-trip time between New Orleans and Pittsburgh from 100 to 30 days. Nor was competition lacking. In 1819 some 60 steamers plied between New Orleans and the Falls of the Ohio at Louisville. The latter was the effective head of navigation from New Orleans. Until the opening of the Portland Canal in 1830 very few steamers attempted to pass the falls, preferring to transship their cargoes to other craft that operated upstream of the rapids.

The development of the western river-steamer design took some years. The *New Orleans* had generally followed the deep-draft designs of the Hudson River steamers which, as we have seen, limited her operation to the Lower Mississippi. But the Mississippi and Ohio are much shallower than the Hudson and needed a new design. The first element appeared in 1813 on board Daniel French's little *Comet:* a lighter-weight, high-pressure engine that permitted the reduced draft necessary for shallow-river navigation. The following year French's more successful *Enterprise* startled the West by ascending from New Orleans to Louisville in 25 days and to Pittsburgh in 34 by taking advantage of shortcuts provided by high water in the rivers. That high water also permitted her to steam all the way to Brownsville on the Monongahela.

The second element, placing the boilers on the main deck, first appeared in Henry Shreve's *Washington* of 1816. In either that vessel or the *George Washington* of 1825 Shreve introduced a horizontal cylinder with pitman arm. This reduced the headroom necessary for the engine and permitted its installation on the main deck. The *George Washington,* as well as the *Emerald* built in Smithtown, Kentucky, the same year, moved the cabins onto a second, raised deck.

The third element, the shallow draft, flat bottom, appears to have been a gradual development. It was not, as has often been claimed, a Shreve contribution on the *Washington* or *George Washington.* The former, indeed, may have been the deepest draft of all early steamers, and the latter, while pointing towards shoalness, drew nearly as much water as the eastern boats.

Until about 1830 all vessels were heavily built like coastal sailing craft, which they outwardly resembled even to bowsprits. Yet there were constant complaints about the poor construction of the vessels and the recklessness with which they were operated. Any study of the mortality of western river steamers will bear out that accusation. Snags, rocks, and shifting sandbars took the heaviest toll, but boiler explosions and fires followed close behind. The earliest reported boiler explosion occurred on the *Washington* in 1816, but similar disasters became increasingly frequent in later years as boiler pressures rose to 100–150 psi, where they remained until the appearance of steel boiler plates in the 1880s.

Imperfect as it was, the steamer represented the most practical public transportation for people and goods moving between river ports. Following their initial appearance in 1818 on the route between Cincinnati and Louisville, express passenger steamers or packets came to dominate travel. If they had sufficient means, passengers could travel in relative luxury in private cabins. When lacking in funds they could ride as deck passengers and pay for part of the passage by working in the wood crews that periodically brought fuel on board from great stacks of firewood maintained along the banks. As valuable as the passenger packet may have been, it was as a cargo carrier that the steamer had its greatest value to the western farmer. It permitted him greater freedom in the timing of his shipment of produce to New Orleans and so reduced the price of goods brought upriver from the Crescent City that they no longer were luxuries.

The arrival of the steamboat did not mean that flatboats disappeared from the western rivers. They continued to operate down to the Civil War. Over 21,500 flatboats are estimated to have arrived at the New Orleans levee between 1806 and 1857, with 2,792 being counted during the peak winter season of 1846–47. That year they represented 20 percent of the tonnage reaching in the port. After 1820 most of the flatboats seem to have originated on shallow feeder streams that could not float steamboats. In 1828, for instance, between 1,200 to 1,500 flatboats are reported to have descended the White and Wabash rivers in Indiana. The few that did set sail from the banks of the major streams, often manned by professional crews, commonly served owners or shippers who could not afford steamboat shipment. It was on one of these that Abraham Lincoln made his well-known voyage to New Orleans. Keelboats succumbed to steam competition earlier than flatboats. They were driven from the New Orleans—Louisville trade by about 1825 but held on longer on smaller streams. As late as the mid-1840s St. Louis registered an average of 55 arrivals a year.

2. The Steamboat Age

The superiority of the steamboats quickly demonstrated itself. They hastened the settlement of the West by opening the markets necessary to bring economic health to the new settlements. By 1820 steamers regularly ran from New Orleans to Louisville in ten to fifteen days. The wood-gulping, steam-coughing, cargo-hauling packets were now launched on their golden voyage, which continued for most of the next two decades. During the 1830s, however, the market grew saturated, and profits fell until they became negligible if not nonexistent.

Economists like to point out that the steamboat caused a surge of productivity on the rivers that permitted New Orleans— Louisville freight rates to drop from $5.00 to $0.25 per hundred pounds between 1815 and 1860. Down stream rates fell from $1.00 to $0.32 during the same years. While much of the decline reflected the impact of competition, a substantial portion also resulted from the greater efficiency brought about by faster trips, quicker turnarounds, and a longer shipping season. The latter was six months in 1830 but stretched an additional ninety days during the next two decades.

The growth of steamboat tonnage was phenomenal. In 1856 the 123,869 tons registered on the Mississippi and its 44 navigable tributaries surpassed that of the total steam fleet of Great Britain. The impact can be seen from a different point of view in the value of goods reaching New Orleans from upstream. It doubled every decade from 1820 to 1860:

1820	$ 12,637,000
1830	$ 22,066,000
1840	$ 49,764,000
1850	$ 96,898,000
1860	$185,211,000

The spread of feeder services was equally rapid. Steam service on the Cumberland River reached Nashville in 1818, Florence, Alabama, in 1821, and Knoxville in 1822. The first steamer worked her way up the Arkansas River in 1820. Two years later an enterprising captain brought his vessel to Little Rock, and in 1827 another steamer pushed her way up to Fort Gibson in modern Oklahoma. During the 1820s and 1830s other steamers initiated service on the Green, Kentucky, Barren, Scioto, Miami, Licking, Big Sandy, and Kanawha rivers. The advance up the Red River in Louisiana was slower because of its "raft," an 160-mile long tangle of trees, branches, and other debris that restricted traffic to the lower reaches. It was temporarily opened by James B. Eads in 1832–38 but closed again during the 1840s and was not finally cleared until 1873. Ironically, almost immediately the dominant cotton trade of the area moved to the recently opened Texas and Pacific Railroad.

After 1830 river transport faced competition from canals and railroads, which channeled increasing amounts of goods, especially western grain, into direct east-west movement. This caused New Orleans to lose its dominance as the transshipment point of eastern goods headed west and vice versa. It made up for that loss with increased cotton shipments from the river plantations and the upriver movement of coffee and West Indian goods like sugar and

The Civil War steamer *Chattanooga* was similar to other light-draft craft that ran on the smaller streams such as the Wabash, Tennessee, and Arkansas. Official U.S. Navy Photograph

molasses. Indeed, by 1860 the canals and railroads had almost completely driven New Orleans from the east-west trade. This was not realized by many southerners who counted on the closing of the Mississippi to create strong pressure in the North for a political settlement favorable to the slave states in 1861. Those wishful thinkers assumed that the western states would find the loss of the New Orleans outlet so damaging that they would return to their historical alliance with the South.

The western river steamers quickly developed their own lore and lingo. Most American know that Mark Twain took his pen name from a call of the Mississippi boatman, but few know the measurement system from which it was derived.* A mark in the riverman's dialect was a fathom; therefore Mark Twain was two fathoms or twelve feet, plenty of water in which to navigate most of the pre-Civil War steamers. While the everchanging contours of the river bottom were a constant threat to the vessels churning the

---

*Quarter less mark, 4½′; mark, 6′; quarter mark, 7½′; half mark, 9′; quarter less twain, 10½′; mark twain, 12′; quarter twain, 13½′; half twain, 15′; quarter less tyree, 16½′; mark tyree, 18′; quarter tyree, 19½′; half tyree, 21′; mark four, 24′.

coffee-colored water, snags were even more dangerous. Not only did disaster lurk among the floating trees and limbs—which is the narrow meaning of the word—but also from sawyers, trees that came to the surface or remained submerged according to the effect of the current. Sawyers were often sleeping, i.e., underwater, for long periods. The immobile planters, which had one end jammed into the bottom, the bank, or a bar, offered an even greater danger.

Better than nearly any other river town St. Louis mirrors the history of transportation on the great central waterway. It had been settled by French fur traders in 1764 but grew slowly until the Louisiana Purchase. Although in 1810 it contained a mere 1,400 inhabitants, the settlement had undeniable natural advantages. Perched atop the first high ground south of the mouths of the Illinois and Missouri rivers, it overlooked the start of the deep channel on the Mississippi. For that reason, and because the Des Moines Rapids restricted the size of upper-river vessels, it became the transshipment point for the upper Mississippi trade. Because of its location, St. Louis also served as the entrepot for a web of commerce that stretched along the Missouri and its tributaries into the Rocky Mountains.

Prior to 1817 no steamer attempted to thread its way through the shifting channels of the Mississippi above its confluence of the Ohio. In that year the little *Zebulon M. Pike* arrived from Louisville after a six-week voyage but seems not to have remained in the area. Neither did the *Maid of Orleans,* which appeared the following year from Philadelphia and New Orleans. Once these pioneer craft proved the feasibility of reaching St. Louis, others followed. The Missouri city rapidly became the commercial center for the upper Mississippi River and for the country westward to the Rocky Mountains. As noted earlier, since the river shoaled appreciably above St. Louis the large downriver boats had to transship their cargoes at her levee. Until the Ohio and Mississippi Railroad arrived in 1855, St. Louis was strictly a river city receiving its supplies and exporting nearly exclusively by water. Her merchants brought manufactured goods from the Ohio River ports and distributed what she did not use to settlements in Iowa, Illinois, and Missouri. As the trans-Mississippi grain fields entered production during the late 1830s and 1840s, St. Louis became a grain center second only to Chicago. At the same time she continued to dominate the fur trade as the headquarters and depot of the American Fur Company.

In 1846 observers reported that 663 steamers arrived at the St. Louis levee from the upper Mississippi (about half carrying lead from Galena, Illinois), 395 from New Orleans, 420 from Ohio River ports, 446 from the Illinois River, and 256 from the Missouri River. A further indication of the volume of traffic on the levee can be glimpsed in the effects of the fire that broke out on the steamer *White Cloud* during the evening of May 17, 1849. It consumed 214 other steamers, 9 flatboats and barges, as well as fifteen city blocks, causing $5.5 million in damages.

Contributing mightily to St. Louis's prosperity was its proximity to the lead-mining region around Galena, Illinois, and Dubuque, Iowa. The famed Henry Shreve, as a youth, had initiated lead shipments in 1810 when he took a keelboat load to New Orleans. For the next sixteen years the mines's output moved, usually to St. Louis, on other keelboats. Then steamboats took over the growing trade. In 1828 they carried 13 million pounds. Twenty years later, after the Iowa mines were opened, the trade had risen to 55 million pounds. It was then worth $1.5 million, triple the value of St. Louis's trade with Santa Fe and five times that of her renowned fur trade. Nevertheless, the riverborne lead trade collapsed in 1854 when the Galena and Chicago Railroad began service. During the decade of the 1850s the character of St. Louis's commerce shifted as railroads also detached most of the traditional flour and provision trade. A growing movement of local produce and a new commercial hinterland along the upper Mississippi and the Missouri somewhat offset the loss.

The flood of German forty-eighters and Irish escaping the potato famines contributed to the health of the Mississippi passenger trade down to the Civil War. Many immigrants took passage from Europe to New Orleans and then made their way upriver to St. Louis, Cincinnati, and other river towns. The poorer or more thrifty reduced their $4 deck passage fare by toting wood on board at the fuel stops. Others found permanent work. In the 1850s observers estimated that half the deck crews were Germans or Irishmen. So great was the passenger traffic at St. Louis that in 1859 thirty-two steamers regularly carried passengers from New Orleans and another thirty-six ran to Cincinnati. The following year St. Louis record keepers noted 3,149 arrivals and departures from her levee and the movement of a million waterborne travelers through the city.

In 1823 the 188-foot *Virginia* pushed her way upstream to Ft. Snelling at the foot of St. Anthony's Falls in present-day

Minneapolis-St. Paul. Regular service developed slowly because of the shoal water on the Des Moines Rapids. Upriver navigation surged, however, following the entry of steamers into the Galena lead trade in 1826 and the movement of loggers and settlers into the great timberlands of western Wisconsin and southern Minnesota. The first Minnesota sawmill opened in 1839. Steamers from St. Louis offered the isolated river settlements their only contact with the outside world, and by 1844 packets regularly ran between St. Paul and St. Louis. A tremendous jump in activity along the upper river occurred in the decade of the 1850s, when the number of arrivals and departures at St. Paul rose 1,000 percent.

Initially, cargo on the upper Mississippi moved nearly exclusively upriver since the main export crop of the upper valley was lumber that easily floated downstream in great rafts. As early as 1828 a steamboat line ran to the Rock River, and a small steamer even churned a further 150 miles up the lesser stream when the water was adequate. We do not know when the first lumber from the Wisconsin forests floated downstream to St. Louis although there is evidence that it may have been at least in 1822. Timber rafts descended from the Chippewa River in 1831 and from the Wisconsin shortly afterwards. As the lumberjacks spread northward they began to work the Minnesota forests, but little timber cut above the Falls of St. Anthony reached St. Louis. Most was absorbed by the huge mills at Minneapolis and St. Paul. Rafts were the usual form of shipping for lumber on the Mississippi and its northern tributaries. Normally the logs were brailed together into a unit about 700 feet long and 135 feet wide called "half a raft." It drew about 18 inches and was handled by a crew of ten to twenty men. The record raft was 1,625 feet long and 275 feet wide. Because of several difficult stretches of the river, efforts were made early in the lumber trade to find better ways of handling the ungainly rafts. In 1844 Stephen B. Hanks, a cousin of Abraham Lincoln, began towing rafts through a tricky portion of the river. Specially fitted towboats came into general use by 1863 to speed the wood downstream. A more effective method of controlling the rafts appeared during 1866 in the *Le Clair.* She was the prototype of a class of specialized raft steamers whose powerful stern wheels and large capstans allowed them to act in effect as large rudders in controlling the course of the tow. They permitted larger tows.

An estimated 46,974,220,170 feet of timber moved downstream in rafts between 1830 and 1916. They had a value of approximately $704 million. The reports of watchers at Rock Island give a better sense of the magnitude of the traffic. In 1873 they counted 680 rafts and eleven years later 1,056. Those rafts fed 75 sawmills between the Falls of St. Anthony and St. Louis. The largest clusters were at the two ends and at Winona, Minnesota, La Crosse, Wisconsin, Dubuque, Clinton, and Muscatine, Iowa, Rock Island, and Hannibal, Missouri. Although the construction of locks and dams and the bridging of the river combined with railroad competition to restrict their utility, Mississippi timber rafts continued to make the downriver voyage until 1915. Between 1871 and 1909 most of the rafts were operated by the Mississippi River Logging Company, a consortium of lumber companies.

The upper Mississippi River freight and passenger service was an intensely difficult and competitive business. By 1857, however, it was dominated by the Minnesota Packet Company, which operated 99 steamers. In 1861 the company passed into the hands of William F. Davidson, who for the next twenty years controlled the lines serving Wisconsin and Minnesota. Davidson ultimately went bankrupt attempting to compete with the railroads, which after the Civil War stretched their steel tendons throughout the area drained by the river. The peak traffic year was 1892, when 5,498 steamers, 1,000 barges, and 2,000 rafts passed Winona.

Equally important were the Minnesota and Red rivers, which fed the wheat from the townshipwide farms of western Minnesota to the flour mills of Minneapolis and St. Paul. The earliest steamer on the Red River began operation in 1859, but until about 1878 her successors found their chief activity in ferrying cargoes to the Canadian settlements around Fort Garry. Southbound wheat shipments replaced local trade during the next decade although the construction of the Great Northern Railroad in 1878–89 increasingly syphoned away business. The Minnesota River, which enters the Mississippi at Minneapolis, served as the chief artery for the wheat flowing from the western farms. Its heyday was the decade of 1873 to 1883; thereafter the growing rail network absorbed most of its traffic.

3. Federal Assistance

Federal interest in the western rivers developed slowly since it was submerged in the larger question of federal aid for internal improvements. That changed in 1820 when Congress authorized a survey of possible improvements of the Ohio and Mississippi rivers. Carried out in 1821 under two able army engineers, Brigadier General Simon Bernard and Lieutenant Colonel Joseph G. Totten, it recommended construction of a canal around the Falls of the Ohio; installation of dikes to deepen the channels over shoals and bars; and removal of snags and other obstructions from the Mississippi. Nothing resulted from the proposals in the face of President James Monroe's doubts about the constitutionality of federally funded internal improvements.

In 1824, however, the climate of opinion shifted to favor federal assistance. Congress enacted the General Survey Act, which created an advisory Board of Engineers for Internal Improvements in an effort to provide orderly development. The board's recommendations primarily concerned eastern canals but also responded to the needs of the westerners. As a result, during its 1824 session Congress appropriated $75,000 to support dredging of six bars on the Ohio River and to start snag removal. The law assigned responsibility to the Army's engineers. Two years later the river improvements projects were combined with harbor improvements in a single rivers and harbors works bill, a practice that continues to the present and has helped create some of the most notorious of all log-rolling politicking in Congress. It has been one of the important factors in creating the great political power of the Army Corps of Engineers.

In 1826 Henry Shreve became Superintendent of Western River Improvement, and in 1829 he completed the prototype snag boat, the *Heliopolis*. She was a catamaran steamer with a heavy ram affixed to the bow so she could butt embedded trees and break them off underwater. The steamer carried a strong steam-powered winch to haul the freed trees onboard where they could be cut up. In her first encounter with a jumble of snags she cleared the notorious collection at Plum Point, Tennessee, in eleven hours. Within two years Shreve had eliminated all the major submerged forests on the Mississippi. The Ohio, Cumberland, Arkansas and Missouri rivers quickly followed. One great obstacle remained, the 160-mile-long "Great Raft of the Red River." That tangle of jumbled timber took from 1833 to 1839 to clear. In his honor the city that grew upon the site of his base camp took the name Shreveport. Shreve worked diligently to cut off bends in the Mississippi, but his improvements ruined the entrances to the Red, Ouachita, and Atchafalaya rivers. They had to be repaired at considerable cost in time, effort, and money.

The levees of larger river towns were scenes of feverish activity during the packet era. This rare photograph shows Vicksburg, Mississippi, probably in 1864, when the *James Watson* (left) and *White Cloud* (right) were in government service. Official U.S. Navy Photograph

In 1845 a River Improvement Convention met at Memphis, followed by a second two years later. Like the later conventions of 1851, 1866, and 1867 the assemblies lobbied for such improvements as deepening the channels at the mouth of the Mississippi to permit larger vessels to reach New Orleans; improvement of the channel of the Mississippi, notably deepening that between New Orleans and St. Louis to eight feet; and removal of the Rock Island Rapids and Falls of the Ohio. They met with success. In 1850 Congress authorized a survey of the lower Mississippi in order to determine what improvements were needed. The Delta, or Humphreys and Abbot survey, as it is commonly called, was completed just before the Civil War. It included recommendations for the flood prevention levees that became the mark of the postwar river banks as well as other efforts, especially at the river's mouth, to increase the velocity of water in the channel in an effort to scour it of bars.

The most notable use of federal funds on the Ohio was in the Louisville and Portland Canal around the Falls of the Ohio. Although the two-mile-long work was built by a private concern, about half of its capital came from a federal contribution. When opened in 1830 it allowed easy through passage from Pittsburgh to New Orleans. No longer was the Mississippi system fragmented into two relatively distinctive parts. In the first full year of operation 416 steamboats, 46 keelboats, and 357 flatboats transited the canal. Even so, until the completion of the dam system on the Ohio during the 1920s, year-round navigation was not possible because of the low-water months. Although the record low level in the river came during 1838, low-water problems in the 1850s were more persistent. They were years of drought that caused the river to be too shallow for extensive navigation between December of 1854 and March 1855 and between January and March 1856.

Different federal assistance appeared in the Steamboat Act of 1852, which codified the rules of passing; limited the maximum pressures that could be used in engines, and established other safety regulations. As a result the number of boiler explosions dropped from an average of 10 a year before its enactment to 4 a year immediately afterwards. Deaths fell from about 240 to 45 per year.

Despite strong political pressure the federal government did not take over the hard-pressed Louisville and Portland Canal until 1874. That was part of efforts to have the critical passage of the Falls of the Ohio enlarged and coincided with Colonel W. E. Merrill's proposal for the construction of wicket (movable) dams to maintain water depth along the Ohio River. Congress authorized the first, Lock 1 at Davis Island below Pittsburgh, in 1879. It was completed in 1885 and proved the practicality of wickets. Nevertheless, no additional works were approved until 1910.

Much attention instead focused on the upper Mississippi because of its grain and timber trades. There improvement began in 1867–77 with the construction of the Des Moines Rapids Canal. Other Corps of Engineers projects initiated at the same time at Rock Island and south of St. Paul established a 4½-foot channel. In 1905 Congress authorized a 6-foot depth north of St. Louis and an 8-foot one from there to the Ohio. That involved building 27 dams during the next nineteen years. In 1874 Congress ordered that an 8–10 foot channel be maintained in the lower Mississippi and five years later established the Mississippi River Commission to oversee the well-being of the river and its shipping.

The federal efforts to improve the river occurred at a propitious time for St. Louis. Its economy had yet to recover from the wartime destruction of its trade with New Orleans. It suffered a second blow during the 1870s and 1880s with the arrival of Chicago-centered railroads on the upper Mississippi and the Missouri, which syphoned away much of St. Louis's northern trade. The railroads even carried the bulk of traffic leaving St. Louis. In 1871 steamers hauled 770,498 tons from her levee, but railroads loaded 919,812 tons. In 1895 the tonnage was down to 303,335 tons by water and 5,349,347 tons by rail while ten years later the figures were 90,575 and 15,225,973, respectively. Nor was St. Louis alone in the loss of river trade; in 1880 arrivals in New Orleans were less than 75 percent of the number they had been in 1860.

Superficially, the one bright spot for western waters transport was the revival of the long-distance passenger trade after the Civil War. It followed the construction of a group of new express steamers. The *Natchez* and *Robert E. Lee* were only two of the best known. Their fabled race from New Orleans to St. Louis in 1870 was in effect the last fling of a dying breed. With the railroads offering faster and better service on many routes, the long-distance express steamer soon faded into history books. Their heyday, and their peak of ostentatiousness, occurred during 1867–1885. The gaudiest boats sailed the lower reaches of the Mississippi, where the rail competition was least. Although the luxury packets fought hard against the railroad, it was a losing battle because of the faster service offered by the land route. The final blow was the great ice flow of 1918, which destroyed $6 million worth of vessels including many of the surviving passenger craft. By World War II the only vessels left were a handful of cruising steamers. Most of those soon disappeared, leaving only the *Delta Queen,* a former Sacramento River boat, to keep the tradition alive. In 1976 she was joined by the *Mississippi Queen,* the first river passenger steamer to be built in forty years.

4. Missouri River

The Missouri River, the second of the great tributaries of the Mississippi, played a major role in the development of the West, but the irregularities of its flow and its bed limited the traffic it carried. Active use of the river, despite its difficulties, was another instance of the willingness of the pioneers to resort to water routes whenever possible. During the fur-trading period the American Fur Company and its St. Louis-based successors maintained their chief posts along the river or its navigable tributaries. This allowed them to collect the pelts during the winter and ship them to market on the spring floods in locally built pirogues and mackinaw boats. The trip was difficult at best. Islands, bars, snags, and rocks awaited the unwary boatman. The westbound trade goods normally moved out in mackinaw or keelboats during late February or early March when the ice went out of the river. This allowed the boats to reach, say Fort Benton, between May and July and make a return trip before winter arrived.

As the army moved out on the plains to shield the frontier from the ranging Indians, commerce pushed up the river. The first steamer on the Missouri was the *Independence* in 1819. That year also saw the Yellowstone Expedition of Major Stephen H. Long. Of his three steamers only the shallow-draft, serpent-bowed *Western Engineer* proved successful. Because of the slowness of its valley to attract settlers, very few commercial steamers operated on the Missouri during the 1820s. For instance, the first packet between St. Louis and Independence, at the head of the Santa Fe Trail, did not enter service until 1829. Nevertheless, the American Fur Company steamers pushed farther and farther westward on the upper river. They reached Pierre, South Dakota, in 1831; Fort Union, Montana, the following year; the Milk River in 1853; and Fort Benton, below Great Falls, Montana, in 1859.

Fort Benton was the effective head of navigation although an occasional vessel pushed on to the Great Falls. The post was 3,600 miles from St. Louis and only 200 miles from Helena, where gold was discovered in 1862. The Missouri River route naturally became the prime route to the Montana gold fields. Five-sixths of the mining equipment and most of the miners used it. At its height in 1856 about 2,500 men, 20,000 mules and oxen, and 600 wagons shuttled goods from Fort Benton to Helena.

As long as the Montana mining boom continued the steamers earned fantastic profits. One made $66,000 on a single voyage in 1866. The Missouri River lines also carried large shipments for the army, which during the later 1860s and 1870s built a series of new posts on the plains under a policy of restraining the nomadic

The Missouri River steamer *Expansion* loads grain. Most shipments on western rivers originated at similar small landings. Bureau of Reclamation Photograph, Courtesy of the National Archives

tribes. As the Dakota wheat fields came into production the west-ward push of settlement contributed another source of business.

By 1868 the effect of the rail competition could be felt. That year the Chicago and Northwestern reached Sioux City, Iowa, which replaced St. Louis as the starting place for much of the river service. Since Sioux City drew on Chicago rather than St. Louis for its goods, the shift was a double blow for the Missouri city. The following year the Union Pacific laid track to Ogden, Utah, from which a relatively easy wagon route ran to Montana. That ended most river-freight shipments to Montana. In 1872 the Northern Pacific reached Bismarck, North Dakota. It effectively diverted Dakota wheat to the Minneapolis mills and shifted the base of steamboating to Bismarck. The final blow to Missouri River traffic came in 1887 when the Great Northern reached Helena. Although Bismarck continued to serve as a wheat-gathering point for the railroad, the amount traveling by water declined drastically after 1916. In 1924 the long-dominant Benton Transportation Company suspended operations, and twelve years later the last local steamer drew its fires.

The residents of the lower Missouri valley fought hard to secure improvements in the channel at least as far as Sioux City. In 1887 they secured an $850,000 appropriation and three years later the establishment of a Missouri River Commission to plan and coordinate the improvements. It accomplished little, although Congress in 1910 authorized a 6-foot channel as far as Kansas City. Before the improvements were completed the focus of the Corps of Engineers work on the river shifted to flood control dams connected by a 9-foot channel below Sioux City. Authorized in 1940 the new system was completed in the 1970s at which time the river carried about three million tons of cargo, roughly half of that bulk farm produce.

5. The Modern Period

Coal provided the largest portion of the cargoes that rode the western rivers in the late nineteenth and early twentieth centuries. It was a trade, however, that grew slowly until just before the Civil War. The earliest recorded shipment occurred in 1806 from the mines around Pomeroy, Ohio, to Cincinnati. Eight years later the much more important Pittsburgh shipments began. They were well established by 1819. Shipments from western Kentucky to Mississippi river ports started a decade later. Even so, in 1855 the trade had a value of only about $100,000. Until the 1850s, coal moved in large barges or flatboats that in their fullest development could carry 575 tons and required a crew of 23 or 24 men. Normally they floated downstream with the current, but by 1854 towboats had begun to handle groups of them.

The 1850s saw the start of large coal shipments from Pittsburgh. They also witnessed the rise of the coal ports along West Virginia's Kanawha River, where the mines, especially those producing the oil-bearing cannel coal, boomed. The cannel coal trade lasted less than two decades because the petroleum wells that came into production in the late 1850s provided the raw material for better and cheaper illuminants. After the Civil War, West Virginia continued to mine bituminous coal in great quantities, but most of it moved to the coal pockets of Newport News and Norfolk rather than westward.

Although the Civil War distrupted trade, the damage was short-lived. Well-built two-way barges pushed by towboats appeared during the war years and quickly took over the trade. As a result forty steamboats worked fulltime in 1869 hauling cargoes of coal downstream from Pittsburgh, and another sixty found employment locally. By 1880, 90 million tons of coal moved on the Ohio. Thirty million tons of it headed for Cincinnati, 12 million to Louisville, and 8 million to New Orleans.

Most towboats operated only during the daytime prior to the 1880s because of the dangers of night navigation. That changed in the 1870s, when the Lighthouse Board began installation of navigation range lights or day markers along the shore. Nevertheless it was 1882 before warning lights were required on bridges. It was also in the late 1870s that steamboats were first fitted with the electric searchlights that one newspaper boasted could "illuminate the river almost as bright as day for a distance of five miles ahead."

Despite the growth of the coal shipments, total trade dropped from 28.3 million to 26.4 million tons between 1889 and 1906. The decline came chiefly in lumber, grain, and cotton. The former fell from 9.2 million tons to 515,000; grain from 1.7 million to 514,000; and cotton from 896,000 to 147,000 tons. The reasons are complicated. Not only did the railroads extend their rails to cities formerly serviced by the steamers alone but the post-Civil War service offered by the rebuilt southern rail network was faster. On top of this the railroads established highly discriminatory rates, especially on joint tariffs with water-transport companies. After 1876 the lower Mississippi shippers lost much of their remaining cotton trade when stronger cotton presses permitted railroads to stow 47 bales in the space formerly occupied by 22. As a result many freight packets rotted in seldom-visited backwaters or lost their engines to become wharfboats.

Between 1870 and 1891 the number of New Orleans-owned steamboats dropped from 455 to 128, and their tonnage declined from 46,000 to 20,000. Barges took over much of the remaining traffic. In the 1880s they carried a third of all cargo on the lower river. The same period saw the stern-wheeler, which was better adapted to handle tows, replace the side-wheeler. During the decade, coal shipments rose from 8.5 million to 11 million, and the distribution of trade changed radically. Upper Mississippi shipments, which particularly felt the impact of the trans-Mississippi railroads and their connection through Chicago to the eastern rail network, fell from 6.3 million to 1.1 million tons.

The increase in power of towboats went on apace to take advantage of the economy of scale. The great steamer *Sprague* built in 1904 set a record by pushing a tow of 56 barges from Cairo, Illinois, to New Orleans. The tow measured 1,132 feet by 312 feet and contained 53,000 tons of the black diamonds. During 1905 the Kanawha Valley coal mines in West Virginia alone dispatched nearly a million and a half tons of coal by water. Most of it went to Cincinnati for transshipment by rail to users elsewhere in the Midwest. By 1915 the Pittsburgh long-distance coal trade had ceased since the local steel mills consumed nearly all the coal dug in western Pennsylvania. The downriver trade, therefore, originated in the fields of Alabama, Illinois, Indiana, West Virginia, and Kentucky.

In 1895 a group of men interested in the health of their waterway formed a lobbying organization, the Ohio Valley Improvement Association. In 1909 they and other western shippers and owners used a "Rivers and Harbors Congress" to pressure the federal government into improvements on the western rivers. Despite the removal of the Red River raft by Shreve, the building of the Mississippi River jetty by Eads, and the creation of a 4¹/₂-foot channel in the upper Mississippi, the rivermen argued that the federal government had done little to assist navigation. Only 2,500 miles of 6-foot-deep channels existed on the main stream. The meeting induced Congress to authorize a 9-foot channel the following year. It was accomplished by a system of dams on the Ohio and by dredging on the Mississippi. The network of Ohio River dams, which ultimately cost $150 million, was not completed until 1929. It consisted of 41 movable or wicket dams that would be laid flat in periods of high waters and raised in low ones. Five other dams had fixed walls. All had 600-foot-long locks. The 9-foot channel was also extended to the Ohio's major tributaries, in most cases with their own dam network. The deeper channels permitted use of barges having 8-foot-deep holds that could carry at most three times as much as their older sisters. As a result the Ohio River handled 22 million tons of cargo in 1929, compared to only 7.3 million in 1915.

One benefit of the 9-foot channel was that for the first time the Ohio River ports had year-round service to the South. After the Illinois River was canalized in 1935, river service to Chicago also became feasible. Another benefit, well appreciated by those living within sight of the dams, was the fairylike effect of night lockings as the searchlight of the towboat picked out the web of piping atop the decks of the oil barges.

During World War I the federal government, in keeping with its actions relating to oceangoing shipping and the railroads, seized all floating equipment on the Mississippi and the Warrior River systems. Both the vessels and service deteriorated under government operation, so in 1924 Congress attempted to rectify the situation. It created the Inland Waterways corporation to operate the government-owned river vessels. The Corporation undertook a rebuilding of the fleet, initially replacing the worn-out barges with a new more efficient design. In 1929–31 the corporation began construction of a series of able towboats powered by Diesel engines employing tunnel-screw propulsion. The latter placed the propellers inside a shroud installed in a spoon-shaped recess in the vessel's bottom. The design revolutionized towboats and revitalized the industry. Modern versions of the tunnel-screw towboat may exert over 10,000 horsepower and handle tows of 40 or more barges. The record tow, set in 1981 by the *Miss Kae-D,* involved 72 barges.

Spurred by the demands of World War II, flood-prevention imperatives, and political considerations, Congress in 1944 enacted the Flood Control Act, which among its provisions established a 12-foot channel for the Mississippi River along with a series of upriver dams and downstream improvements. It is a project still uncompleted. The larger tows made possible by the more efficient towboats required fewer dams and larger locks on the Ohio. In 1954 the Corps of Engineers began reconstruction of the waterway, at a cost expected to run well over $1 billion when all the nineteen dams are completed. All will have two locks, one 1,200 feet long and the other 600 feet. Each of the dams will have a lift of 23 feet. The importance of coal as a cargo is demonstrated by the rise of Huntington, West Virginia, the outlet for the Guyandot Valley coal mines. In 1980 it handled 10 million tons of cargo, nearly all coal, a volume second only to Pittsburgh among the Ohio River ports. About 35 percent of all river cargoes today consist of petroleum products in trades not competitive with the railroads. Coal represents another 25 percent, most of that moving to plants not serviced by railroads.

As has been true on most inland waterways, the river carriers have historically suffered from railroad efforts to eliminate them.

Often in cooperation with a railroad-dominated Interstate Commerce Commission, the land carriers have sought to establish minimum rates on water transport, impose waterway-user charges, and sometimes have inhibited the introduction of more efficient waterborne technology. They have traditionally sought to put prohibitive rates on rail-water interchanges and generally striven to kill off the water-based competition. As a result, inland water commerce is largely restricted to bulk cargoes. Government support of inland waterways has slackened. In 1953 the Inland Waterways Corporation passed to private owners, and in 1982, as a part of its efforts to place the entire navigation system "on a starvation diet," the Reagan administration proposed restricting the funds to operate the waterways. Although defeated by the industry's congressional supporters, the administration has made no secret of its intention to force inland shippers to pay the cost of building and operating the waterways. In this instance, as in many others, the proponents of government withdrawal from direct support of the economy overlook the benefit to the public derived from the inland waterways. It remains the most efficient and ecologically inexpensive method of moving large quantities of goods.

Chapter Six

INLAND SEAS

T HE GREAT EXPANSE OF THE UNITED STATES CONTAINS THOUSANDS OF lakes and ponds, but most claim attention only from local historians, anglers, and the surrounding property owners. A few merit our consideration because they have played a significant role in the history of the nation and reflect a further facet of the maritime impact upon the story of the American people. The most important were the Great Lakes, but in the Northeast Lake Champlain, Lake George, and New York's Finger Lakes played critical roles; while far to the west, the Great Salt Lake of Utah served as a major transportation link for a short but important portion of the West's history.

Exploration of the interior of North America occurred throughout the colonial period and into the national one. The eastern rivers and lakes, as well as those of the continent's heartland, played a major role in shaping the routes through which the continent became known. The French fur traders and clerics who sketched in the map of so much of the continent did so in canoes and bateaux that floated upon the fresh waters of the continent's interior streams and lakes.

1. Lake Champlain

The first large expanse of freshwater encountered by Europeans as they traversed the interior of North America was Lake Champlain, the 100-mile-long stretch of blue water marking the eastern edge of the Adirondack Mountains. It was initially visited by Samuel de Champlain in 1609, scarcely eight weeks before Henry Hudson's ascent of his river brought him to within fifty miles of the lake. Although the lake and river formed a natural, nearly all-water, route between New York and Montreal, Lake Champlain served as a buffer area between the Dutch-English and the French spheres until 1731. Then the French built a fort at Crown Point that touched off a struggle for control of the waterway. It culminated in extensive military operations on and alongside the lake during the French and Indian War of 1754–63.

When the Peace of Paris in 1763 certified British title to the region, Peter Skene and several other former officers who had served there hastened into the area. Skene established a substantial settlement (Skenesborough, modern Whitehall) at the south end of the lake from which his trading schooner supplied the other settlements and the British army's caretaker garrison at Fort Ticonderoga. The schooner and the fort were early targets of the patriots during the during the American Revolution, both being seized within a month of Lexington and Concord. The substantial military role of Lake Champlain during the Revolution, like that which it played in the War of 1812, is not part of our story except as it illustrates the significance of the lake as the only transportation route available in the region until the middle of the nineteenth century.

The shores of Lake Champlain attracted a substantial number of settlers in the twenty-five years after the Revolution. The farming was good, and the area had a natural market at Montreal. This encouraged British and Canadian leaders to attempt to cleave the valley from the United States. They lent support to an independence movement, but it died after the admission of Vermont to the union in 1791. Thereafter, efforts to create a better communication between the Champlain valley and the Hudson and between the upper Connecticut River towns and the settlements along lower stretches of the river took on greater importance.

Between 1790 and 1815 over thirty sailing vessels were built along the Vermont shore of Lake Champlain. They shuttled cargoes among the upper lake settlements and to Whitehall at its south end. In 1808 Lake Champlain became the second body of water to support a commercial steamboat when the *Vermont*'s engineer lit off her boiler. A competing line started work on a second steamer four years later but lost her to the Navy while still on the stocks. What are believed to be her remains are now on display at Whitehall, New York.

The efforts to connect the lake region and New York State started in 1783 when Gideon King, the Burlington entrepreneur who controlled most of the shipping on Lake Champlain, started a line of schooners on Lake George and offered through service to the Canadian border. Because goods had to be hauled by wagon from the head of sloop navigation on the Hudson at Troy to Lake George, the cost of shipping a ton of goods from New York to Plattsburgh at the north end of Lake Champlain was £9 2s. 8d. or well in excess of $75 in modern terms. Passengers and some freight followed an alternate route through Whitehall at least as early as 1787.

Critical in the growth of trade on Lake Champlain was the construction in 1817–23 of the Northern or Champlain Canal. Intended as a tie between Albany and New York City and Montreal and Quebec, its promoters hoped that it would open new markets for New York State goods. The 60-mile long artery followed the Hudson for half that distance before branching off at Fort Edward for Whitehall. Four dams with locks maintained the requisite depth in the Hudson north of Troy while 17 others handled the passage beyond Fort Edward. The construction encountered few difficulties and cost only $18,499 per mile. Although the canal developed enough traffic to remain in operation and to be enlarged and modernized in 1905–18, it never fulfilled the initial expectations and today is used primarily by pleasure craft and petroleum barges.

Consumer goods filled the holds of most northbound craft while those vessels moving southward towards the head of the canal carried more varied cargoes. Agricultural products dominated the trade in the early years but soon gave way to lumber. The latter decreased after the railroad reached Burlington in 1841. As early as the 1820s the iron from mines and furnaces in the Adirondacks and along the New York shore of the lake began to feed the major iron center at Troy and to help supply the demand of the mills around New York City. Those shipments reached their peak in 1885. The bulk of the goods on Lake Champlain moved by sail, although steamboats gained greater importance after the formation of the Champlain Transportation Company in 1826. After 1849 the company offered through-fares to either New York or

Montreal in conjunction with the Saratoga and Washington Railroad, the Rensselaer and Saratoga Railroad, and the Citizens Line steamers from Troy. In 1858 the Transportation Company passed into the hands of chief owners of the Rensselaer and Saratoga and by 1909 to the railroad itself. Passenger traffic did not reach its peak until 1921 but then declined rapidly as good automobile roads traversed the area. After the Great Depression the railroad sold off the steamers, but the new owners quickly disposed of the remaining craft, the last of which, the *Ticonderoga,* now is a major attraction at Shelburne Village, Vermont.

On many of the smaller lakes that are sprinkled among the northeastern states small freight lines developed to tie the settlements along the shores to the collection and distribution points for the goods that they purchased and produced. Some of the lakes saw early appearance of steamers. Lake George in northern New York had one in 1817 and Cayuga in the Finger Lakes acquired one three years later. The second steamer to traverse Lake George was a particularly interesting vessel whose hull, built on an elastic principle, had three layers of boards laid at right angles to each other but without interior framing according to the ideas of an Albany designer. As important as the eastern lakes often were to their regional economies, they played only a limited role in the westward movement of population that was the dominant folk activity of the first half of the nineteenth century.

2. Exploration and Settlement in the Great Lakes Basin

In 1615 the first adventurous Frenchmen, Samuel de Champlain, Étienne Brûle, and Father Joseph Le Caron, glimpsed the Great Lakes as they paddled down the French River towards its junction with Georgian Bay. Within twenty years Jean Nicolet pushed on to Lake Michigan, along whose western shores he discovered Green Bay and the Fox River. Other French fur traders and missionaries followed the Ottawa River—Lake Nipissing route to the great western freshwater seas to ensure French control of the upper lakes. In 1659 Pierre Esprit Radisson and the Sieur des Groseilliers traversed Lake Superior and visited northwestern Wisconsin. Nine years later Father Jacques Marquette established a mission at Sault Sainte Marie while other Frenchmen paddled southward to Green Bay. It was from the Green Bay post that Marquette and the fur trader

Louis Joliet left in 1673 to descend the Fox and Wisconsin rivers to enter the Mississippi. French explorers had now sketched in the general outline of the upper lakes. They continued to extend French presence. The Sieur Duluth in 1679 built a post at the west end of Lake Superior that still bears his name. Twenty-two years later Antoine de la Mothe Cadillac planted a settlement at Detroit on the passage between lakes Erie and Huron. It rapidly became the most important post on the Great Lakes, serving as the entrepot for the upper lake posts.

The decades of the 1670s and 1680s produced a renewed spurt of French exploration. The Sieur de la Salle explored the Ohio River and in 1680 further solidified French claims to the Mississippi River by establishing a post in modern Illinois. That year Father Louis Hennepin ventured up the river as far as the Falls of St. Anthony. Two years later La Salle descended the Mississippi and quickly perceived its great importance. He died while trying to plant a colony in Texas, but French interest in control of the mouth of the Mississippi persisted to culminate in the 1718 founding of New Orleans.

Only a trickle of permanent settlers followed the explorers to staff the trading posts and missions, but they established French control of the Illinois country, the poorly defined region between the Appalachians and the Mississippi that lay north of the Ohio River. By 1724 they had developed a trading route from Lake Erie via the Maumee and Wabash rivers to the Ohio. But those moves set in motion a power struggle that culminated in the French and Indian War. When the French constructed Fort Niagara to protect the portage route between Lakes Erie and Ontario, the British responded with Fort Oswego on the south shore of Lake Ontario in hopes of diverting the western fur trade. The French countered with a new post at Toronto in 1749. The direct cause of the French and Indian War was the French opening of a new route from Fort Niagara via Presque Isle (Erie, Pennsylvania) on Lake Erie, Fort Le Boeuf, and the French, Allegheny, and Monongahela rivers.

Until 1678 the French traders and missionaries relied solely on the large 32–35-foot trading canoes of the northern forest Indians, which could carry three tons of supplies and required a crew of five or six. The first European-style craft to appear were four small 10-ton sloops (probably luggers) built by La Salle at the site of modern Kingston, Ontario, to carry building supplies for a post on the Niagara River. The following year his men built a 60-ton galliot named the *Griffon* along Cayuga Creek within present-day Buffalo, New York. She was the first deepwater vessel constructed by Europeans on the lakes. On her first voyage the doughty little craft carried trade goods to Green Bay, but she foundered on the return trip.

The loss of the *Griffon* failed to halt further construction of deepwater craft on the lakes although little is known of her immediate successors. The next confirmed construction was of a pair of craft, probably schooners, on Lake Ontario in 1725. They were intended for communication between Fort Frontenac (Kingston, Ontario) and Fort Niagara at the mouth of the river of the same name. In 1770 a 40-ton sloop fashioned at the Sault became the earliest decked sailing craft on Lake Superior. She primarily served the copper mines of the northern peninsula of Michigan.

The Anglo-French confrontations of 1750–63 brought a small naval building race to Lake Ontario. The French built at least 13 craft while English carpenters added another 19. After the conquest of Canada 32 government and 15 private craft took to the water between 1760 and 1795 on Lakes Ontario and Erie.

Permanent settlement in the area drained by the Great Lakes and along the routes from Lake Michigan to the Mississippi River

THE
GREAT LAKES

and from Lake Erie to the Ohio River did not increase drastically in the thirty years after the French and Indian War. Independence nominally gave the United States control of the southern shore of the lakes, but actual occupation had to wait until 1796, when the British finally evacuated a string of posts stretching from Oswego to Michilimackinac. American craft did not appear on the lakes until after the transfer of the posts. In 1796 the government purchased a schooner named *Detroit* from the Northwest Fur Company at Detroit and chartered a second one to provide communication with the upper lake posts.

The first vessel built by American labor took shape the following year, but U.S.-flag navigation on Lake Erie developed very slowly. Except for a small settlement started by Moses Cleveland in Connecticut's Western Reserve that was later to bear his name, Buffalo at the lake's outlet, and a handful of smaller groups of homes scarcely worthy of the title of village, the Lake Erie shores attracted few settlers before the War of 1812. Yet in 1816, despite the ravages of the war, the Erie ports and Detroit claimed about 50 vessels totaling 2,067 tons. Nine years later the figures had risen to a steamer and 30–40 sailing craft with a capacity of approximately 2,500 tons.

Two early trade routes to Pittsburgh helped develop shipping on Lake Erie. One shipped salt from Syracuse, New York, via Buffalo to Pittsburgh and the Ohio River settlements. That trade blossomed in the period before the Kanawha Valley salt wells entered large-scale production after the War of 1812. Lake Erie shoppers also participated in the general Pittsburgh-Ohio Valley trade since one trade route brought goods from New York City to Albany by sloop; across New York to Buffalo by wagon; transshipment to Huron, Ohio, by lake vessels; and then movement overland to the Ohio Valley settlements. The complex arrangement was cheaper, although not faster, than the wholly overland route from Philadelphia.

As might be expected, Lake Ontario floated the earliest American lake trading vessels. Not only did it have an established, if small, port at Oswego but the first flourish of settlement in western New York during the decade 1785–1795 added thousands of new residents along its feeder streams. Because the construction of the small and relatively expensive Western Canal opened the Mohawk River-Wood Creek-Lake Oneida route to waterborne trade, Oswego by 1800 had developed a sizable business forwarding goods moving west. Her shippers also carried goods across Lake

Ontario to the Canadian ports and to the Niagara escarpment, notably to Queenston, Upper Canada. So valuable was that trade that in 1806 American merchants who did not share in it built a road to bypass the falls of the Niagara, but their route attracted little traffic until the embargo eliminated its Canadian competition. Most of the goods shipped westward consisted of Indian annuities and military stores; while furs provided nearly all the eastbound cargo.

During 1808–1819 Oswego vessels alone averaged 150 trips per year to Niagara. Some 60 vessels plied the Lake in 1818, by which time timber shipments had begun. The shortage of adequate harbors along the American shore limited the trade's growth and forced shippers to use open roadsteads. As a result they had to raft out the larger sticks and bring off the staves in scows. It was both a dangerous and an expensive procedure. Most of the Lake Ontario lumber found markets at Montreal or Quebec, irrespective of the shore on which it grew.

Prior to the War of 1812 John Jacob Astor's American Fur Company dominated the fur trade the area south of the Great Lakes, but the firm's real importance dates from the postwar years. Not only did it control the dwindling fur trade of Michigan but it moved decisively into the Lake Superior basin in competition with the traders of the Montreal-based Northwest Fur Company. The Montreal firm's Upper Lake trade had been wrecked by the American control of the lakes after 1813, as was the batteau canal it had dug across the Sault in 1798. Astor's men responded to the discomfiture of their competitors with efficiency, although they did not secure complete dominance. In 1817 the American Fur Company's operatives were reported to have hauled a 30-ton vessel across the portage at the Sault for use on Lake Superior. That year they established a post at Duluth. Sault Sainte Marie became as important a post for American Fur as it had for earlier concerns. The company erected warehouses to contain the goods being portaged around the falls. Moreover, large schools of whitefish at the rapids guaranteed a constant supply of food and ensured the proximity of large Indian settlements and numerous missions that formed a large market for the traders.

3. Steam Appears

In 1816 the steamer *Frontenac* flying the British flag appeared on Lake Ontario. The *Ontario,* the first one to stream the Stars and Stripes, appeared the following year. They were the first steamers to operate regularly in waters that had a swell and demonstrated to skeptics the practicality of steam on open waters. The following year the pioneer Lake Erie steamer *Walk-in-the-Water* came down the ways at Black Rock. She proved an operational success from the start, consistently running to Detroit and back in nine to ten days while consuming 36–40 cords of wood in each direction. Nor were her fares cheap. A cabin berth cost:

Buffalo-Detroit	$18.00
Buffalo-Sandusky	$15.00
Buffalo-Cleveland	$12.00
Buffalo-Erie	$ 6.00

But the fare was undoubtedly worth it to those who could afford the cost. The lack of safe harbors or a network of inland communications impeded the growth of steam navigation. Between 1819 and 1826, for example, only an average of one steamer a year passed Mackinac. Not until the latter year did one venture into

A view of Detroit, Michigan, in 1820. The pioneer steamer *Walk-in-the-Water* and the numerous sailing craft hint at the activity of the strategic village. Courtesy of The Peabody Museum of Salem

Lake Michigan, and none operated regularly on the American lake until 1827. Six years later, however, forty-five steamers left wakes on the lakes, and in 1839 sixty-one sought passengers and freight. That was more than the available traffic could support. In 1842, during a period of rate-cutting, thirty steamers in the long Buffalo-Detroit-Chicago service formed an association, one of the earliest efforts to control competition voluntarily. The arrangement rationalized that run but left others overstocked.

In 1842 the *Vandalia* took to the water at Oswego. She was the first screw steamer on the Lakes, the fourth built under the Ericsson patents, and the first large vessel fitted with his invention. She demonstrated both the machinery's ability to operate in rough waters and its lower operating costs when compared to a conventional Lakes paddle wheeler. Not surprisingly, propeller boats very quickly gained a large following on the Lakes.

The volume of cargoes grew steadily, largely because of the settlement of the Great Lakes basin after the completion of the Erie, Welland, and Ohio canals between 1825 and 1832. Most cargo on the lakes moved on sailing craft and would continue to do so until the last decade of the century. In 1835 Ohio exported 543,815 bushels of grain by water. Five years later the figure had risen to 3.8 million, and in 1851 it would reach 12.2 million. Further contributing to the growth of demand for shipping was the arrival of a flood of New Englanders escaping from their dying farms. Although the degree is nearly impossible to determine, the availability of cheap transportation from midwestern farms contributed significantly to the collapse of the New England subsistence farming.

The opening of the Erie Canal in 1825 had immediately opened eastern markets to western grain. Until the Ohio Canal began to tap that state's wheat-growing regions, however, the amounts transshipped at Buffalo were limited. Some astute entrepreneurs made imaginative efforts to ship wheat to market. A schooner sailed to New York City via the Erie Canal in 1826, and in 1843 another voyaged to New Orleans via the Ohio Canal, the Ohio and the Mississippi rivers. Neither experiment was successful since lake craft large enough to be efficient carriers were too big to squeeze through the canal locks. Experience with the canals, however, quickly demonstrated the efficiency of transshipment into specially built canal boats for passage through the artificial waterway. While it would have been technically feasible to build a waterway large enough to accommodate the lake craft, construction would have been prohibitively expensive. Moreover, as the experience with the Welland Canal proved, the size of vessel increased so rapidly during 1830–50 that it would have been impossible to enlarge the long-distance canals swiftly enough.

Occasionally a town, no more fortuitously situated than its neighbors, would undertake a public works project that would give it local commercial dominance. Milan, Ohio, was one example. It had no immediate river, but in 1833–36 it spent $75,000 to build a docking basin and connect it with the Huron River by a two-mile long canal. These public works ensured that across the town's wharfs passed the produce of her hinterland while allowing the local shipbuilders to craft 99 sailing vessels. Milan remained a major grain port for two decades. The bulk of the Ohio shipments, however, continued to rush through Cleveland in an ever greater volume especially after Ohio in 1839 became the nation's leading wheat-producing state.

The small schooner *Franc Miner* of 1885 would not have been out of place in a saltwater harbor. Courtesy of The Peabody Museum of Salem

Not until 1836 did Michigan grain join the stream. Two years later a token shipment of seventy-eight bushels inaugurated shipments from Chicago. Export from Wisconsin started in 1841, moving through Milwaukee. Shipments from the great wheat fields of the northern plains had to await both the settlement of the region, the introduction of red wheats, and the construction of the railroads to the Lake Superior ports. Scarcely more than a trickle moved across the northern lake before 1870.

Grain was not alone in causing the success of the lake shipping. More profitable and certainly more far-reaching was the passage over the Erie Canal of immigrants from New England and abroad to the newly opened western lands. They, and countless others arriving from Europe via the St. Lawrence and the Welland Canal, revived passenger service on the lakes. The influx triggered construction of a large number of new passenger steamers. The 254-feet-long side-wheeler *Empire* built at Cleveland in 1844 was advertised as the largest steamer in the world. The larger and more efficient craft soon forced down passenger fares. By 1848 the charge from Buffalo to Detroit had fallen to $6 cabin or $3 steerage. To Chicago and Milwaukee the fares were $12 cabin and $6 steerage. Freight rates were comparable. Passage times dropped. In the early 1830s fast steamers made the round trip from Buffalo to Detroit in 10 days. In 1851 that time had fallen to 3–5 days.

By 1840 the grain trade via Buffalo and the Erie Canal developed a bottleneck because of the inability of shippers to transfer

An unidentified iron-hulled grain and ore carrier of the late nineteenth century. From *Merchant Vessels of the United States, 1892*

grain fast enough. Shovel and wheelbarrow longshoremen needed two or three days to unload the average 5,000-bushel cargo. Those delays prompted Joseph Dart to build a grain elevator in 1842–43. It followed principles described by Oliver Evans at the start of the century and was an instant success. The steampowered facility could handle 1,000 bushels per hour and store 55,000 at one time.

The impact on Buffalo was felt almost as rapidly. Between 1840 and 1850 it passed both Troy and Rochester in population, growing to 80,000 in 1860. During the late 1840s it handled more grain, flour, and livestock than any other city in the United States. Twenty years later the port required 29 elevators to handle its grain shipments. Oswego, the terminus of one of the branch lines of the Erie Canal, moved into second place as a grain-shipping port although its tonnage was only half that of Buffalo. The ability to handle wheat cheaply and rapidly was further enhanced by the introduction of steam shovels in 1864 to speed the removal of grain from the holds of vessels and reduce the number of longshoremen needed to move it ashore.

No city west of Buffalo held as many as 10,000 people in 1840, but under the stimulus of lake commerce many grew rapidly.

The *City of Cleveland* of 1885 was a noted Cleveland-Detroit passenger steamer that reflected the tendency to retain side-wheel propulsion, which continued well into the twentieth century. From *Merchant Vessels of the United States, 1892*

Twenty years later Cleveland boasted 43,000 people; Detroit and Milwaukee over 45,000; while interior settlements like Dayton, Fort Wayne, Peoria, Dubuque, and Davenport rose to over 10,000 inhabitants. All those expanding cities owed their growth to the grain trade and their location on rivers or canals.

On the Great Lakes as in coastal waters the schooner was the preferred rig. In 1870 there were 1,737 schooners but only 214 brigs sailing the Inland Seas. The reasons were that a fore and aft rig sailed closer to windward, was easier to handle in harbor and canal, and required a smaller crew than a square one. The lake schooner design reached its zenith in the 278-foot, 5-mast *David Dows* in 1881. She carried 140,000 bushels of wheat in a single voyage. But like most of the sailing vessels, the *Dows* soon found herself bobbing at the end of a tow line as a consort or barge. The *Dows*, and most of the other vessels on the Lakes, were built of wood. Iron-hulled craft were slow to appear although both the United States and the Canadian governments had built experimental gunboats of the metal in the 1840s. Only in the 1870s did shipyards able to construct vessels of iron come into existence. But during the next decade the advantages of iron became so evident, and the prices so low, that iron-hulled, bulk-cargo steamers become common. The first, the 287-foot-long *Onoko*, came off the ways at Cleveland in 1882 ready to haul either grain or that new king of the lakes, iron ore.

The grain trade proved to be less of a fixture on the Great Lakes than had initially appeared to be the case. The railroad networks that before the Civil War fed grain ports like Chicago and Milwaukee quickly developed the ability to offer through-shipment from the local elevator to the flour mill or port of export. It played a major, but not exclusive, role in the 19 percent shrinkage of tonnage sailing the Great Lakes between 1868 and 1880.

The 1850s saw an upswing in passenger service as the eastern railroads reached Lake Erie but had not yet finished their ties farther west. Steamship lines, either railroad controlled or backed, sprang up to span the gap between the eastern and western lines. The railroads completed their east-west connections by 1857, just as the nation entered a depression. The twin blows killed most of the passenger lines on the Lakes and created a surplus of vessels.

During the late 1860s and 1870s passenger service gradually revived. The Northern Pacific and Pennsylvania Railroads formed the Anchor Line to connect their Buffalo and Duluth railheads. It ran successfully until the Panama Canal Act in 1912 forced the railroads to give up their steamship lines. Similarly, the Civil War period saw appearance of new local services like the Detroit and Cleveland Navigation Company, whose night boats would remain popular until 1938. On Lake Michigan the Goodrich Transportation Company operated similar services, notably with the *Virginia,* which was called the most elegantly appointed passenger steamer ever built in the country when she took to the water in 1891. The lakes developed extensive package freight lines, frequently as feeders for the railroads or as counterparts of the passenger services. By the turn of the century all the major package lines were railroad owned, but most passenger services remained independent. When the Panama Canal Act in 1912 forced the railroads to dispose of their shipping interests, nearly all the package services became part of the Great Lakes Transit Company controlled by the Buffalo longshoreman and newspaper owner William J. Conners. Although Great Lakes Transit sold off most of its vessels following World War I, it continued some services until 1942.

In the years immediately preceding World War I, tourist trade took on new importance, as it had along the New England coast. The best-known of the tourist lines, the Georgian Bay Line, operated a pair of steamers on cruises from Chicago to Georgian Bay and way points down to the 1960s. The death blows of the Great Lakes passenger vessels were similar to those that killed American service on salt water: labor and safety costs.

Notable among the later passenger vessels were the *Seeandbee,* built in 1913 for the Cleveland and Buffalo run, and the sisters *Greater Buffalo* and *Greater Detroit,* which entered service eleven years later between Detroit and Cleveland. All three were sidewheelers and continued in service into World War II. The *Seeandbee* and *Greater Buffalo* ended their days in Lake Michigan as the world's only side-wheel aircraft carriers. After World War I, lake passenger service declined as the automobile and good roads syphoned off many of these more affluent passengers whose vacation and business travel had earlier been the backbone of the business. While the operators staggered under that blow and the Great Depression shattered the financial underpinnings of all but the strongest lines, passenger carriers had to face the stiffened safety requirements brought about by the *Morro Castle* disaster. Thirty years later, after the *Yarmouth Castle* fire of 1965, even more stringent rules forced the last passenger vessels into retirement.

No town prospered as much from the grain trade as Chicago. Too small to be mentioned in the 1830 census and containing less than 5,000 people a decade later, it reached 100,000 before 1860. Its grain and flour shipments, spurred by the construction of a network of radiating railroads, rose to 100,000 bushels in 1840; over a million five years later; and to 20 million in 1858. Following the discovery of the Michigan salt deposits, Chicago challenged Cincinnati as the hog-slaughtering center of the nation, taking the crown in 1863.

The growth that followed consumed nearly 300 million board feet of lumber annually after 1850, nearly all of which arrived by water from Wisconsin and Michigan ports. The carpenters who built Chicago and the other western towns adopted the balloon frame construction pioneered in the windy city in the 1830s. Its simplified system of plates and studs held together by nails allowed houses to be built for 40 percent less cost than those employing traditional mortise and tenon. Moreover, such structures could be built rapidly by the relatively unskilled carpenters commonly found in most western towns. It is difficult to conceive of the western cities like Chicago, Omaha, or Bismarck being built with traditional methods. Since balloon frame houses relied on a limited number of board sizes, they permitted the mills to cut standardized lumber that stacked and shipped easily.

The western mills not only provided structural timbers but produced large quantities of boards and staves for the eastern market. Helped along by the demand created by the great Chicago fire of 1871, Michigan, Wisconsin, and Minnesota by the 1880s had surpassed Maine as the lumbering center of the nation. In those years Saginaw, Michigan, shipped as much as 900 million feet a year. That rate of cutting rapidly exhausted the forests in lower Michigan, causing the industry to shift its heart westward to Minneapolis and Duluth. The scale of some of the larger logging operations was enormous. The Ontonagon Lumber Company, which began operation in 1881 on Michigan's Northern Peninsula, owned 13,000 acres of forest, and its mill produced 200,000 feet of lumber and 300,000 shingles in a single day. The Diamond Match Company mills turned out 75 million feet of lumber and 30 million shingles annually between 1882 and 1896. In the late 1880s Frederich Weyerhauser and his associates purchased a large tract near Duluth. By 1892 the lumber cut around Duluth exceeded that felled in the massive forests along the Chippewa River. Seven years later Duluth was the leading lake lumber port. Its lumbering heyday lasted but a short time as production declined after 1906. The peak came in 1902 with the shipment of 243 million board feet worth $6,352,876. Not only did lumber shipments play a major role in the development of the Minnesota and Wisconsin ports, they contributed significantly to the prosperity of the eastern terminals of the trade, notably Detroit, Toledo, Cleveland, and Tonawanda, New York.

Although most lumber moved by ship, usually in old schooners or barges, rafts could also be seen as late as 1897. The peak of rafting came in the 1860s, when they were common, especially between Saginaw and Toledo. The largest recorded raft contained 2 million board feet and took 16 days to tow from Bay City, Michigan, to Buffalo in 1875. Rafting was difficult on the Great Lakes because of their short and often irregular seas, which put substantially more stress on the lashings than did salt-water or river voyages.

Shipping on Lake Superior developed slowly. This simply reflected the late development of any trade there beyond fur and fish. Yet the importance of fishing should not be overlooked, since the availability of whitefish played a major role in the American company's establishment of their post at Sault Sainte Marie. The fish there attracted Indians who were usually happy to exchange their furs for trade goods and a supply of dried fish. As a result the Fur Company found itself, almost without thought, involved in the Lake Superior whitefish industry. Its catch grew so large that it exchanged fish for Ohio grain. During the mid-1830s the company built fishing stations around the lake and constructed the supply schooner *John Jacob Astor* to service them. The salting necessary to preserve the fish limited their attractiveness and the company never developed a market large enough to support the project, which died during the Panic of 1837.

Fishing on Lake Superior resumed in the 1850s when settlers finally appeared in sufficient numbers to make it economically viable. After the Civil War, refrigeration transformed the industry into a big business. In the 1880s Lake Superior fishermen shipped 300,000 pounds of fresh whitefish to market annually along with 9,000 half barrels of salted fare. Herring began to be a significant catch in that decade and by 1908 had surpassed whitefish in importance. In the 1920s the lake showed the effects of overfishing, but it was the invasion of lamprey eels and chemicals after World War II that combined to devastate the fisheries. The drastic application of corrective measure and the introduction of Pacific salmon into the Upper Lakes restored some vitality to the industry. The catch rebounded to pass 100 million pounds in 1976 and has continued to grow moderately in the years since.

4. The Ore Trade

The Great Lakes ore trade falls into two distinct eras: copper and iron. The first commenced with the discovery of the Keweenaw Peninsula copper deposits in 1840. The existence of copper deposits had been known since prehistoric times, when they were worked by Indians, but not until the opening of the Keweenaw field did output become sufficient to affect shipping. The first significant movement, which occurred in 1845, totaled some 1,300 pounds. The amount that could be shipped was minimal since it had to be portaged around the falls at Sault Saint Marie. Four years after the Keweenaw find came the even more important discovery of the Marquette iron ore range some sixty miles east of the copper site. But here too the difficulties of transport past the Soo delayed exploitation for a decade.

The construction of the Soo Locks resulted from the efforts of a salesman, Charles T. Harvey, and the support of a small group of eastern businessmen, notably Erastus Corning, the scale-manufacturing Fairbanks brothers, August Belmont, and John Murray Forbes. Pushed to completion in 1853–55 by the driving Harvey, the canal bypassed the rapids to tie the waters of Lake Superior to those of Lake Huron. The motives of the builders were not altruistic. They received 750,000 acres of mineral lands in Michigan's Northern Peninsula, which more than recompensed them for the million dollars expended on the canal. The waterway consisted of two locks 350 feet long, 70 feet wide, and 20 feet deep with a 9-foot lift.

During the first year, 1,449 tons of iron ore passed the locks. From the beginning of the trade the mine operators had to decide whether to ship ore, pig, or finished work from the mines. Their efforts to smelt the ore on site failed for a number of reasons including the difficulty in finding the ironworkers and the distance of the mines from any market for finished iron. They, therefore, decided to ship the ore to southern lake ports, whence it could move to the coal-rich region around Pittsburgh. Cleveland, Conneaut, and Ashtabula, Ohio, and Erie, Pennsylvania, became the chief transshipment ports. But until the Civil War the shipments were small because the Pittsburgh iron industry was in its infancy. Much of the nation's iron production still came from the forges of the Adirondacks and eastern Pennsylvania. After the war, however, iron and steel plants appeared around Detroit and Chicago, using Illinois coal for fuel. Since the blast furnaces also needed large quantities of lime for flux, the limestone quarries of lower Michigan added their stone to the materials heading south. Notable among the latter was the 12 square mile quarry at Rogers City, opened in 1912 by the Michigan Limestone Corporation and still in operation.

The explosion of demand following of the Civil War produced a boom in the Marquette range, which shipped 1,779,000 tons in 1873. That year also the Menominee Range around Iron Mountain, Michigan, added its soft hematite when the Chicago and Northwestern Railroad opened a line to Lake Michigan at Escanaba. By 1880 the port of Escanaba handled 600,000 tons per year. Ore docks made such a volume possible. They fed the ore freighters through gravity tipples or pockets that replaced the traditional but labor intensive wheelbarrows and carts. The first of the new docks appeared at L'Anse, Michigan, on Lake Superior in 1872. It had 80 pockets for sailing craft and 40 more for steamers.

The flow of ore increased greatly after 1885, when the Gogebic Range along the Michigan-Wisconsin border began production, using Ashland, Michigan, as its port. Within a year Ashland outloaded 700,000 tons per year. Mining of the Vermilion Range, near Hibbing, Minnesota, began in 1875, but its major shipments, through Two Harbors, Minnesota, did not start until 1884. The last of the great iron deposits, the Mesabi, lies slightly east of the Vermilion. Although explored as early as 1857 it was not worked until 1891. The mines there shipped their ore through the old lumber port of Duluth. The development of the Mesabi, the greatest of the Lake Superior fields, came slowly in part because its ore was the consistency of fine dust and could not be handled successfully in the furnaces then in use since it would explode if mixed with ordinary ore or if confined during smelting.

The impact of the Lake Superior mines on ore costs was startling. A ton delivered at Cleveland brought $18.00 in 1873 but only $2.95 in 1894. Although there was some decline in ore prices after 1892, most of the reduction came from more efficient transportation. The ore of Lake Superior formed the lifeblood of the furnaces of Pittsburgh, which established America's lead as the world's industrial giant. After the turn of the century the efficiency of lake ore transportation caused the Lackawanna Steel Corporation to construct a mill in Buffalo and United States Steel to open a huge new works at Gary, Indiana, on Lake Michigan.

Meanwhile, the 1890s saw efforts, largely eastern financed, to organize the fragmented mining and shipping operations into combines such as the Lake Superior Consolidated Iron Mines Company and the Bessemer Consolidated Iron Company. (See table 6–1.) After 1891, Lake Superior Consolidated gained control of a large segment of the Mesabi and the Gogebic as well as ore docks, railroads, and a fleet of steamers. Despite the majority of the ore carriers remaining independent of the steel companies, vertical organization had struck the iron industry. Between 1920 and 1955 nearly all ore reaching lake ports originated in Lake Superior. The remaining trickle, in most years under 10 percent of the total, came from the northern Lake Michigan docks. After 1955 the Lake Superior share declined rapidly as the Mesabi mines played out. By 1970 only 73 percent of the ore came from the upper ports. Interest-

Table 6–1. *Iron Ore Shipments* * *from Lake Superior Ports*

1855	1,449	1895	10,429,037	1935	28,362,498
1860	114,401	1900	19,059,393	1940	63,712,496
1865	236,208	1905	33,476,784	1945	75,715,174
1870	830,940	1910	42,618,747	1950	78,206,247
1875	891,257	1915	46,318,747	1955	89,170,531
1880	1,908,745	1920	58,527,675	1960	73,073,210
1885	2,466,642	1925	54,081,247	1965	78,627,674
1890	9,003,725	1930	46,583,033	1970	87,098,210
				1980	55,241,832

*In 2,240 lb. "gross tons."

Sources: Marine Review, XXXIII (Feb. 22, 1906), 26; Lake Log Chips, IX (March 28, 1981), 1.

ingly, between 1920 and 1955 the destinations of these shipments also changed. Those bound for Lake Erie ports decreased from 77 percent to 61 percent while that bound for Lake Michigan docks, notably at Gary, rose from 19 percent to 28 percent.

The ore shipments initially moved by conventional 700–800-ton sailing craft and an occasional steamer. In 1869 the *R. J. Hackett,* the first specially designed ore steamer, appeared. During the next decade the unique requirements of the ore trade caused the development of special cargo-handling facilities. Because of the short season, vessels had to load and unload as rapidly as possible. The need for speed hastened the development of mechanical loaders and unloaders. The new equipment in turn dictated that the vessels have all possible deck space clear and that the engines perch on the stern. There they were out of the way and eliminated the need for a long shaft alley that destroyed the straight sides and flat floors of the holds. The design first appeared in the iron-hulled *Onoko* during 1882. She carried 3,000 tons of ore. While the channels between the lakes were dredged deeper as the size of vessels increased, the danger of grounding continued. It encouraged shallow draft, which in turn dictated a flat bottom and full model in order to gain maximum capacity. As a further protection against groundings, lake designers quickly adopted double bottoms. Since the distance between ports was so short, most craft offset the capacity lost to the double bottom by small coal bunkers.

The persistence of cheap lumber retarded the acceptance of iron hulls, although the first, USS *Michigan,* appeared in 1842. Widespread use did not begin until the 1880s. The first steel-hulled steamer, the *Spokane,* took to the water in 1886. Despite a fear of the brittleness of steel plate on the part of some owners the new material caught on, especially for package freighters. During the late 1890s steel vessels became common, but the peak of construction awaited the next decade. Between 1901 and 1910, 297 large ore freighters took to the lakes. Their construction coincided with the introduction of pneumatic riveting in which the Great Lakes yards played a leading role. In 1899 a group of the Lakes yards combined to form the American Ship Building Company. It was one of the largest shipbuilding firms in the world and dominated ore carrier construction for the next seventy-five years. It continued active on the lakes until 1985.

Demands for ore were so great that during the latter years of the nineteenth century shippers attempted to increase their capacity by employing consorts, unpowered but usually rigged barges, towed by a regular steamer. The concept died when larger and more efficient steel-hulled steamers entered service. Some far-sighted operators recognized that the easiest way to meet the demands was to improve the efficiency of unloading the ore carriers. In 1867 J. D. Bothwell, a Cleveland dockmaster, tripled his off-loading speed by replacing horse-powered winches with steam driven ones. Alexander E. Brown followed in 1892 with an unloader that used cables running from ship to dock to carry buckets of ore directly from the hold. He later developed an automatic grab bucket that gulped five tons per bite. The next, and longest-lasting, improvement was George H. Hulett's invention in 1899 of a 15-ton-capacity clamshell bucket attached to a tilting vertical arm that could be lowered directly into the hold.

The Hulett unloaders became standard unloading gear once ship designers included larger, 24-foot hatches on their craft. The first so fitted was the *James H. Hoyt* in 1903. She was followed the next year by the 560-foot *Augustus B. Wolvin*. The *Wolvin* was an innovative vessel with 33 hatches capable of receiving the Hulett buckets and a hold kept completely clear of obstructions by the use of large arched plates between the hatches. Her inner bottom and side tanks were designed to create a hopperlike hold. This permitted her to carry 10,245 tons of ore. The insatiable demand for ore caused the construction of ever larger vessels, reaching 605 feet in the *J. Pierpont Morgan* of 1906 and 625-feet twenty years later with the *W. Grant Morden*. She was not exceeded until the first of the post-World War II giants, the 675-foot *Wilfred Sykes* in 1950. She was dwarfed four years later by the 710-foot *George M. Humphreys*. The final stage of development came in the *Stewart J. Cort* of 1975. She was the first of the "thousand footers." During the 1960s and 1970s the potential for saving in crew costs caused an experimental return to barges. That urge culminated in Litton Industry's ill-fated automated yard, Erie Marine, which built only one 974-foot barge specially designed for pushtowing. It has not been repeated.

One major innovation to enter the ore trade during the last two decades has been self-unloading, in which a freighter is fitted with a set of conveyor belts that gather the ore in the hold and move it up to a pivoting, boom-mounted belt that moves it ashore. Self-unloading is faster and cheaper than using a Hulett, especially since the big bucket machines are reaching the end of their useful lives. The first experimental self-unloaders entered service during the latter years of the nineteenth century, and a very successful installation appeared on the limestone carrier *Wyandotte* in 1908. An improved system was fitted to the *Carl D. Bradley* in 1927. Since the conveyors needed a dry cargo to avoid clogging, they worked well with limestone but could not be used for iron ore until the introduction of taconite in the 1950s. Since then nearly all the ore carriers built have been self-unloaders, and several older boats have received similar conversions.

The increase in the size of the carriers hauling grain and ore from the Lake Superior ports forced a series of enlargements of the Soo locks. The Wetzel Lock, first filled in 1881, was 515 feet long with a 17-foot depth. In 1896 the Poe Lock opened, 800 feet long, 100 feet wide, and 22 feet deep. Its Canadian counterpart which opened the preceding year, was longer at 900 feet but narrower at 60 feet. The growing length of the ore boats forced the addition of a new set of American locks at the time of World War I. The 1,350-foot-long Davis Lock opened in 1914 and the duplicate Sabin Lock five years later. They remain the longest locks at the Soo, although the MacArthur Lock built during World War II is more commonly used today because of its 31-foot draft. That depth is repeated in the new 1,200-foot-long Poe Lock, which opened in 1968 and permitted construction of the "thousand footers."

During the winter of 1974–75 the lakes remained open the year around for the first time in history. It was an effort to take advantage of the taconite pellets that now make up a major portion of the iron being shipped from the Lake Superior fields. Unlike pure ore, which contains enough moisture to freeze during cold weather, taconite pellets are round and dry. The winter shipments continued until 1985 when the costs of maintaining the Soo locks and the aids to navigation in winter and the reduced flow of ore caused its abandonment. The shipments of taconite declined from 56 million tons in 1979 to 23 million in 1982. At the same time the production at the traditional steel centers in the Great Lakes states dropped. With the appearance of the efficient thousand-footers the number of active vessels declined drastically. In 1975 there were 95 ore carriers sailing from the Lake Superior ports. In 1985 that number had declined to 47. But the size of individual cargoes rose. The 1000-foot *Columbia Star* loaded a record cargo at Escanaba of 70,001 tons of taconite pellets on August 2, 1986.

While ore generally flowed down the lakes to the Illinois and Ohio ports, small coal shipments began moving uplake as early as

1842. Most was burned for heat rather than for refining, and the initial shipments traveled as ballast on returning grain vessels. Coal movement remained limited prior to the Civil War but developed rapidly thereafter. By 1900, the Central States consumed a fifth of all anthracite mined in the nation. It normally moved by rail or canal to Buffalo for transshipment by lake vessel to western ports. In 1898 Buffalo reported receipts of 4,225,000 tons of anthracite, of which half was transshipped; over a million tons to Chicago and half a million to Milwaukee and to Duluth and Superior. The shipments were attracted by the low rates charged on bulk return cargoes to the Upper Lakes.

Within the past two decades the coal trade has changed dramatically. American coal flows north to fuel Canadian power plants and steel mills, especially those close to Toronto and along Lake St. Clair. A second, wholly new trade, developed as utilities in the Great Lakes basin shifted from oil to low-sulfur western coal for their boilers. Huge quantities of the coal move out of Superior, Wisconsin, and Thunder Bay, Ontario, to down lake ports, 6.3 million in the record year of 1979. During the fall of 1978 the all-time record single cargo—68,553 tons of western coal—passed from Superior to the Detroit Edison's plant at St. Clair, Michigan.

The long finger of Lake Michigan cutting across the natural rail route east from Minneapolis-St. Paul and Milwaukee led the railroads serving those cities to consider train ferries to avoid the long trip through Chicago. The idea was not new. Train ferries had operated in the United States since 1837 when the *Susquehanna* began carrying trains across her namesake at Havre de Grace, Maryland. During the 1880s various Michigan railroads investigated ferry service across Lake Michigan in order to tap the Minnesota and Wisconsin grain trade. They discovered that the route was feasible provided the vessel had sufficient ice-breaking capacity to operate in the winter. That problem was solved in 1888 by Frank E. Kirby in his plans for the Straits of Mackinac ferry *St. Ignace*. In 1892 the Ann Arbor Railroad opened a line between Frankfort, Michigan, and Memoninie, Wisconsin, with the wooden *Ann Arbor No. 1,* designed by Kirby. The Flint and Pere Marquette Railroad countered five years later with their all-steel *Pere Marquette,* which served as the model for all the Great Lakes car ferries built in the next thirty years. Not until the *City of Saginaw 31* and *City of Flint 32* of 1929–30, which combined both rail and automotive capacity, did the design change. The faster service offered by the direct routes served by the car ferries kept them profitable into the early 1970s. Thereafter, the cost of operation of the vessels and shifts in traffic patterns caused them to lose money and the railroads to threaten abandonment.

5. St. Lawrence Seaway

Critical to any direct service between the lakes and the Atlantic was an ability to bypass the Great Falls of the Niagara River and the dangerous and difficult rapids on the St. Lawrence River between Ogdensburg and Montreal. The easiest bypass route for both lay in Canadian territory. The earliest canals around the St. Lawrence rapids floated batteaux and Durham boats only. That prohibited extensive shipment of goods above Ogdensburg because no steamer then in use could breast the rapids west of there. The problem persisted until the building of the Beauharnois and Lachine Canals in 1842–48 permitted passage of vessels 200 feet long and drawing 9 feet. This and the earlier (1825–29) construction of the Welland Canal around Niagara Falls opened navigation to the saltwater ports around the world. One of the earliest craft to transit the canals, and certainly one of the most colorful ever, was the brigantine *Eureka*. She left Cleveland in 1849 with a company of gold seekers bound to San Francisco. Few other craft ventured into salt water during the midnineteenth century while oceangoing vessels normally shunned the lakes because of the 200-foot-length limit and the nine-foot depth of the Canadian locks.

Local traffic found the waterways immensely helpful. In the later years of the nineteenth century the Canadians built additional St. Lawrence canals until the network included six separate systems containing 26 locks between Cardinal, Ontario, and Montreal. Unfortunately, however, the system was not enlarged to a 270-foot length and 14-foot draft until 1909. That, combined with the 261-foot length and 14-foot draft on the Welland prior to 1932, ensured that the craft that plied between salt and fresh water remained appreciably smaller than the economically optimum size.

The small size of the canals limited the use that could be made of both the Canadian and American shipyards fronting the lakes during World Wars I and II. In both wars they were restricted to the construction of small warships like submarine chasers and minesweepers or small freighters. During World War I the American yards turned out 90 small warships and 448 copies of a standard design 251-foot steel freighter known as "Lakers" in honor of their birthplace. They were the largest vessels that could safely pass the St. Lawrence Rapids. During World War II fewer craft were constructed although the lake yards delivered 119 large warships, 264 landing ships, and 129 oceangoing freighters or tankers along with a mass of smaller craft. Most of the larger vessels, including submarines, destroyer escorts, and landing-ships tanks, went to sea via the Chicago Drainage Canal and the Mississippi River, a difficult and slow voyage but one necessitated by the limitation of the Canadian canals.

The problems of wartime use of the lake's facilities and the restriction on overseas trade that the small locks imposed convinced the United States and Canadian governments that a new and much larger route had to be built. Constructed in 1954–59 as the St. Lawrence Seaway, it offers a 27-foot-deep channel and locks capable of handling craft up to 730 feet by 75 feet and drawing up to 25 1/2 feet. Under the seaway system seven locks raise vessels the 227 feet to Lake Ontario. Then an additional eight Welland locks lift them the 572 feet necessary to reach Lake Erie. Most of the vessels built to seaway dimensions since its opening have been Canadian since they can haul Canadian grain eastward and return with cargoes of Labrador iron ore. American vessels cannot share in grain movement and lack the necessary east-bound cargoes. Nevertheless, foreign trade tonnage on the Great Lakes rose from 35.2 million tons in 1950 to a peak of 69.2 million tons in 1977. The paucity of American flags among those traversing the seaway has created political problems, especially demands for higher tolls. They appear attractive to many legislators as a means of reducing the operating subsidy provided by the United States Treasury and as a means of ensuring more work for American craft. Unfortunately, the solution overlooks the shortage of cargoes for American vessels east of Lake Ontario and the difficulties of American saltwater craft in competing with foreign craft.

Although it is the healthiest segment of the American merchant marine, the Great Lakes fleet has followed the same pattern as the deepsea and coastal carriers. Despite its role in opening the

West to settlement and in the industrial burgeoning of the nation, the American Great Lakes merchant marine has lost traffic to other carriers because of relative costs, government regulation, and shifting national priorities as well as new trade patterns.

Chapter Seven
FISHING

RICH FISHERIES DREW THE FIRST EXPLORERS TO NORTH AMERICA. There is ample circumstantial evidence to suggest that the initial trips to North America by English and possibly Portuguese navigators were the direct result of their awareness of the teeming fishery on the Grand Banks. Since the definitive evidence that the Grand Banks were known to western European fishermen prior to Columbus's voyage is lacking and may never appear, the exact date of the initial visit to North America by a European in the modern period will probably never be known. Our earliest hard evidence places Breton and Basque fishermen on the Grand Banks in 1504 in such numbers as to make journeys there, and possibly to the mainland beyond, during the preceding decade a virtual certainty.

English interest in the northern lands waned in the early sixteenth century. Apparently the barrenness of the Newfoundland and Labrador coasts and the ability of British fishermen to secure adequate catches off Iceland kept them away from the North American fishing grounds. On the other hand, large numbers of Portuguese, Breton, and Basque seamen did visit the region, using the coastal glades of Nova Scotia and Cape Breton Island for flake yards. In the later years of the sixteenth century, English fishermen returned to the northeastern coast. This resulted in their shift during the last quarter of the century from wet to dry packing in order to reduce dependence on French and Portuguese salt. They developed a good market for dried cod among the Catholic population bordering the Mediterranean. As a result, by the end of the century the English sent two hundred vessels a year to the Grand Banks. Inshore fishing along the New England coast where cod grew to as much as twice the size of those found off Newfoundland was under way by 1602. The English fishermen soon established temporary bases at convenient points along the coast to repair and occasionally to construct craft.

Commercial fishing in the seventeenth century, as in the whole colonial period, meant cod fishing. Cod was the only fish with two very important attributes. Salted and air dried, it could survive both long sea voyages and slow journeys overland without further deterioration. This made it a cheaper source of protein than salt pork or beef whether on the frontier or in the sugar islands of the Caribbean. In addition, cod was the only fish of its day considered acceptable for daily eating. This ensured a steady enough market to warrant large-scale fishing. On the other hand, vessels fishing the Banks and North American coastal waters had to cure their cod on some convenient coast since uncured fish could not be kept for long voyages.

Two methods of curing were common. Wet curing was practical only if the fisherman was relatively close to home because the fish were salted on shipboard after being split and gutted but taken to shore for drying. The second and more prevalent dry method involved splitting, gutting, and lightly salting the fish on shore before spreading them on flakes (raised boughs and brush) to dry. In either case the end product was a hard, stiff, almost indestructible and nearly unpalatable slab that could be made into a delicious dish once properly soaked and prepared. Although the dry method used less salt and permitted a vessel to carry more fish, in effect it required two crews: one to fish and a second to dry. Less common were corned or "cor-fish," packed whole in brine; or the premium-priced "dun fish," which took their name from the color caused by alternately burying and drying the cod until it mellowed. Unblemished fish, the best of the standard cure, sold in Catholic Europe for about 50 percent premium over the still wholesome but less well formed, discolored, or salt-burned "refuse fish," which formed the staple of the West Indies trade.

Other fish were sometimes taken. Pickled mackerel and herring served as bait or occasionally as slave food in the West Indies. Halibut, for which there was no market, was sometimes smoked by the fishermen for their own use. Specialty-fish packing began in

A Maine flake yard during the late nineteenth century. It is smaller but more substantial than those erected in less inhabited areas. The principles of salting and drying, however, remained the same. Courtesy of the Maine Maritime Museum

1632 with the curing and packing of salmon on the Androscoggin River in Maine. It found a ready market in London. Somewhat later a small sturgeon fishery also developed on the Maine coast.

The largest early seventeenth-century fishing craft reached 200 tons in size and carried up to 50 men, but the average vessel was about a quarter of that size. Nearly all the crew operated on a lay system whereby the owner and the fishermen split the proceeds of the voyage. Although the apportionment changed over the years, in the early period it was approximately one-third for the owner, one-third to the vessel to cover food, outfitting, and salt, and the final third to the crew as wages. The usual method of fishing called for the vessel to anchor in 25 to 60 feet of water while the crew lined the rail, each tending two lines. As the fisherman unhooked a fish from one of his lines, he removed the tongue, which he turned in each evening as proof of the number caught since that determined his share of the profits.

1. The Colonial Experience

Although Boston initially evinced little interest in fishing, the North Shore villages of Salem, Beverly, Marblehead, and Gloucester amply demonstrated their origins as fishing settlements. In the late 1630s Rev. Hugh Peter of Salem recognized that the prosperity of his neighbors rested in the salt water at their doorstep rather than the rocky soil beneath it. He promoted fishing as the economic base of the Massachusetts settlements. As a result, a few hardy mariners visited the Grand Banks but not until the middle of the century did many New England fishermen venture as far as Sable Island or Newfoundland. Most of the New England cod came from inshore waters, particularly along the Maine coast. The Massachusetts General Court in 1639 hastened the growth of the industry by exempting fishing vessels, gear, and curing yards from taxes for seven years. As a result, Bay Colony fishermen marketed 300,000 dried fish in 1641.

The phenomenal growth of inshore fishing continued during the next two decades. In 1664 Boston claimed 300 fishing boats, mostly small one- and two-man craft, and in the same year a reported 1,500 men fished off the Isle of Shoals on the New Hampshire-Maine border. In part the Massachusetts concentration on the nearby fisheries reflected a fear of attack from French predators, especially after King William's War (1689–97). It was a situation that would not change until after Queen Anne's War in 1713.

Nor were the French the only assailants faced by the fishermen. During 1675–77, while the rest of New England underwent the devastating King Philip's War, Abenaki Indians, under a leader quaintly called Rogue Mugg by the English, raided Saco and New Dartmouth, and attacked the Sagadahoc settlement. In the latter year the Indians even struck the fishing fleet off the Maine coast, capturing thirteen Salem fishing ketches. Although never able to organize such an undertaking, Mugg considered using his prizes to attack Boston. In 1722–24 another wave of Indian attacks resulted in the capture of twenty-two vessels, eight of them in the Fox Island Thoroughfare of Penobscot Bay. Yet, as serious as these losses were, those to the weather were consistently greater.

During the eighteenth century the operations of fishing fleets at Newburyport, Portsmouth, Gloucester, Salem, and Boston developed a standardized pattern. Vessels generally made three trips per year to the fishing grounds, staying out a month or more each time. By 1700 dried codfish had become the mainstay of the Massachusetts export market. The best fish, usually taken on the first voyage of the year, weighed about 40–50 pounds and normally were sold on the Spanish or Portuguese markets. The "middling" fish had a market in Virginia, Jamaica, and the Portuguese Atlantic islands while the remaining "refuse" fish found their way to the other British West Indies islands as slave food. The colonists drew their salt for curing from the Tortugas and the Turks Islands in the Caribbean, the Cape Verdes, Portugal, and various Bay of Biscay ports. The problem of a reliable and easily reached native source of salt haunted the American fishing industry down to the introduction of refrigeration.

In 1720 the exports to the south of Europe amounted to about 100,000 quintals worth some £80,000, while ten years later the volume had risen to 230,000 quintals, which brought the traders £138,000. The increase testifies to the rapid growth of the fishing fleet after the Treaty of Utrecht opened the Nova Scotia coast and the departure of cod from Newfoundland waters. In the decade before the Revolution approximately 665 New England vessels (25,630 tons) fished for cod. This gave employment to 29,500 men ashore and afloat, roughly 20 percent of the male population over sixteen years of age.

2. The Sacred Cod

In 1784 Massachusetts hung the "sacred cod" in its House chamber as a symbol of the importance of the fishery to the state. The gesture nearly became an empty one. The maritime warfare of the Revolution devastated the fishing fleet. Hampered by limited capital to replace vessels and gear, disrupted markets, and the loss of expertise brought on by seven years of idleness, the industry rebounded slowly. Even the fishermen who did return to the sea faced sharply reduced earnings. The distress of the New England fishermen was so evident that one speaker at the South Carolina constitutional ratification convention used it as an argument for the acceptance of the new federal government.

The central government that the South Carolinian expected to relieve the distress of the fishermen nearly completed their ruin. The 1789 duties on molasses, rum, hooks, lead, cordage, hemp, twine, salt, and other fishing needs threatened to drive the remaining fishermen ashore. Political pressure from New England produced a reduction on the molasses duty and a bounty of 5 cents a quintal on exported salted fish. The latter was designed to offset the duty on salt, which still came almost totally from abroad. The palliatives proved ineffective, and in 1792 Congress adopted a direct bounty, the first enacted by the new nation. It provided an annual payment to each vessel and her crew of $1.00–$2.50 per ton, depending on the size of the craft up to a maximum of $170. The crew received ⁵/₈, apportioned according to their percentage of the catch, and the owner the remainder.

The incentives worked. The Massachusetts fishing fleet which totaled about 25,000 tons in 1790, reached 42,746 in 1798 and 57,465 in 1807. Approximately 8,000 fishermen worked the fleet. Exports during the same period also rose to about $2 million, flowing chiefly to Spain and the West Indies. Since the bounty was so successful, Congress repealed it in 1807 along with the tariff on salt. The lawmakers, however, very quickly learned an important political fact of life. It is extremely difficult to separate a vested interest from its benefit once it has tasted federal subsidy. In 1813 Congress reinstated and enlarged the bounty to $2.40–$4.00 per ton.

The restoration of the fishing fleet coincided with the appearance of a new vessel, strong, cheap to build, and easy to handle. The Chebacco boat, as it came to be called, carried a schooner or double-cat rig without headsails. The 24–45-feet-long hull had a distinctive appearance because its high bulwarks culminated in a high bustle or pinky stern. Most of the new craft worked on Jeffries or Stellwagon Banks in the Gulf of Maine, although a venturesome few sailed on the Sable Island or the Grand Banks. Before the 1807 Embargo restricted voyages, about 75 percent of the catch came from the close-in banks or the Labrador coast. Only about a quarter came from the Grand Banks.

The right of Americans to fish in Canadian water and dry the catch along the uninhabited stretches of coast was not settled in the treaties at the end of either the Revolution or the War of 1812. It continued to haunt Canadian-American relations throughout the nineteenth century. In 1818 British and American diplomats solved a number of the outstanding problems between the two neighbors, including, they thought, the fisheries dispute. The British agreed to grant American fishermen the liberty to fish and dry along limited portions of the Labrador and Newfoundland coasts. Although considerably less than the "right" to fish those waters that the New Englanders desired, the agreement continued the conditions that had existed de facto since the end of the Revolution.

Coincident with the 1818 arrangement, Congress provided a subsidy of 2 cents per pound for cod landed by American fishermen. The following year Congress added a second incentive by raising the annual bounty paid owners to $3.50–$4.00 per ton. In keeping with the belief that the fisheries were the cradle of the merchant marine and navy, the law stipulated that the payments go only to vessels whose master and 75 percent of the crew were United States citizens. The subsidies triggered a prolonged growth in the fishing fleet, from 37,000 tons in 1815 to 72,000 in 1820, 98,000 in 1830, 104,000 in 1840, 152,000 in 1850, and a record 163,000 in 1860.

The resultant invasion of their waters angered Canadian fishermen, who both officially and privately harassed the boats from below the St. Croix. In 1852 the situation had so deteriorated that Massachusetts fishermen requested naval protection. The following year the navy responded with a fishery protection force under Commodore W. Branford Shubrick. A diplomat of the highest order, he arranged a truce between the two factions. The tensions declined further after the signing of a reciprocity treaty the following year.

Although the treaty triggered a small increase in the fishing fleet, the skirmishing over sectional interests killed the fishing bounty in 1858. Its impact was delayed by the demands of the Civil War. Thereafter a general decline hit the fisheries. Canadian fish entering the country duty free under the reciprocity treaty made increasing inroads into the market. Dissatisfaction became so great that the United States denounced the treaty in 1866, the same year that Congress abolished the last vestiges of the fishing bounty. The Treaty of Washington in 1871 restored free access to the Canadian-caught fish but whether it hampered the resurgence of the American fishing fleet as much as late nineteenth-century American writers claimed is doubtful. It solved some, but by no means all, of the problems of American vessels fishing off the Canadian coast. The United States in 1884 denounced the fisheries provisions of the treaty but was unable to negotiate a new one acceptable to the New Englanders. This became less important as the Americans shifted to other grounds and stayed out of Canadian ports.

The majority of the fishermen in the first half of the nineteenth century hailed from Massachusetts. By the 1840s Gloucester had established her place as the premier fishing port in the country. After midcentury the Maine-based tonnage surpassed that of the Bay State. Although Gloucester still led every port in the number of its fishing craft, nearly every Maine seacoast village maintained a fleet. Unlike the Massachusetts fishermen, who followed no other occupation, the Mainers tended to be small farmers who fished when conditions permitted and farmed when they did not.

Along with the growth in size of the fishing fleet came shifts in vessel design. About 1820 the older Chebacco boats gave way to the "Essex pinky" or jogger, a strongly but roughly built, sharp-sterned vessel, generally schooner rigged, about fifty feet long. They were good inshore boats, able to ride a sea well. A decade later the pinky began to give way in the ports north of Cape Cod to a low-quartered, square-sterned schooner. The new craft behaved well in the rough waters of Georges Bank and served admirably in the new dory method of fishing that came into vogue during the 1850s. Fast "sharpshooter" and "clipper" schooners able to rush their catch to market entered the fishing fleets in the decade before the Civil War. Unfortunately, their instability made them dangerous in storms. As a result, heavy losses occurred whenever an unexpected tempest hit the fishing fleet. In 1846 twelve Marblehead craft went down in a single gale on Georges Bank, but the worst disaster was the "American" or "Yankee Gale" of October 1851. It wiped out a large part of the Gloucester fleet as it sought refuge in Chaleur Bay on the Gulf of St. Lawrence. The storm reportedly covered the north shore of Prince Edward Island with the wrecks of lost craft.

After 1831 a growing number of vessels fished the rich waters of Georges Bank. Previously, fishermen had believed that any craft anchoring on the banks would be pulled under by the currents that rushed across those shoals. Now that experience showed such was not true, the great Georges fishery began. Nevertheless, Georges Bank remained an exceptionally dangerous place. The most profitable fishing there came in the winter, and the best grounds were along the east side, where strong currents and gales could cause the sea to break heavily on the shoals. As a result, vessels anchored on the bank took a bad beating and risked being dashed to pieces if their ground tackle parted. Yet it was the closest major fishing ground and permitted the northern New England fishing vessels to make five trips or "fares" annually. Usually these started in March with a trip to the grounds off Sable Island, then one later in the

Gloucester harbor during its dory fishing period. Note the dories stacked on the deck of schooner in the foreground, which has hoisted both fore and main staysails. National Park Service Photograph Courtesy of the National Archives

spring to Brown's Bank, two to Georges, and a final one to Sable Island for winter cod. Despite the extended fishing period, the income of individual fishermen remained low. Although a success-ful fisherman could make $800–$1,000 per year, wages in 1852 averaged only $76.89 per hand including the federal bounties.

Considering the conditions of the trade, it is surprising that the New England vessels could find crews at all. In practice they were increasingly manned either by part-time sailors, especially in Maine, or by foreigners, usually from the Canadian maritimes or the Portuguese Atlantic islands. The manning problem was scarcely unique to the fishing fleet. It applied to all areas of the merchant marine and to the navy as well. By 1830 the opportunities of westward movement and the enticement of factory employment with its relatively high pay absorbed the bulk of the manpower that hitherto had gone into seaborne occupations. The movement away from the sea undoubtedly reflects the difficult working and living conditions as well as the necessarily long absences from the traditional rhythms of work, rest, and play. This increasingly made factory work, despite its long hours, often difficult conditions, and sometimes poor pay, appear more appealing than a modern generation, raised on tales of industrial horror and the romance of the sea, assumes. Neither did men still living only a very short distance from the land find it as unappealing as many of their city-smothered descendants have, to strike out for new, richer farm lands and the opportunities of the West.

Conditions at sea changed, not necessarily for the better, in the late 1850s as dory fishing came into common use. Instead of handling lines cast over the sides of the fishing schooner, the crew took to double-ended dories in search of the elusive fish. They still used hand lines to catch, but the new method proved faster. The clinching example of the superiority of the new method came in 1858 when the schooner *American Eagle* boated 900 quintals of fish on Georges Bank in the same time that nearby traditional handliners got only 160. The rule of thumb quickly developed that dory fishing was three times as efficient as hand-lining.

Long-lining, or trawling as it was called in America, arrived from Scotland in the mid-1840s but its use remained limited to the Cape Cod halibut fishermen before 1865. As developed on the banks after the Civil War the trawl lines, usually four to six to a dory, were 300 fathoms long and carried 300 hooks. They were anchored at one end. While the dory moved along the line, one of the occupants removed the fish and the other rebaited the hooks. Purse seining, which at the outbreak of the Civil War had just begun to be used for some of the smaller species, notably mackerel and menhaden, did not gain great popularity until late in the century.

Cod and mackerel fishing, the staple trades of the pre-Civil War era, declined drastically during the war and after. This reflected the competition of cheaper food fish like oysters, salmon, sardines, herring, and shad plus the effects of opening the American market to the Canadian catch. Nearly all the Maine ports dropped Grand Banks fishing altogether, while in Massachusetts only Boston and Gloucester continued working them. The period also saw a change in the state of the fish marketed. In 1850 Maine fishermen began to use ice to preserve their catch. This opened the New York market to fresh cod for the first time. The introduction of icing resulted in fresh fish providing a third of the sales in 1888 and 75 percent twenty years later. After the turn of the century the growing demand for fresh fish stimulated the introduction of gasoline engines into the inshore fishermen to permit them to deliver their catches faster. On the larger deepwater vessels, icing kept the catch fresh.

The shift to Georges Bank for much of the American fish supply hastened a change in the design of deepwater fishing vessels. Much of the fishing exposed the craft to the miserable and dangerous winter storms that wrecked havoc among the old clipper fishermen. They were too narrow and shoal to ride easily in a seaway. Under the prodding of Captain Joseph William Collins of the United States Fish Commission, a new spoon-bowed, broader-beamed, seaworthy design appeared in Gloucester during the early 1880s. Owners there purchased 221 of the new schooners between 1885 and 1895. This was the peak of the "trawl-lining" or dory fishing, "Captains Courageous" period on the banks. Not only Gloucester but Boston, Portland, and Rockland, Maine, sent large fleets to sea. Some idea of the diversity that crept into fishing in the 1890s can be seen in the report that in the spring of 1895 the Gloucester fleet had 95 vessels working inshore for the fresh fish market; 79 hand-lining on Georges; 51 dory trawling on the Grand Banks; 3 in the salt halibut trade; 15 seining for mackerel; 20 seeking herring for freezing; 42 catching fresh halibut; and 60 still fitting out.

Late nineteenth-century technological developments led to other changes in the industry. The most far-reaching appeared in the early 1890s with the introduction of frozen fish. Its discovery came accidentally when a Provincetown, Massachusetts, fisherman named D. F. Small in 1892 built a freezer to process the local whiting for bait and found he had an even larger market in the inland west. Others followed, but the great spread of frozen fish did not come until after Clarence Birdseye's experiments in quick-freezing during the 1920s. The greatest growth in demand of frozen fish came after World War II, when home refrigerators fitted with large freezer compartments became common.

A second nineteenth-century technological development was the introduction of the trawler, or as the New Englanders usually termed them, draggers. They changed both the method of catching and its ecological impact. The traditional trawl, or long-lining, by the proper choice of hook size selectively took only the largest fish. Trawling, which uses a net whose mouth is kept open by a beam or stick, catches in its pouch or otter all fish too large to escape through the mesh and thus rapidly diminishes the number in an area.

The initial dragger, the *Resolute,* appeared in 1891. Not a success, she was followed by the *Spray,* a full-powered, steel-hulled version, in 1905. The new design numbered the days of the traditional "Gloucester schooner" although auxiliary gasoline engines, whose use was pioneered by the *Helen Miller Gould* in 1900, and the first of Thomas B. McManus's classic knockabout (bowspritless) vessels appeared two years later. Schooners continued to be built into the 1920s, but most lost their masts to become mundane diesel trawlers before the end of their lives. A fine example of one of the later Gloucester boats, restored to her schooner condition, is the Mystic Seaport's *L. A. Dunton.* A bluenose counterpart, less extensively restored, is in Boothbay Harbor's Schooner Museum.

3. Other Fish

As the nineteenth century moved towards its midpoint, fishermen began to seek species other than cod. Mackerel can be wet-salted, like herring, beef, or pork, but prior to 1819 few were packed. Two years earlier the economics of the fishery changed. The Rockport, Massachusetts, schooner *Defiance* first worked the mackerel fishing grounds off Cape May, New Jersey. They proved to be exceptionally valuable since the catch could be delivered directly to New York. The mackerel were so heavily fished there and on the northern (Maine) grounds that in the peak year of 1831 about 450,000 barrels were put down at ports in Maine, Massachusetts, and New Hampshire. But then, as now, mackerel fishing was a very fickle business, for unlike the cod, which feeds at the bottom and must be fished on shoals and banks, the mackerel is a surface feeder and ranges over a much wider and less predictable stretch of water. For instance, between 1831 and 1840 and between 1851 and 1860 mackerel shunned northern New England waters. During the years between they were so numerous between Sandy Hook and Block Island that they created a significant living for many Connecticut fishermen. In the early 1880s, when mackerel returned to Maine, the introduction of the purse seine allowed them to be netted in such quantities as to glut the market with nearly 300 million pounds.

The general acceptance of fresh fish caused fishermen to switch to species such as halibut, haddock, and pollock, which had earlier been ignored because they did not salt well. Halibut became the staple of the Cape Cod fisherman since their runs to and from the fishing grounds were short. In 1846 they began using ice to preserve the catch. The idea quickly caught on elsewhere. Following the Civil War halibut fishermen began to go farther afield for their catch. In 1866 they extended their grounds from the Grand Banks northward to Greenland and Davis Strait. Within a decade they were operating off Iceland. The growth of the live fish trade after the 1890s also brought the appearance on the market of scrod, a species that does not exist. Scrod was a trade term applied to young cod or haddock, too small for salting in the traditional manner, which quickly earned a reputation as a delicacy among certain segments of the public.

In colonial days, river-running alewives and shad served as fertilizer until their attractiveness, when fresh, as a food made them too valuable to be used to implant nutrients in the New England loam. Menhaden or pogy* replaced them. After about 1812, moreover, substantial quantities of pogy oil began to be used as a paint base. In 1850 the first efficient pogy press appeared to improve the separation of the oil from the fish and the conversion of the residue or chum into fertilizer. Steam plants followed in 1866, and the industry grew rapidly. In 1877 some 60 plants in New England produced about 3 million gallons of oil and over 51,000 tons of fertilizer. Then the menhaden disappeared from waters north of Cape Cod. By 1880 nearly all the factories had closed, their stench gone from the air of coastal Maine in time to avoid fouling the noses of the ever growing gaggle of summer rusticators. But not so for the inhabitants farther south. In 1880 New York factories alone produced over a million dollars worth of menhaden products only to be forsaken as the fish continued to move southward. At the start of the twentieth century the Ameri-

*Also called porgy, fatback, mossbunker, old wife, bony-fish, hardhead, white-fish, bug-fish, chegog, or yellowtail shad, depending on the locality.

can Fisheries Company, which monopolized the Long Island production, had to cut back to four plants.

As the pogy shifted south so did the fish oil industry. The earliest factory to operate on the Chesapeake appeared in 1866 and the first in the Carolinas in 1868. While after 1884 the pogy plant operators faced growing competition from other oils and guano-based fertilizers, the industry remained strong. Reedville, Virginia, its center, is one of the towns in the United States that lays claim to having produced the greatest number of millionaires per capita.

Even today more tonnage of menhaden are caught than any other fish. The oil still commands a market as a specialized paint base while also being exported to Europe to make margarine. Meal is now largely used as poultry and swine feed. In 1984 the catch exceeded 2.8 million fish, about four and a half times the take in the "peak years" of the 1870s. Although the industry has remained largely southern based, the elusive fish have begun to reappear in large numbers in Long Island Sound.

Halibut were noted on Georges Bank in 1819 but attracted little attention until about 1830. Since the fish cured poorly, fishermen sought it generally only during the winter, when it could be shipped on ice. In 1861 Gloucester had 75 vessels fishing for halibut, but as late as 1860 they accounted for less than 16 percent of the tonnage of the port's fishermen. Despite the increased use of ice, the proportion of the Gloucester fleet catching halibut remained constant throughout the remainder of the century.

Herring began to reach the market in quantities during the second quarter of the nineteenth century, although plants in Maine had begun smoking them in small quantities as early as 1808. Between 1845 and 1865, Lubec alone produced half a million boxes a year. That was but a small portion of what was to come. The industry exploded after George Burnham in 1865 started a cannery in Eastport that canned herring as a substitute for European sardines. Within a decade 10 sardine canneries operated in Maine. By the end of the century that number had risen to 50. The Maine canneries relied on both native fishermen and on the Gloucester fleet for their fish. The latter specialized in frozen fish initially caught off southern Newfoundland, where in the winter of 1870-71, for instance, 118 Gloucester schooners fished. The local fishermen viewed the Americans as poachers and in 1878 attacked a group of

Gloucester fishermen anchored in Fortune Bay. Although both governments succeeded in preventing the incident from getting out of hand, it clearly illustrated the animosity that Americans fishing in Canadian waters provoked. Nevertheless, sardine packing continued to grow. The record of 201 million pounds caught in 1902 stood until 291 million pounds were landed in 1980. That figure has not been exceeded. In 1985 the eleven canneries in Maine alone produced 30 million cases of sardines.

Since they are surface-feeding fish, mackerel are difficult to locate and follow no predictable migration patterns. As might be expected, their pursuit becomes a business beset with years of famine as well as feast. The record catch was 147 million pounds, gathered in 1881. Thereafter the take dropped drastically to 16 million in 1900 and has ranged between 2 and 5 million pounds since. American sturgeon had a short history as a food fish. They were infrequently caught before 1870, but during the next decade new methods of preparation of sturgeon roe permitted its substitution for caviar. The resulting demand was so great, particularly in Europe, that the price rose from $10 per keg in 1885 to $40 in 1890. The result was a classic example of the effects of overfishing. The sturgeon catch fell from 15 million to 1 million pounds between 1890 and 1910.

The ecological consequences of the Industrial Revolution were early recognized by river fishermen, who saw their catches decline as dams blocked the upstream movement of anadromous fish and the effects of pollution began to be felt. One of the earliest incidents was the construction of the Holyoke Dam on the Connecticut River in 1849, which stopped the upstream movement of shad. It reduced the catch on the Connecticut from 500,000 to 50,000 fish in forty years. In 1867 the four states bordering the river agreed to build fish ladders around the Connecticut River dams and to restock the stream with shad and salmon. The steps were only temporarily successful because of the inability to control pollution, especially from paper mills, until the midtwentieth century. The restoration of purity to the Connecticut has progressed to a point that shad have returned in sufficient numbers to permit the appearance of a small commercial fishery during their spring migration. Much the same restoration of fish runs occurred in other eastern rivers during the 1970s and 1980s although in some, notably the Hudson, the presence of polychlorinated biphenyls (PCB) has complicated the process.

The decline of catches in the rivers also focused attention on artificial fish breeding. In 1859 Stephen H. Ainsworth developed a method of collecting trout eggs and spawn that was widely followed. After the Civil War both salmon and shad were raised successfully in hatcheries but the numbers were too small to offset the destruction wrought by man and pollution. Nevertheless, state fish hatcheries appeared in most states by the turn of the century although they generally served only to stock ponds and streams with game fish.

In 1870 Congress, disturbed by the state of the fish stock and the fishing industry, created the United States Fish Commission. Its origins were in the work done by Spencer F. Baird and other scientists at the Smithsonian Institution. The commission collected statistics of fish stock and catches, experimented with new fishing methods, and investigated fish biology. Although Fish Commission scientists went so far as to fit out railroad cars to carry fish fry to the West Coast and successfully introduced both striped bass and shad into western waters, they could not transplant the lobster.

A small, but at the time lucrative, fishery started about 1825 when Connecticut fishermen began gathering live fish along the Florida coast for the Havana market. They transported their catch in specially built, welled smacks. Only the most hearty entered that particularly dangerous trade, which faced not only lonely, poorly charted waters but also the animosity of the coastal Indians, who frequently attacked the fishing craft and destroyed the lighthouses that had just begun to appear along the coast of the peninsula. The trade collapsed in 1835 when the Spanish authorities in Havana imposed a high tariff. About the same time as the Havana trade died, Pensacola fishermen began catching red snapper along the Gulf Coast. Once refrigerated shipping became possible the market rapidly expanded, attracting both schooners and fishermen from New England waters.

Another Florida fishery in its infancy in the middle years of the century was sponge gathering. Prior to about 1850 all sponges used in the United States were imported from the Mediterranean or the Bahamas. Then a rapid rise in prices induced Key West and Tarpon Springs fishermen to enter the trade. It developed slowly until Greek surf divers arrived in 1884 to work the deeper water not accessible to the traditional harvesting methods using hooks on long poles. In 1908 the harvest reached 622,000 pounds per year. In the late 1930s Tarpon Springs became the sponge capital of the world, only to be rocked by an assault of red tide that nearly wiped out the beds. The harvest fell from 628,000 pounds in 1936 to 201,000 in 1941. After World War II, as the industry sought to regain its production, it had to confront the cheap plastic imitation that eliminated most of the market for the natural product. In 1966 only half a dozen sponge vessels sailed out of Tarpon Springs although the next decade saw a moderate recovery.

4. The Pacific Fisheries

Pacific Salmon are anadromous fish that spawn in the rivers along the Northwest Coast from the Arctic Circle to central California. There are five species, all commercially attractive: sockeye or red, chinook or king, coho or silver, pink or humpback, and chum or dog salmon. Traditionally, some varieties had been smoked by the Yakima Indians, who traded their surplus to interior tribes.

When the Hudson's Bay Company established its posts in the Northwest the traders relied on salted or pickled salmon for their winter food supply. This caused a Boston trader to experiment with a small shipment in 1831 that was not well received by eastern housewives. Despite the inauspicious start, a steady trade did develop. In 1852 the industry moved onto more solid ground when a commercial fishing center sprang up at Seattle, Washington. The first permanent salmon-packing plant was built at Oak Point on the Columbia River in 1861, followed in five years by a second one at Eagle Cliff farther upstream. They triggered a growth so rapid that by 1883 the 39 Columbia River salmon canneries produced half a million cases a year. Nevertheless, by the end of the decade leadership passed to those in Alaska. In self-protection, the Columbia River plants consolidated into the Columbia River Packers Association in 1889. It helped little since the Alaska canneries produced 4 million cases in 1912 and a record 8.5 million in 1936.

As early as the turn of the century, specialists began to worry that the salmon were being overfished and their stocks shrinking. Conservationists secured legislation requiring the canneries to maintain hatcheries to replenish the fish stock but could not force compliance. In more recent years the claims of the local Indian tribes of treaty rights to use nets across rivers bearing salmon

bound for breeding grounds have reduced the number of adult fish
in the rivers and forced limitation on sport fishing. The Indians
argued in turn that the real culprits were the offshore commercial
fishermen. In 1974 the courts awarded half the catch in Washington state waters to the Indians. Irrespective of the cause, the stock
of salmon in the Pacific Northwest dwindled in the single decade
1963 to 1973. Overfishing clearly played a major role. For example, in 1970 the largest catch in twenty-one years, 396.7 million
pounds, were taken by the fishermen, a crop worth $143 million
when it left the canneries. The 1980s, however, saw a revival of
the industry that during 1980–84 averaged over 600 million
pounds taken in both Northwest and Alaskan waters.

Particularly colorful in the history of the salmon industry was
the fleet of vessels maintained after 1893 by the Alaska canning
companies. Most were old Downeasters unable to earn a living on
routes dominated by steam freighters but adequate to carry supplies and cannery workers to the fishing station along the Alaskan
coast and to haul canned salmon back to warehouses in San Francisco, Portland, or Seattle. As late as 1927 the Alaska Packers Association of San Francisco still owned 14 square-riggers, but by 1930
steamers had replaced them all. Two survive as museums—The
Star of India at San Diego and the *Balclutha* at San Francisco.

Although salmon have continued to be the leading Pacific
food fish, others have grown in value. As the Atlantic halibut catch
declined, Pacific Northwest fishermen took up the slack after 1910
and even shipped the bulk of their take to New England. Cod first
attracted western fishermen in 1863. Soon as many as twenty
schooners, barkentines, and brigantines left San Francisco, and
later Puget Sound, each spring on annual trips to the Aleutians,
Shumagins, and even into the Sea of Okhotsk. In time the Pacific
dory-fishing fleet gave way to trawlers, as it had in the Atlantic.
The last schooner sailed north in 1950. She was the three-masted
C. A. Thayer, now preserved at San Francisco. Extensive cod fishing areas in the Gulf of Alaska and Bering Sea still exist and have
not been as overfished as the comparable Atlantic areas.

At the turn of the century, California fishermen exploited an
enormous resource of pilchards for sardines but the temporary failure of the run in 1903 induced some canners to seek other raw

material. Local bluefin tuna offered one possibility. The tuna packers developed a small but steady market. During the next twenty years the tuna fleet grew gradually, as did the size of individual craft and the fishing grounds they traversed. Not until a San Pedro packer accidentally cooked some albacore whole and discovered "white meat tuna" did a large market develop. The modern tuna industry dates its beginning to the construction of the 112-foot "tuna clipper" *Atlantic* in 1926 by Campbell Machine Company in San Diego to a design of Manuel Madruga. By 1930 the large, long-range craft were common. They ranged as far south as the equator. Once brine refrigeration came into use just before World War II the clippers traveled farther and stayed away from home longer.

Albacore tuna appeared off the Northwest Coast in large numbers in 1938. It was a propitious appearance for the Columbia River Packers Association, which had been confronted with declining salmon runs. The association shifted its production increasingly from salmon to tuna until as Bumble Bee Seafoods it is currently one of the major tuna packers in the world.

In part, the Columbia Rivers Packers' successful shift to tuna canning was tied to the shifts in consumption that occurred following World War II. The tuna packing industry expanded its production from 4.2 million cases in 1940 to 9 million in 1950 and 11.8 million in 1956. The increasing demand was reflected in the growth of the tuna fishing fleet. It grew from 75 vessels, capable of carrying 8,445 tons in 1945, to 225 vessels with a capacity of 50,000 tons six years later. Most hailed from San Diego. About 75 percent of the catch was taken by boats using poles, lines, and live bait. In 1956 nylon nets and the power block appeared. They revolutionized tuna fishing, eliminating the traditional live-bait method. In 1959–61 the number of seiners catapulted from 44 to 114 while bait boats declined from 141 to 44. Despite the entrance of Japanese and other fishermen into the market, the American catch in 1970 totaled 393 million pounds. It then plunged to 240,000 tons, worth about $118 million in 1985. The decline resulted from a combination of ecological legislation attempting to protect porpoises, strong foreign competition, high costs, and a declining United States market. But one of the most important influences in the decline, as well as one of the most difficult to solve, was the embrace of the 200-mile fishing limit by Mexico and other nations. This froze United States vessels out of substantial portions of the prime tuna grounds in the Pacific. As a result only one canning plant remained in operation in San Diego in 1985.

5. Shellfish

In colonial times oysters abounded in the brackish coastal waters along the Atlantic Coast west of Rhode Island with significant beds beneath New York, Cheaspeake, and Delaware Bays. Immense quantities came from the Brooklyn shore of the East River, Manhattan Island, up the Hudson to Ossining as well as around Keyport, New Jersey, the mouths of the Raritan, Hackensack, and Newark Rivers, and Staten Island. So prized were Delaware Bay and New York oysters that by the end of the eighteenth century those waters already suffered from overfishing. When a New Haven, Connecticut, dealer discovered that opened oysters could be shipped in watertight kegs for long distances he initiated a booming trade. By 1836 a thousand men and three hundred boats dredged for oysters in Long Island Sound near New Haven alone. During the second quarter of the century the Connecticut port's fishermen harvested and sold the shells for grinding into lime. Express shipment by stage, canal boat, and packet allowed New York, New Haven, and later Baltimore packers to reach consumers as far west as St. Louis by 1850. It also destroyed any hope of conserving the New York harbor beds.

Prior to 1820 the Chesapeake Bay beds had been exploited for local consumption only because of the prohibitive cost of moving oysters to New York for processing. In 1850 a Connecticut processor moved his plant to Baltimore. Others followed, and the Chesapeake oyster trade grew so rapidly that within two years Baltimore was dispatching 400–500,000 cans a year to market. Despite the damage wrought by the Civil War, in the 1870s the Baltimore packers handled 10 million bushels of the bivalves. By the end of that decade half of all oysters harvested in the United States came from Maryland waters.

The Chesapeake Bay oystermen were a notably truculent group who fought each other over private oyster beds. So violent was the warfare between Virginia and Maryland watermen that the two states had to intervene in 1877. The settlement shifted 23,000 acres of the best beds to Virginia control. Some Marylanders, however, refused to recognize the agreement and continued to work those beds. The conflict culminated in 1895 in a pitched battle between the oystermen of the two states. Only after 1910, when the disputed beds gave out, did a peace of sorts finally descend. Maryland waters generally declined in productivity after 1900 in comparison to Virginia despite efforts at oyster culture and a prohibition against mechanical harvesting or powered boats.

Overfishing as well as changing industrial and agricultural patterns along the Chesapeake's tributaries brought a gradual decline in the size of the harvest during the first half of the twentieth century. Even so, the industry remained relatively stable until 1967. Then the cumulative effect of the manmade chemicals flowing into the bay forced the closing of most of the beds. The oyster industry has not recovered. Its harvest continues to hover about one million pounds, insufficient to support even the diminished number of boats and watermen who visit the beds.

In Long Island Sound, pollution began to destroy the beds in the 1880s. By the end of the century those along the Connecticut shore had to be abandoned. Since then the oyster harvester has worked only off Long Island. Unlike Chesapeake Bay, where mechanical dredging was outlawed, the Sound oystermen began using steampowered dredges about 1900. Within five years the value of the harvest increased 100 percent to $2.8 million. Fifty years later suction dredges that could harvest 1,500 bushels per hour appeared, but careful reseeding of the beds has kept them productive.

The second significant crustacean seafood to develop into a major trade during the first half of the nineteenth century was the lobster. Not commercially important before 1830, lobsters were used locally along the New England coast as fertilizer. They were so plentiful along the rocky Maine shore that the normal method of catching them was by hand as they moved through the rockweed in shallow water. Maine's lobsters acquired a commercial value once Boston traders introduced them to the Massachusetts market. One vessel carried about 52,500 lobsters to Boston in 75 trips during 1841. Once again it was a trade that depended upon icing of the live product since uncooked, dead lobsters are toxic.

In 1843 the canning of cooked lobsters began at Eastport, but the industry developed slowly, and only three plants sent forth pungent clouds of steam a decade later. After the Civil War, however, the nation's appetite for exotic foods blossomed. Lobster, then as now, was one of the more commonly bought delicacies. So many young lobsters, preferred for canning, were taken in Maine waters that in 1879 the state imposed conservation measures. It limited the canning season to April through July and four years later forbad using lobsters less than nine inches long. The following year all of the New England states outlawed retention of females carrying eggs. Even so, the demand was so great that the price doubled from five to ten cents a pound during the 1870s. In 1891 Maine cut the season further and in 1895 increased the minimum size to ten and a half inches. Because of the obvious decline in the supply of lobsters during the 1880s, both federal and state agencies initiated experiments in their artificial propagation. The hatcheries achieved little success until 1905, when they began holding the eggs until past their helpless larval stage.

The size of the catches in the 1880s were so huge that the 30 million pounds (25 million from Maine alone) hauled in 1889 were not matched until 1968. Throughout most of the intervening years the catch dropped steadily, reaching its low point in 1933 at a mere 9 million pounds. It consistently rose again, climbing to 41.8 million in 1984 and 42.3 million pounds in 1985. The rise in landing during the 1970s resulted from the introduction of new deepwater techniques that allowed the exploitation of new grounds in the Gulf of Maine.

The shrimp fishery is another great success story. As late as 1915 shrimp found a market only among the Cajuns of the Gulf Coast and Orientals. During the 1920s and 1930s, however, shrimp moved rapidly from an esoteric delicacy to the traditional festive appetizer and a relatively common, if expensive, fish dish. The catching of shrimp at the same time has grown into a major fishery that in 1975 lauded 347 million pounds despite growing friction with Mexico over fishing rights to many of the richest shrimping grounds. In the late 1970s the shrimp fishermen along the Gulf of Mexico were jolted by the influx of displaced Vietnamese who rapidly, but not always peacefully, took over a major segment of the industry. Although the catch peaked at 357 million pounds in 1981, it retreated to 302 million in 1984.

6. The Conservationist Urge

The impetus for the protection of the offshore fisheries came from several sources. Environmentalists, disturbed over the depletion of the stock of individual species and the general assault on the aquatic food chain, formed one vocal group. American fishermen who saw their portion of the catch off the Atlantic Coast fall from 92.6 percent in 1960 to 48.8 percent in 1974 composed another strong political pressure group. Yet the common explanation of foreign overfishing is only part of the story. American fresh-fish consumption is growing but is still too small to support the re-equipping of the fishing fleet with modern equipment or the re-cruiting of younger seamen. Moreover, if the marine biologists who think that the stock of fish off North America is falling as a result of overfishing are correct, the likelihood of developing an industry able to attract the necessary private capital looks dismal. The prospects for federal assistance in an era of financial strin-gency are scarcely bright, so Americans will probably continue to eat increasing amounts of foreign-caught fish. In any event, many marine biologists fear that the haddock have been reduced below the level needed to reproduce and that yellow tail flounder and cod are in close pursuit.

Clearly contributing greatly to the overfishing of many species are the techniques employed by East European, German, and Japa-nese fishing fleets. Their large fleets of fish-processing ships and trawlers using large-capacity, fine-mesh nets tend to sweep up, or vacuum clean, whole areas of the sea. Too few fish escape to rees-tablish by natural means the local stock especially of cod, capelin, and pollock. Moreover, since uses could be found for nearly all fish caught, little incentive exists to fish selectively. An example is mackerel, whose stocks dropped 96 percent between 1968 and 1978.

As the ecological impact of the vacuum cleaner operations became clear, various halting steps to salvage the remaining stocks occurred. Some proved successful, some not. The International Halibut Commission rationalized halibut catches off Alaska and British Columbia, and the Inter-American Tropical Tuna Commis-sion has been remarkably successful in protecting the stock of Pacific tuna. In 1950 the Northwest Atlantic Fisheries Act imple-mented a quota system established by the International Convention for the Northwest Atlantic Fisheries, but until 1971 enforcement only affected United States vessels. In 1954 a similar North Pacific Fisheries Act passed Congress. Not until the Bartlett Act of 1964, however, did American law establish any criminal or civil penalties for foreign craft fishing off the American shores, and even then it applied only to activities within the three-mile national limit or to creatures of the continental shelf. The regulation was extended to a nine-mile-fisheries zone beyond the three-mile limit in 1964. Since many fishermen and legislators believed that the 12-mile limit was too short, they secured the passage of the Fisheries Conservation and Management Act in 1976. It provided for a 200-mile wide band along the coast in which quotas for fish to be taken are set by eight regional councils. Foreign-flag operators received quotas only after those for American vessels had been set. The law was a defeat for the State Department, which had hoped to hold off the legislation until after the completion of the complex law of the sea negotiations at which the United States wished to limit national waters to nine or twelve miles. The legislation was an outstanding example of Congress bowing to local pressures at the expense of national objectives.

Another result of heavy lobbying, this time by environmental groups, was in the Marine Mammal Protection Act of 1972 intended to prevent the killing of porpoises caught in nets of tuna boats. The act restricted the fishing by American vessels to a 5-million-square-mile area stretching from Santa Barbara, California, to the Chilean Coast. The effect in the view of American operators was to price them out of the market. Their response was to shift deep-sea tuna boats to foreign flags, which were not hampered by the restrictions. New equipment like fine-mesh nets and new techniques such as backing down to swim porpoises out of the nets brought some accommodation between the environmentalists and the tuna industry, but it did not restore American registry to the vessels transferred abroad or bring back jobs to San Diego's fishermen and cannery workers.

7. Whaling

Probably no portion of the American maritime industries has its image as firmly set in the mind of the average American as whaling. Whether envisioned as Captain Ahab pursuing his white whale, the danger-enshrouded Nantucket sleighride, or simply the elegant beauty of a nineteenth-century whaleboat, whaling has retained a romance that only the clipper ship and the Mississippi River packet can approach. Yet the reality of whaling was different: long hours of dirty and dangerous work on board crowded, stinking vessels for wages that would have made a slave weep. Whaling, nevertheless, had great economic significance prior to the Civil War because the oil tried from blubber served both as an illuminant and a lubricant; ambergris formed the base for perfumes; and whalebone ended up as corset stays.

Well before Leif Ericksson's mist-shrouded voyage, Norse seamen hunted whales. About the year 1000 the trade gained its most notable early practitioners when the Basques of the northern Iberian peninsula began assailing the great packs swimming in the Bay of Biscay. In 1527 Basque whalers appeared in the waters off Newfoundland; fifty years later 20–30 craft worked those waters. The Basques dominated whaling until the Dutch exploited the Spitzbergen grounds in the seventeenth century. During the eighteenth century the center of whaling shifted westward to Greenland and Davis Strait. After Parliament in 1733 began granting bounties to whalers, the moribund British fleet revived to such a degree that in the decade before the American Revolution the Union Jack dominated Greenland waters. American-built and -manned vessels contributed significantly in that revival.

The earliest recorded British attempt to establish whaling in the New World was the 1614 expedition of John Smith, which discovered the great fisheries off the coast of Maine and traced the coast of New England in detail. Although he reported a great number of whales, Smith's tales of a greater richness in cod diverted attention and capital in other directions. Nevertheless, many early British coastal settlements envisioned whaling as a possible source of income and offered support to the industry. One example of the official aid is the 1639 Massachusetts law exempting whaling vessels from taxes and their crews from military service during the whaling season.

In the seventeenth century whaling meant boat whaling in pursuit of the coastal right (whalebone) whales. In the whaling communities, lookout stations kept a watch for the approach of a whale. Once sighted, the lookout called the boat crews in the neighborhood who put to sea in pulling boats to harass the animal and kill or drive it ashore. If possible, the carcass was towed or forced ashore near the try works and stripped on the beach. This followed the pattern already worked out by the Indians and varied little from that used by the Basques. The Indians' role in whaling was substantial. On Long Island they commonly manned the boats; at Nantucket and elsewhere local Indians developed special skills as harpooners; and the traditional double-ended whale boat drew upon the Indians' graceful and functional canoe for inspiration.

It is impossible to establish the date or location of the earliest full-time whaling in the colonies, but we know the English on Nantucket practiced it as early as 1640. The Nantucketers were probably not the first and certainly not the most successful seventeenth century practitioners. Full-time boat whaling apparently started along the shores of outer Long Island where local Indians had practiced it before the arrival of the white men. In the early deeds to the lands they sold to the whites, the natives consistently reserved to themselves a portion, if not all, of any stranded whales. In 1644 the town of Southampton on the eastern end of the island organized groups of citizens to report and dispose of stranded whales. With good reason the men who were assigned the odorous and onerous task of cutting up the generally stinking carcass received a double share of the proceeds. The earliest recorded organized boat-whaling company appeared in Southampton in 1650. Within the next two decades several others appeared in outer Long Island. We know that in 1687 the Southampton and Easthampton whalers tried out 2,148 barrels of oil, worth about £2,255, a sizable trade for that date. In 1707 the take had risen to about 4,000 barrels.

The crown authorities also looked upon the fortuitous arrival of drift whales as a source of revenue. In 1665 the new English overlords in New York declared drift whales to be royal fish and demanded a fifteenth of the oil for the colony. This brought on one of the earliest colonial taxation struggles when the towns in eastern Long Island ignored the law and sent Samuel Mulford to London to try to enlist support of the home government. The mission failed; but Mulford's method of fending off the pickpockets in the metropolis was successful—he lined his pockets with fishhooks. Less controversial, and more common, was Eastham, Massachusetts's 1662 decision to use the proceeds from the sale of drift whales to support a minister.

As the techniques of whale gathering developed and resources grew, boat whaling gave way to whaling in shallops and sloops. The techniques remained much the same while the vessels became stronger, more seaworthy, generally worked in pairs, and could stay at sea up to a week. Whaling developed into a major industry at Nantucket in the latter half of the seventeenth century. There the Gulf Stream, and therefore, grazing whales, came closest to the United States coast. In 1672 Nantucket contracted with the experienced Easthampton, Long Island, shore whaler James Loper to teach the techniques of the larger island, but he never appeared. In 1690, however, Ichabod Paddock from Cape Cod did move to the island, bringing knowledge of harpooning and the methods of the mainland whalers.

In 1712 the whole industry changed markedly through chance. Captain Christopher Hussey in one of the small Nantucket sloops was blown well offshore in a storm. There he discovered a new deep-sea species of whale, the sperm, which, although without usable whalebone, produced oil of unsurpassed quality and great quantity. Spermaceti oil, which came from a roughly two-by-six-foot "case" or hollow in the whale's head, was both lighter and purer than that of the right whales usually caught inshore. Sperm oil burned brighter than any other luminant until kerosene

During the nineteenth century whalers frequently operated in close proximity to each other. Here the *Coral*'s boats pursue several whales while two other vessels pass nearby. Note the harpooner standing in the bow of the whaleboat. Courtesy of the Peabody Museum of Salem

appeared on the market after the Civil War. Hussey's accidental catch was so successful that by 1715 Nantucket had six large 30–40-ton sloops cruising in deep waters in search of the sperm whales. Some now-forgotten Nantucketer about this time added a brick trywork, which freed the whalers for longer voyages since they did not have to worry about stowing great slabs of rancid blubber. Nearly as important was Benjamin Crabb's invention in Rehobeth, Rhode Island, of a process for making spermaceti candles that were both easier to ship and use than the bulk oil. As a result the demand for sperm oil and its products gave Nantucket such an economic boost that in 1775 it could claim 150 whalers at sea.

Once the existence of the sperm whale was known, Nantucket and other whalers spread out through the Atlantic Ocean in search of the creatures. Some, predominantly from Provincetown, Massachusetts, pushed into Davis Strait in 1732–46, and others in the next decade entered Baffin Bay. After the conquest of Canada, fishing in the hitherto French-controlled Gulf of St. Lawrence beckoned. Ten vessels tried those waters in 1761 with such success that three years later there were 80 seeking whales there. After the 1764 lifting of duties on whalebone sent to England, exports there grew rapidly, reaching 112,971 pounds in 1770.

The most venturesome colonial whalers were those from Nantucket. In 1774 the brig *Amazon* under Captain Uriah Bunker crossed the equator and worked the Brazil Banks. Not surprising, the leading port before the Revolution was Nantucket although Boston, and Swansey in Massachusetts; Providence, Warren, and Riverton in Rhode Island; New London in Connecticut; and Sag Harbor on Long Island also sought the great mammal.

Since the best market for most of the whaling products, both oil and bone, was in England, many of the whalers either sailed directly there to dispose of their catch or shipped their cargoes there. This helped provide the vessels to carry English goods to the American market although occasionally, as was the case of that carried by the infamous Boston teaship *Dartmouth* (a homeward bound Nantucket whaler), the goods were not in demand.

The price of oil rose steadily: it brought £7 per ton in 1730, £21 in 1753; and £45 in 1775. The price rise was matched by the growth of the American whaling fleet, which in 1775 amounted to 300–400 vessels employing about 5,000 seamen. They processed at least 45,000 barrels of spermaceti oil; 8,500 barrels of right whale oil; and about 75,000 pounds of bone. The Revolution destroyed this fleet, especially the ships sailing from Nantucket. The islanders, mostly Quakers who wanted no part of the unpleasantness, were exposed to assaults from both sides. One hundred thirty-four whalers fell to British cruisers and another 15 were lost at sea, so that when peace came Nantucket had only 28 fit for sea. Moreover, many of the island's inhabitants scattered. The British induced or forced many captured crewmen to take berths on their South Atlantic whalers while others sought refuge on the mainland or in France and Nova Scotia.

Although the first vessel flying the Stars and Stripes to enter a British port after the Revolution was the Nantucket whaler *Bedford* carrying refined sperm oil, the conditions facing the whaling industry remained precarious until after the War of 1812. Massachusetts tried to help its whaling ports by offering bounties to their citizens of £5 per ton on white spermaceti oil, 60 shillings per ton on brown or yellow sperm oil, and 40 shillings per ton on whale oil. Although the bounty helped, recovery came slowly because the wartime shortages had caused most Americans to shift to tallow candles, and they were loath to return to the more expensive spermaceti ones. On top of that the British placed a prohibitive duty on imported sperm oil that eliminated the best prewar market. Although sales to France started in 1789, they soon disappeared in the upheavals of the French Revolution.

Boston initially led in fleet size, but by the end of the decade of the 1780s Nantucket and New Bedford were rapidly closing. Neither of the southern Massachusetts ports had a physical advantage over Boston, but they had a unique Puritan Yankee-Quaker heritage that produced merchants with qualities of courage, hardiness, parsimonious thrift, shrewdness, perseverance, ingenuity, and independence that, when combined with a business sharpness that bordered on the unethical, made them uniquely suited to the whaling industry.

Nantucket whaling captains again took the lead in expanding the hunting grounds. In 1789 they learned of the vast herds of sperm whales in the Indian Ocean. Two years later six other Nantucket whalers rounded Cape Horn to try the Pacific grounds earlier discovered by fellow islanders sailing a British ship and confirmed by the Hudson, New York, whaleship *American Hero*. The latter returned with a record cargo of over 2,000 barrels of sperm oil. The six were the first of many as the Pacific grounds grew into the major source of whales during the early nineteenth century. Outside of tropical waters, most of the catch was right, humpback, and gray, or "whalebone whales," whose oil was inferior to that of the sperm.

The whaler was an unlovely vessel. Bluff-bowed and heavily built with compact, easily handled rigs, weatherbeaten in appearance, and often trailing yards of weed from her foul bottom, she could scarcely be mistaken for anything else, especially if one got within smelling distance. Since impregnation with oil tended to preserve their timbers, whalers frequently had long lives. The *Rousseau* operated for 97 years, and the *Maria* lasted from 1782 until 1872. They normally carried four graceful double-ended whaleboats, each about thirty feet long, three swinging from davits on the port side and one on the starboard. Spares sat on deck or were stowed knocked down.

When searching for a whale the whaleboats were rowed by five oarsmen while a mate handled the steering oar. The forward oarsman, known as the boat steerer, was also the harpooner. Once he had placed on iron in the whale, the boat steerer exchanged places with the mate, who wielded the killing lance. Techniques changed little over the years although technological developments appeared occasionally. The most important single invention came in 1848 from the ingenious New Bedford, Massachusetts, Negro blacksmith Lewis Temple. It was a toggle harpoon with a removable shaft. Temple ran his line through a hole in the head of the harpoon so that any pressure from the whale would cause the head to "toggle" or turn 90° to become even more firmly embedded. During the 1850s the explosive head, which killed the whale instantly, appeared. It was promoted and refined by Captain Thomas Welcome Roys.

As might be imagined, the cost of outfitting a whaler for a two- or three-year voyage surpassed the capabilities of most men in the seaport town; nor could even the wealthy permit so much capital to be tied up for so long. Therefore, most whalers were owned in shares by a group of investors. The *Beaver,* one of the first six crafts actually to pass Cape Horn, cost $10,212 to fit out. She carried a crew of seventeen and three boats. Later craft cost as much as $20,000 to fit for a single voyage. Yet the profits could run as high as 350 percent. The *Lagoda* of New Bedford averaged 98 percent profit in six voyages between 1841 and 1860. Her next two yielded 219 percent and 363 percent.

Contrary to popular notion, the whalers shipped few experienced seamen especially after the 1830s, since they were too prone to rebel against the appalling conditions on board. Instead, whaling skippers recruited green farm boys and filled out their crews with skilled boat-handlers from the Azores, Canary, Cape Verde, and Hawaiian islands. They "advertised in Boston, New York, and Buffalo," as Burl Ives sings, where agents forwarded the recruits to New Bedford. Under the most humane and considerate of captains, which was almost a non sequitur among whaler commanders, life was rough, dirty, and monotonous; under any other kind it was a living hell. On the other hand, the captains and mates, nearly all of whom were native-born Americans, were superb technicians with a commanding knowledge of the industry.

Although the Nantucket Indians had made a name for themselves as whalers in the later colonial and early national period, they died out by 1822. The Chilmark Indians of Gay Head, Martha's Vineyard and Montauk Point, Long Island, became even more noted as boat steerers. The period of highest incidence of Negroes and Indians in the crews was the first two decades of the nineteenth century. It has been estimated that in 1820 12.5 percent of the crews were full-blooded Indians and between 25 percent and 37.5 percent were Negroes or Indian half-breeds. Rather than pay their crews on a fixed basis, whaleship operators, like the owners of fishing vessels, allotted the seaman a lay or portion of the money earned by the vessel during the cruise. Although the amounts varied slightly depending on the owner (who usually retained about $3/5$) and the period, the following are illustrative:

Captain	$1/18$	Able-bodied Seaman	$1/75$
Mate	$1/27$	Negro Seaman	$1/80$
2d Mate	$1/37$	Green hand	$1/120$
Boat steerer	$1/48$		

Generally the earning of the seamen were less than their counterparts in the merchant marine and in comparable unskilled occupations ashore. A green hand could expect as little as $55 for a four-year voyage—while his captain might bank $2,350. This contributed to the increasing disinclination of men who had any choice to sign on a whaler. Why should they undergo the trials of a whaler's existence when they could work in a factory at a job little if any more unappealing and come home every night?

By 1804 Nantucket had become the most important whaling port, but the outbreak of the War of 1812 again dealt a blow to her fleet. Half were war casualties. The fleet recovered after 1814 but not with the vigor that New Bedford exhibited. By 1823 the mainland port had gained the leadership. The reason was basically physical. As the pursuit of their quarry took whalers farther and farther from home, they grew in size. Nantucket lacked the capital to dredge the bar that restricted entrance into the port; and the alternative steps like camels or lifting pontoons were inadequate and too slow to attract large vessels. Along with this, a number of the second and third generation of merchants and shipowners left the island for the greater opportunities of the New York commission business. Others had moved to the more protected environs of Hudson, New York, where a short whaling boom occurred in 1830–45. Despite its disadvantages and a population of only about 9,000, Nantucket in 1843 sent 88 whalers to sea.

While the struggle for supremacy between Nantucket and New Bedford and later between the latter and New London continued, whaling captains expanded the areas of their hunting. In 1818 Captain George W. Garner in the *Globe* of Nantucket located the Peruvian or "offshore" grounds in the Pacific; two years later the Nantucketer *Mars* followed some British whalers into the Japanese grounds. In 1835 Captain Barzillai T. Folger of Nantucket took the *Ganges* into the Gulf of Alaska, or Northwest Coast, grounds. They proved to be rich in right whales, while in 1843 a pair of New Bedford vessels found the great bowhead packs off Kamchatka. Five years later Captain Roys sailed the Sag Harbor whaler *Superior* through the Bering Straits into the bowhead ground of the Bering Sea, the last of the great fishing grounds to be opened.

The whale oil and bone market boomed during 1830–60. Sperm and whale oil dominated the lighting market while whalebone found a great demand for corset stays, whips, and umbrellas. The utter efficiency of the American whalers soon gave them a near monopoly of the world's whaling. In the year 1842, 652 of the world's 882 whaling craft flew the American flag. In 1838 the value of oil and bone landed in the United States was nearly $2.5 million and would remain more than $2 million for thirty-eight of the next forty years. The whaling fleet reached its maximum size of 735 vessels of 23,189 tons in 1846, when the industry employed, directly or indirectly, about 70,000 people.

Why did the decline set in them? The primary cause was eco-logical. Whales had been overfished (about 10,000 per year) so owners found costs of operation rising faster than the price of oil. The efforts to offset the rising costs by shifting to barks that needed smaller crews scarcely had even a palliative effect. More successful was the move of a growing portion of the whaling fleet to San Francisco to take advantage of its proximity to the Pacific grounds. Nearly as important as overfishing was the appearance of petroleum-based illuminants and lubricants. The Pennsylvania and West Virginia oil fields came into production in 1859 and 1860, while after the Civil War kerosene rapidly displaced sperm and whale oil as a lamp fuel and paraffin, a distillation residue, pro-duced much cheaper candles than spermaceti. Lubricants distilled from the heavier fractions of petroleum proved to be both cheaper and much superior for most purposes to sperm oil.

As the demand for whale oil faded, bone became more signifi-cant. After the Civil War the change in female fashion to wasp waists brought a demand for corsets that needed whalebone and especially baleen from bowheads for stays. Not until spring steel came into use about 1904 did the demand for bone decrease. If a third reason for the decline of whaling is needed, it can be found in the general decay of the American merchant marine, which co-incided with the post-Civil War rejection of the sea. Although widely known, the Confederate depredations were not as decisive as some writers have claimed. The *Shenanadoah* did destroy twenty-five vessels in one raid, but the total loss of whalers during the war was only fifty. That would not have been an insurmounta-ble replacement problem had the owners so wished. But they found that other investments, notably in railroads and industry, offered better returns and less risk.

With attention fastened elsewhere and few replacements being added, the American whaling fleet gradually shrank as vessels were lost or worn out. In 1870, the year that the last Sag Harbor whaler sailed, and the year after Nantucket's final one departed, 299 were still active. A decade later the number had fallen to 174. By 1910 there were only 36. The last sailing whaler departed in 1927. The Norwegian-developed technique of hunting whales with explosive harpoons fired from small, maneuverable steam- or diesel-powered craft was introduced on the West Coast about 1910. To be fully effective, the Norwegian-style whaling required a number of

Following the Civil War many whalers shifted their base of operations to San Francisco because of its proximity to the Pacific whaling grounds. Note the whaleboats that have been landed on the wharf. National Park Service Photograph Courtesy of the National Archives

hunter vessels and a processing vessel or shore station. The large investment required ensured that only very tentative efforts would be made by Americans to follow the new system, and the last American factory ship went out of commission shortly after World War II. In 1950, when the Whaling Convention Act applied international whaling quotas to Americans, only the museum ship *Charles W. Morgan* at Mystic Seaport remained of the once mighty fleet.

8. Sealing

One of the lesser trades attracting American seamen was sealing. There are three families of seals: walruses, eared seals, and earless seals. The walrus, while occasionally sought by sealers, has chiefly been exploited by Alaskan natives for its ivory and meat. The fur seal is the most common of the eared seals although the sea lion is also a member of the family. The earless seals include the hair seal and the large seal elephants.

Sealing began soon after the Revolution when a Boston vessel took 13,000 hair seal pelts in the Falkland Islands that sold for fifty cents each in New York. In 1790 both New Haven, Connecticut, and Nantucket merchants sent vessels there to secure pelts for sale at Canton. In 1797, when the first American vessels visited the sealing grounds at Más Afuera, one of them exchanged its seal skins in China for $260,000 in merchandise while another cleared $52,300 on a single voyage. By 1804 the seal hunters had shipped at least 3 million pelts to Canton alone and effectively destroyed the Más Afuera rookery.

In 1819 Edmund Fanning promoted a voyage to seek new sealing grounds farther south. He discovered those in the South Shetland Islands. The following year, during a second exploring expedition, the *Hero* under Captain Nathaniel B. Palmer became the first vessel to sight Antarctica, November 17, 1820. Since the South Shetlands turned out to be a relatively poor hunting area, sealing declined in the South Atlantic. Thereafter, the sea elephants of the Antarctic became a target. The sea elephant hunt prospered between 1840 and 1870, but by that time the huge mammals were virtually extinct. A United States-Japan-Britain-Russia treaty of 1911 prohibited further attacks, with the result that the sea elephant has made a limited recovery. Meanwhile the American whaling fleet in Hudson Bay between 1860 and 1880 took about 10,000 hair seals.

After the purchase of Alaska, attention turned to the great fur seal rookery in the Pribilof Islands. In 1870 the government leased the right to take skins there to the Alaska Commercial Company for $55,000 per year and $2.625 per pelt. In twenty years the company took 1,977,377 seal skins from the islands; the payment of $6,290,614.60 nearly equaled the $7.2 million that the United States paid for all of Alaska. The great numbers of animals attracted numerous foreign, chiefly Canadian, sealers who practiced pelagic sealing in the waters beyond the three-mile limit. Since the sex of swimming seals is extremely difficult to determine, many of those shot from the decks of the sealers were pregnant females who often also left a defenseless pup ashore. This reduced the size of the herd so rapidly that the United States in 1886 unilaterally closed the entire Bering Sea to seal hunting with guns. Seven years later it closed a 120-mile diameter zone around the rookery to any hunting. Since international law did not then recognize the unilateral right of a nation to close international waters, the United States faced recurrent diplomatic problems until the North Pacific Sealing Convention of 1911 internationalized the ban.

Since 1917 as the Pribilof herd regained its strength, the United States Bureau of Fisheries has annually hired local Aleutian Island hunters to kill a limited number of surplus young male seals. This has kept the herd within manageable size. The proceeds from the sale of the pelts has been divided among the United States, Japan (to 1940), and Canada as signatories of the 1911 Convention.

Even more than the other aspects of the fishing industry, whaling and sealing have demonstrated the dangers of overfishing and the destructiveness of man's ignorance, or worse, of the food chain. They do not argue for the theory that man's awareness of his long-range best interests serves as a brake on his rapaciousness. On the other hand, there is some evidence that we do not know enough about the food chain in the ocean to establish the levels at which it is mortally damaged. Even so, fishing needs to be rationalized on an international scale and not by hysterical adoption of local political solutions like 200-mile fishing limits.

Chapter Eight
TURNING INWARD

A RAPID DETERIORATION OF THE DEEPWATER MERCHANT MARINE coincided with the Civil War. In addition to 105,000 tons seized or destroyed by Confederate raiders, nearly 800,000 tons fled to foreign flags between 1861 and 1865. Their departure accompanied the loss of American domination of many trade routes. The decline had begun earlier. The California trade, as we have already seen, died as a premium route in the mid-1850s although the general shipping boom hatched by the Crimean War cushioned the fall. More important in the long run were shifts in shipbuilding economics. The great coastal forests of northern New England vanished under the bite of the woodsman's axe. Each tree felled increased the costs of the builders. After the Civil War, wooden building south of the Merrimack, except for small craft, dwindled away. New York built her last large wooden craft in 1869; Boston in 1881; and Newburyport in 1883. Only a few large schooners that came from Long Island yards in the 1880s and 1890s countered the trend.

More devastating was the shift to iron and steel hulls, which had begun in Britain. The technological advantages of metallic hulls had been amply demonstrated in the two decades before 1860, but the greater initial cost inhibited adoption. Thereafter the situation was reversed as new, cheaper methods of production came into use. In the United States, conversely, not only did the iron industry develop more slowly but the plants concentrated on rails and structural shapes not adaptable to shipbuilding. What little marine iron and steel was produced carried a high price tag that could not be offset by importation of European-made ones because of the high tariffs that American manufacturers secured after 1864. As a result British owners could buy iron hulled steamers for one-third of the American price.

Tying in with the decline in domestic demand and the rise of nonmaritime interests was a decline in leadership of American designers. The day of the clipper had passed; technological superiority now resided with the British builders, who shaped iron and steel plates into the mightiest carriers of bulk cargoes yet seen and converted masses of inert metal into throbbing power plants. Moreover, the day of the sailing ship was fast closing. In 1869 the Suez Canal opened. It forbad passage by sailing craft, thus precluding their utilization on the routes to Australia and the Orient. Although the sailing craft would continue to haul bulk cargoes like grain from Australia and coal to bunker the steamers churning through the Suez, fewer and fewer were built.

Even the cotton export trade passed out of American hands after the Civil War. In 1865 United States vessels handled a 37.5 percent smaller segment of the trade than they had in 1860. Three groups of vessels handled the bulk of the trade: British iron-hulled steamers; Canadian-built wooden sailing craft; and former American sailing craft flying the Red Duster or other European flags. Even here the greater efficiency of steel-hulled steamers powered by the vastly more efficient multiple-expansion steam engines quickly cut into the markets available to sailing craft. The more innovative American owners like Charles Morgan and C. H. Mallory and Company shifted to similar vessels even in the protected coastal trade despite the higher initial costs.

Hastening the decline of the foreign-trade merchant marine were the increasing expense of American flag operation as a result of relatively high American wages; difficulties in recruiting seamen among a population who found life ashore more attractive than in the cramped forecastle; and the increased costs of operation caused by high tariffs on imported goods, including even the emergency repairs made in foreign ports. Congress, under the control of the industrialists after the Civil War, refused to grant relief either through subsidies to the operators who faced foreign competition or by permitting American registry of foreign-built vessels.

The story of Boston's efforts to secure favorable railroad rates illustrates another influence affecting the maritime history of the late nineteenth and twentieth centuries. The last quarter of the nineteenth century brought the amalgamation of individual railroads into systems. Nearly all of the combinations resulted from efforts to tap the grain fields of the West. As late as 1881 some 73 percent of all eastbound tonnage on the trunk lines of the United States was grain bound for export. This induced a series of rate wars that culminated in 1882 in a common rate schedule under which Boston- and New York-bound produce paid the same rates while goods bound for Baltimore were charged three cents per hundred pounds less and those headed for Philadelphia two cents less. Despite being a day closer to Europe, Boston could not offer cheap enough rates to attract substantial grain shipments to its elevators. No more successful were its efforts to secure a major slice of the Canadian grain trade. In desperation, Boston shippers resorted to a new rate war in 1909–12 but were forbidden by the Interstate Commerce Commission to charge railroad rates less than those to New York. That mortally wounded Boston's effort to develop a major western trade. The coup de grace came in 1916 when the North Atlantic Conference equalized all transatlantic rates for ports between Portand and Norfolk. In 1920 the Shipping Board extended the equality to Gulf ports as well. That destroyed all vestiges of Boston's natural advantage.

The lower returns from shipowning also frightened off potential investors, as did the slowness of the industry to adopt corporate structures. A final contributor to the decline was a phenomenon common in American business of that and later periods. The second generation of business leaders who came upon the scene in the 1860s and later were not as willing to spend twenty-four hours a day operating their business, as had their fathers. William H. Webb, one of the last survivors of the older generation, complained that the new generation did not know what it was to start from scratch and would not live with their business as had their elders. An 1874 writer in *Harpers Monthly* noted:

> Nowadays men buy ships as they get real estate, or set up a bank, or marry a wife even, on speculation, with no further interest or aim in the venture than simply to make as much money as they can in the quickest possible time, and to run the greatest risks of loss to others compatible with a very great profit to themselves.

Between 1865 and 1890 a number of half-hearted attempts to revive the merchant marine, especially the overseas portion, occurred. Nearly all were direct operating subsidies like the $150,000 per year bestowed upon the Pacific Mail's transpacific line in 1865. Others, including the recommendations of the Lynch Report of 1870 and Secretary of the Navy George Robeson's 1872 proposals, involved construction subsidies to benefit the builders and the suppliers of iron and steel. They were not enacted.

1. The Decline of Overseas Trade

Although the United States focused inward, it did not and could not totally abandon foreign contacts, nor could it allow them to pass entirely into the hands of its trading partners. Latin America continued to attract attention as a potentially large market, but like China it never developed the volume that its promoters predicted. Nevertheless, three Latin American trades prospered. The traditional Baltimore and New York coffee trade with Brazil and Central America continued to grow, especially after the establishment of the United States and Brazil Mail Line in 1864, which received subsidies from both governments. Lumber exchanged for hides and tallow at the Rio de la Plata ports, notably Buenos Aires, gave steady employment to a small number of the larger schooners. The most important South American trade in the late nineteenth century was in guano.

Prior to the German development of synthetic nitrates during World War I, guano was the principal known source of nitrogenous fertilizers. It existed in great, readily accessible quantities along a relatively narrow band of the South American coast where the Humboldt Current swings close to shore. There the rich harvest of fish had over the centuries attracted great flocks of birds whose droppings accumulated into depths of as much as forty-eight feet in the virtually rainless climate. The guano was dug by Chinese coolies, often held in virtual slavery and transported to South America under almost slave-ship conditions, as well as by peons, and occasionally Peruvian criminals. The powdery, smelly, dusty cargo was loaded by chutes onto launches or, if possible, directly into the holds of the vessels in which seamen universally agreed was one of the most uncomfortable experiences of their lives.

Between 1851 and 1872 Peru shipped 10 millions tons of guano with a value of $20–30 million, most of it in United States vessels. The trade came to be a refuge for the wooden sailing craft crowded off the California and other deepwater trades. The nearly insatiable demand of American farmers for guano-derived fertilizers led Congress as early as 1856 to authorized United States citizens to take peaceful possession of any guano bearing island not already possessed by another nation. By 1880 about 80 islands, including Baker, Howland, and Jarvis, had been claimed. The majority were in the Pacific although a few, like Navassa, were Caribbean islets. Most were never exploited.

A Central American fruit trade started after the Civil War since many tropical fruits could safely ripen during the voyage. In 1869 the schooner *Trade Wind* landed a cargo of Honduran bananas at New Orleans to initiate traffic that by 1872 had risen to a schooner a day. Five years later S. Oteri and Company rebuilt a tug for the trade and in 1880 added the specially designed refrigerated steamer *S. & J. Oteri*.

Three years later the Standard Steam Navigation Company, one of the leading firms in the Boston-West Indies fruit trade, maintained its own plantations and rail systems along with a large fleet of passenger-carrying reefers. The latter soon acquired the title of the Great White Fleet from the glistening color of their hulls and superstructures. United Fruit operated lines from Cuba, Jamaica, Colombia, Honduras, and the Canal Zone to New York, Boston, New Orleans, and the West Coast. United Fruit, under the capable leadership of Sam Zemurray, reached its zenith in the 1930s. It survived World War II in good shape, but poor leadership and an antitrust suit in 1958 forced it to relax its tight control of the banana trade. Changes in operation after the divesture suit and the introduction of refrigerated container service in the 1970s ended American flag operation of its vessels.

Other Central American and Caribbean trades prospered before World War I. Philadelphia's "Red D"-line steamers to Venezuela developed a lucrative trade and then shifted their base to New York. The Havana lines multiplied as American investment grew in Cuban sugar and cattle. The Panama Railroad, having disposed of various corporate buccaneers prior to the Civil War, operated the land leg of the isthmian route to California at a profit until the completion of the transcontinental railroad. In 1881 it passed into the control of the French Panama Canal Company and a dozen years later started its own steamship line to New York with American flag vessels. In 1904 the United States government purchased control of the line along with the other assets of the Canal Company. Despite losing most of its vessels to war service in both world wars, it continued passenger operation until 1961.

After the acquisition of Puerto Rico and the removal of the duty on goods arriving from there in 1901, traffic expanded rapidly. It was handled by the New York and Puerto Rico Steamship Company, a line controlled by Charles W. Morse, which in 1908 joined the Atlantic, Gulf, and West Indies (AGWI) combine, and A. H. Bull and Company, which by 1930 had achieved domination of the route.

The most important of the South American shipping firms grew directly from the guano trade. In 1865 William R. Grace, an Irish-born shipper of Peruvian guano, moved to New York. He gradually enlarged his business and in the 1890s started his own line between New York to the west coast of South America using British flag vessels. In 1913 William R. Grace and Company initiated sailings between the west coasts of the two continents using American craft. Its "Santa" boats quickly earned a solid reputation for service and dependability plus a following as cruise liners, especially in the years between the two World Wars. Grace sold its shipping routes in 1970 to the Prudential Lines, which in turn disposed of the passenger service to the Mississippi Shipping Company's Delta Line. Delta has continued the service, which offers the only noncruise passenger sailings under the United States flag.

After the Civil War the North Atlantic service to western Europe remained the premier maritime route. As we have already noted, for a variety of economic reasons American lines had been shouldered out of all but the cargo and immigrant trades before the Civil War. In 1865 the Baltimore and Ohio Railroad (B & O) tried to lure Irish immigrants to Baltimore, but the vessels of the Baltimore and Liverpool Steamship Line, former coastal liners just released from navy service, offered little to attract passengers. The railroad after three years changed its strategy to join the North German Lloyd and the North American Steamship companies in a service using German-flag craft. The B & O tried a third time in 1880 by offering joint service with the British Johnston Line. It too soon collapsed.

No more successful was the 1866 effort of several German immigrant houses in New York to establish the North American Lloyd, which acquired several old, wooden, pre-Civil War paddle steamers. The New York and Bremen Steamship Company followed in 1867, but it lasted only a few crossings. In 1867 a group of Boston investors formed the American Steamship Company. It ordered a pair of superb wooden-screw steamers, but costs mounted faster than expected, and passengers preferred British iron hulls. The experiment died after three sailings.

The next effort came in 1871, when Philadelphia capitalists backed by the Pennsylvania Railroad established a line to Queenstown and Liverpool seeking immigrants. It ordered four large iron-hulled steamers from William Cramp and Sons. They were the first modern deepwater passenger craft built in the United States and compared well with the similar European craft although they were somewhat expensive to operate. Unfortunately for its promoters, the line ran in competition to the well-established Belgian flag (but U.S. owned) Red Star Line as well as having to overcome the longer voyage to Philadelphia. The line never developed either the business that its leading spirit, the importer Clement A. Griscom, envisioned, nor that the railroad hoped. In 1884 it was purchased by the International Navigation Company, the parent concern of the Red Star Line.

The post-Civil War period saw the development of an arrangement that would have been unthinkable in the Golden Age of American merchant marine: the American-owned foreign-flag vessel. In 1866 Williams and Guion, the operators of the Black Star Line of sailing packets from Liverpool, formed the Liverpool and Great Western Steamship Company. Although the vessels were British-built and flew the Red Ensign, the line was largely American owned and the vessels American commanded. Generally known as the Guion Line, it was successful as a emigrant and freight line until 1875. Then it abandoned its unglamorous past to build express liners. Three of them, the *Arizona, Alaska,* and *Oregon,* held the North Atlantic Blue Ribbon in succession between 1879 and 1884. The line could not attract enough passengers to survive the transition to a luxury carrier and failed in 1894.

The next flag of convenience line to be established had a distinguished career. In 1873 Philadelphia investors formed the International Navigation Company to sail between Antwerp and

Philadelphia as the Red Star Line employing streamers flying the Belgian flag. Despite the advantages of foreign-flag operation, the line was not profitable and passed into the hands of its bondholders. They reorganized it, adding the American Line in 1884. Three years later International Navigation added the well-established British Inman Line. In 1892, in order to preserve the line's American mail contract, International Navigation secured permission from Congress to transfer Inman's crack liners *City of Paris* and *City of New York* to United States registry. In turn, it agreed to build two others in American yards. Those were the highly successful *St. Louis* and *St. Paul,* which joined the two former Inman liners to form a new American Line.

Another flag of convenience line set sail in 1882 when Bernard Nadal Baker, with the support of the Pennsylvania Railroad, established the Atlantic Transport Line to carry cattle and cargo between London and Baltimore on freighters flying the British flag. In 1892 it added passenger service to New York, but during the Spanish-American War it sold all its vessels to the army for

Although Scottish-built, the *City of Paris* flew the American flag after 1892. In 1889 she had won the transatlantic speed record. Official U.S. Navy Photograph

service as transports. Atlantic Transport replaced them with a quartet of large cargo-passenger vessels in the early years of the twentieth century. Their loss in World War I hobbled the company, which died during the Depression.

In the most significant effort before World War I to organize large foreign-flag operations, J. P. Morgan, with advice from Griscom and Baker, established the International Mercantile Marine Company (IMM). It gathered under one ownership the Red Star, Atlantic Transport, Dominion, Leyland, White Star, and American Lines as well as majority interest in the Holland-American Line. After working out agreements with the German transatlantic lines, the combine controlled or was allied with all the significant transatlantic operators except Cunard and the French Line. Nevertheless, the Morgan effort failed. Hard hit by the shipping slump that followed the panic of 1907 and by a decline in earnings of White Star after the loss of the *Titanic* in 1912, the company went into receivership.

World War I revived IMM, but after the war it sold most of its foreign lines to concentrate on its American holdings. In 1915 it had established an intercoastal service (Panama-Pacific Line) and in 1931 purchased the transatlantic United States Line from the government. It acquired the transpacific Roosevelt Steamship Company the following year. Despite its size, the concern could not make money during the Depression, so the Morgan interests withdrew, leaving the remains in the hands of the able Philip A. S. Franklin. Such was the short and inglorious career of the most ambitious American attempt to form an international shipping combine.

Nor were the American efforts to attract vessels to the Stars and Stripes more successful. As part of his stimulation of American investment and trade with Latin America, Secretary of State James G. Blaine prodded Congress into subsidizing the steamship lines that he hoped would bind together the two hemispheres. But Blaine's political magic could produce at best only very moderate payments. In 1891 Congress authorized payments of $0.66²/₃ to $4.00 per mile on outbound voyages, none on return. This was far too scanty to attract bidders for most routes, and only eleven of the projected 53 mail contracts even received bids. The twin problems of high building and high operating costs could not be conquered at a time when American builders were 40–75 percent more expensive than British yards.

Efforts to rebuild the merchant marine received renewed impetus at the turn to the twentieth century. The Spanish-American War demonstrated the lack of American vessels available for use as transports and as auxiliaries to the new navy. When the Navy Department attempted to find the colliers necessary to haul coal to its squadrons, it had to purchase British craft; and when the War Department needed transports to carry General William H. Shafter's force to Cuba it had to requisition the bulk of the eastern coastal passenger vessels. In order to secure the deepwater transports and supply ships for the troops sent to the Philippines, emergency legislation had to be enacted to permit the transfer of the necessary craft from British registry. In the eyes of the nationalists and imperialists who dominated the nation, this major blot on the American image had to be corrected. The concern magnified after the Boer War absorbed so many North Atlantic craft that shipping rates rose. The problem was not assuaged by the 1904 passage of the Cargo Preference Act, which reserved military cargoes to American flag craft. Even when the successful Round-the-World Cruise of the American battle fleet in 1907–1909 again demonstrated an inability to supply our own fleet on foreign seas, Congress was not moved. In 1908 it refused even to limit trade with the Philippines to American vessels.

The arguments centered around the poles of free ships, i.e., open importation of foreign-built craft, and of subsidies large enough to make the American-built and -manned craft competitive on the world market. The supporters of each position tended also to divide along party lines, with Democrats generally favoring free ships and Republicans arguing for subsidies. Since the Republicans controlled both Congress and the White House from 1897 until 1913, the first alternative received little consideration. The issue was, and still is, complex. Since American yards were 40–75 percent more expensive than foreign ones, free or lightly taxed entry of foreign-built craft could destroy the industry unless some areas, like the coastal trade, were restricted to American construction. Yet cheaper craft would not solve the problem of the higher wages paid American seamen. That could be accomplished only by greater productivity or by offering superior service that could command a premium, as had the clippers in their heyday. Conversely, subsidies could make the American shippers more compet-

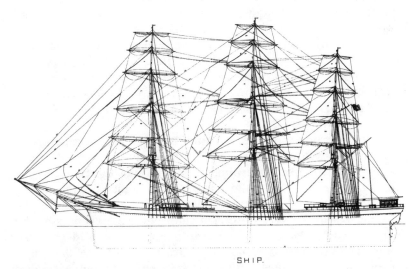

SHIP.

The sail plan for the "Down Easter" *Henry B. Hyde.* From *Merchant Vessels of the United States, 1892*

itive but only at a high price to the taxpayer and a less obvious one to efficiency and innovation.

The Free Ships advocates gained a partial victory in the 1912 Panama Canal Act, which opened American registry to foreign-built vessels less than five years old. Since the bill offered no subsidies or other inducements sufficient to offset the higher wages of American seamen, no owners shifted their craft. Two years later, as a result of the outbreak of World War I, the age limitation was lifted. As a result 148 vessels (530,000 tons) shifted their flag between August 1914 and July 1915, but nearly all were already American owned. Despite the shipping shortage of 1915, which created pressures, purchase of foreign vessels to enlarge the American-flag cargo capacity, legislation to accomplish it ran into strong congressional opposition and never reached the floor. The shortage of American-controlled vessels able to move American goods did, however, lead to the creation of a federal agency, United States Shipping Board, to resuscitate the merchant marine.

The commercial impetus of World War I opened or strengthened American involvement in overseas markets. For instance, the

National City Bank of New York greatly eased transactions below the Rio Grande by acquiring branches in Latin America. Other commercial and investment firms, hopeful of taking advantage of Europe's involvement in World War I to expand American markets in China and Latin America, increased their overseas outlets. One of the most ambitious came into being in 1915 when a consortium led by the Stone and Webster Corporation formed the American International Corporation to stimulate American engineering enterprises abroad.

These efforts to revive the American merchant marine in the half century following the Civil War illustrate two cross currents common to American maritime history during the past century and a quarter. The first is the already noted flight from the American flag in order to reap the benefits of lower operating costs, cheaper construction, and foreign subsidies. The second was the periodic awakening of the American nation and its leaders to the importance of a strong merchant marine flying the Stars and Stripes. In the late nineteenth century its rationale took a number of forms:

1. The belief that a major nation should have a large merchant marine;
2. The realization that the country needed a merchant marine under its own flag in order to guarantee it access to raw materials and markets;
3. The awareness that a good business could be developed by those willing to enter the field;
4. The utility of large liners and plodding freighters as reinforcement and auxiliaries of the navy.

Hawaii, which played such a major role in the development of American trade with the Orient and served so gracefully as a refreshing pause in the dull lives of whalers, was a natural candidate for sailing or steam packet service from California. But it did not work out so in practice. At least three efforts between 1854 and 1866 to establish such a service failed. In 1867 the California, Oregon, and Mexican Steamship Company finally received the mail contract, which provided the consistent traffic necessary for a healthy shipping line. The contract passed through several hands until it reached the outstretched tentacles of Pacific Mail. In 1896 the transpacific firm introduced a Honolulu stop on their San Francisco to Sydney line. Meanwhile, the Reciprocity Treaty of 1876 had opened the United States to Hawaiian sugar, which caused Claus Spreckel to organize the Oceanic Steamship Company five years later. It operated a successful service from California to Hawaii and the South Pacific in conjunction with New Zealand's Union Steamship Company.

After annexation of the islands, the passenger travel and sugar exports so increased that in 1901 Captain William Matson formed the Matson Navigation Company. Within seven years he had absorbed all his sailing competitors and in the following year built the passenger steamer *Lurline*. During the 1920s Hawaii became a resort center and drew competition for Matson in the form of Los Angeles Steamship Company. The latter ran into bad luck and in 1926 sold out to Matson, as did Spreckel's Oceanic Line four years later. Matson successfully reentered the passenger trade after World War II, despite the competition of the airlines. Efforts by less well-entrenched operators to join the trade between 1953 and 1957 failed. They lacked Matson's general freight and bulk-sugar carrying capacity. Although Matson stopped passenger service in 1978, the islands are not devoid of American-flag passenger vessels. Since 1980 American Hawaii Cruises have operated two former American Export Mediterranean liners on cruises out of Honolulu.

The great expectations of oriental trade that Americans have always held, however wistfully, dominated the political activities of the United States in the Far East during the middle years of the nineteenth century. They were preeminent in the successful American efforts to maintain the territorial and political integrity of the Celestial Empire. Hope of trade fueled the boilers that generated the pressure for Matthew C. Perry's and Townsend Harris's opening of Japan. In part Perry's Japanese expedition looked to the establishment of an American transpacific steamship line. However, no such line appeared because the traffic necessary for an unsubsidized line did not develop.

In 1865 Congress finally agreed to provide $500,000 per year to Pacific Mail to maintain the long-sought service. In return the line built four magnificent 280–foot wooden side-wheel steamers—the *America, China, Great Republic,* and *Japan.* While they were the largest wooden commercial steamers ever built and surpassed even the Collins steamers in the quality of their construction and appointments, which included a joss house and opium den for the Chinese steerage passengers, they left the ways already obsolete. Contemporary European craft had iron hulls and screw propellers. Nevertheless, using its Panama connector, Pacific Mail could offer New York-Yokohama service in 42 days, and New York to Hong Kong in 50 days.

In 1871 Pacific Mail passed into the control of a shady stock-market operator, Alden B. Stockwell, who succeeded in having the annual subsidy doubled to $1 million in return for bimonthly service and an agreement to build a pair of new iron, screw steamers. Rumors, never proved although generally believed, reported that the line spent $900,000 in its lobbying efforts. Whether or not the figure is true, the heavy handedness of Pacific Mail's agents left a continuing bad taste in the mouths of many Congressmen and contributed to their reluctance to vote other maritime subsidies.

Irrespective of the financial and political maneuverings, the two steamers, appropriately named *City of Peking* and *City of Tokio,* both products of John Roach's Chester, Pennsylvania, yard, were an indication of what American shipyards could produce if given the opportunity. Similar in size and appearance to the two leading transatlantic craft, the White Star Line's *Britannic* and *Germanic,* they were the last word in luxury. But because of the growing competition from foreign vessels and the degeneration of Pacific Mail into a financial football, its leadership of the service to the Orient passed into other hands. A good example of the difficulties faced by Pacific Mail came in 1875. The line received a $4 million annual subsidy from the Central Pacific and Union Pacific railroads to keep rates high. When Pacific Mail tried to force an increase in the subsidy by threatening to carry transpacific cargo bound for the East Coast directly to Panama for transshipment over the Panama Railroad, Leland Stanford, Jay Gould, and others established the Occidental and Oriental Steamship Company. Using chartered British vessels, the new line ruthlessly brought Pacific Mail to the verge of bankruptcy. Between 1875 and 1880 the Robber Barons who controlled or sought to control Pacific Mail used it as a pawn in their struggles over control of the transcontinental rail line. In 1880 Pacific Mail again reached an accommodation not only with the railroads but with Occidental and Oriental. The latter continued in the transpacific trade until 1908.

In the long run, however, the problems of Pacific Mail were primarily those of foreign competition. In 1887 the Canadian Pacific Railroad established a Vancouver-Yokohama-Hong Kong line with former Cunard liners. Then in 1896 even more damaging competition began when Nippon Yusen Kaisha (Japan Mail Steamship Company) instituted its transpacific service.

Pacific Mail remained competitive in the transpacific trade only by using Chinese crews with American officers. In 1915 this changed when the Seamen's (LaFollette) Act halted shipping of Chinese crews by requiring that 75 percent of the members of any ship's department be able to understand English. It was part of the effort by Andrew Furuseth's National Seamen's Union to force low wage crews off American vessels. Beyond this, the prohibition in the Panama Canal Act against a railroad operating competing rail and steamer lines forced the Southern Pacific Railroad, which now owned Pacific Mail, to sell it. Despite its problems, Pacific Mail prospered during the shipping boom of World War I. When the shipping depression of 1920–21 hit and the Dollar Steamship Company in 1924 underbid it for the Shipping Board's transpacific route, along with the new vessels to operate it, Pacific Mail folded. In 1926 it sold its name, flag, and good will to Dollar.

Dollar operated the transpacific service during the 1920s but allowed its profits to flow into stevedoring companies owned by the Dollar family. As a result, in 1938 the company defaulted on the mortgage payments due to the government for the vessels. The Maritime Commission foreclosed and reorganized the line as a government-owned corporation, the American President Line. After the new concern earned sufficient money during World War II to liquidate its indebtedness, the Dollar family then brought suit to reclaim their stock. In 1952 they settled for $9,180,000, which was half the proceeds of the sale of the line to private operators. After World War II American President and freight lines like Pacific Far East kept the American flag visible on the Pacific trade routes. Increasingly that became difficult. In 1964 American President abandoned its round-the-world passenger service, and in 1973 it sold its last transpacific liner. The company continued as a freight operation, and five years later absorbed Pacific Far East, which had gone bankrupt as a result of trying to introduce lighter-on-board-ship (LASH) service.

2. The California Grain Trade

During the decade of the 1860s California developed into one of the world's great granaries. Her soil produced a flinty wheat, hard and dry enough to withstand the voyage to a Europe whose ever increasing factory population consumed ever more imported grain. As a result, the wheat-growing area, initially concentrated in the San Joaquin Valley, spread southward as far as San Pedro and north-

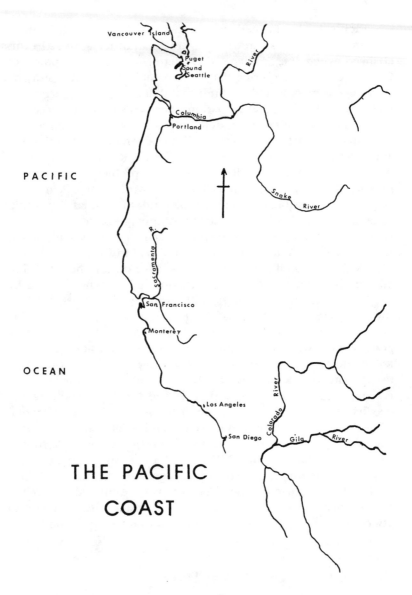

THE PACIFIC
COAST

ward into the Willamette Valley of Oregon and the Palouse area of
Washington. In 1869 some 200 flour mills dotted the waterways of
California. San Francisco, the base of operation for wheat king
Isaac Frielander, served as the spout from which poured the
golden harvest.

The first export of grain from California occurred as a direct result of the dislocations of the Crimean War. In 1855 the clipper bark *Greenfield* took a cargo to New York, but few followed her. A mere 1,087 tons of wheat and 58,926 barrels of flour left the Golden State in 1860, but the following year Donald McKay's *Great Republic* carried a full cargo to Liverpool. That changed the market. Within five years the value of exported wheat exceeded $1.75 million. In 1866 it skyrocketed to over $6.7 million. The peak came in 1882 when 559 vessels hauled 1,128,031 tons of wheat and barley plus 919,898 barrels of flour out of the state.

Despite its growth the trade passed increasingly out of American hands. As early as 1869 it was clear that American wooden-hulled craft could scarcely compete against European iron-hulled vessels. During the entire decade of the 1870s only 379 square-riggers left the ways in the great Maine yards. In those years the bulk of the Maine yards, like the surviving wooden builders elsewhere in the country, shifted to smaller, generally fore- and aft-rigged craft for the coastal trades in coal and general cargo. The exceptions were a handful of yards around Bath that built large, square-rigged, relatively swift, deepwater cargo carriers that came to be called the "Down Easters." Although not as fast as the clipper, they were still swift and able to carry bulk cargoes like grain. Some made fast passages. In 1888 the *Henry B. Hyde* ran from San Francisco to New York in 88 days. She averaged 124 days in fourteen trips, a record matched by few clippers. Despite being the zenith of American wooden cargo-ship design, the Down Easters retarded the decline of the American participation in the California grain trade only slightly. Many factors contributed. One was the downgrading of American wooden hulls by British insurance inspectors, which resulted in much higher insurance premiums than European metallic-hulled craft and gave an additional advantage to the European craft. What this meant is clear in table 8–1.

In what was the last gasp of American competition, Arthur Sewall and Company of Bath in 1890–92 built four large grain carriers. The *Rappahannock* was a 3,185–ton, three-skysail yard ship fitted with double topgallants which spread 14,000 square yards of canvas. The other three were four-masted barks (sometimes called shipentines although the term did not stick). The largest was the *Roanoke* of 1892, which at 3,359 tons was the second largest wooden sailing ship ever built in the United States. Some idea of her size can be imagined from the report that she consumed 1,250,000 board feet of yellow pine, 24,000 cubic feet of

Table 8–1. *Grain Trade Sailing from San Francisco*

Year Fiscal	Grain vessels	No. flying U.S. flag.
1872–73	339	136
1875–76	174	82
1880–81	356	224
1881–82	559	154
1884–85	371	116
1889–90	284	55
1891–92	273	39

Source: Basil Lubbock, The Down Easters *(Boston, 1929), 3.*

oak, 98,000 treenails, and had 550 hackmatack knees. A 2,000-ton vessel would have consumed only 950,000 feet of timber. Although the last American wooden full-rigged ship, the *Aryan,* did not go down the ways at Phippsburg below Bath until the following year, the Sewall quartet represented the final attempt to build mammoth wooden hulls. The maximum size had been reached.

Starting with the *Dirigo* in 1894, the Sewalls turned to steel. But the cost of construction proved to be so high that American metallic-hulled sailing craft never played a major role in international commerce. The only substantial exceptions were those built for Standard Oil's case-oil fleet. The last steel-hulled, full-rigged ship, the *Atlas,* was built for that trade although she ended her days as a salmon packer. Is it any wonder then, that when the San Francisco Maritime Museum sought a grain carrier, that they had to settle for the iron-hulled, Scotch-built *Balclutha?* Yet, she more properly commemorates the trade than would an American wooden wall. The assault on the grain trade forced American owners increasingly to seek refuge in the protected coastal trade where schooners, with their smaller crews, were the rule.

Almost as soon as the transcontinental railroad joined its two sections at Promontory Point in 1869, the faster service attracted much of the package and express business. In 1870 New York shipped $15.3 million in goods to San Francisco by water and received $3.15 in return. Ten years later the figures had fallen to $2.6 and $2.85 million, respectively. By 1909 water shipments constituted only 10.5 percent of the westbound and 5 percent of the eastbound traffic between the two great ports. In very large part this reflects the ownership or traffic arrangements between the railroads and the lines serving the two ports. The rates were so advantageous to land shipment and the business left to the maritime shippers under the traffic agreements so limited that it ensured the near collapse of waterborne service between the two coasts.

Although the advantage of the railroads superficially seems clear-cut, it was not substantial for goods that paid no premium for speed. Although shipments destined for the opposite coast had to be unloaded, carted across the Isthmus, and reembarked, or hauled around Cape Horn, those carried by railroads had to contend with the lack of a national rail system and the resulting necessity for shunting back and forth between different lines. For bulk goods that could not easily be shipped by rail, the long voyage around Cape Horn still provided the only viable route. Since the distances were too great for a steamer to cover without coaling, the cost in both time and money of fuel stops along the South American

The *John Englis* of 1896 ran between New York and Portland, Maine, until converted to a hospital ship during the Spanish-American War. Her appearance was similar to most other coastal passenger steamers of the period. Author's collection

coasts eliminated steamships from that trade until the end of the century. The inherent disadvantages of the Cape Horn or the Central American routes ensured western support for the construction of a transisthmian canal.

Between 1899 and 1914 much of the remaining intercoastal trade passed into the hands of a new concern with very imaginative leadership. Following the extension of American coasting laws to Hawaii, an experienced group of New York, San Francisco, and Honolulu shipping operators, agents, and sugar merchants formed the American-Hawaiian Steamship Company to provide steamship service between the East Coast, San Francisco, and Honolulu. The firm proved a success from the start, operating nine modern steel freighters by 1906. The following year it began transshipping cargoes over the newly opened railroad across the Isthmus of Tehuantepec in Mexico rather than carrying them around Cape Horn. This cut the time of passage from sixty to twenty-six days. Although all the technical problems of transshipment had not been solved before the opening of the Panama Canal in 1914, the traffic boomed. The line's westbound shipments increased from $5.5 million in 1907 to $62.4 million in 1913 while the eastbound proceeds jumped from $5.88 million to $32 million.

The Panama Canal's opening allowed the line to offer through shipments although it also brought a number of competitors. In its first year of operation the canal served six new American intercoastal lines sailing 27 vessels. The most important was Lewis Luckenbach, who before 1913 had operated an East Coast freight line that relied heavily on barges. In 1913 Luckenbach instituted a New York-San Francisco service in conjunction with the Panama Railroad. When through service became feasible he shifted to his own craft. In February 1915 he offered a sailing each way every ten days, half as frequently as American-Hawaiian.

During World War I all the shipping lines temporarily abandoned intercoastal service because of the greater profits found in the war-generated trades. Both American-Hawaiian and Luckenbach returned to the intercoastal trade in 1920. The former came under the control of W. Averell Harriman. He embarked on an ill-conceived expansion program just as the route attracted a number of smaller concerns that acquired surplus Shipping Board freighters at bargain prices. Although wounded, American-Hawaiian survived until returned to health by the shipping boom of World War II. She emerged from the war with a strong cash position but did not use the money to reestablish the intercoastal run. The intercoastal shippers now had to face not only the postwar inflation of costs, especially labor, but a hostile Interstate Commerce Commission, which continued its tradition of favoring railroads and truckers over the shipping lines. As a result American-Hawaiian departed from the trade in 1953 and Luckenbach nine years later. Most of their smaller competitors did not last that long.

3. The Eastern Coastal Trades

Other than the expected dislocations associated with the hostilities, the eastern coastal trade survived the Civil War little changed from the years immediately preceding. The northern routes had not only suffered little from the conflict but had added one significant link—the Boston-New York direct service instituted by the Neptune Line in 1863—and enlarged others. The cotton trade suffered from the destruction and dislocations of the war. As the cotton plantations adapted to the new economic life of the South, the trade revived, although less rapidly than anticipated. In part the cause was that the resuscitated southern railroads attracted increasing amounts of cotton that in former years would have moved by water. Moreover, the postwar period saw extension of rail lines into the river valleys like the Apalachicola, Tombigbee, and Alabama, where they quickly eliminated the antebellum river shipping systems.

Although the coastal fleet contained 1,775,000 tons of shipping in 1890 and 2,100,000 ten years later, it carried only a small portion of the nation's trade. In 1906, for instance, the Atlantic and Gulf coastal trade carried 64 million tons, of which 41 million consisted of coal, lumber, stone, sand, and other mineral products. Yet the 64 million tons were only 7 percent of the tonnage carried by the railroads. Nevertheless, coastal shipping, which was five times as large as that employed in foreign voyages, was a major factor in the economic health of several ports, notably of Boston. There it permitted shippers to bypass the rail congestion at New York and other centers.

In Maine and to a lesser degree along Long Island Sound the growing vacation trade began to have impact. The opening of great resort hotels and boarding houses in the White Mountains and Maine brought droves of rusticators who sought respite from the pressures of modern life through communing with raw nature. The easiest route for many vacationers bound for the White Mountains was to take a Long Island Sound steamer to New London, whence special trains carried them to the majestic splendor of Jackson and Crawford Notch. Those bound for Poland Springs and other southern Maine points commonly used the Maine Steamship Company's service to Portland because it eliminated the time-consuming and irritating shift of baggage, wives, and children from South to North Stations in Boston. Those bound for the Down East resorts like Bar Harbor, Camden, Boothbay Harbor, and the myriad of islands and landings in between had no choice except water movement since the railroad had yet to reach nearby depots. In some cases that would not occur until the early years of the twentieth century.

The coastal passenger steamers in all areas followed a similar pricing system. They charged a low basic fare and added fees for cabins and meals. Even on the night runs fares were cheap. In the 1890s the Fall River Line charged $2 fare plus $1 and up for cabins. Since most steamship lines complemented rather than competed with the railroads, few rate wars resulted. Most of those, when they did occur, came on waters like Long Island Sound, which were well populated with competing steamer lines. Out of the series of wars and peace settlements that occupied much of the period between 1867 and 1881 the Fall River Line of the Old Colony Railroad Company emerged dominant on the longer Sound run although lesser lines still operated from Connecticut ports and the Metropolitan Steamship Company offered "outside" service between Boston and New York around Cape Cod.

The persistence of steamboat service on Long Island Sound reflected the geography of the area. The shore rail line was broken by the Thames and Connecticut rivers. The latter was not bridged until 1870, while train ferries were required across the Thames for some years more. The main impact of the railroads, and especially the newly developed sleeping cars, was to eliminate those lines operating slow, small steamers without affecting those employing fast, well-outfitted, and dependable vessels.

The growth of the cotton and woolen textile, boot and shoe, and paper industries in central and southern New England markedly influenced in the health of the Sound lines. Even the inland mills marketed most of their wares through New York houses, New Hampshire sending a third of its cotton goods there, for instance. Indeed, one of the strengths of the New York merchandising houses was their ability to receive rapid shipments from the factories in order to fill unexpected orders. This ease of access permitted the New York merchants to keep their stocks low and avoid metropolitan warehousing costs. Conversely, the speed and reliability of the rail-water service in New England kept the mills there competitive down to World War I despite high labor costs and increasingly obsolescent plants. Throughout most of the nineteenth century, the steamship lines on the Sound offered better express service than did the railroads. Passenger service also constantly expanded, reaching its peak during the first seven years of the twentieth century, but it never recovered from the panic of 1907 and the arrival of the automobile.

As the demands on the Long Island Sound lines for consistent and safe service grew, they turned to iron-hulled steamers. The earliest appeared in 1867 when the Norwich Line placed the *City of Lawrence* in commission. Six years later the Metropolitan Line contributed the highly successful *General Whitney,* a miniature deepwater liner for the outside route between Boston and New York. By the 1880s the Sound lines had all turned to iron. In 1883 the Fall River Line added the noted *Pilgrim,* the first vessel on the Sound to be lighted throughout with electric lights, the first commercial vessel in the United States to have a double bottom, and the first to have her machinery and boiler spaces completely enclosed in metal. She was followed at the end of the decade by the *Puritan* and in 1890 by the *Plymouth,* which boasted the largest beam engine ever built. The apex of the Sound boats arrived in 1908 in the Fall River Line's famed *Commonwealth,* a 438-foot-long steel beauty, which continued in service until the death of the firm in 1937.

The closing decade of the nineteenth century marked the appearance in New England of the amalgamation and rationalization that had already struck the railroads and many industries. The New York, New Haven, and Hartford Railroad came into being in the 1870s when the New York and New Haven leased the Hartford and New Haven. In 1892 the New Haven amalgam acquired the Providence and Stonington Steamship Company, itself a combination of the old Stonington and Providence lines to New York. The following year the New Haven leased the Old Colony Railroad, which brought with it control of the Fall River Line. Five years later the lease of the New York and New England added the New York and

The Fall River Line's famed *Plymouth* of 1890. Like contemporary passenger liners on the Great Lakes, she had a beam engine and side wheels. From *Merchant Vessels of the United States, 1892*

New London Steamboat Company. The 1898 acquisition of the Norwich line completed the railroad's control of all routes east of New Haven. Under the New Haven's management the Sound lines were in the words of a modern historian "a productive monopoly" that supplemented the service available on land. Unfortunately, the New Haven's management also saw the Long Island Sound lines as pawns in their larger design of a New England rail monopoly.

Between 1901 and 1905 Charles W. Morse of the Kennebec River ice trade collected the "eastern" or Maine lines into the Eastern Steamship Company. In 1905 he added the Metropolitan Line and combined his holdings as the Consolidated Steamship Company. Morse's objective was control of all major steamship lines between Maine and Texas. He acquired the Clyde Steamship Company, New York and Texas Steamship Company (Mallory Line), New York and Cuba Mail Steamship Company, and New York and Puerto Rico Steamship Company during the next two years. This was a challenge that the New Haven could not permit, so it moved decisively into the arena by purchasing, sub rosa, the Maine Steamship Company, which operated between Boston and Portland and was still reeling under the loss of their *Portland* in the classic

A good example of the smaller coastal steamers was the *Kennebec,* which served on the run between Boston and Bath, Maine. She later operated on Long Island Sound and the Hudson River. Courtesy of Maine Maritime Museum

November 1898 storm off Cape Cod. More openly, the railroad acquired the Merchants and Miners Company to counter Morse's southward expansion.

The New Haven also entered the Boston-New York outside Cape Cod service by establishing the Merchant's Line in 1908 with three fast new steamers to oppose Morse's Metropolitan Line. The latter responded with the even faster *Harvard* and *Yale.* Meanwhile, the panic of 1907 hit Morse full force, driving his Consolidated Line into receivership. Morse's successors split his empire into three groups; the Atlantic, Gulf, and West Indies (AGWI) Lines, which included the Clyde, Mallory, New York and Cuba Mail, and New York and Puerto Rico services; Eastern Steamship Corporation in Maine; and the Metropolitan Line handling the Boston-New York "outside" run. The latter passed into the hands of the New Haven in 1911 and the following year was peddled to Eastern Steamship.

It was a bad purchase, and by 1914 the Eastern Steamship was bankrupt. Its able receiver Calvin Austin restored health by selling off most of the vessels during World War I and resuming only limited service after the war. As cheap construction loans became available under the Merchant Marine Act of 1924, Eastern built a group of fine small coastal liners: the *Yarmouth, Evangeline, Acadia, St. John* for service to Bay of Fundy ports and the *Boston* and *New York* to operate between those two cities. The Maine feeder services retracted as highways absorbed greater and greater portions of the tourist trade, ceasing altogether in 1936. The six new vessels went into World War II service, but only the first two returned. Using them, Eastern ran an unsuccessful Boston-Yarmouth, Nova Scotia, line during 1948–54. They were the last sailings of the New England coastal fleet.

The opening of the long-discussed, privately financed Cape Cod Canal in 1914 strengthened the coastal trade by cutting Boston-New York passage time by 25 percent and eliminating the rough outside passage. Initially limited to vessels of 15-foot draft and low speeds, the canal did not see extensive use until deepened and widened two years later. Thereafter, it served as the preferred route for all but the largest of deep-sea craft.

Other factors began to alter the traditional maritime activity on Long Island Sound. The New Haven Railroad's collection of maritime services had been acquired with little concern about their cost since the railroad's management, led by the abrasive Charles S. Mellen and its financial backer J. Pierpont Morgan, assumed that the efficiencies produced by rationalization would produce a significant jump in profits. They did not, and the New Haven's lines never developed enough business to support their indebtedness. A further latch on the coffin of the monopoly closed in 1912 when the Panama Canal Act forbad railroads to own competing maritime services. The New Haven promptly dismantled its holdings. The Maine Steamship Company went to a reorganized Eastern group while the Merchants and Miners and Fall River lines became independent. Although all the Sound services, like the West Coast lines and to a lesser degree the Maine lines, suffered dislocations from government requisitioning of vessels during World War I, most survived into the 1920s. Even so, the Sound lines carried only half as much cargo in 1921 as they had in 1917.

During the 1920s, as the inroads of automobiles, and trucks began to be felt on the short runs, they closed. The Depression of 1929, the automobile, the new fire-protection requirements added after the *Morro Castle* disaster in 1934, as well as the growing demands of the labor unions, killed all service by 1937.

After its recapture of independence, Merchants and Miners regained its reputation for quality and profitability. In 1915 it operated twenty-two steamers and a schooner on its traditional routes between Boston and Baltimore. Nineteen years later it still operated nineteen steamers, including five built in 1923–26. When its vessels went to war in 1941 the line ceased operations and did not attempt to restore service after the war.

The longer coastal services resumed after the Civil War. In 1866 Charles Morgan reestablished his line between New Orleans and Texas, carrying cattle, hides, and cotton. The following year the Old Dominion Steamship Company emerged from a consolidation of existing New York-Norfolk services while in 1872 Henry Winsor started the very successful Boston and Philadelphia Steamship Company (Winsor Line). In the 1870s Morgan built his private port at Brashear, Louisiana, in an effort to outflank his competition by placing his base astride the route from Texas. It was an innovative and daring step but destined to failure within twenty years because of the cost of keeping open a deepwater channel through Berwick Bay. In 1878 Morgan took advantage of the recently deepened South Pass entrance to the Mississippi to add a New York-New Orleans line. By then he had already shifted heavily to railroads and was reducing his maritime commitments. Ultimately, his Louisiana and Texas Railroad and Steamship Company passed to the Southern Pacific, which operated the steamship division at a reduced scale down to World War II.

Morgan, whose Texas base was Galveston, ran into opposition from Charles H. Mallory, a Connecticut sailing-ship operator who had shifted to steam and opened a line to Houston as early as 1868. This sparked the long and intense great trade war between the two towns. The opening of the Houston Ship Canal in 1914 following close on the heels of Galveston's devastating hurricane, ratified Houston's victory and brought with it direct passenger service to New York and Philadelphia. The real importance of the Houston

No. 10. FORE-AND-AFT THREE-MAST SCHOONER.

The three-masted schooner, a main-stay of the coal trade. If the three masts were of equal height, the rig was commonly called a tern. From *Merchant Vessels of the United States, 1892*

Ship Canal, however, came with the opening of oil refineries along its shores after World War I.

On the Chesapeake Bay, steam service lasted longer than elsewhere. Since railroads were late in entering the eastern peninsula, the coastal settlements relied on steamboats and an occasional trading schooner to move their shipments of wood, oysters, and tobacco to market or to bring them the necessities and luxuries of everyday life. Various small feeder lines, many railroad controlled, appeared, but the Baltimore Steam Packet Company (or Old Bay Line to use its more common name) remained, as it had before the Civil War, the dominant force although occasionally facing stiff competition from concerns like the Baltimore and Virginia Steamboat Company and the Chesapeake Steam Ship Company. The managers of the Old Bay Line, like Charles Morgan in Texas, early recognized the superiority of iron hulls and turned to them nearly exclusively after the 1870s.

The four-masted schooner *Inez N. Carver* about to be launched from the New England Company yard in Bath, Maine. Courtesy of Maine Maritime Museum

Even after the completion of the railroads to Albany and Troy, the steamboat remained the preferred means of travel between the Hudson River ports because of the relative comfort, especially for travelers electing to use the night boats. Nevertheless, the importance of the river rested primarily in its prosaic bulk cargo shipments. Between April and December, inhabitants along its banks could watch a constant progression of big canal boat tows, as many as six barges abreast and stretching for a half mile, following a puffing paddle-wheel tug. One observer described the tows as resembling a floating town with streets formed by the long lines of level decks on which squatted awning-adorned cabins resplendent with shining windows and bright green blinds. Nearly all traffic moving east across the Erie Canal had New York for its destination. After the midcentury very seldom did a grain and other bulk barge stop at the upriver ports unless bound for the docks of Boston.

Prior to the Civil War the most commonly used coal was anthracite from northeastern Pennsylvania. Its popularity followed the introduction of cast-iron heating stoves early in the century and the increasing use of steam to power factories no longer able to locate water power. In 1850 Boston imported only 189,571 tons of coal, but fifty years later the figure had leaped to 4,708,147 tons. Throughout the nineteenth century and most of the first half of the twentieth, the northeastern seaboard received nearly all its coal by water.

The Reading Railroad, one of the leading anthracite producers, experimented unsuccessfully with steam colliers before the Civil War. In 1868–74 the Reading tried again, building fourteen new colliers and adding to its own docks and storage yards in New England. In the 1880s the railroad shifted to more efficient barges.

Before World War I most of the coal consumed by East Coast communities traveled by schooner. The five-masted *Edna Hoyt* takes on cargo at the great coal pier at Newport News, Virginia. Photo by William T. Radcliffe, courtesy of The Mariners Museum of Newport News, Va.

They proved especially useful in Long Island Sound, where a single tug could handle as much as 27,000 tons at a time. Barges, however, were unsatisfactory in the rough waters beyond Point Judith, Rhode Island. As a result, the longer trade was handled by coastal schooners and a few steam colliers until the first decade of the twentieth century.

In 1881 the Chesapeake and Ohio Railroad opened its line to the West Virginia bituminous coal fields; two years later the Norfolk and Western tapped the Pocahontas field. These made Newport News and Norfolk, Virginia, on opposite sides of Hampton Roads, the leading coal ports in the nation. Some indication of the rapid growth of the bituminous trade can be seen in the coal imports into Boston at the end of the decade: 1,637,000 tons of anthracite and 915,000 tons of bituminous. Most of the coal bound for Boston and other East Coast ports moved by schooner. The bituminous fields opened at a propitious time in American industrial growth although the appearance of the pioneer smoke-abatement laws in 1893 had a limiting effect. Not only did the new steel and fabrication plants consume unheard-of quantities of coal but the appearance of electric trolley cars and interurbans created a many-fold increase in the demands upon the coal-fired generating plants.

One direct result of the growing demand for coal was an enlargement of the vessels hauling the black diamonds. During the 1870s the three masted schooner was the workhorse of the coal trade. Most had masts of equal height, a rig that came to be known along the coast as a tern. The shift from two to three masts represented an effort to reduce the area of the individual sails to one that could be handled by the small crews that the schooners carried while increasing the total sail area sufficiently to move the larger craft at a reasonable speed. During the decade of the 1870s the average size of three-masters grew from about 500 to 920 tons. By the end of the decade a "donkey" steam engine appeared on the decks of the *Charles A. Briggs* as an aid in the hoisting the sails and anchor and to operate windlasses and pumps, as one had two decades earlier on the *Great Republic*. Other vessels quickly adopted the crew-saving iron donkey.

The next logical development was a shift from the tern to a four-masted craft. It began in 1879 with the conversion of the steamer *Weybosset* to a four-masted schooner. The following year Goss, Sawyer, and Packard, one of the leading Bath yards, produced the 995-ton, four-master *William L. White.* Sixty-seven more of the big craft came down the ways before the end of the decade. The need for still larger vessels led to the five-masted schooner *Governor Ames* in 1889. Some 55 others followed. The highest development of the coastal schooner, the six-master, did not appear until the Camden, Maine, yard of Holly M. Bean launched the *George W. Wells* in 1900. She could haul 5,000 tons in one load. Yet the six-masters were efficient. The largest of them, the *Wyoming,* required a crew of only twelve. With the six-masters, both wooden hulls and big schooners reached their greatest practical size. The freak *Thomas W. Lawson,* Fore River shipyard's steel-hulled, seven-master schooner, proved so unhandy that the experiment was not repeated.

Although 1907 was a good year for the big schooners they soon lost much of the trade to barges and a new generation of steel-hulled steam colliers. The reasons are a good example of the interrelationship between seemingly unrelated events. The "custom of the port" at Hampton Roads was that vessels loaded in turn as they arrived. This meant that a vessel might lay idle for several days before taking on cargo since colliers tended to arrive earlier than they could load. Under those conditions it made no sense to operate steam colliers with their high crew, power, and amortization costs. In 1909 the Virginian Railroad completed its Sewalls Point coal piers. For the first time Hampton Roads had surplus coal-loading capacity, and within two months the Coastwise Transportation Company ordered a pair of 8,000-ton steamers. By 1915 the trade had attracted 16 steamers whereas few schooners joined the coal fleet after 1909. Sailing craft would continue to handle a dwindling portion of the trade down to the Depression, but it was largely restricted to that with ports not normally served by barges or colliers.

Most of the schooners were owned in shares by a group of investors, but some large sailing fleets existed. The largest, Crowell and Thurlow, formed in 1900, owned as many as 100 vessels at its peak. In 1912 Crowell and Thurlow began to shift to the bigger, more efficient powered craft. The economies of scale caused the largest New England coal company, Koppers Coal Company, in 1924 to create a shipping concern—the Mystic Steamship Company. It embraced the steamers of Crowell and Thurlow as well as the fleet of the New England Fuel and Transportation Company. Mystic operated through World War II and maintained a limited flow of coal to northeastern power plants into the 1960s.

Coal remained almost exclusively a coastal trade until after World War II. What limited exports did occur went to Canada and the West Indies although Britain, beset by a union's strike, purchased 11 million tons in 1926. While Newport News was the preeminent coal-shipping port, New York increasingly developed a transshipment trade with its satellite ports. In 1902 that totaled 10 million tons, largely anthracite, but in 1911 the figure had risen to 25 million, most of it bituminous. No better indication of the decline of the northeastern Pennsylvania fields and the domination of the southern Appalachian ones can be found than the report that coal shipments from Philadelphia in 1911 amounted to only 7 million tons, two-thirds of that bituminous.

Frederick Tudor inaugurated the trade in ice in 1805 when he first cut blocks at Saugus, Massachusetts, and shipped them to Martinique. His experiment proved so successful that he extended operations to Charleston in 1817, Savannah the next year, and New Orleans in 1820. His most-famed shipment was that to Calcutta in 1833—200 tons of ice, which arrived 70 percent intact. Initially, most of the ice came from Massachusetts ponds, although a well-organized trade existed as early as 1835 between northwestern Pennsylvania and the lower Mississippi River ports. Similar ice-harvesting operations along the Hudson River supplied New York City from huge ice houses that could hold as much as 200,000 tons of ice.

Very little ice came from Maine before the Civil War. The earliest shipment, a fortuitous one from Pittston on the Kennebec River to Baltimore in 1826, was followed by a few small shipments to New York, but as late as 1848–49 only 10,000 tons passed out of the mouth of the Kennebec. In 1860 James L. Cheeseman, a former Hudson River ice merchant, began cutting ice on the Kennebec. He revolutionized the industry by supplying his workers with improved cutting tools and mechanizing the handling of the blocks. During the Civil War, Cheeseman sold so much ice to the federal government that the amount shipped from the river tripled between 1860 and 1863, when it reached 30,000 tons. Philadelphia's Knickerbocker Ice Company purchased the Kennebec operation in 1868 and pushed its growth over the next three decades. In the peak year of 1890 forty-eight gigantic ice houses graced the banks of the river between Bath and Augusta. They shipped 1,441,000 tons while their competitors along the Penobscot dispatched an additional 1,651,000 tons. That year the Maine ice houses employed 25,000 men and required the services of 1,000 houses during the harvesting season.

Initially ice moved to market in the holds of old schooners unable to compete on more challenging routes. This changed when in 1889 Benjamin M. Morse's Knickerbocker Towing Company ordered the first of over 160 large barges with which it quickly gained control of the ice-shipping trade. In 1899 Morse's son Charles merged all the ice companies serving the Boston, New York, Philadelphia, Baltimore, and Washington markets into the single mammoth American Ice Company, but it was the dying gasp of the natural ice industry. Artificial ice and home electric refrigeration had arrived. As a harbinger of things to come, no ice left the Kennebec after 1900. The last shipment from Maine occurred a decade later since the Hudson could now supply the declining demands of the metropolitan areas.

Two little-remembered trades that employed large numbers of vessels—lime and granite—centered upon a small section of Maine's Penobscot Bay. On the mainland near the shipbuilding towns of Thomaston and Rockland were limestone beds that produced rock that could be calcified or burnt into lime for mortar. As early as 1734, lime kilns in Thomaston shipped their product to Boston. In 1828 the kilns operating there needed 89 vessels to take their product to market. In 1880 production reached 1,800,000 casks. Since a kiln burned 30 cords of wood each time it was fired, a flotilla of small, roughly built schooners, sloops, and brigs scoured the shores and islands of the bay for kiln-wood and scraps from sawmills. A second fleet of "Johnny wood-boats" brought fuel from New Brunswick as early as 1848. The lime normally flowed to market in Boston, New York, and Europe in the holds of schooners. Like the ice traders, many were old craft, no longer suitable for their original trades, very tightly calked in hull and deck since the lime, once wet was very flammable. Traditionally the lime carriers returned with salt to preserve the fish caught by the Maine farmer-fishermen. Although some lime production continues to the present, the effective end came with a March 3, 1907, fire that destroyed most of the kilns.

In the 1830s several of the islands in Penobscot Bay, notably Hurricane, Vinalhaven, and Little Deer, began to ship granite for the curbs, buildings, lighthouses, breakwaters, and monuments of the East Coast. By 1890 Maine could claim production of more granite than any other state in the Union. The twin advantages of the Penobscot Bay quarries, proximity to deepwater moorings and cheap water movement, were difficult to overcome. The granite schooners were easily recognized by their set of heavy booms needed to hoist the heavy blocks, broad beam for stability, and low bulwarks to ease loading. Although most stone moved in relatively small blocks, an occasional one was very large. In the 1870s one of the Vinalhaven quarries shipped to Troy, New York, at the head of river navigation on the Hudson, a block 60 × 5 × 5½ feet that weighed 165 tons.

Bangor remained the world's leading lumber port through most of the last quarter of the nineteenth century. Her position gradually weakened as the consumption of easily accessible timber increased costs to the point that Canadian and Florida lumber could compete on the eastern market. In the twentieth century the Maine lumbering operations shifted to pulpwood, and paper mills sprang up along the clear, swift-flowing inland rivers of the Pine Tree State. Great log drives downriver to the pulping plants replaced the ride to Bangor's docks while, below the plants, contaminated wash waters fouled the rivers and the fresh air with their unmistakable marks. Nor were the Maine rivers unique in their destruction. The Connecticut and the Hudson suffered as grievously, but none so horribly as the Kanawha in West Virginia, which hosted twenty-miles of chemical plants.

The southern yellow-pine forests attracted few lumbermen before 1880 because of the fancied superiority of northern white pine for structural and shipbuilding timbers. However, the decline of the northern forests after 1880 allowed pine lumber from southern Georgia and northern Florida to flow outward from Jacksonville, Pensacola, and Mobile. Not only did the terns and four-masters that carried the lumber haul it to the metropolitan Northeast but they serviced a large secondary trade with Cuba and the West Indies. One interesting variant of the trade developed after 1908 in which Philadelphia merchants shipped coal south in barges to New Bern, North Carolina, and exchanged it for lumber for the homeward trip. The southern lumber trade continued to rely on water shipment until the Depression of 1929. It never returned wholeheartedly to sea thereafter.

Insofar as sailing craft were concerned, the coal trade had died by 1921. With its demise the price of big schooners plummeted. In 1929 a four-master that cost $200,000 to build in 1918 could be purchased for $5,000. Most of the dwindling fleet of schooners hauled lumber to Miami in the mid-1920s as the Florida city underwent its first great land boom, or carried railroad ties from southern ports to Boston and New York. Smaller schooners and terns carted bulk goods and pick-up cargoes to smaller ports normally ignored by the coastal steamers. The last commercial schooner went down the ways at Stonington, Maine, in 1938. She was a small, 55-ton local trading craft that scarcely evoked even a memory of the great wind-propelled trading fleets.

4. The Western Coastal Trades

Although much of the local freight of San Francisco Bay was handled by a fleet of scow schooners that first appeared in the 1850s, the traffic moving down the rivers emptying into it was controlled by the California Steam Navigation Company. The line had begun on the Sacramento River but had spread its control throughout the bay region. Its magnificent steamer, *Chrysopolis,* which entered the Sacramento River service in 1860, set a standard of opulence that more than equaled that of the palatial Hudson River boats of the era. In 1869 the Central Pacific Railroad purchased the company. Three years later the railroad gained a monopoly of service on the Sacramento River by acquiring an interest in the California Pacific Railroad. This ensured that the movement of goods from inland points to the various railheads around the bay would remain firmly under control of the railroads. The Central Pacific, however, faced competition in the late 1870s as the Southern Pacific built northward through California. In 1879 it constructed the *Solano,* a massive train ferry capable of carrying both a train and its locomotive, which saved an hour in crossing Suisun Bay. About 1900, the Santa Fe Railroad instituted its own ferry service between San Francisco and its railhead at Richmond. Five years later the Key Route interurban line began its own cross-bay passenger ferries. The Key Route built to a peak in 1930. Soon afterwards the Great Depression and the opening of the Oakland and Golden Gate bridges eliminated need for the ferries.

Although the Pacific Mail rebuilt its San Francisco-Panama fleet with iron-hulled steamers in 1873–75, it paid little attention to the California coastal service. The local trade, therefore, rested in the hands of Goodall, Nelson, and Perkins, a firm organized for that purpose in 1861. During the centennial year the line reorganized as the Pacific Coast Steamship Company. The new name was appropriate. It dominated the coastal trade from Victoria in British Columbia to San Diego in California although competitors, usually tied to one of the northern transcontinental railroads, appeared from time to time. In 1881 the company passed into the hands of the Oregon Improvement Company.

Despite the paucity of good harbors along the California coast, most of the state's commerce had to move by water since the Pacific coastal range inhibited the construction of roads and the rail network had not yet spun its steel web. As a result, bitter political feuds developed between coastal settlements hoping to win state and federal support for the harbor improvements that they assumed would make them the regional trade center. Perhaps the most noted of these were the thirty-year struggle of San Pedro to become the port for Los Angeles, and San Diego's long fight for recognition as a major port.

Three bulk trades that developed in the last quarter of the nineteenth century left indelible marks on western shipping. The opening of the King County, Washington, coal mines in the 1870s created a collier trade between the Puget Sound ports and San Francisco in which the Oregon Coal and Navigation Company and the Pacific Improvement Company played major roles. By 1881, shipments for the San Francisco market alone reached towards 200,000 tons. A direct result of the coal trade was the Lake Washington Canal at Seattle. The coal mines were within easy carrying distance of fresh-water Lake Washington east of Seattle. If colliers could be loaded there, it would eliminate the heavy repair costs of the wharves along Seattle's *teredo* (shipworm)-infested waterfront. Although work started in 1893, constructing a canal connecting the lake and Puget Sound proved too great for local resources and had to be finished during 1911–17 by the Army Corps of Engineers.

Better remembered, however, was the massive movement of lumber from the northern California, Oregon, and Washington forests southward, eastward, and ultimately to the Orient. It began in a small way before the Civil War when enterprising San Francisco businessmen established sawmills in the northern California redwood country. Logging took a jump in volume when West Coast railroad building created a great demand for ties. As along the East Coast, coastal schooners served the trade. Generally two- and three-masters, they had shallow draft to enable them to work the coves and anchorages at whose head so often stood the sawmills. Two good examples still exist: The *C. A. Thayer* of 1895 at San Francisco and the *Wawona* of 1897 at Seattle. About 1880, auxiliary steam schooners began to be built for the lumber and produce trades. Their small (about 100 horsepower) plants sat aft and discharged smoke through thin funnels. The auxiliaries soon developed into full-powered steamers known locally as "steam schooners." The steam schooners initially were "single-ended," meaning that their cargo-handling gear was all forward of the machinery. The *Wapama* is an example now on exhibit in San Francisco. "Double-ended" steam schooners first appeared in 1905,

Lumber carriers from Europe and California await cargoes on a snowy day in 1905 at Port Blakeley, Washington. Despite the size of the wharf, few mechanical loading facilities can be seen. Courtesy of the National Maritime Museum

but their heyday did not come until World War I. In that configuration the machinery remained in the conventional midship location with cargo stowed both fore and aft.

These doughty little craft squeezed into the dog-holes of the redwood coast of northern California, where they lay moored bow and stern but always at the mercy of a sudden gale. They frequently loaded from overhead cables because the inlets were too small and their shores too rocky to use piers. Other craft, generally larger, braved the fogs of Puget Sound to carry away the produce of half a thousand sawmills.

Some of the lumber cut along the banks of the Columbia River moved to San Francisco or San Diego in great log rafts. When initially used in the last years of the nineteenth century, they were cigar-shaped collections of wood 600 feet long, 60 across, and 26 feet deep, which contained as much as 4 million board feet. Later versions grew to 900 feet in length and 7 million board feet in volume. Rafts continued to be towed southward until World War II despite the dangers of fire and breakup. In the coastal waters of the Northwest logs were handled in massive booms, the largest of which contain 2 million board feet. In the decade between 1880 and 1890 production increased 350 percent to 2 billion board feet. Thereafter, the growth of water shipment slowed as reductions in railroad rates allowed the land carrier to attract large shipments.

Nearly as important was the grain trade of Washington and Oregon. It had already made its mark before the Civil War, as mentioned earlier, but the real outpouring had to await the construction in 1873 of the Oregon City locks on the Willamette River, which opened direct barge shipment from the upper reaches of the river to Portland.

On the Columbia River, the Cascades and the Dalles broke up river service into three distinct segments. The earliest, naturally, ran from below the Cascades to Astoria. It saw its first steamboat in 1851 while two years later enterprising operators made use of the newly opened mule-powered portage railroad at the Cascades to ship a steamer in sections to the Upper Cascades. She ran to the Dalles. At the end of the decade the steamer *Colonel Wright* pushed her way through the swift-flowing current between the Dalles and upriver points. During the Idaho and Montana gold rush she gained fame in the 1860s by traversing the Snake and Clearwater rivers nearly to the gold fields. She offered a more convenient, if more expensive, route to the mines than the Missouri

River steamers. They seldom got within 125 miles of the mines. Between 1878 and 1896, locks were built around the Cascades, and in 1915 the Celilo Canal opened the Columbia as far as Priest Rapids and the Snake all the way to Lewiston, Idaho. The latter attracted little traffic during the ensuing six decades. In about 1945 a tug and barge demonstrated the feasibility of bringing out grain by water, but not until the Lower Granite Dam opened in 1975 to make possible barge service to Lewiston did large shipments start.

Local shipping in the Northwest early developed a structure. In 1861 the operators on the Columbia and Willamette rivers formed the Oregon Steam Navigation Company, which quickly monopolized shipping on those two waterways. Aside from the normal package-freight trade and local passenger service, Oregon Steam Navigation provided the means of bringing to Portland the wheat grown in the Willamette and Umpqua valleys. By 1868 that grain had begun to find a market in Australia, and two years later Oregon achieved stature as a major wheat-growing state. Further strengthening the Oregon Steam Navigation Company were the Upper Columbia River and Montana gold strikes since the line controlled the easiest means of moving goods to them—the portage railroad around the impassible Cascades passage. Henry Villard purchased Oregon Steam Navigation in 1879 to use it as a feeder for his Northern Pacific Railroad. He consolidated the Columbia River line with his Oregon Railway and Navigation Company, which ran express steamers from Portland to San Francisco. About 1904, Oregon Railway and Navigation passed into the control of the Union Pacific Railroad, changing its name to the San Francisco and Portland Steamship Company.

Portland faced substantial disadvantages as an ocean port because of its location 90 miles up the Columbia River, at whose mouth a huge and constantly shifting bar existed. It restricted entry to vessels drawing more than 15–18 feet. In 1894 a jetty was completed on the south side of the entrance in an effort to scour out a deeper passage. Its northern sister was completed in 1917. Together they created a 55-foot channel depth that was more than adequate until the arrival of supertankers in the 1970s. It is a marginal depth for the large tankers and bulk carriers of the 1980s, which often draw the same 55 feet.

Early service to Alaska, chiefly by the Pacific Coast Steamship Company, was limited because of the small population there although a substantial summer tourist trade to Sitka developed in the 1880s. The initial gold strike occurred around Juneau in 1880, but it created little traffic. After 1890 Seattle increasingly supplanted San Francisco as the entryway to Alaska. It was Seattle at which the *Portland* arrived on July 17, 1897, with the news that set in motion the great Klondike Gold Rush. At the height of the rush anything that could be renovated sufficiently to float northward carried fortune seekers. In February 1898 alone, 44 different craft entered Skagway, the port for the gold field. Out of the scramble the Alaska Steamship Company (controlled by the Guggenheim interests which owned the Kennecott copper mine) emerged as the dominant line. It served primarily to bring out the copper from the Kennicott mine and incidentally as Alaska's tie to the lower forty-eight states. After the mines played out, the general cargo traffic proved insufficient to support the line, and it ceased operations in 1971. Since that time the cargo bound for the northern state—whether intended for the southern panhandle or the oil fields north of the Arctic Circle—has traveled by barge. As a result the Pacific Northwest is home to the world's largest concentration of tugs and barges.

The great name in Pacific Northwest shipping during the first half of the twentieth century was Hubbard F. Alexander. A Seattle shipowner who started in the Alaska trade, he built his small Alaska-Pacific Steamship Company and its successors into the leading coastal service north of Los Angeles. In 1910 Alexander arranged with the Pacific Navigation Company to offer through-billing from Los Angeles to Seattle in conjunction with his San Francisco-Seattle Admiral Line, which gave him a great advantage at a time of intense competition along the coast. In 1912 five lines offered Pacific coastal passenger service. Two years later the number climbed to eleven. Most traversed only the California coast, where poor roads made water travel imperative, but others ventured into longer services. The best-known vessels and certainly the fastest were the Northern Pacific Steamship Company's *Great Northern* and *Northern Pacific*. Built in 1914–15 to run in competition with the Southern Pacific Railroad's Shasta Limited, they dashed from Flavel, Oregon, at the mouth of the Columbia River, to San Francisco as swiftly as the train covered its route from Portland.

In 1916 Alexander acquired the venerable Pacific Coast Steamship Company, renamed his combined operation the Pacific Steamship Company, but still sailed it as the Admiral Line. Its move to leadership was aided by the outbreak of World War I, which diverted the *Great Northern* and *Northern Pacific* into federal service. After the war the Admiral Line continued its domination, especially following acquisition of the *Great Northern,* appropriately renamed *H. F. Alexander.* Nevertheless, rail and truck competition and a bad rate war in 1929 took their toll. Alexander fled into retirement in 1931, and two years later his successors sold out to the Dollar Steamship Company. The new owners had little time to enjoy their prize before being hit by the West Coast maritime strike of 1934 and the greatly increased safety requirements that followed the *Morro Castle* disaster. The two combined to finish off nearly all the surviving coastal operations, even the profitable San Pedro-San Francisco express service of the former East Coast liners *Harvard* and *Yale.* In 1936 Dollar abandoned both passenger and freight service along the coast.

Despite the demise of long-distance passenger service along the Pacific Coast, commuter runs persisted. On San Francisco Bay they were ended by the construction of the Golden Gate and Transbay bridges in 1936–37. Service on Puget Sound was long

The express liner *H. F. Alexander* competed with the fastest trains between Portland, Oregon, and San Francisco. Official U.S. Navy Photograph

handled by a group of small steamers known locally as the Mosquito Fleet. Most of those lines passed into the hands of the Black Ball Line of the Puget Sound Navigation Company, which in 1929 operated 17 different routes. Its service contracted as roads and bridges were built to tie the isolated island settlements together and with the Seattle-Tacoma metropolitan center. In 1950 the state of Washington purchased the Black Ball routes and has since operated them as a state ferry system.

5. Labor

Prior to 1865, labor legislation concerning seamen primarily reinforced discipline and ensured the maintenance of order on the not illogical premise that life at sea required unquestioning obedience from the crew. This concept remained acceptable so long as both the owners and the ships' officers treated the crews with reasonable care and avoided taking unfair advantage of them. These limitations succumbed during the Golden Age to the pressure to squeeze every penny of profit from each voyage and to owners and officers who found nothing immoral in taking unfair advantage of their crews. Either as a result or coincidentally, that change came at a time when native-born Americans abandoned the sea and crews became composed of foreign-born seamen, frequently non–English-speaking. By the mid-1880s informed observers estimated that 90 percent of the seamen on deepwater American vessels were foreign-born. Many of those, it must be noted in justice to the rough and tough bully mates and other officers of the American merchant marine, were among the poorest examples of mankind that could be dredged up from the ports of the world.

In part because of the character of the men attracted to the nineteenth-century merchant marine, organizations to ameliorate conditions of life afloat and ashore sprang up in various ports, notably New York. Before 1825 nearly all grew out of religious activities. In 1816 the Marine Bible Society appeared in New York, to be followed in short order by the Port of New York Society for Promoting the Gospel Among Seamen and the more concisely named New York Marine Missionary Society. The city boasted a Mariner's Church in 1820, and the following year the New York Bethel Union, a sailor's religious organization, initiated a program of services held on board individual vessels in the port. Despite, or perhaps because of, their assaults on drinking and prostitution, the religious societies met a general apathy. Even so, they undoubtedly did more for the well-being of seamen than any other group, especially the inadequate marine hospitals maintained by the federal government. In 1828 the American Seamen's Friend Society formed in New York as a general seamen's benevolent society. It soon established a badly needed Seamen's Bank for Savings, which still exists but is no longer restricted to sailor depositors. American Seamen's Friend Society operated the Home for Colored Sailors and subsequently one for whites.

The earliest Federal intervention into the conditions of service for seamen came with the 1850 act outlawing flogging on merchant craft. It would be nearly another quarter century before Congress acted again. In 1871 physical conditions on board some vessels had reached the point that Congress belatedly authorized the revocation of the licenses of officers found guilty of mistreatment.

Meanwhile, New York State in 1866 attempted to correct another abuse by requiring the licensing of sailors' boardinghouses. It caused a reduction of those horror houses, little better than thieves dens, from 169 in 1863 to 90 in 1872. The boardinghouses were commonly operated by "crimps," shipping masters who provided boarding and lodging to sailors at high rates and collected large advances on the sailors' pay upon delivering them to captains in need of hands. Thus the unlucky seaman was already indebted to the ship when he signed on. He seldom was paid until the end of the voyage, so the inflated price of any clothing or material he purchased from the ship's slop chest was deducted from his pay on discharge. He therefore went ashore at the end of a voyage with very little cash, which he commonly blew on an orgy of high living, only to find himself befuddled, broke, and back in the clutches of the crimp.

Congress reinforced the assault on the crimps with the Shipping Commissioners Act of 1872, which provided that shipping articles (the papers that set pay and conditions of service signed by all seamen before joining the crew) had to be signed in the presence of a federal shipping commissioner to ensure that the seaman had not been shanghaied, i.e., forcibly or unknowingly signed on by a crimp to collect the sailor's advance. The law, moreover, required that the seaman be paid off in person, but the provision turned out to be less effective than anticipated. During 1884 Congress in the Dingley Act attempted to close the loopholes by prohibiting advances on wages and limiting allotments to close relatives. Two years later, however, the boardinghouse keepers secured an amendment which largely nullified the law by permitting their payment as "original creditors."

One of the running complaints of late nineteenth-century seamen was their liability for arrest as deserters if they left their vessel, no matter how bad the conditions, before the end of the voyage. The coastal seamen in 1874 were the first to secure exemption. This was confirmed in the 1895 Maguire Act, which also set controls on the use of allotments and prohibited the attachment of a sailor's clothing by his debtors. In the *Arago* case of 1897, however, the Supreme Court limited the application of the law by exempting the coast-wise legs of foreign voyages from the nonimprisonment provisions. The court, noting the nature of work at sea and the shipping articles, held that the thirteenth Amendment's prohibition against involuntary servitude did not apply to seamen. The White Act of 1898 in direct response to the *Arago* decision, formally abolished imprisonment for desertion in American and nearby waters so long as the sailor was a United States citizen, which only half were. More important in the lives of most sailors, however, were the provisions that forbad the corporal punishment such as that meted out by the "bully mates" who heretofore had relied on their fists, belaying pins, and handspikes to enforce discipline.

The final step in the legal freedom of the seaman came in the Seaman's or LaFollette Act of 1915. It halted imprisonment for desertion in American or foreign ports; gave the seaman the right to demand half of his earned wages at any way port where cargo was handled; greatly improved the conditions of work and safety; established the two-watch system for sailors and the three-watch system (four hours on, eight hours off watch) for the black gang; and required that three-quarters of the men in any department must be able to understand English. The law was the result of the effective lobbying of Andrew Furuseth of the International Seamen's Union. Furuseth hoped that the legalization of ship-jumping would cause low-paid foreign seamen to desert in American ports and thereby drive up the international wage level to American standards. This, of course, would make American shipping once again competitive and, Furuseth hoped, create more jobs for the members of his union. The effect of the law was negligible, if not actually counterproductive. For example, it forced Pacific Mail to give up Chinese crews on their transpacific vessels, with the result that the line simply abandoned the service, and when the World War I shipping boom collapsed so did Pacific Mail.

The earliest reported strike occurred in 1850 when crews who had deserted from vessels at San Francisco came back from their fling at gold prospecting to find that the captains had cut wages. Since enough men to man the vessels had filled their craw with gold seeking and were ready to return to sea, the strike failed. So did a strike by longshoremen the following year for higher wages and shorter hours. Although sporadic strikes for higher wages occurred, chiefly at San Francisco, none succeeded. In part this reflected the relatively high wages paid American seamen. In 1872 the *Scientific American* observed that an American first-class engineer earned $240 per month while his British counterpart received but $80. Nearly as striking was the $40 per month paid American ordinary seamen. His British counterpart got only $12.50.

Even so, unionization took root in the maritime trades during the last quarter of the nineteenth century much as it did in other branches of American industry. American maritime unionization has its roots in the Social-Democratic labor movements in northern and central Europe. It had its greatest success among the seasonally employed and heavily Scandinavian seamen of the Great Lakes, where the Marine Engineers Beneficial Association formed in 1875 and the Lake Seamen's Union three years later. The Lakes owners displayed more tolerance for the organizations than did their saltwater counterparts and chose to work with the labor organizations rather than against them. As a result the Lakes have had an enviable record of labor peace.

On the West Coast, where unions were strongest because of a relative scarcity of workers, the Longshore Lumbermen's Protective Association formed in 1880 among the men handling the lumber-schooners. In 1885 some of the lumber schooner crewmen formed the Coast Seamen's Union as a part of Karl Marx's International Workingmen's Association, but the union soon forsook its radical origins. The following year the Pacific Steamship Sailors' Union appeared. The two combined in 1901 as the Sailors' Union of the Pacific under the leadership of the dedicated and energetic Andrew Furuseth. Furuseth dominated the Sailor's Union of the Pacific and the National (later International) Seamen's Union, the national umbrella union for all marine crafts established by the American Federation of Labor in 1892, until the rise of a new generation of radical leaders during the turbulent 1930s.

One of Furuseth's problems, along with his uncompromising support of the craft union concept, was his running feud with the longshoremen's union. Not until the 1930s would the two unions cooperate, but when they did they were able to place the West Coast shipping industry in such a straightjacket that it has yet to recover. Although the NSU could claim 115,000 members in 1920, it did not have the strength to withstand the collapse of the World War I shipping boom and the hostility of the West Coast longshoremen. In 1921, the Shipping Board proposed a 15 percent reduction in the high war-induced wages, abolition of the three watch system, elimination of overtime, and a reduction in subsistence as a means of restoring the competitiveness of American vessels. The International Seamen's Union (ISU) and the Marine Engineers staged a six-weeks-long strike but lost when the longshoremen refused their support. The result was that between 1921 and 1934 the American merchant marine operated on an open shop, or occasionally a company union, basis. ISU membership fell by nearly 67 percent, and wages dropped 50 percent.

Although there were few labor troubles between 1921 and 1934, except in local situations, the employers did not use the time to develop solutions to the industry's obvious labor relations problems. Neither did they take steps to win the loyalty of their employees. Wages were kept low while living conditions ranged from bad to terrible. Particularly irritating to the seamen were the continuous discharge books, known to union members as "fink" books, in which the master of a vessel could enter comments on the performance of a seaman. Without his book a sailor could not get a job, yet with it he was at the mercy of the whims of unscrupulous captains. Longshoremen detested the daily "shape up" at which foremen, often capriciously or corruptly, picked their gangs. The shipowners compounded their problems in 1933 by ignoring the unions in drawing up the industry code called for in the National Industrial Recovery Act. This naturally played into the hands of the radicals in the maritime labor movement, already discontented over the ineffectiveness of Furuseth's leadership.

The arrival in Washington of the New Deal brought changes in maritime labor relations. The federal government shifted from supporting the owners to siding with the unions in most disputes. The rout of the old system began in the National Labor Relations Act of 1935 and was completed the following year by the Merchant Marine Act. The latter wrought fundamental changes in life on board ship by tightening licensing requirements and requiring the three-watch system at sea in all departments. It mandated wholly American citizenship for the crews on subsidized cargo vessels and 90 percent of those on board subsidized passenger craft. The regulations drastically upgraded the accommodations and conditions of work of the seafarers. But the law did not eliminate the hated "fink" book, although its use became optional after 1938. The new militancy spawned by the Depression and the New Deal's pro-union stand brought a resurgence of union power. Between 1934 and 1937 the West Coast longshoremen, now formed into the International Longshoremen's and Warehousemen's Union under the leadership of the militant radical Harry Bridges, and the seamen led by the equally militant Harry Lundeberg brought the shipping industry to its knees.

The successes of the unions went far beyond simple correction of abuses. The Pacific longshoremen, for instance, struck 450 times between 1935 and 1956 to force employers to accept featherbedding practices. As late as 1961 the Pacific Maritime Association, the employers' organization, paid the longshoremen $29 million in order to get the union to agree to eliminate some of the worst featherbedding. On the East Coast the longshoremen practiced nearly as poor citizenship. Many of the New York City locals passed into the hands of racketeers who called strikes as a means of extorting money from the shippers and ultimately forced the formation of the Port of New York Authority as a means of combating crime on the waterfront. In Boston the longshoremen by 1960 had gotten so far out of control, even of their own leadership, that they staged local strikes over nearly any minor provocation, such as attempts to enforce rules against smoking in cargo holds.

6. Shipbuilding

Building costs rose rapidly during the Civil War. A 1,200–ton vessel could be built in Maine before the war for $47 per ton. After the war the price was $75 per ton, and even in the depression at the end of the war decade it did not drop under $68. The builders argued that the costs were kept high by the price of materials, especially the timbers imported from Canada. The same difficulties faced iron shipbuilders since much of their material had to pass through the tariff curtain with its high rates. The impact of the tariff on American building costs was hotly debated during the 1870s and 1880s by politicians, builders, and ironmakers. The builders generally, but not universally, claimed that they were competitive with the Europeans except for raw material costs. Other observers suggested that the iron building yards did not push actively for relief because of fear that dropping rates or giving drawbacks for shipbuilding materials would also open the way for Congress to reduce the rates on foreign-built craft. Others, like the Philadelphia builder Charles Cramp, believed that the problems of the American builders were chiefly poor design and inferior engines. His experience went far to prove his point.

Whatever the reason, the shipbuilding industry declined. Wooden yards continued profitable only in Maine and in the lumber areas of the West Coast, where the proximity of great forests or the accessibility of Canadian or southern oaks and pines allowed shipbuilders to carry on their traditional labors. The two great metropolitan wooden shipbuilding centers, New York and Boston, ceased significant production by the end of the 1860s. New York, already a high-cost building area because of the need to import every stick of timber at least 150 miles, received a coup de grace when her shipwrights struck in 1866 for an eight-hour day. She built her last large wooden vessel in 1869. Boston, which had no advantage over Maine, had effectively dropped out of wooden building before the Civil War and made only a limited effort to construct iron hulls.

Wooden vessels represented the bulk of those coming off the ways throughout the nineteenth century, although the day of the wooden sailing ship had long since turned to dusk. Even so, production in the United States remained over 500,000 tons a year during the 1870s, more than twice Britain's wooden hull output. The last wooden square-rigger slid down the ways in 1893. Coastal schooners, fishermen, work craft, and pleasure boats continued to take shape in a myriad of yards, as they would into the middle years of the twentieth century, but the deep-sea trade demanded larger and stronger craft. A handful of iron- and steel-hulled square riggers joined the fleet after 1893; the last, the steel-hulled, case-oil carrier *Atlas* in 1902. She was fated to spend much of her life at the end of a tow line.

One of the problems facing the American iron-hull builders, as well as engine manufacturers, was the preoccupation of the United States ironworks with railroad iron, rails, nails, and structural shapes for bridges. Few American mills could roll the shapes or plates required by the shipbuilders, and those that did demanded high prices. Despite the general impression left by polemic writers of the late nineteenth and early twentieth century, most American coastal steamers were iron-hulled after the 1870s. Nor should it be overlooked that the *City of Peking* and *City of Tokio*, which John Roach built for Pacific Mail in 1875, were the equal of any liner then in operation. Only the *Great Eastern* exceeded them in size.

Although British builders experimented with plates rolled from Bessemer steel in the early 1860s, the difficulty in achieving uniformity of strength delayed widespread use. In the latter part of the following decade, better, open-hearth, steel plates became available and were quickly adopted by British and continental yards. In the United States their high cost inhibited use. In 1883 John Roach, one of the most innovative of the post-Civil War American shipbuilders, began rolling steel plates for use in his yard at Chester, Pennsylvania. The following year he added a mill to produce open-hearth and crucible steels. This permitted him to build the first American steel-hulled merchantman, the *Alaskan* of the Oregon Railway and Navigation Company, in 1883 and win the contract for the first four vessels of the new navy. During the 1880s other mills began to forge heavy steel shapes, like crank-shafts for western river boats, but the capacity remained limited. As late as 1887 both Cramp and the Union Iron Works in San Francisco ordered propeller shafts abroad. The development of a sizable new market in heavy steel forgings, armor, and plate as a result of the rapid reconstruction of the navy during the four decades following 1883 induced steelmakers to invest in the plant necessary to produce the material needed by the shipbuilders. The difficulties in securing American steel at competitive prices have persisted to the present.

In one area, however, the United States did play an early role—petroleum tankers. In 1861 the brig *Elizabeth Watts* carried the first cargo of oil in wooden barrels to Europe. Two years later the British-registered *Ramsey* introduced tanks. Modern tankers, however, date from the German-American Petroleum Company's British-built *Glückauf* of 1885. The earliest American counterpart, the *Standard*, appeared three years later by Roach for John D. Rockefeller's Standard Oil Company. Standard Oil gradually built a large fleet of tankers and case-oil carriers, the latter being particularly useful in hauling kerosene to the large Chinese market, and experimented with barges on transatlantic runs between 1905 and the First World War. Initially, tankers carried finished products only, but in 1892 Standard started shipping crude oil by water. This not only increased safety but permitted the building of refineries near the market which offered clear economic benefits.

The great growth in tankers, however, came between 1914 and 1923 when the United States tanker fleet jumped 1,400 percent in numbers and 2,500 percent in tonnage as a result of the nearly insatiable thirst of the internal combustion engine and its spread throughout the nation and the world. In 1923 the amount of oil shipped east from California jumped 7,392,000 tons. As the world's oil companies moved farther and farther afield in their search for new sources, the demand for tankers rose. So did their size. After 1930 the opening of the East Texas fields shifted American tankers from Mexican and Caribbean runs to the shuttle between the Gulf and the East Coast refineries. Because of their operating costs, American flag tankers remained heavily concentrated in the protected trades from the Gulf and California until the decline of those fields in the 1960s, and then in the massive transit of Alaskan oil during the 1970s and 1980s.

Great changes also occurred in motive power. The original low-pressure, square boilers operated only to about 50 psi. before their structural weaknesses became evident. Therefore, during the 1870s cylindrical "Scotch" boilers became common since they could handle the increase of pressure to about the 70 pounds that was required by the two-cylinder compound engines then coming into use. The Scotch boiler had numerous advantages. It could be made from standard sheets, tubes, and rods, which permitted easy repair. Strong and able to withstand much abuse, they had the twin disadvantages of high weight and a long delay in raising steam because of the large amount of boiler water to be heated. As the engineers developed triple and quadruple expansion engines that utilized higher pressures to drive the additional pistons, boilers became stronger, but most retained a basically Scotch design since it could withstand pressures up to about 250 psi. In all of this civilian American designers played a minor role. They generally followed the lead of their European counterparts in both boiler and engine design.

In a few areas American engineers led. Prior to 1886 all launches relied on steam power. Then Frank Olfeldt patented a design in which a burner used naphtha both as its fuel and the source of gas to drive the pistons. Since the naphtha could be cooled and reused, the engine was essentially a closed circuit. This was a godsend to American steam-launch owners because it removed them from federal steamboat regulations, which required them to hire a licensed engineer to run the engine, an impossible cost for owners of 25–80 foot launches. It also offered a new market for what heretofore had been a petroleum waste product. Olfeldt transferred manufacturing rights to Charles Seabury, who established the Gas Engine and Power Company at Morris Heights on the Bronx side of the North River. The plant operated in conjunction with Seabury's hull-building operation, which resulted in the shipbuilding concern with what is undoubtedly the longest title in American maritime history: The Gas Engine and Power Company and Charles L. Seabury and Company Consolidated. After the turn of the century, however, the naphtha engines lost favor to the safer and more easily operated gasoline engines.

Along with the introduction of gasoline engines for small craft came the installation of diesel engines in larger craft. The initial development of the diesel came in Europe, especially in Germany, although the earliest commercial deep-sea installation appeared from the Danish yard of Burmeister and Wain. The chief impetus for the development of diesel engines, however, came from its adoption by the navies of the world as the surface power for their submarines. During and immediately following World War I the Shipping Board and a few private owners experimented unsuccessfully with semi-diesel engines. Regular diesels began to enter extended civilian use in the 1920s, when the war-promoted developments became available. As power increased, so did the number of installations. By the outbreak of World War II the diesel had effectively driven the reciprocating steam engine from new construction. The attractions of the diesel were several: It required a smaller engine room crew, it used relatively cheap fuel oil, and was simpler to operate.

One area in which the Americans participated in the technological development was the steam turbine. Although developed initially in England by Sir Charles A. Parsons and in Sweden by Carl G. P. de Laval in the 1880s, American electrical generator manufacturers soon took over. In 1897 the General Electric Company purchased the rights to a pressure-compounding design developed by Charles G. Curtis that proved better adapted to land-based than marine use although a number of shipboard installations were made. The Westinghouse Machine Company, on the other hand, acquired the rights to the Parsons designs. Because of the near impossibility of producing satisfactory reduction gears, all early turbines were direct drive even though this produced a higher than desirable propeller speed. The problem was one of achieving the constant and equal tooth pressures necessary for heavy-duty gearing, and it would not be solved until the introduction of floating teeth after World War I. Westinghouse attempted to solve the difficulty by using the turbines to drive dynamos that in turn powered motors that drove the propellers at more efficient speeds. Use of turbo-electric drives, as they were known, was largely restricted to American vessels. The best-known installations were in large naval vessels like the battleships of the *New Mexico, California,* and *West Virginia* classes and the aircraft carriers *Lexington,* and *Saratoga.* Experience proved, however, that the turbo electric and the later diesel-electric installations were less desirable than geared turbines. This became especially true as the more efficient superheated steam and higher pressures came into use.

Part of the increase in pressures and in temperature grew out of the increased use of oil for fuel. Here, American owners and engineers, especially on the Pacific Coast, played pioneering roles. Aside from various limited experiments beginning in the 1860s, the initial significant trial of oil came in 1902 on the Oceanic Steamship Company's liner *Mariposa* and the Matson freighter *Enterprise.* They proved so successful that the American-Hawaiian Steamship Company adopted oil for its new passenger-freighter *Nebraskan,* built in 1904. Her gain of $500 per day in reduced operating expenses, reduced bunkering time, and additional cargo revenue brought its rapid incorporation in new construction.

The American shipbuilding industry had a spectacular growth in the last decade of the century, largely as a result of the construction of the new steel-hulled "White Fleet" for the navy and the replacement of obsolescent vessels by commercial operators. William Cramp and Sons, then the preeminent Delaware River yard, moved from their crowded Kensington yard to a larger and more efficient one in South Philadelphia. On the West Coast, Union Iron Works enlarged its capacity. Three entirely new yards, two of them larger than any in the country, began production during the 1890s. Newport News Shipbuilding and Dry Dock Company was an offspring of the Chesapeake and Ohio Railroad and the godchild of its owner, Collis P. Huntington. It occupied ground near the great

C&O coal docks and rapidly became the nation's largest and most productive yard, as it remains today. The second concern, New York Shipbuilding Corporation, established its works in Camden, New Jersey, across the Delaware River from Philadelphia. Laid out by a group of highly skillful engineers, it was designed to make maximum use of the newly developed electric-powered cranes and hoists as well as the pneumatic riveting techniques developed in the Great Lakes yards. On Baltimore's harbor, the Maryland Steel Company erected a third major steel yard.

Considering the dynamism of the industry and the embrace of corporate concentration by much of the industrial and banking leadership of the nation, it was only a matter of time before someone or group attempted to form a single dominant shipbuilding concern. There were two significant efforts. One succeeded; the other did not. The successful one was the American Ship Building Company, which dominated but did not control construction on the Great Lakes. The other was a fiasco that illustrates the pitfalls of combination. The United States Shipbuilding Corporation was promoted in 1899–1901 by John W. Young, although Charles M. Schwab, the young, energetic, and very able head of Bethlehem Steel, emerged as the leading figure. Young gathered together four medium-sized eastern coast yards along with Union Iron Works and Bethlehem Steel. Unfortunately for the promoters, and the investors, the yards had been acquired at prices not warranted by either their working capital or their prospects. Therefore, the United States Shipbuilding collapsed into bankruptcy in 1905. From the debris the Bath Iron Works and Hyde Windlass Company arose again independent, and Schwab created a new, enlarged Bethlehem Steel Company that absorbed Union and two of the eastern yards. That launched Bethlehem on its shipbuilding voyage, which continues to the present.

At the outbreak of World War I the major steel shipbuilders were limited to fourteen, plus a handful of smaller ones that concentrated on yachts, tugs, or coastal craft. The shipping boom that preceded America's entry into World War I brought into being a handful of new yards, but most of the construction was handled by established firms. After American entry and the need for the "Bridge of Ships" became overwhelming, the country moved into a crash shipbuilding program. New yards were built, new techniques developed, and vessels rushed to completion, most too late for wartime service.

Since it was assumed that house carpenters could be readily trained as ship carpenters, a series of contracts were let in 1917 to hastily formed concerns in the Pacific Northwest and New England to produce both big schooners and wooden steamers. The program nearly collapsed because of the inexperience of the managers, most of whom knew little of maritime construction; the difficulty in converting the carpenters, and shortage in the East of sufficiently large timbers. Very few of the vessels remained active after the shipping market contracted in 1921.

Steel shipbuilding, however, proved exceptionally successful. Since most of the existing steel yards were filled with navy or private contracts, the Emergency Fleet Corporation (EFC), the government's merchant shipbuilding arm, had to locate hitherto untapped sources. The EFC of necessity ordered most of its steel vessels from concerns that had never built a vessel. The largest single contract went to the American International Corporation, the trading and engineering firm controlled by Stone and Webster. American International built and operated the largest shipyard ever attempted, a 50-way plant on Hog Island in the Delaware River adjacent to Philadelphia. Since traditional building methods were too slow to produce the vessels as rapidly as needed, American International and two other large EFC yards functioned only as fabrication centers, subcontracting portions of the vessel to bridge and structural steel shops around the United States and Canada. The resulting vessels were not pretty; their lines were made as straight as possible in order to speed production, but they proved seaworthy and reliable. They formed the core of the merchant marine between the wars, and many survived until after World War II when a new generation of standard-design freighters replaced them.

World War I first introduced widespread use of arc welding in shipbuilding. It was limited to repair work but gained both in stature and in experience as a result of the work done to resuscitate the German craft taken over in American ports after our entry into the war. In most cases the repairs involved extensive welding to return their damaged engines to service. Not until 1928 would welding come to play an important role in construction, but two years later the first all-welded cargo vessel went down the ways. In 1938 the Ingalls Shipbuilding Company established at Pascagoula, Mississippi, the nation's first yard designed to build only welded vessels.

The fifty years that followed the Civil War offered little hope for a revival of the merchant marine. The timorous efforts at restoration in the 1890s and before World War I proved that the nation's political leadership was not willing to expend the massive funds necessary to support a large American-flag, foreign-trade merchant fleet. Nor was it evident that the various special interests, in and out of the industry, were yet willing to abandon their privileged positions to ensure a healthy maritime trade.

Though the frontier-expansion period of the nation's history had passed, and with it the channeling role of the waterways, their maritime impact remained. Tankers hauled the bulk of the nation's petroleum and its products; colliers brought the coal that warmed New England and the Middle States; riverboats with their tows of barges carried coal, stone, and grain on the Mississippi, on the Hudson, on the Columbia, and elsewhere; ore carriers trundled the riches of the Mesabi to the steel mills of Pittsburgh and Gary, Buffalo, and Chicago; and a flotilla of local steamers scudded about the bays and lakes of the continent like so many water bugs carrying weary city dwellers and their families to their rustic paradises, summer cottages, and whimsical retreats.

Chapter Nine

CRASH PROGRAMS FOR SURVIVAL

ALTHOUGH SOME ECONOMIC NATIONALISTS AND IMPERIALISTS DURING the rise of the United States to international prominence championed an enlarged deep-sea merchant marine, they achieved scant success in transmitting their concerns to the general public. Most Americans, their horizons broken by waving grain, factory smokestacks, or towering trees forgot the role of the oceans, rivers, and lakes in developing the nation and frequently in carrying themselves to their homestead. The nation stood with its back to its waterways and exalted the ribbons of steel with their coal-gulping locomotives that pulled strings of cars hither and yon like so many worker ants. That view ignored both the efficiency of water transportation and its critical role in the economic health of the country. Twice within the first half of the twentieth century, Americans would feel the price of their failure to remember those basic truths.

The outbreak of World War I created opportunities for American shipping that the country had not seen since the Napoleonic era. Unfortunately, unlike a hundred years earlier, the foreign-trade merchant marine was inadequate to benefit fully from American neutrality. Indeed, the merchant marine was so limited that it could not even handle the needs of the nation itself.

1. The United States Shipping Board

President Woodrow Wilson, even before the war began, had complained of the inadequacy of an American merchant marine that

297

carried less than 10 percent of the nation's foreign trade. An enlarged merchant marine was critical to his economic program of lower tariffs, a broadened capital base for the nation, and increased foreign trade. Wilson seized on the shipping dislocations of 1914–15, which upset American foreign trade patterns, to further his aims.

In January 1915 the president suggested formation of a federal shipping agency. Initially rejected by Congress, the proposal after reshaping by Secretary of the Treasury William G. McAdoo was adopted the following year. The Shipping Act of 1916 created a federal agency, the United States Shipping Board (USSB) to promote, investigate, regulate, and administer the shipping industry. Recognizing the small size of the shipping community, Congress empowered the Board to create a $50 million government corporation to purchase and operate vessels. Although envisioned as a means of equipping the United States to carry on neutral commerce in wartime, the project stirred little interest. The bipartisan five-man board was not organized until late in January 1917. From the start the Shipping Board was hampered by rapid turnover in membership, which reflected as much as anything its low political standing. Of the thirty-five men named commissioners between 1917 and 1933, only twelve served for more than three consecutive years. The provision that none of the commissioners would be drawn from the shipping industry ensured that they had scant knowledge of the industry even when they stayed long enough to learn their job.

In one of its earliest actions the board prohibited the transfer of American craft to foreign flags, although it did not secure the right to commandeer foreign-flag vessels building in United States yards until June. Meanwhile the board created the Emergency Fleet Corporation (EFC) to build and own the vessels required to meet America's shipping needs. William Denman, the San Francisco admiralty lawyer who chaired the Shipping Board, soon found himself in conflict with General George W. Goethals, the builder of the Panama Canal and the General Manager of the Corporation, over the latter's role. In July the president forced both to resign and brought in Edward N. Hurley to run the Board and navy engineer Rear Admiral George W. Capps (replaced in December by Charles Peiz) to run the Corporation. Peiz and Charles M. Schwab of Bethlehem Steel, who assumed Goethals's role in January 1918, gradually brought order to the maritime program. During the summer of 1917 the Shipping Board took over enemy vessels and neutral Dutch craft in American ports, and in the autumn it requisitioned all vessels over 2,500 tons in order to control their use.

The major activity of the Board and its subsidiary Corporation was building the "Bridge of Ships" to France, the largest industrial undertaking yet conceived by the United States. An administrative organization had to be created, and since the managers had no previous experience to guide them, they had to learn as they went. Whole new yards as well as housing and transportation for the workers had to be built. Under the circumstances unnecessary delays, great waste, much needless activity, and numerous clashes of personalities and policies were unavoidable. Not surprisingly, the program took so long to get started that less than a sixth of the projected 3,000 vessels were completed before the armistice.

Complicating the Corporation's construction program was the single overriding reality that navy orders filled nearly all the existing ways. Before it could produce the vessels for the bridge the EFC had to create new yards or enlarge existing ones and design ships capable of mass production. Two solutions emerged. One involved building yards that would be little more than massive assembly points for vessels whose components could be subcontracted to steel fabrication plants in less congested areas. Three huge assembly yards containing 90 ship ways dominated East Coast production: American International Corporation of Hog Island below Philadelphia (50 ways), Merchant Shipbuilding Corporation at Bristol above Philadelphia (12 ways), and the Submarine Boat Corporation at Newark, New Jersey (28 ways). The other solution, used widely by the Great Lakes yards and the hurriedly constructed yards for steel-hulled craft on the West Coast, was repetitive or serial construction that took advantage of the economies of mass production. Therefore during the fall of 1917 the Corporation prepared standardized plans for vessels in eight sizes between 3,500 and 9,600 deadweight tons.

The enormity of the task is difficult to visualize. In January 1917 the United States had 37 yards building steel and 24 building wooden seagoing vessels on 235 ways. On January 1, 1919, the country boasted 77 yards building in steel, 117 in wood, 2 composite or mixed yards, and 7 others fabricating concrete hulls. Together they contained 1,020 ways. The new yards were scattered along all the coasts since the wooden building yards sprang up

USS *Pecos,* a Shipping Board tanker that was assigned to the Navy.
Official U.S. Navy Photograph

wherever it appeared likely that they could develop a source of
raw materials. But the major activities were more limited. On the
East Coast the new yards concentrated in New York Harbor and the
Delaware River; on the Gulf at New Orleans, Mobile, and in northern Florida; the Pacific yards clustered at Los Angeles, San Francisco Bay, Seattle, and Portland. Seattle, alone, contributed 26.5
percent of all EFC tonnage.

The new methods speeded up production. Great Lakes Engineering Works built the 3,500-ton *Crawl Keys* at their Ecorse,
Michigan, yard in 37 days, and the Seattle yard of Skinner and
Eddy turned out eight vessels with building times between 78 and
92 days. Most spectacular, however, was Hog Island's successful
launching of five vessels on May 30, 1919. Nor should it be assumed that new methods produced poor vessels. The "Hog Islanders" formed the backbone of the cargo fleet of the 1920s and
1930s. Many continued through World War II, as did the large
passenger-cargo liners that began life as troop transports, and in
some instances returned to that duty.

The wooden shipbuilding program proved less successful. Although 500 wooden vessels were ordered, 200 had to be canceled.

The basic design drawn by Theodore E. Ferris of a single screw, coal-fired steamer of about 3,500 tons deadweight tonnage was a good one, but the program was treated as a stepchild at EFC. Many of the contracts went to inexperienced builders who proved incapable of overcoming the three great obstacles to the program: the need to secure 1.5–1.7 million board feet of lumber for each vessel, the shortage of experienced labor, and bureaucratic disinterest. As a result, none of the vessels was finished before the spring of 1918. Part of the disinclination of the EFC to push the wooden program was the realization that steel for shipbuilding would become available once the fabrication plants began operating. The probable availability of steel also limited the technologically successful ferroconcrete building experiment. Even so, most of the steel vessels were delivered in 1921 and 1922. By the latter year the United States had spent $3.3 billion and possessed the world's largest merchant marine (13.5 million tons), about 22 percent of the world's shipping and five times the size of that flying the American flag in 1914. Unfortunately, the United States had neither a shipping industry to absorb the craft nor trade routes to give them employment. Moreover, American shipowners had not solved their traditional problem of high wage costs despite a comparatively greater rise in the pay of the foreign seamen during the war.

In 1920 Congress enacted the Jones, or Merchant Marine, Act in an effort to close some of the holes in the 1916 legislation. The new law established terms and conditions for the sale of government-owned craft to private operators. It also directed the USSB to determine what lines should be established to promote coastal and foreign shipping and authorized the sale or charter of vessels to operate them. The bill's authors hoped that the provision for charters would entice private operators to gain experience in managing the government-owned lines, after which they would purchase them. The act set the long-term objective of the Shipping Board as "whatever may be necessary to develop and encourage the maintenance of a merchant marine . . . sufficient to carry the greater portion of its commerce and serve as a naval military auxiliary in time of war or national emergency ultimately to be owned and operated privately by citizens of the United States." That remains the basis of United States policy, from which springs the subsidy programs that ensnared the government ever more tightly in the affairs of the maritime industry until 1983.

Like many other pieces of economic legislation passed in the halcyon days leading to a return of normalcy, the 1920 act assumed continuing favorable business conditions. It was not to be. By the end of the year, time charter rates had fallen to $1/3$ their summer levels, and in 1922 they sank to prewar levels. With 10 million tons of shipping (17 percent of the world's tonnage) idle, the Shipping Board's sales program died unborn since it asked unrealistic prices of $200–250 per ton for vessels that could be built in American yards for $185 per ton and in Britain for $125–150. Even dropping prices to $30 per ton could not move vessels in the glutted market. In November 1923 USSB abandoned its individual vessel sales in favor of developing routes in hopes of selling them to their managers when better times returned. But this forced the board to subsidize the operators and built up deficits of $52 million in 1922, 35 million in 1923, and $16 million in 1924. The losses naturally increased pressures to transfer the lines to private ownership.

Under the circumstances there was little incentive to build new vessels. As a result American craft, most of them of wartime construction, grew progressively more expensive to operate and less efficient than their foreign competitors. An example of this was the slowness of American deep-sea craft to shift to diesel power. The diesel engine had undergone great development during World War I because of its use in submarines, and by 1919 manufacturers offered engines of sufficient size and reliability to power large freighters and liners. The diesel offered several advantages over steam plants. Although no smaller than a steam installation, its 30–50 percent lower fuel requirements reduced operating expenses and bunker space. The engine started easily and could be brought under full load almost immediately while a steamer's boilers took hours to reach operating pressure. The diesel required a smaller engine room force and no expensive high-pressure piping. It discharged a cleaner exhaust. Even though American fishing and harbor craft and large yachts turned ever more frequently to the diesel power after the war, large installations were few. This remained true until the American South African Line built the *City of New York* in 1931 although an experimental Shipping Board program in the mid–1920s refitted several existing freighters with diesels and American-Hawaiian Line used them on their *Missourian* and *Californian*.

American shipping could be competitive if it had good leadership and proper promotion. Matson Navigation Company was a striking example. It had its roots in the Hawaiian sugar and pineapple trades. By 1925 it had developed frequent service between the West Coast and the islands and had close ties to the "Big Five" concerns that dominated the Hawaiian economy. In 1926 Matson purchased the venerable Oceanic Steamship Company and turned it into a highly profitable South Seas tourist vehicle. It drove British competition from the Australia-Hawaii-California run and severely cut into business on that between Canada and Australia. A second success story came from the Farrell Line, which in 1925 purchased the Shipping Board's service to South Africa. Using imaginative promotion of both passengers and cargoes, the line developed into one of the strongest of the smaller shipping concerns before World War II and maintained its position into the 1970s.

Most other new deep-water lines failed. In 1919 W. Averell Harriman established a United States-flag transatlantic service in conjunction with the German war-devastated Hamburg-American Line. Harriman's United American Lines vessels quickly surrendered to the high cost of American registry and the strictures of the Volstead Act and switched to Panamanian registry. Neither could the vessels compete in the North Atlantic against the *Aquitania, Berengaria,* and *Leviathan.* They found steady employment bringing immigrants from the Mediterranean. Even so, the returns were small, and in 1926 Harriman abandoned the field, selling out to the resurgent Hapag.

Longer-lived was the Shipping Board's effort to capture part of the prestigious North Atlantic trade. Among American spoils from World War I was the big German liner *Vaterland,* which in honor of her size became the *Leviathan* in American service. In 1920 the Shipping Board established a New York-Bremerhaven service with stops at the Channel ports. It was operated by the U.S. Mail Line. The following year the Shipping Board itself took over the service, calling it the United States Line. Because the *Leviathan* lacked a comparable partner to give a balanced service, and since most travelers were disinclined to use dry American vessels, the line found no buyer until 1929. The purchaser, hard hit by the Depression, defaulted on its purchase agreement two years later, and the line returned to government hands. In 1932 a new group closely connected to the International Merchantile Marine purchased it.

United States Lines operated the premier passenger vessels in the American merchant marine until 1969: *Manhattan* (1931), *Washington* (1932), *America* (1939), and the record-smashing *United States* (1952). The line's efforts to attract passenger traffic was hampered by the moderate size of its vessels, World War II, and the arrival of transatlantic air service following that conflict. The line continued as an innovative cargo handler on its traditional North Atlantic runs and in 1984 began a round-the-world cargo service.

Other new American shipping lines had more mundane origins. Henry Ford established his own line to speed Model T's to foreign markets and to ensure a smooth flow of raw materials to River Rouge. James A. Farrell of United States Steel started the Isthmian Line as a protection against European shipping rates. Bethlehem Steel operated the Calmar Line of ore carriers to haul iron from its Venezuelan mines while most American oil companies owned tankers to move both crude and finished petroleum.

The more seamy side of the shipping lines of the 1920s can be seen in the activities of Henry Herberman, a warehouse operator, who rose to president of Export Steamship Company. Established in 1919 to operate in the Mediterranean trade, the firm passed into Herberman's control in 1920. Five years later Export purchased the Shipping Board's Mediterranean services and their vessels for $1,062,000, about 30 cents per dollar of cost. Despite its low initial expenses, the line lost money until it secured a good mail contract in 1928. That contract obligated the line to build four new passenger-freight combination vessels, later renowned as the Four Acres; but they cost more than the route would support, and in 1931 the line defaulted on its payments. It then became clear that Herberman had lavished gifts on officials and had been the recipient of improper favors from the Shipping Board. In 1934 the Board threatened to reclaim the line but did not act for a variety of reasons, notably that it had no purchaser. Finally in 1935 a new syndicate did take over and rehabilitated the line. Renamed the American Export Line in 1938, it has survived to become one of America's best-known maritime enterprises. In 1978 American Export became a division of Farrell Lines.

2. The Failures of the Twenties

Since the 1920 Merchant Marine Act brought no construction of vessels and private operators showed scant inclination to do so on their own, Congress in 1924 established a $25-million revolving construction fund under control of the Shipping Board. Even the relatively cheap government funds attracted only coastal line operators who ordered 14 small and medium sized vessels to replace worn-out passenger tonnage or that lost in World War I. Four years later Congress tried again. It refused to enact direct subsidies but increased the fees paid for carrying mail up to thirty times the old rates. That served as a modest subsidy. The 1928 law also increased the building fund to $250 million. Those provisions brought the construction of 42 new vessels, 25 of them passenger craft for intercoastal or overseas service. The quality of the vessels proved to be exceptional, three of them seeing half a century of service under the American and other flags.

The law was poorly drawn. It lacked standards for determining the size of the subsidy and did not require competitive bidding. Moreover, it gave statutory preference to established concerns, which effectively nullified any competition. Even more amazing, it did not require the operators to use their increased income to build new craft. Moreover, the Shipping Board had little taste for administering the law and neglected to develop standardized criteria or procedures. As a result nearly all the contracts went to existing lines at the maximum rate. This brought down the wrath of congressional and public critics. In 1933 Congress gave the president the right to cancel or modify any mail contract not in the public interest. More important in the long run, the scandal brought about an investigation by a Senate Select Committee chaired by Hugo L. Black of Alabama.

Black's massive investigation exposed the shady dealings, stock manipulation, other improprieties, and general opportunism of many operators along with documenting the failure of the law to resuscitate the merchant marine. Black's indignant report proposed ending all assistance to shipping operators, but cooler heads, notably Postmaster General James A. Farley, prevailed. They secured support from President Franklin D. Roosevelt for a policy designed to protect American peacetime foreign commerce from unfair competition by the foreign-dominated shipping combines or conferences; to secure the United States a merchant marine sufficient to conduct its trade during a war to which it was not a belligerent; and to provide auxiliaries for the Navy in time of war. Roosevelt also accepted the notion of direct subsidies for construction and operation. Nevertheless, the resultant Merchant Marine

Ace of 1936 was largely a Congressional product, little influenced by the presidential fascination with naval and maritime affairs.

3. The Maritime Commission

The congressional debate over the 1936 act showed scant interest or attention to the rationale of the new program or even to the question of whether the United States needed a merchant marine at all. Not surprisingly, therefore, the law contained both subsidy and nonsubsidy provisions. During its consideration the argument mainly swirled around its role in creating more jobs. The subsidy proponents, largely nationalists and protectionist, won a requirement for 100 percent American citizenship among the crews of subsidized freighters and 90 percent on passenger vessels along with payments to equalize operating and construction costs with those of foreign competitors. The law authorized loans of up to 75 percent of the cost of a new vessel at 3½ percent for twenty years. Since a subsidy had been an anathema to stalwart Democrats since the Civil War, the legislation provided for recapture of any profits that averaged more than 10 percent during a five-year period. In keeping with the New Deal's efforts to legislate improved working conditions, the law established a three-watch system with an eight-hour working day in port and spelled out minimum standards for quarters. It established a five-member bipartisan United States Maritime Commission charged with regulatory, promotional, and operating functions.

Roosevelt chose as first head of the commission the strong-willed Wall Street operator Joseph P. Kennedy. Other members were the highly regarded Vice-Admiral Henry A. Wiley; a top-flight naval engineer, Rear Admiral Emory Land; Thomas Woodward, a respected Shipping Board lawyer; and former Congressman Edward Moran of Maine. Kennedy successfully negotiated the replacement of all the mail contracts with operating subsidy agreements. When Kennedy left the commission in 1937 Land replaced him and headed its operations through World War II.

One of the commission's first objectives was the refitting of the merchant marine with new vessels. It proposed to construct 500 vessels by 1947. Although Congress ignored that ambitious plan, the commission in 1938 received authority to build 150 craft. The delays inherent in developing new designs delayed the

The Navy modified many Maritime Commission hulls for wartime service. The USS *Clay* was a standard C3 freighter fitted as a transport for amphibious assaults. Official U.S. Navy Photograph

start of construction until 1939. The designs were ingenious. As a means of reducing the unit cost of new vessels, the board's naval architects and engineers developed a series of standard designs in various sizes that could be modified to meet the needs of individual operators. The plans designs were for 7,200, 9,000, and 12,000 deadweight-ton freighters designated C1, C2, and C3; a new North Atlantic Liner (*America*) to replace the *Leviathan;* and a standard tanker. From these modest beginnings stem such subsequent complicated design designations as C3–Sl–N2, C1–M–AV1, or C5–S–78a.* In 1940 the obvious necessity for quick construc-

---

*The designations followed a standard pattern: Type (P, passenger; C, cargo: T, tanker, etc.) and length category (1, 2, 3, etc.)—power plant (S, steam; M, Diesel) and number of screws if carrying over twelve passengers—design number or special modification.

tion of large numbers of freighters for wartime service led the Maritime Commission to start a second, "Emergency," building program. Unlike the earlier commission-sponsored craft, these were not intended for postwar service. The design (designated EC2–S–C1), which was specially adapted for mass production became world famous as the Liberty Ship. After an initial 60 vessels for Britain, another 2,580 were constructed between 1942 and 1945 along with 130 modified sister ships specially fitted to carry tanks, aircraft, coal or oil. The ubiquitous Liberty Ship could be built rapidly, using workers without shipbuilding experience and the subassembly methods developed during World War I. When finished the 441-foot, 6-inch steamers carried 9,146 tons, a cargo equal to a train of 300 freight cars. Their easily acquired reciprocating engines drew steam from a pair of oil-fed boilers, the whole power plant being chosen for ease of procurement, durability, and simplicity of operation.

As had occurred in World War I, the Emergency design and later Victory (VC2) freighters poured forth from newly built yards: notably the South Portland, Maine, works of the New England Shipbuilding Corporation, the Fairfield Yard in Baltimore operated by Bethlehem Steel; the Delta Shipbuilding Company at New Orleans managed by American Ship Building; the four-yard complex at Richmond, California, operated by Henry J. Kaiser Company; and Kaiser's yards at Swan Island, Portland, Oregon, and Vancouver, Washington. The ways of the existing yards were apportioned between the navy and the Maritime Commission. Although most contributed warships to the war effort, a small number continued to produce merchant craft in order to provide the vessels needed for the permanent merchant marine. Many of the latter, however, donned navy uniforms for the duration as transports, cargo carriers, and aircraft carriers.

Since the shipyards, whether new or expanded, were seldom sited in areas of massive unemployment, they played a major role in the great folk movement of workers that is one of the notable sociological marks of World War II. At their peak the shipyards employed 800,000 workers, and their suppliers another 596,000, most recruited from homes far afield. About 20 percent of the workers in the San Francisco Bay yards, for instance, came from Oklahoma, and perhaps half of the employees at the larger Bay yards hailed from the states of Oklahoma, Arkansas, Texas, or Missouri. As the demands of the draft continued to call men, they

The *Meredith Victory,* one of the mass-produced Victory ships, riding high but dressed for visitors at Seattle, probably in the 1950s. Courtesy of the Maritime Administration

were replaced by women who not only kept the home fires burning but the shipyards open. In 1944 about 17 percent of all shipyard workers were women, and in some yards the rate was much higher. At the Oregon Shipbuilding Company at Portland, Oregon, for instance, it reached as high as 25 percent. The women undertook skilled and semiskilled tasks that heretofore had been male preserves. In shipbuilding they first appeared as welders; then as laborers and electricians. By the end of the war they had entered most of the other crafts. Their acceptance varied widely. Nevertheless, the barrier of sex discrimination had been rent by the rod of Winnie the Welder.

The production of the yards was staggering. In 1942 some 5.4 million tons came down the ways. The following year that figure bounded to 12.5 million, the highest it would ever reach. Thereafter shifting priorities dropped merchant ship output to 8 million tons in 1944 and 6.3 million in 1945. The yards alone represented an investment of $15 billion. During the war years they sent to sea 2,418 Liberty Ships of all types; 527 Victory Ships; 216 small C1–M–AV1 freighters; 301 C2 types; and 163 C3 size freighters. As a result, in 1945 5,529 vessels, totaling 56,797,700 deadweight tons, flew the American flag.

On February 7, 1942, President Roosevelt established the War Shipping Administration (WSA) as the agency responsible for wartime ship operation and for the administration of the shipping priorities. Nominally independent of the Maritime Commission, it was directed exofficio by the chairman of the commission. Although the Maritime Commission retained responsibility for the regular and wartime building problems, most of its other activities passed to the WSA. It undertook a huge training program to provide the officers and men required by the new vessels. Such a program had begun in 1942 with the establishment of the U.S. Merchant Marine Academy on the former Walter P. Chrysler estate at Kings Point on Long Island, New York. By the end of the war Kings Point, the seven training ships, and the schools at Sheepshead Bay, Long Island, St. Petersburg, Florida, and Avalon on Catalina Island, California, Fort Trumbull, Connecticut, and Alameda, California, trained 270,000 seamen and 10,000 officers. Another 23,000 received refresher training, along with 7,500 radio officers and 5,300 pursers.

When the reckoning of the costs was completed it showed that 733 United States vessels had fallen victim to the dangers of war and 5,638 American seamen had died or disappeared. Heroes or overpaid slackers, the American seamen and their doughty vessels had kept the supplies and men flowing onto the battlefields, to the war plants, and to American homes. Yet almost as soon as the shooting stopped, the merchant marine again resumed its slide into oblivion.

Chapter Ten

THE YEARS OF STRUGGLE

SℐNCE ALMOST HALF OF THE BRITISH, FRENCH, GREEK, DUTCH, AND Norwegian merchant fleets, along with nearly all of those flying the Japanese and German flags, disappeared during World War II, the United States emerged from the conflict with 60 percent of the world's tonnage. In 1946 about 130 shipping companies operated 4,500 American commercial vessels. They represented about a threefold increase in operators and a fourfold growth in vessels since 1939. Under the circumstances the American shippers had a field day, although about 70 percent of their cargoes were either relief or military supplies not destined to continue for long into the future.

In a piece of great altruism, the Merchant Ship Sales Act of 1946 opened the bidding for surplus Maritime Commission craft to foreign owners as well as Americans. Between 1946 and 1948 United States owners bought 746 vessels at bargain prices while another 1,000 went abroad at a higher figure. Thus the United States played a major role in restoring sea legs to the traditional maritime powers in Europe. With their lower operating costs the Europeans, and later the Japanese, began to regain their traditional markets. This forced American owners to rely ever more heavily on government cargoes—primarily relief cargoes that gave way after 1950 to shipments generated by the Korean War. By 1954 the foreign-aid shipments had dwindled to 12 million tons, of which about 800 shiploads or 8 million tons were available to American vessels.

The postwar years witnessed efforts to reassert American leadership at sea. The Maritime Commission attempted to establish American presence on the North Atlantic seaway. In 1952 the United States Lines took delivery of the heavily subsidized liner *United States*. She reached 38.25 knots on her trials and made her first eastbound crossing in a record 3 days, 10 hours, and 40 minutes and returned in 3 days, 12 hours, and 12 minutes, also a record. The North Atlantic Blue Ribbon had returned to American hands for the first time since the *Baltic* had seized it in 1854, but the days of the express liner were fast closing. Airplane travel by the 1950s was fast becoming the preferred mode of travel across the Atlantic. United States Lines sent the great liner on her last crossing in 1969. She has since languished in lay-up despite periodic proposals to refurbish her for cruise service. The last American liner in transpacific service, the *Mariposa* on the San Francisco—Sydney run, ceased operating in 1978.

In conjunction with the Atomic Energy Commission, the Maritime Administration constructed a nuclear-powered combination freight and passenger vessel, the *Savannah,* in 1962. She was intended both as an experiment and a demonstration of the potential of the maritime nuclear power plant. The *Savannah* was an experiment not repeated since neither the public nor the industry was attracted to the high-priced white whale. She exists today as a museum ship at Charleston, South Carolina.

The coastal trade did not recover after World War II. Most of the traffic that had been lost to rails, trucks, and barges never returned. The reasons were numerous: better roads, greater flexibility of trucking, the sharp rise in port costs—notably longshoremen's charges—and the 1940 placement of coastal shipping under regulation of the Interstate Commerce Commission, which had traditionally demonstrated its prorailroad bias. Despite many wishful thoughts, articles in newspapers, and a few design projects, only the Baltimore-Norfolk, Washington-Norfolk, and Boston-Yarmouth, Nova Scotia, passenger runs survived the war, as did the local services on Puget Sound. They all died within fifteen years of the return of peace. By 1950 only about 150 privately owned vessels remained in the coastal services where 440 had sailed before the war. Of those, about 50 handled the traffic with Hawaii, Alaska, and Puerto Rico. In 1963 the coastal fleet had fallen to 100. Twenty years later its number was down to 44 freighters.

1. Reshaping Policies

Dissatisfaction with the Maritime Commission's dual administrative and regulatory roles resulted in its revamping in 1950. A new Federal Maritime Board (FMB) took over the regulatory and the quasi-judicial functions while administrative activities passed to a Maritime Administration that was placed in the Commerce Department. The separation proved to be more theoretical than real since the same individuals served as chairman of the FMB and head of the Maritime Administration until 1961. Then the differing functions were further recognized by replacing the FMB with two agencies: a Maritime Subsidy Board charged with subsidy concerns and a Federal Maritime Commission responsible for regulatory matters.

Despite this more rational arrangement of the maritime agencies, the American-flag merchant marine continued its decline. The Merchant Marine Act of 1970 attempted to bring more status to the Maritime Administration by having its head serve concurrently as Assistant Secretary of Commerce for Maritime Affairs. It was the first time that maritime interests had acquired a subcabinet representative. Finally, in 1981 the Maritime Administration was shifted from the Department of Commerce to the Department of Transportation in a change that reflected more of a shift in the focus of the Department of Commerce than an effort to find a more congenial home for the merchant marine agency.

In the Cargo Preference Act of 1954 the government attempted to overcome the decline in opportunity for American freighters by requiring "Ship American" provisions in the contracts for the sale of surplus grain that controlled the movement of the American grain reserves to starvation areas overseas. In 1958 a general worldwide glut of shipping caused a drastic drop in rates and forced many vessels to lay up. The reduced demand permitted many freighters operated by the scheduled lines to move into the surplus grain trade either to find employment or to fill out cargoes. This further depressed the opportunities for the tramp or non-scheduled carriers. Many vessels, notably the now marginal Liberty Ships, headed for scrapyards, but others hastened to join the flight to foreign registry, where operating costs could be lowered through smaller crews, lower pay, and less restrictive work rules.

The Flag of Necessity vessels, as their owners called them—or as they are more commonly termed, Flag of Convenience vessels— tended to gravitate to Liberian, Panamanian, and Honduran registry. The shift was tacitly supported by the American government, which took no significant steps to halt it.

By 1962 government cargoes accounted for almost two-thirds of all tonnage carried by American vessels. That portion rose as the Vietnamese War intensified, but it declined nearly as rapidly after 1973 as United States participation in the war ebbed. Meanwhile, the Nixon administration recognized that only drastic action would prevent the American Flag from becoming one of those missing from the seas of the globe once peace returned. In part the plan recognized that nonsubsidized American-flag operators could not afford to replace their vessels that by then were twenty-five years old or more and were no longer competitive on the world shipping market. They simply did not have the capital to build replacement vessels in the United States, and the American ship registration laws prohibited construction abroad. At the same time many of the world's major ports were so congested that the itinerant or tramp freighters had difficulties discharging and loading cargo. This allowed the scheduled lines, which had ready access to facilities, to offer noticeably better service. It also permitted foreign tramp owners with their significantly lower operating costs to underbid both American subsidized and unsubsidized vessels on cargoes to many ports. The 1970 law, therefore, extended operating and building subsidies to nonscheduled bulk carriers who hauled ores, coal, and grains.

The law committed Congress to subsidize the construction of 300 new vessels for the American merchant fleet between 1971 and 1980. That made it the most energetic peacetime shipbuilding effort ever enacted in the United States. The law prescribed a sliding scale of subsidies in an effort to promote efficiency and competition. It was successful in driving down construction subsidy costs and in forcing operators to phase out their foreign-flag operations. The legislation, however, was not as successful in enlarging the number of vessels under the American flag. During 1972–79 only 83 vessels were built under its provisions. Thirty of them were large oil tankers ordered at the height of the petroleum boom of the early 1970s and delivered during its collapse.

Much of the failure of the Nixon administration's 1970 plan

was the direct outgrowth of the devastation of the world's economy by the unilateral escalation of petroleum prices by the Organization of Petroleum Exporting Countries. Not only did the OPEC price rises sharply reduce the movement of oil and produce a world surplus of tankers but it so upset the economies of much of the world that many have yet to recover. Many of the nations that have struggled to their feet have done so only at the cost of restricting their foreign trade. This has greatly delayed the recovery of the world's merchant marines. Since they are among the last to benefit from a shipping boom because of their high costs, the United States shipowners still face a dreary world. Many of the weaker firms have been driven ashore or into bankruptcy courts; few in 1986 could claim a profit.

One obvious result of the decline in construction of replacement vessels is an ageing merchant marine. The privately owned vessels still flying the United States flag in 1983 averaged twenty-three years in age while those riding at their moorings in the government's boneyards had earned a rest at thirty-five years. In comparison, foreign craft averaged only thirteen years in age. Equally frustrating was the failure of the Omnibus Maritime Regulatory Reform, Revitalization, and Reorganization Act of 1979, envisioned by its proponents as the vehicle to restore vitality in the shipping industry by freeing it of the shroud of debilitating governmental control. As might be expected from legislation with such a title, however, the law proved to be a disjointed collection of provisions that primarily reflected the competition of political forces within and without the industry. Enacted with little guidance from the White House, it mirrored the continuing refusal of Congress to view the merchant marine as a critical aspect of national defense.

2. New Technologies

Technologically, the years after World War II were significant in the world's marine. New hull forms along with the introduction of lighter and tougher materials like aluminum and fiberglass, new propulsions systems, and better antifouling paint created more efficient designs and faster vessels. The *United States* and the *Savannah* were merely two examples. New cargo-handling equipment like shipboard gantry cranes and high-capacity pumps reduced time in port. Larger vessels, which permitted more efficient use of crew, fuel, and port facilities, changed the profile of shipping and the ports it visited. Moreover, aircraft and the automobile eliminated nearly all passenger traffic except for cruising vacationers.

Despite its small stature as a carrier of the world's goods, the United States introduced a large number of innovative designs and services during the forty years following the end of World War II.

Containerships. These are vessels fitted to carry shipping containers. Containers offer several advantages over traditional shipping methods. They can be loaded at an inland point; placed on wheels and hauled to shipside; then hoisted off their wheels and stowed on board ship either in the hold or on deck. Since containers can be loaded and unloaded quickly, the turnaround time in port is decreased, thereby increasing the efficiency of the vessel. Containers also overcome several other problems inherent in break bulk shipments. No longer must each package be considered as a single shipment, nor must it be handled several times during movement. Since delays in break bulk shipments are fre-

The *Hawaiian Progress* of the Matson Line, a successful containership design. Courtesy of the Maritime Administration

quent, the shipper has to assume that all shipments will take the longest time, which translates into larger inventories and more goods in transit. By using containerships, more precise shipment schedules can be established and more frequent departures offered. Since cargo handling costs rose to as much as 30 percent of a vessel's operating revenue during the 1960s, the ease and speed of handling containers took on a great significance. In some ports, notably in South America, the theft problem was so large that break-bulk shippers had to resort to radical measures like shipping right and left shoes separately. Containers solved that. They could be loaded at the shipper's door and unloaded at the consignee's. The containers could be moved as trucks and never had to be repacked, hence were relatively safe from theft. But the greatest advantage is speed. While most of their advantage results from their faster turnaround time, some of the containerships are among the fastest in the world. In August 1973 the *Sea-Land Exchange* established a new record for a westbound North Atlantic crossing which was 48 minutes faster than that of the *United States*. The relative efficiency of the containership when compared with a traditional break-bulk carrier is substantial. It has been estimated that a break-bulk freighter with an annual lift capacity of 156,000 tons could move 560,000 tons on the same route as a containership.

Small, experimental containers were tried on the West Coast by the Pacific Steamship Company during the 1930s, but the concept did not attract a following for another twenty years. A few experimental trailer-hauling services using surplus navy landing ships operated in the aftermath of World War II, but none prospered. Alaska Steamship Company successfully experimented with small containers that could be stored in the holds of its vessels in 1953. The following year Pan Atlantic Steamship Company, a subsidiary of McLean Trucking Company later to call itself Sea-Land Service, Incorporated, converted a freighter to carry standardized containers that could be lifted on and off the vessel and stacked on the deck. Two years later Matson Navigation Company made a comparable conversion of one of its vessels on the West Coast-Honolulu service. In 1959 the Grace Line converted two of its freighters to handle containers on runs between eastern United States ports and South America. Sea-Land pioneered the use of containers in the transatlantic trade during 1966. It was quickly copied by other American and foreign firms, notably United States Lines. Speeding the transformation was the 1961 acceptance by shippers of standardized 20- and 40-foot containers with common fittings. These allowed their interchange among lines in much the same fashion that cars move among railroads.

Lighter Aboard Ship (LASH) Vessels. One of the most interesting and potentially efficient variations of the container idea was the LASH vessel. In them cargo was first loaded on board standardized lighters at a factory or terminal that could be anywhere on a navigable stream. The lighter would then be towed to a LASH terminal to be taken on board the ship and carried either to the terminal nearest its destination or offloaded at sea near its destination and towed to shore. It appeared to be a particularly flexible system since a LASH vessel did not have to enter a port to discharge and because the lighters were often loaded at low-volume ports or at off-peak hours. The first LASH vessels came off the ways in 1970, but the system proved less effective than expected because longshoremen's contracts produced excessive costs at the terminals. The first line to build LASH vessels, Pacific Far East Lines, failed,

The stern of the LASH carrier *Robert E. Lee* of the Waterman Line showing her stern gate and massive crane structure. Courtesy of the Maritime Administration

and its vessels were subsequently converted into conventional containerships. LASH craft have been more successful in service with Delta and Lykes lines in the Gulf of Mexico.

Roll-on, Roll-off (RoRo) Vessels. An outgrowth of the World War II landing craft and the prewar sea trains, the roll-on, roll-off vessels are fitted with ramps or elevators that permit trucks, trailers, and other wheeled or tracked vehicles to be rolled on and off. Ro-Ro craft are more flexible than standard container vessels in that they can generally accommodate any size object that can be wheeled on board, but they are not as efficient users of their cubic capacity.

Liquid Natural Gas (LNG) Carriers. During the 1970s the expected depletion of American natural gas supplies caused several of the threatened gas companies to investigate the possibility of importing liquified gas. The gas was carried in special refrigerated tanks that maintained temperatures of $-160°$ to $-163°$ Centigrade. The first of those vessels, the *LNG Aquarius,* was built in 1977. A small number of others appeared, but the problems of designing a satisfactory tank and a safe offloading terminal, along with the discovery of additional native sources of gas, have limited the number of LNG carriers under the American flag.

Other special or experimental designs have appeared to serve specific needs. An interesting development has been the integrated tug-barge combination (ITB). It involves a barge with separate tug whose bow is thrust into a notch at the stern of the barge. This results in a very rigid combination that is appreciably cheaper to construct than a regular bulk vessel. The first two have hauled petroleum from the Gulf Coast to New England, and a third traverses the Great Lakes.

3. Causes of the Decline

What is responsible for the decline and virtual demise of United States merchant shipping? Many people and many interests share the blame.

Labor unions have demanded exorbitantly high wages, superior working conditions, inflated manning scales, and other benefits that have not been offset by high productivity. The unions for too long concentrated on short-term benefits for their members at the expense of the long-term health of the industry and the future well-being of their membership. One result often has been the attraction of more workers to the industry than it can support. Owners have too frequently bought peace from turbulent workers by paying the direct and indirect wages demanded by the unions, assuming that the increased costs could always be passed along to the shipper and by him to the consumer. Yet the poor labor relations of the industry have made it difficult to attract the capital necessary to revitalize the shipping lines and to contest the competition of foreign shippers or competing methods of shipment.

Government regulation did not encourage efficiency, frequently rewarded the noninnovative, and surrounded the operator with a deadening cocoon of paper, inhibition, and prohibition. Conversely the unchecked competition let loose by deregulation has bred an ever greater search for short-term profit.

Government regulators were unwilling to attack the basic causes of American noncompetitiveness.

Management preferred to be regulated rather than innovative while ownership judged its success purely in terms of short-term gain.

Industrywide public relations fiascos commonly appeared to demonstrate interest only in finding the maximum federal subsidy and a guaranteed cargo at top rate.

Administrators imposed no penalties on subsidized vessels carrying preference cargoes.

The airlines are able to offer faster passenger and express service.

The Interstate Commerce Commission has been apathetic towards the plight of American coastal shipping.

Equally important were four factors that contributed to the conditions that produced the rapid decline of both domestic and foreign services:

1. The inherent inflexibility of a subsidy system that restricted recipients to outdated trade routes and modes of operation vulnerable to competition from alternative transportation systems,
2. Subsidies that tended to breed political restrictions, such as the requirement for repairs in American yards,
3. The high operating costs that have hurt the noncontiguous states and possessions and limited the domestic market of some industries such as Pacific Northwest lumber,

4. The role of conferences as policemen of the various trade routes resulted in higher rates on American exports than imports.

On the other hand, many operators believe that they have been damaged by antitrust laws that bar participation in the closed conferences that control most of the cargoes in trades not involving American ports. Such conferences are designed to prevent oversupply of vessels for their routes and to arrange for cargo sharing. In theory, at least, they permit conference members to carry larger cargoes per voyage. The argument is that the open conferences (to which any steamship company may belong) are oversupplied with vessels and, as a result, the American lines get less than a fair share of the shipments.

On a cost-benefit basis the American merchant marine has been a good investment. The total maritime subsidies dispensed since 1789 have been less than those lavished on agriculture in 1985 alone. On the other hand, it has been estimated that the merchant marine contributed $11.3 billion in "quantifiable benefits" to the nation between 1958 and 1967 alone at a cost to the government of $2.7 billion. Much of the benefit has come from the shipment of American grains abroad under the cargo-preference acts. Generally those government-subsidized cargoes flow at higher rates than a private voyage. For instance, when the Soviet Union and the United States negotiated the details of the 1975 wheat sales, the Russians agreed to pay $16 per ton to move the grain from American to Soviet ports. This represented a jump of $6.50 per ton from earlier agreements. Since American craft needed $12–13 in order to break even, it was the first time that the grain carriers had a profitable contract.

For many operators the salvation to their impossible situation—caught between high costs and low return—has been to turn to foreign-flag operation. Leaving aside those of the unions, who suffer a loss of berths for their members when a vessel breaks out a foreign flag, what are the advantages and disadvantages? First, foreign registry usually reduces the already short supply of jobs for American seamen since few will sail for the wages offered on foreign craft. This contributes to a surplus of American seamen that intensifies the instability of the labor market at a moment when its very volatility inhibits the infusion of new capital, which would create new jobs. Second, the earnings of the vessel remain abroad except when the owners choose to repatriate them. Unrepatriated earnings contribute little to solving the balance of payments problem. Third, the taxes that American registry would direct to the United States treasury are diverted elsewhere or absorbed as profit. Indeed, one of the great attractions of Flags of Convenience/Necessity is the provision in American tax law that exempts American-owned foreign-flag vessel earnings from taxation so long as foreign taxes are paid. In the PanHonLib countries these taxes are virtually nonexistent, and such American taxes as are collected are imposed on the profits only when and if they return to the United States as dividends.

A final issue that the expatriate vessels raise is their availability in wartime or other emergency to the United States. In 1983 American owners managed 26.3 percent of the world's shipping. While the proponents of foreign operation insist that those vessels are under "effective control" of the United States, most other observers question the ability of the American government to make such agreements stick. During the Vietnam War the United States was not always able to secure vessels from the effective control pool in the numbers required. The problem was not major, but it was a nagging one and raised questions about the utility of the concept.

How can these vessels be repatriated? One knowledgeable observer has recommended:

1. Closing the tax advantages to foreign registration; primarily, this involves eliminating the deferral of income tax payments.
2. Permitting construction and repair of vessels abroad.
3. Achieving greater efficiency of management and productivity in order to offset the high operating costs.

Most of the problems faced by the American merchant marine boil down to the single issue of costs and the inability to offset these costs through increased productivity or innovation. In the contemporary world, technology is too mobile to permit innovation to give the United States shippers much help. This we have seen in the adoption of the containership by European and Oriental shippers as soon as American lines demonstrated the practicality. Therefore, productivity has to become the hallmark of the

American shipper, but here he must contend with nearly insurmountable factors. In 1936 American seamen earned slightly less than comparative factory workers but the wage increases of World War II boosted seagoing wages to 50 percent above those in the factory. By the late 1960s that differential had risen to nearly 200 percent. Yet manning scales are still so high that even the most efficient vessels cannot compete with foreign craft. Clinton Whitehurst estimates that the wage cost of an American-flag vessel exceeds those of foreign craft by a margin of as much as three to one.

How did this boost in wages occur? Largely through the militancy of the marine unions. In 1946 they forced overturning of the pay formula established by the Wage Stabilization Board to gain an average 72.5 percent increase. In 1948 the West Coast ship lines bought peace with the shipboard unions by accepting union hiring halls, only to find themselves being whipsawed in the 1950s as the individual unions demanded parity in both wages and fringe benefits.

Adding to the wage costs, but applying both to foreign and domestic vessels, were those of longshoremen. In New York the racketeers moved in after World War I and stole or extorted millions from shippers. As late as October 1975 the port still held its place as the "most graft ridden port in the nation," in the opinion of the *New York Times*. On the West Coast, operators paid Harry Bridges's ILWU $29 million between 1960 and 1966 to permit the mechanization of the docks. It is no surprise, therefore, that the industry quickly adopted the easily handled and relatively theft-proof containers. Yet the price exacted by the longshoremen for their use was horrendous. Although only seven men are needed to load and unload containers, East Coast shippers have to employ a full gang of twenty-one.

Even so, the ability of the American shippers to stand up to the unions is limited by the nature of the industry and its realities. The chaotic collective bargaining conditions in the industry have caused the operators to call for compulsory arbitration since under the present mediation rules the unions risk nothing in a strike. The employers are not unified in their dealings with the unions, and most are financially too weak to survive a long shut-down. It has been estimated that not more than six companies could survive a 100-day maritime strike.

Adding to the problem is the growing age of the American merchant seamen, who now average an even fifty years. Younger men have been repelled by the stagnation in the industry; poor working conditions as compared to those ashore; the indifference of many of the companies; as well as the rapaciousness of the unions. Moreover, in some areas, notably among engineers, the licensing agencies have become lax, in large part because of manpower shortages. As a result the American seaman tends to be relatively uneducated and to possess few skills easily marketable ashore. Without statesmanship on both sides of the labor bargaining table there is little hope for the revival of the deepwater marine. Both labor and management must recognize that not only jobs and profits but the continued existence of the industry, and the economic health, if not survival, of the country demand an increase in productivity, innovative leadership, and above all stability.

Immensely complicating the efforts to revive the merchant marine following World War II was the belief, most clearly spelled out in the Project WALRUS Report of 1959, that the next major war would be thermonuclear. Since that disaster would presumably leave the nation without an industrial base, all thought of preserving a wartime shipbuilding capacity faded. For two decades after the Korean War little government aid went to maintaining a civilian shipbuilding capacity. Moreover, the accession to power in the Department of Defense of budget managers under Robert McNamara caused the navy to concentrate its orders in the few yards capable of serial production and assembly-line techniques. As a result the building capacity in the country withered rapidly despite the increased demands for shipping generated by the Vietnam War.

Despite the experiences of the two Asian conflicts in which the combatants had to be carried there by water and supplied by a bridge of ships from the United States, national planners have shied away from committing the nation to the investment necessary to restore life to the shipbuilding industry or to ensure the continuance of a viable merchant marine. This becomes ironic when one considers the dependence of the military's contingency plans throughout the world on the flow of supplies brought by merchant vessels. The experience of the past twenty years underlines the reality that those merchant vessels may not be available in the emergency if they fly other than the Stars and Stripes.

Yet, given the verities of the American economy, the merchant marine cannot be resuscitated cheaply nor with a single infusion of money. No recent administration has been willing to commit itself to such a program when confronted with the other demands on its limited budget. Most have talked loudly about the problem and have hoped that it would disappear. In 1982 the Office of Management and Budget circulated a staff memorandum that questioned the need for a merchant marine at all. In an administration like that of Ronald Reagan, which was publicly committed to enlarging the American role abroad and to a strengthening of the merchant marine, the proposal received scant formal attention. Yet that administration's removal of construction differential subsidies and the lifting of the prohibition on foreign construction of United States-flag vessels has brought civilian construction almost to an end. Through all the discussions over the means for restoring American control of her foreign-trade carriers, one preeminent fact evaded most of the public and many of their political leaders: The United States has to import a growing list of critical raw materials without which her industry cannot survive. Tungsten and tin have always been imported, but in the 1980s the United States also imports over 95 percent of its annual consumption of bauxite, titanium, manganese, and sugar. The raw-material import problem dwindles in comparison to our energy deficiencies since less than 3.5 percent of the oil arriving from abroad does so on American vessels.

4. Future Directions

The greatest remaining potential untapped source of many of the world's minerals lie in or under the sea. How great concentrations occur under the waters of the globe we do not know but are rapidly learning. At least fifteen elements exist in the ocean itself in sufficient concentration to permit extraction of more than $1 worth per a million gallons of water. At the present time only magnesium, salt, and bromine are commercially viable products. Table 10–1 gives an indication of the relative quantities of dissolved solids in the oceans.

The Law of the Sea Treaty has started the movement making the mining of the sea feasible, even if the United States government chose not to recognize the rules. It has defined national waters, zones of exploitation, and even the safeguards necessary to exploit those waters. Yet the rapid depletion of accessible land-encased raw materials has hastened the rate of intrusion into the seas. No longer does the 200-meter depth established in the Geneva agree-

Table 10–1. *Minerals in Sea Water*

Element	Avg. tons per cubic mile
Chlorine	89,500,000
Sodium	49,500,000
Magnesium	6,400,000
Sulfur	4,200,000
Calcium	1,900,000
Potassium	1,800,000
Bromine	306,000
Carbon	132,000
Strontium	38,000
Boron	23,000
Fluorine	6,100
Rubidium	570
Iodine	280
Barium	140
Zinc	47
Arsenic	14
Copper	14
Uranium	14
Manganese	9
Silver	1
Lead	0.1
Gold	0.02

Source: *J. L. Mero,* The Mineral Resources of the Sea *(New York, 1965), 26–27.*

ments of 1958 represent a viable line. Significant amounts of phosphorite, which yields fertilizer, exist in many places in the world including off the California coast. Deepsea mining of manganese nodules has been conducted off Florida, the Carolinas, and Hawaii. Other exploitable amounts clutter the sea bottom at other locations around the world. Nickel, cobalt, and copper can also be found. Despite its present prominence in the press, mining of the sea bottom is not new. Beach and bottom gravels and sands have been used since before recorded history to build beach and shore structures; Goodnews Bay in Alaska has provided nearly 90 percent of the United States requirements for platinum since 1935; and placer gold is common throughout the American West. Nevertheless, sea-mining technology is still in its infancy.

Several areas in United States waters also hold considerable potential for oil and gas development. Although the initial efforts to exploit them were failures, the Baltimore Canyon off the coast between New Jersey and North Carolina, parts of the historic fishing grounds of Georges Bank, and the Blake Plateau Basin off the Georgia and Florida coasts appear promising to petroleum geologists. A fourth region is in the waters adjacent to Prudhoe Bay field. Until these deepwater fields, which are covered by up to 3,000 feet of water, are explored in greater detail we cannot tell what riches, if any, they contain nor if their exploitation is possible with the technology presently available.

The ecological problems raised by the offshore field, whether in deep or shallow water, are great and well known. Rigs do have accidents; pipelines do leak; and wells do act up. The question is rather, can the environmental damage be reduced to acceptable limits—and what are the limits? We really do not yet have the information to make a nonemotional evaluation. What are the long-term effects of various sizes and types of spills? What are the long-term damages or benefits of a sea area dotted with oil rigs? We know that they are not all bad. Fish do congregate around rigs, but are the quantities sufficient to attract more than sport and small-scale commercial fishermen?

This question naturally moves quickly into the issue of tankers and tanker terminals. For example, there is no oil refinery in all of New England despite the region's overwhelming dependence on petroleum for energy. How do we balance the natural objection of natives and politically potent summer residents to the intrusion of large new industrial complexes into the midst of their idyllic shoreline? Yet there are no areas left in New England with sufficient depth of water and available space for a refinery that do not touch some sensitive political nerve. The efforts, for instance, to place the refinery in as out of the way and difficult to use location as Eastport, Maine, or to construct an off-loading point at the Isle of Shoals in New Hampshire illustrate the absurdity of the situation.

The proposal to open a terminal along the Middle Atlantic coast capable of handling the deep-draft, ultralarge crude carriers (ULCC) face the same difficulties, despite the fact that the United States does not possess a harbor adequate to handle the giants, which draw up to 100 feet. Sooner or later, the imperative need for petroleum carried in the most efficient manner will cause the United States to develop a few ports to handle the huge vessels. The problem is one of balancing the need against a locality's desire not to have the port and refinery put in its backyard. The decision will be a political one, undoubtedly reflecting the strength of the competing exclusionary groups. At best, the solution will not be cheap. In 1972 the estimates for an artificial island off-loading point about eight miles off Delaware Bay was estimated to cost $500 million for a facility able to handle 100 millions tons annually. Today the cost would probably be triple that. Currently, the most flexible and cheapest system to install is a single-point system in which the tanker to be discharged moors to a buoy that contains both the hose and ground tackle. Such buoys can be operated safely in depths as great as 120 feet; one utilizing 42–48-inch pipe can pump 650,000 barrels per day and handle any fluid. But protection for the vessels lying at the mooring will have to be built at great cost.

Much the same problems have developed on the West Coast, especially around Puget Sound, over the delivery of the 2 million barrels of oil per day that flows into Valdez, Alaska, through the Alaska Pipeline. Although the physical conditions are nowhere near as formidable as at Eastport, the waters that must be traversed at the start and finish of the voyage are notoriously difficult and frequently fog-shrouded and the size of tankers limited by legislation.

One of the greatest, but commonly overlooked, causes of the deterioration of ocean, lake, and river environmental quality has been tourism. Since World War I tourism has shifted from the rustication of a few relatively well-to-do connoisseurs of the unspoiled to a mass industry. In some areas, notably Maine, Florida, and parts of Michigan and California, it has become the dominant economic force. Hence, tight restrictions on development of waterfront areas, limitation of the number of tourists, or competence testing of boaters have consistently met with disfavor. Moreover, both the tourists and those who cater to them traditionally have believed that they were rugged individualists who resented violently any efforts to restrain their activities. Yet beach erosion, dune bulldozing, inadequately treated sewage, and overcrowding have wrought havoc on the very shorelines that the perpetrators supposedly extolled. In the process entire stretches of beach have disappeared and valuable property and buildings have been unnecessarily washed away by erosion, flood, and storm. In the United States strict legislation has appeared recently to protect shore areas, but few other nations have followed our lead except very timorously.

Equally devastating has been the deterioration of the waters polluted by oil and gasoline spilled from poorly maintained pleasure craft; garbage heaved overboard by "who cares" operators; and trash littering the bottom and the surface deposited by a generation of boaters whose affection for the sea equates with the showiness of their fiberglass success symbols. Steps to bring the devastation of the lakes, rivers, and seashores beloved by the vacationer under control have begun, but whether they will overcome the American tradition of despoiling our natural beauty spots remains unsettled.

Most modern Americans look upon the seas and the waterways as an ecological concern, which in part is correct, but they too often overlook the evergrowing economic and political role that marine transport plays in the health of the nation. The reality of life today is that the United States is more dependent on the sea and on its waterways than it has ever been in its history. As a nation that has been profligate with its raw material and energy, it must import to live, and as a nation that imports it must export to retain economic vitality. Since American safety is inseparably bound to that of the industrial nations of Europe and Japan, the United States must retain the capacity to project its national might to those distant locales where collective security may be assailed. All of this can be done only by exploiting the sea routes, and it can be done assuredly only in vessels flying the Stars and Stripes. Our ancestors built upon the sea's routes and the sea's creatures in constructing their new nation. We and our children must look on the seas, in the seas, and under the seas for the future welfare of the United States.

FURTHER READING

T HE FOLLOWING REPRESENTS ONLY A PORTION OF THE LITERA-
ture on American maritime history and should not be considered
the full bibliography for this study. Many other works, too periph-
eral, too specialized, too old for inclusion, were consulted. However, all major sources are included. Since the intent of this list is
to point readers towards further studies in areas of particular interest to them, few works published before 1920 are included unless
they have been recently reprinted. Works marked with an asterisk
are of special value to students of American maritime affairs.

Most of the general histories of the American merchant marine
are out of date, but two have recently appeared: *Robert A.
Kilmarx (ed.), *America's Maritime Legacy* (Boulder, 1979), and
*James M. Morris, *Our Maritime Heritage* (Washington, 1979).
The best of the earlier works are Willis J. Abbot, *The Story of Our
Merchant Marine* (New York, 1919); George Weiss, *America's
Maritime Progress* (New York, 1920); F. C. Bowen, *America Sails
the Seas* (New York, 1938); and *Winthrop L. Marvin, *The Ameri-
can Merchant Marine* (New York, 1902). Samuel W. Bryant, *The
Sea and the States* (New York, 1947), Eloise Engle and Arnold Lott,
America's Maritime Heritage (Annapolis, 1975), and Clayton Bar-
row, *America Spreads Her Sails* (Annapolis, 1973), are more recent but heavily navy-oriented. Benjamin W. Labaree (ed.), *The
Atlantic World of Robert G. Albion* (Middletown, 1975), contains
a group of valuable interpretative essays.

330

Among the general histories of trade and transportation the following have valuable sections on waterborne commerce: Archer B. Hulbert, *The Paths of Inland Commerce* (New Haven, 1920); Edward C. Kirkland, *Men, Cities, and Transportation* (2 vols., Cambridge, 1948); *Oscar Osborn Winther, *The Transportation Frontier* (New York, 1964); *Balthasar H. Meyer (ed.), *Transportation in the U.S. Before 1860* (Washington, 1917). Nor should a student overlook the numerous maritime topics covered by the talks reprinted in the Newcomen Society pamphlets. The volumes of National Waterways Studies of the Army Corps of Engineers (Washington, 1983) vary in quality but trace both maritime history and manmade river and harbors improvements.

General maritime bibliographies are led by *Robert G. Albion, *Naval and Maritime History: An Annotated Bibliography* (4th ed., Mystic, 1972). Between 1952 and 1958 Albion also contributed "Recent Writings in Maritime History" to *The American Neptune*. Edward Sloan III, "Maritime History: A Basic Bibliography," *Choice*, VIII (September 1972) surveys more recent writings, as do the periodic lists prepared by Charles R. Schultz, *Bibliography of Maritime and Naval History: Periodical Articles* (Mystic and College Station, 1971–   ).

Far and away the most useful of the general maritime historical periodicals is *The American Neptune* (1941–   ). The *Newsletter* of the North American Society for Oceanic History (1976–   ) carries news of meetings, recent developments in the field, and publishes lists of museums, bibliographies, and similar short items. *Sea History* (1980–   ) is the quarterly of the National Maritime Historical Society. Other maritime historical journals, more specialized or shorter lived, include *Log Chips* 1948–54), *Steamboat Bill* (1939–   ), and *Inland Seas* (1944–   ). *Mariner's Mirror* (1911–   ) should be consulted despite its English orientation. Occasional historical articles appear in most maritime and yachting periodicals. Nor should the maritime columns in the seaport newspapers be overlooked. Their value varies greatly with time and place. During the early nineteenth century *Niles National Register* (1811–49) contained much material not readily available elsewhere. Since 1859 the *Scientific American* has contained numerous maritime-oriented articles. Short biographies of significant maritime figures appear in *Dictionary of American Biography* (22 vols., 1928–64).

Many pictorial histories deal with America's role at sea. The best include Alexander Laing's trio, *American Ships* (New York, 1971), *American Sail* (New York, 1961) and *The American Heritage History of Seafaring America* (New York, 1974); and Edward V. Lewis and Richard O'Brien, *Ships* (New York, 1965). Nor should the reader overlook Ralph Henry Gabriel, *Toilers of the Land and Sea* (New Haven, 1926) and Malcolm Kier, *The March of Commerce* (New Haven, 1927) in the Pagent of America series. Gordon Newell and Joe Williamson's series of West Coast photo histories, *Pacific Coast Liners* (Seattle, 1959), *Pacific Lumber Ships* (Seattle 1961), *Pacific Steamboats* (Seattle, 1958), and *Ocean Liners of the 20th Century* (Seattle, 1969) contain a wealth of information, as do Jim Gibbs, *Pacific Square Riggers* (Seattle, 1969), *West Coast Windjammers* (Seattle, 1968), and Richard M. Benson, *Steamships and Motor Ships of the West Coast* (Seattle, 1968). Few volumes are as striking as Robert A. Weinstein, *Tall Ships on Puget Sound* (Seattle, 1978), which reproduces the work of photographer Wilhelm Hester.

Vessel design is treated historically by Howard I. Chapelle, *American Sailing Craft* (New York, 1939), *History of American Sailing Ships* (New York, 1935), *American Small Sailing Craft* (New York, 1951); E. P. Morris, *The Fore and Aft Rig in America* (New Haven, 1927); and *Historical Transactions of the Society of Naval Architects and Marine Engineers* (New York, 1945). Special types are studied in *George W. Hilton, *The Night Boat* (Berkeley, 1968); Marion V. Brewington, *Chesapeake Bay Log Canoes and Bugeyes* (Cambridge, Md., 1963); and Howard I. Chapelle, *The Baltimore Clipper* (Salem 1930), *The American Fishing Schooner* (New York 1973), and *The National Watercraft Collection* (2d ed., Washington, 1976).

Among the more attractive volumes studying aspects of the maritime culture in the United States are: *John Wilmerding, *A History of American Marine Painting* (Boston, 1968); Hans J. Hanson, and *Art and the Seafarer* (New York, 1968); *Joanna Colcord, *Sea Language Comes Ashore* (Cambridge, Md., 1944) and *Roll and Go* (New York, 1938; reissued in 1964 as *Songs of American Sailormen*); *Frederick Pease Harlow, *Chantying Aboard American Ships* (Barre, 1962); and Henry R. Skallerup, *Books Afloat and Ashore* (Hamden, 1974).

Local Histories

Regional and port histories vary widely in quality from serious and exhaustive studies in the tradition of Samuel Eliot Morison and Robert G. Albion to the merely filiopiestic. The best and most generally available are listed below.

A book that belongs in the library of every student of New England maritime history is *Robert G. Albion, William A. Baker, and Benjamin W. Labaree, *New England and the Sea* (Middletown, 1972). More specialized are *John F. Leavitt, *Wake of the Coasters* (Middletown, 1970), and Giles M. S. Tod, *The Last Sail Down East* (Barre, 1965). *William Hutchinson Rowe, *Maritime History of Maine* (New York, 1948), John M. Richardson, *Steamboat Lore of the Penobscot* (Augusta, 1941), and George S. Wasson, *Sailing Days on the Penobscot* (New York, 1932) have recently been reprinted. *William A. Baker, *A Maritime History of Bath, Maine and the Kennebec River Region* (2 vols., Bath, 1973) is a successful and monumental study of one of the great shipbuilding areas. William G. Saltonstall, *Ports of the Piscataqua* (Cambridge, Mass., 1941), treats the New Hampshire ports.

Massachusetts basks in the luminescence of *Samuel Eliot Morison, *Maritime History of Massachusetts* (Boston, 1921, 1961), one of the classics of American historiography. Individual Massachusetts ports have extensive coverage in James B. Connolly, *The Port of Gloucester* (New York, 1940); James D. Phillips, *Salem in the Seventeenth Century* (Salem, 1933), *Salem in the Eighteenth Century* (Salem, 1937), and *Salem and the Indies* (Boston, 1947); and Ralph D. Paine, *Ships and Sailors of Old Salem* (Boston, 1923). *W. J. Bunting, *Portrait of a Port* (Cambridge, Mass., 1971) and the Works Progress Administration, *Boston Looks Seaward* (Boston, 1941) treat Boston.

Except for Virginia B. Anderson, *Maritime Mystic* (Mystic, 1962), and Marilyn E. Weigold, *The American Mediterranean* (Port Washington, 1974), no general account of either shore of Long Island Sound exists. James P. Baughman, *The Mallorys of Mystic* (Middletown, 1972), describes the maritime role of one Connecticut family long associated with shipping; William Leonhard Taylor, *A Productive Monopoly* (Providence, 1970) takes an unusually balanced look at the marine activities of the New Haven Railroad while Edwin L. Dunbaugh, *The Era of the Joy Line* (Westport, 1982), is a perceptive study of the New Haven's short-lived Providence—New York competitor. Roger Williams McAdam, *Floating Palaces* (Providence, 1972) is an illustrated history of the Fall River Line that incorporates his earlier (1937) *The Old Fall River Line*.

The best history of a single port is *Robert G. Albion, *Rise of the Port of New York* (New York, 1939). Very similar is Richard C. McKay, *South Street* (New York, 1934). Unlike the two preceding works, the Works Progress Administration, *A Maritime History of New York* (New York, 1973), covers the whole history of the port. More specialized studies are Robert Miller, *The New York Coastwise Trade 1865-1915* (Princeton, 1940), and W. J. Lane, *From Indian Trail to Iron Horse* (Princeton, 1939), which traces the struggle for dominance in the New York—Philadelphia corridor.

Francis Burke Brandt, *The Majestic Delaware* (Philadelphia, 1929) and *David Budlong Tyler, *The Bay and River Delaware* (Cambridge, Md., 1955), tell the Philadelphia maritime history in text and pictures. Particularly useful for its economic interpretations is Diane Lindstrom, *Economic Development in the Philadelphia Region, 1810-1850* (New York, 1978). Neither should a reader overlook the maritime passages in Russell F. Weigley (ed.), *Philadelphia* (New York, 1982), a model local history. Baltimore and Chesapeake Bay have also attracted a number of good studies. The most useful include *Alexander Crosby Brown, *Old Bay Line* (Richmond, 1961), and *Steam Packets on the Chesapeake* (Cambridge, Md., 1961); *Robert H. Burgess, *This Was Chesapeake Bay* (Cambridge, Md., 1963); Marion V. Brewington, *Chesapeake Bay* (Cambridge, Md., 1953); Robert H. Burgess & H. Graham Wood, *Steamboat Out of Baltimore* (Cambridge, Md., 1968); and William L. Tazewell, *Norfolk's Waters* (Woodland Hills, Calif., 1982).

Maritime histories of the South Atlantic and Gulf coasts are scarce. They are the areas of American maritime history most in need of study. *James P. Baughman, *Charles Morgan and The Development of Southern Transportation* (Nashville, 1968), is important while Ulrich B. Phillips, *History of Transportation in the Eastern Cotton Belt* (New York, 1908), remains useful.

Pacific Coast maritime histories are numerous and range widely in value. Among the best are *Giles T. Brown, *Ships That Sail No More* (Lexington, 1966) covering the coastal trade 1910–40; Wytze Gorter and George H. Hildebrand, *The Pacific Coast Maritime Shipping Industry, 1930-1948* (2 vols., Berkeley, 1952–54); Eliot Grinnell Mears, *Maritime Trade of Western United States* (Stanford, 1935); Jack McNairn & Jerry McMullen, *Ships of the Redwood Coast* (Stanford, 1945); John Haskell Kemble, *San Francisco Bay: A Pictorial History* (New York, 1957); Felix Reisenberg, *Golden Gate* (New York, 1940); William Martin Camp, *San Fran-*

cisco: Port of Gold (Garden City, 1947); *H. W. McCurdy and Gordon Newell, *The Maritime History of the Pacific Northwest* (3 vols., Seattle, 1966–77); James H. Hitchman, *The Port of Bellingham, 1920–1970* (Bellingham, 1972). The Northwest lumber trade is covered in Edwin Freeman Comer and H. M. Gibbs, *Time, Tide, and Timber* (Stamford, 1949), and Thomas R. Cox, *Mills and Markets* (Seattle, 1974). Mifflin Thomas, *Schooner from Windward* (Honolulu, 1983), is a valuable study of Hawaiian interisland shipping.

General histories of the Great Lakes with a maritime orientation include: *James C. Mills, *Our Island Seas* (Chicago, 1910); Dana Thomas Bowen, *Lore of the Lakes* (Cleveland, 1946); *Walter Havinghurst, *Long Ships Passing* (New York, 1961); and the recently reprinted although sometimes unreliable *John Mansfield, *History of the Great Lakes* (2 vols., Chicago, 1899). The individual lakes have good histories in the American Lakes series: *Fred Landon, *Lake Huron* (Indianapolis, 1944); *Harlan Hatcher, *Lake Erie* (Indianapolis, 1945); and *Arthur Pound, *Lake Ontario* (Indianapolis, 1945). For twentieth-century activities the annual reports and monthly bulletins of the Lake Carriers Association are useful. Specialized studies include *John G. Clark, *The Grain Trade of the Old Northwest* (Urbana, 1966), and Knut Gjerset, *Norwegian Sailors on the Great Lakes* (Northfield, Minn., 1928). Still Bayard, *Milwaukee* (Madison, 1965) is a recent history of a lake port. Surprisingly, neither Chicago, Cleveland, Buffalo, nor any of the Lake Superior ports has an adequate maritime history. Good pictorial studies include James Barry, *Ships of the Great Lakes* (Berkeley, 1973); George W. Hilton, *The Great Lakes Car Ferries* (Berkeley, 1963); Harlan Hatcher and Erich A. Walter, *A Pictorial History of the Great Lakes* (New York, 1963).

The volumes of the Rivers of America series provide excellent impressionistic introductions to the histories of individual rivers. Walter Havinghurst, *Voices on the River* (New York, 1964), is similar. For the western rivers a good place to start is *Charles Henry Ambler, *History of Transportation in the Ohio Valley* (Glendale, 1932). W. Franklin Gephart, *Transportation and Industrial Development in the Middle West* (New York, 1909), is older but still useful as is Archer B. Hulbert, *The Ohio River* (New York 1906). Leland D. Baldwin, *The Keelboat Age on Western Waters* (Pittsburgh, 1941), recounts the story of riverboating before the steamboat. The best study of the steamboat is *Louis C. Hunter,

Steamboats on the Western Waters (Cambridge, 1949). Erik F. Haites, James Mak, and Gary M. Walter, *Western River Transportation* (Baltimore, 1975), is a valuable but heavily statistical study of the 1810–60 period. More restricted is Joseph R. Hartley, *The Economic Effects of Ohio River Navigation* (Bloomington, 1959). Henry Sinclair Drago, *The Steamboaters* (New York, 1967), is popular as is Edward C. Quick, *Mississippi Steamboatin'* (New York, 1926). Many pictorial histories exist. Among the most useful are Fritz Timmen, *Blow for the Landing* (Caldwell, Id., 1973) and Frank Donovan, *River Boats of America* (New York, 1966). *Leland R. Johnson, *Fall City Engineers* (Washington, 1979), is a study of the role of the Corps of Engineers in the Louisville District and for this book the most useful of the Engineer District histories.

Edith McCall, *Conquering the Rivers* (Baton Rouge, 1984), and Florence L. Dorsey, *Master of the Mississippi* (New York, 1941), are biographies of Henry M. Shreve. Dorsey's *Road to the Sea* (New York, 1947), deals with the engineer James B. Eads. E. W. Gould, *Fifty years on the Mississippi* (St. Louis, 1899), is a combination of memoirs of an early riverman and extracts from contemporary accounts. William J. and Robert W. Hull, *The Origins and Development of the Waterways Policy of the United States* (Washington, 1967), is a publication of the national Waterways Conference. F. G. Hill, *Roads, Rails, and Waterways* (Norman, 1958), studies the broader topic of federal support of transportations. Frederick Way, Jr., has given thumbnail histories of most Mississippi river steamers in *Directory of Western River Packets* (Swickley, Pa., 1950), *Directory of Western River Towboats* (Swickely, Pa., 1954), and *Way's Packet Directory, 1848–1983* (Athens, Ohio, 1983).

The upper Mississippi River is treated separately from the river below St. Louis in *William J. Petersen, *Steamboating on the Upper Mississippi* (Iowa City, 1937), and Mildred L. Hartsough, *From Canoe to Steel Barge on the Upper Mississippi* (Minneapolis, 1934). The lumber rafts on the Mississippi are covered in Walter A. Blair, *A Raft Pilot's Log* (Cleveland, 1930), Charles Edwards Russell, *A-Rafting on the Mississippi* (New York, 1928), and William Gerald Rector, *Log Transportation in the Lake States Lumber Industry, 1840–1918* (Glendale, Calif., 1953). The Missouri River has also received considerable attention, notably in *William J. Petersen, *Steamboating on the Missouri River* (Iowa City, 1955), and Jerome E. Petsche, *The Steamboat Bertrand* (Washington, 1974), an archeological study of a recently excavated wreck. The Columbia River is covered in Fred W. Wilson and Earle E. Stewart, *Steamboat Days on the Rivers* (Portland, Ore., 1969), and Randall V. Mills, *Stern-Wheelers Up Columbia* (Lincoln, Neb., 1977). Arthur E. Knudson, *Sternwheels on the Yukon* (Kirkland, Wash., 1979), is a memoir of a little-known trade.

Good general histories of canals include: Henry Sinclair Drago, *Canal Days in America* (New York, 1972); *Carter Goodrich, (ed.), *Canals and American Economic Development* (New York, 1961); Alvin Harlow, *Old Towpaths* (New York, 1926), a popular history; and the useful but out of date Archer Butler Hulbert, *Great American Canals* (2 vols., Cleveland, 1904). Despite its title, Albert Fishlow, *American Railroads and the Transport of the Ante-Bellum Era* (Cambridge, Mass., 1965), contains a substantial amount of maritime information. The Erie Canal has attracted considerable attention, including *Ronald E. Shaw, *Erie Water West* (Lexington, 1966); Madeline Sadler Waggoner, *The Long Haul West* (New York, 1958); George E. Condon, *Stars on the Water* (Garden City, 1974); Harvey Chalmers II, *The Birth of the Erie Canal* (New York, 1960); and *Nathan Miller, *Enterprise of a Free People* (Ithaca, 1962). *Julius Rubin, *Canal or Railroad* (Philadelphia, 1961), studies the responses of Philadelphia, Baltimore, and Boston. *Walter S. Sanderlin, *The Great National Project* (Baltimore, 1946), is a fine treatment of the Chesapeake and Ohio Canal. Barbara N. Kalata considers the Morris Canal in *A Hundred Years A Hundred Miles* (Morristown, N.J., 1983) while Alexander Crosby Brown, *Dismal Swamp Canal* (Chesapeake, Va., 1967) and *Juniper Waterway* (Charlottesville, 1981) recount the histories of the Dismal Swamp and Albermarle and Chesapeake canals. Harry N. Scherber, *Ohio Canal Era* (Athens, Ohio, 1968); Frank Trevorrow, *Ohio's Canals* (Oberlin, Ohio, 1973); Paul Fatout, *Indiana Canals* (West Lafayette, Ind., 1972); and James William Putnam, *The Illinois and Michigan Canal* (Chicago, 1918), treat western responses to the Erie Canal. *Ralph D. Gray, *The National Waterway* (Urbana, 1967) traces the history of the Chesapeake and Delaware Canal. Dorothy Hurlbut Sanderson, *The Delaware and Hudson Canalway* (Ellenville, N.Y., 1965) is the best long study of an eastern coal canal. Mary Stetson Clark, *The Old*

Middlesex Canal (Melrose, Mass., 1974) and Christopher Roberts, *The Middlesex Canal* (Cambridge, Mass., 1938) study that Massachusetts waterway.

Colonial Period

The background to the age of exploration is discussed from various points of view in many books. Notable among them are *J. H. Parry, *The Age of Reconnaissance* (New York, 1967) and *The Discovery of the Sea* (New York, 1974); Charles E. Nowell, *The Great Discoveries and the First Colonial Empires* (Ithaca, 1954); Edmundo O'Gorman, *The Invention of America* (Westport, 1972); G. V. Scammell, *The World Encompassed* (Berkeley, 1981); and *John Parker, *Merchants and Scholars* (Minneapolis, 1965), a provocative collection of essays. *Richard W. Unger, *The Ship in the Medieval Economy 600–1600* (Montreal, 1980) is an excellent and valuable discussion of the development of naval architecture down to the period of exploration.

For the voyages of discovery themselves *Samuel Eliot Morison, *European Discovery of America* (2 vols., Boston, 1971–74) is the best starting point. Morison's *Admiral of the Ocean Sea* (2 vols., Boston, 1942) is the classic biography of Christopher Columbus; his *Christopher Columbus Mariner* (Boston, 1955) and *Portuguese Voyages to America in the Fifteenth Century* (Cambridge, Mass.,1940), are valuable as are David B. Quinn, *England and the Discovery of American* (New York, 1974) and *Set Fair for Roanoke* (Chapel Hill, 1984), and K. G. Davies, *The North Atlantic World in the Seventeenth Century* (Minneapolis, 1974).

Among the better studies of colonial maritime affairs are: James F. Sheperd and G. H. Walton, *Shipping Trade and the Economic Development of Colonial North America* (Cambridge, England, 1972); Stanley F. Chyet, *Lopez of Newport* (Detroit, 1970); *W. T. Baxter, *The House of Hancock* (Cambridge, Mass., 1945); *Byron Fairchild, *Messrs. William Pepperell* (Ithaca, 1954); Bernard and Lotte Bailyn, *Massachusetts Shipping, 1697–1714* (Cambridge, Mass., 1959), a statistical study; Christine Leigh Heyrman, *Commerce and Culture* (New York, 1984) concentrates on Gloucester and Marblehead; Bernard Bailyn, *The New England Merchants in the Seventeenth Century* (Cambridge, Mass., 1955); Arthur L. Jensen, *The Maritime Commerce of Colonial Philadelphia* (Madison, 1963), another statistical study. *Robert G. Albion,

Forests and Sea Power (Cambridge, Mass., 1926), and Joseph J. Malone, *Pine Trees and Politics* (Seattle, 1964), discuss naval stores and imperial forest policies. Philip C. F. Smith (ed.), *Seafaring in Colonial Massachusetts* (Boston, 1980); *Oliver M. Dickinson, *The Navigation Acts and the American Revolution* (Philadelphia, 1951) is a standard study. Robert Pares, *Yankees and Creoles* (London, 1956); Arthur Pierce Middleton, *Tobacco Coast* (Newport News, 1953); Leila Sellers, *Charleston Business on the Eve of the American Revolution* (Chapel Hill, 1934); Benjamin W. Labaree, *Boston Tea Party* (New York, 1964) and *Patriots and Partisans* (Cambridge, Mass., 1962) discuss narrower aspects of the colonial maritime experience; Gary B. Nash, *The Urban Crucible* (Cambridge, Mass., 1979), describes the role of the northern seaports in the coming of the Revolution.

Although much has been written about slavery, little original research has been undertaken on its maritime aspects. The most useful are: *W. E. Burghard DuBois, *The Suppression of the African Slave Trade to the United States of America* (New York, 1898, 1904); Philip D. Curtin, *The Atlantic Slave Trade* (Madison, 1969); *Daniel P. Mannix and Malcolm Cowly, *Black Cargos* (New York, 1965; and George F. Dow, *Slave Ships and Slavery* (Salem, 1927).

The Golden Age

Ralph D. Paine, *The Old Merchant Marine* (New Haven, 1919) in the Chronicles of America series is still useful. David T. Gilchrist, *Growth of Seaport Cities* (Charlottesville, 1967), reprints the proceedings of a valuable but inconclusive economic history symposium. Individual trade routes are considered in: *Alfred W. Crosby, Jr., *America, Russia, Hemp, and Napoleon* (Columbus, Ohio, 1955); Charles Oscar Paullin, *American Voyages to the Orient* (Annapolis, 1971); Kenneth S. LaTourette, *Voyages of American Ships to China, 1984–1844* (New Haven, 1927); Foster Rhea Dulles, *The Old China Trade* (Boston, 1930) extends to 1844; *James A. Field, *America and the Mediterranean World* (Princeton, 1966) covers 1776–1882; *George E. Brooks, Jr., *Yankee Traders, Old Coasters, and African Middlemen* (Boston, 1970); *Adele Ogden, *The California Sea Otter Trade* (Berkeley, 1941) covers 1784–1848; Robert Kingery Buell and Charlotte Northcote Skladal, *Sea Otters and the China Trade* (New York, 1968), is a popular history.

Individual shipowners and merchants of the period are covered most satisfactorily in *James B. Hedges, *The Browns of Providence Plantations* (2 vols., Providence, 1952, 1968); *Kenneth W. Porter, *The Jacksons and the Lees* (2 vols., Cambridge, Mass., 1937) and *John Jacob Astor* (2 vols., Cambridge, Mass., 1931); Robert Bennett Forbes, *Personal Reminiscences* (Boston, 1878); and *Wheaton J. Lane, *Commodore Vanderbilt* (New York, 1942).

The transatlantic trade rivalry has been discussed in numerous books. Those of greatest utility are: *Robert G. Albion, *Square Riggers on Schedule* (Princeton, 1938); *Carl C. Cutler, *Queens of the Western Ocean* (Annapolis, 1961); *N. R. P. Bonsor, *North Atlantic Seaway* (Prescot, Ariz., 1955); *David Budlong Tyler, *Steam Conquers the Atlantic* (New York, 1959); Warren Tute, *Atlantic Conquest* (Boston, 1962); Frank C. Bowen, *Century of Atlantic Travel* (Boston, 1930). *Norman S. Buck, *The Development and The Organization of the Anglo-American Trade 1800–1860* (New Haven, 1925) is a broader economic study. The best study of the steamers themselves for the period down to 1870 is *Cedric Ridgely-Nevitt, *American Steamships on the Atlantic* (Newark, Del., 1981). Less detailed is Frederick E. Emmons, *American Passenger Ships* (Newark, Del., 1985) covering 1873–1983. *John M. Brinnin, *The Sway of the Grand Saloon* (New York, 1972) are social histories. Marcus Lee Hansen, *The Atlantic Migration* (Cambridge, Mass., 1940) and E. C. Guilett, *The Great Migration Since 1770* (Toronto, 1937), concentrate on the immigrant traffic.

*Carl C. Cutler, *Greyhounds of the Seas* (New York, 1930) and Arthur H. Clark, *The Clipper Ship Era* (New York, 1910), are the standard studies of the clipper ship; *Octavius T. Howe and Frederick W. Matthews, *American Clipper Ships* (2 vols., Salem, 1926–27) contains histories of individual vessels; Alexander K. Laing, *Clipper Ships and Their Makers* (New York, 1966) is more popular. Oscar Lewis, *Sea Routes to the Gold Fields* (New York, 1949) recounts the difficulties of the '49ers who came by sea while *John Haskell Kemble, *The Panama Route* (Berkeley, 1943), is the history of that complicated transisthmian route.

Civil War and After

*George W. Dalzell, *The Flight From the Flag* (Chapel Hill, 1940) studies the impact of the Civil War; Alfred Basil Lubbock, *The Down Easters* (Boston, 1929) treats the vessels of the California grain trade, 1869–1929; Frederick C. Matthews, *American Mer-

chant Ships 1880–1900 (2 vols., Salem, 1930–31) traces the histories of individual vessels; Neale Haley, *The Schooner Era* (New York, 1972), Paul C. Morris, *American Sailing Coasters of the North Atlantic* (Chardon, Id., 1973), W. J. Lewis Parker, *Great Coal Schooners of New England* (Mystic, 1948), and William H. Bunting, *Steamers, Schooners, Cutters, and Sloops* (Boston, 1975), all study aspects of the East Coast coastal trade.

Dorrell Hanenor Smith and Paul U. Betters, *The United States Shipping Board* (Washington, 1931), is the standard study while Edward N. Hurley, *The Bridge to France* (Philadelphia, 1927), describes his World War I activities. *W. C. Maddox, *Building the Emergency Fleet* (Cleveland, 1920) is the best survey of the World War I building program.

Two studies describe the state of the merchant marine at the start of the Maritime Commission period: *Editors of Fortune, *Our Ships* (New York, 1938), and *U.S. Maritime Commission, *Economic Survey of the American Merchant Marine* (Washington, 1937). Walter A. Radius, *U.S. Shipping in Transpacific Trade* (Stanford, 1944) is a case study covering 1922–38; Frank O. Braynard, *The Leviathan* (7 vols., New York, 1972–84) describes the queen of the interwar American merchant marine. Robert G. Albion, *Seaports South of Sahara* (New York, 1959), traces the history of the Farrell Line while Thomas McCann, *An American Company* (New York, 1976), and John H. Melville, *The Great White Fleet* (New York, 1977), recount the rise and fall of the United Fruit Company; Willima L. Worden, *Cargoes* (Honolulu, 1981) chronicles the rise of the Matson Line. Lucile McDonald, *Alaska Steam* (Anchorage, 1984) is a valuable pictorial history of the Alaska Steamship Company.

World War II merchant marine studies, with some notable exceptions, are not impressive. The best are: *Emory S. Land, *Winning the War with Ships* (New York, 1958); *Frederick C. Lane, *Ships for Victory* (Baltimore, 1951); R. Carse, *The Long Haul* (New York, 1965); Felix Riesenberg, *Sea War* (New York, 1956). John G. Bunker, *Liberty Ships* (Annapolis, 1972); L. A. Sawyer and W. H. Mitchell, *The Liberty Ships* (Cambridge, Md., 1974) describe some of the vessels which fought the war at sea.

Fishing and Whaling

Still valuable but out of date are: B. B. Goode, *The Fisheries and Fishing Industry of the United States* (7 vols., Washington, 1884–

87), especially Section V, and Raymond McFarland, *A History of the New England Fisheries* (Philadelphia, 1915). *Edward A. Ackerman, *New England's Fishing Industry* (Chicago, 1941), is also dated but still useful. Robert J. Browning, *Fisheries of the North Pacific* (Anchorage, 1974), is more modern. Harold A. Innis, *The Cod Fisheries* (Toronto, 1954) covers activities on both sides of the St. Croix. Andrew W. German, *Down at T Wharf* (Mystic, 1982), offers a pictorial history of the Boston fishing fleet with informed commentary. John M. Kochiss, *Oystering From New York to Boston* (Middletown, 1974), is a detailed study of the development and present state of that fishery. Carl I. Wick, *Ocean Harvest* (Seattle, 1946) describes the Pacific coastal fisheries. Arthur F. McEvoy, *The Fisherman's Problem* (New York, 1986), is a pathbreaking environmental history of the California fisheries which appeared too late to benefit this study.

*Alexander Starbuck, *A History of American Whale Fishing* (2 vols. Waltham, Mass., 1876) is the classic study. Edouard A. Stackpole, *The Sea Hunters* (Philadelphia, 1953), and Frances Downes Ommanney, *Lost Leviathan* (New York, 1971), are the best recent histories. Stackpole's *Whales and Destiny* (Amherst, 1972), covers the international struggle for supremacy in the southern whaling area, 1785–1825. Good pictorial coverage can be found in *George F. Dow, *Whale Ships and Whaling* (New York, 1946). Specific areas are covered in Frances Diane Robotti, *Whaling and Old Salem* (New York, 1962); *Everett J. Edwards and Jeanette Edwards Rattray, "*Whale Off*" (New York, 1932), describing shore whaling; Frederick P. Schmitt, *Mark Well the Whale* (New York, 1971) about Sag Harbor. Elmo Paul Hohman, *American Whaleman* (New York, 1928), studies the seamen who sailed the whalers. Frederick P. Schmitt, Cornelius de Jong, and Frank H. Winter, *Thomas Welcome Roys* (Charlottesville, 1980), is the biography of an important American whaling innovator. Briton Cooper Busch, *The War Against the Seals* (Montreal, 1985) is a broad and incisive study of the seal fishery.

Shipbuilding

There are no recent histories of the shipbuilding industry in the United States. Older works include: *Henry Hall, *Shipbuilding Industry in the United States* (Washington, 1884) and Roy W. Kelly and Frederick J. Allen, *The Shipbuilding industry* (Boston, 1918). *William A. Fairburn, *Merchant Sail* (6 vols., Center Lovell, 1945–

55) contains a wealth of information. *F. G. Fassett, *The Shipbuilding Business in the United States* (2 vols., New York, 1948) is extremely valuable while *Society of Naval Architects and Marine Engineers, *Historical Transactions, 1893–1943* (New York, 1945) has several very useful articles. Clinton H. Whitehurst, Jr., *The U.S. Shipbuilding Industry: Past, Present, and Future* (Annapolis, 1986) concentrates on current problems.

The preeminent study of colonial shipbuilding is *Joseph A. Goldenberg, *Shipbuilding in Colonial America* (Charlottesville, 1976). William A. Baker in *Sloops and Shallops* (Barre, 1966) and *Colonial Vessels* (Barre, 1962) studies colonial designs and building techniques. Local historians have reported the output of individual ports with varying success. Among the best are: *H. G. Inches, *Great Lakes Wooden Ship Era* (Vermilion, Ohio, 1962); *David Budlong Tyler, *The American Clyde* (Newark, 1958); *John H. Morrison, *History of New York Shipyards* (New York, 1909); and the classic *William A. Baker, *A Maritime History of Bath, Maine and the Kennebec River Region* (2 vols., Bath, 1973).

Of the histories of individual builders and firms the most useful are C. Bradford Mitchell, *Every Kind of Shipwork* (New York, 1981), a history of the Todd organization; Howard J. Balison, *Newport News Ships* (Newport News, 1954); Alexander Crosby Brown, *The Good Ships of Newport News* (Newport News, 1976); Richard C. McKay, *Some Famous Ships and Their Builder Donald McKay* (New York, 1920); *Richard J. Wright, *Freshwater Whales* (Kent, Ohio, 1969), an account of the American Ship Building Co.; and Charles Preston Fishbaugh, *From Paddle Wheels to Propellers* (Indianapolis, 1970), an extensive history of the Howard Shipyards in Jeffersonville, Ind. Although really useful biographies of shipbuilders are scarce, the best include; A. C. Buell, *Memoir of C. H. Cramp* (Philadelphia, 1906); Cerinda W. Evans, *Collis Potter Huntington* (2 vols., Newport News, 1954); L. Francis Herreshoff, *Captain Nat Herreshoff* (Yonkers, N.Y., 1953); Cynthia Owen Philip, *Robert Fulton, A Biography* (New York, 1985); *Leonard A. Swann, *John Roach* (Annapolis, 1965); and Edward W. Sloan, *Benjamin Franklin Isherwood* (Annapolis, 1965). Special aspects of the industry are treated in Katherine Archibald, *Wartime Shipyard* (Berkeley, 1947), a sociological study; *Marion V. Brewington, *Ship Carvers of North American* (Barre, 1962); Samuel Eliot Morison, *The Ropemakers of Plymouth* (New York, 1950); and Virginia Steele Wood, *Live Oaking* (Boston, 1981).

The standard histories of the development of steamships in

America are: *Fred M. Dayton, *Steamboat Days* (New York, 1925); *John H. Morrison, *History of American Steam Navigation* (New York, 1903). George Henry Preble, *A Chronological History of the Origins and Development of Steam Navigation* (Philadelphia, 1883), is older but still useful. More general histories of the development of steam navigation can be found in *James Flexner, *Steamboats Come True* (New York, 1944; reissued in 1962 as *Inventors in Action*); *H. Philip Spratt, *The Birth of the Steamboat* (London, 1958); S. C. Gilfillian, *Inventing the Ship* (Chicago, 1935); Henry S. Dickinson, *Short History of the Steam Engine* (London, 1938); and Edgar C. Smith, *A Short History of Naval and Marine Engineering* (Cambridge, England, 1937).

Carl D. Lane, *American Paddle Steamboats* (New York, 1943) is brief but well illustrated; Erick Heyl, *Early American Steamers* (6 vols., Buffalo, 1952–69) illustrates and traces the history of selected vessels. Eric Hofman, *The Steam Yachts* (Tuckahoe, 1970), studies a popular but specialized portion of maritime history. Norman J. Brouwer, *International Register of Historic Ships* (Annapolis, 1985), describes the vessels maintained as museums or candidates for such use. Lists of vessels with varying amounts of information are found in the official *Merchant Vessels of the United States*, issued annually since 1867 and in greater detail in American Bureau of Shipping, *Record of American and Foreign Shipping,* also issued annually since 1867. For steam vessels a very useful unofficial list covering the period before 1867 is William M. Lytle, *Merchant Steam Vessels of the United States* (Mystic, 1952, 1976).

Seamen

There are several accounts of shipboard life and of the maritime labor movement but none is wholly satisfactory. The most useful are: *James C. Healy, *Foc's'le and Glory Hole* (New York, 1936; Alexander Laing, *Clipper Ship Men* (New York, 1944); R. N. Dillon, *Shanghaiing Days* (New York, 1961); *Betty V. H. Schneider, *Industrial Relations in West Coast Maritime Industry* (Berkeley, 1958). Charles Rubin, *The Log of Rubin the Sailor* (New York, 1973), and William L. Standard, *Merchant Seamen* (New York, 1947), view the labor story from the extreme left wing; John G. Kilgour, *The U.S. Merchant Marine, National Maritime Policy* *and Industrial Relations* (New York, 1975) and *Joseph H. Ball, *The Government Subsidies . . . Labor Unions* (Washington, 1966), present the management point of view. *Hyman Weintraub, *Andrew Furuseth* (Berkeley, 1959), is the biography of the great figure in maritime labor. John J. Collins, *Never Pay Off* (New York, 1964), traces the history of the Independent Tankers Union while *Joseph P. Goldberg, *The Maritime Story* (Cambridge, Mass., 1958), treats the National Maritime Union. Hartley K. Cook, *In the Watch Below* (New York, 1937), studies the life of off-duty seamen. *Robert Straus, *Medical Care For Seamen* (New Haven, 1950), and Labor-Management Committee, *Medical and Hospital Care for Merchant Seamen* (2 vols., Washington, 1964), lay the ground work for studying the health of seamen. Linda Grant DePauw, *Seafaring Women* (Boston, 1982), surveys the roles of women at sea over the centuries but memoirs of the wives of sea captains like James W. Baldwin (ed.), *The Log of the Skipper's Wife* (Camden, Me., 1979) and Julianna FreeHand (ed.), *A Seafaring Legacy* (New York, 1981), are more colorful.

Business Aspects

The basic book for any understanding of the interrelationships between the maritime industry and public policy is *John G. B. Hutchins, *The American Maritime Industry and Public Policy, 1789–1939* (Cambridge, Mass., 1941). Less far ranging are: A. D. Rathbone IV, *Shall We Scrap Our Merchant Marine?* (New York, 1945); Wytze Gorter, *U.S. Shipping Policy* (New York, 1956); Gerald R. Jantscher, *Bread Upon the Waters* (Washington, 1975); *Samuel A. Lawrence, *U.S. Merchant Shipping Policies and Politics* (Washington, 1966); Lloyd W. Maxwell, *Discriminating Duties and the American Merchant Marine* (New York, 1926); *Paul Maxwell Zeis, *American Shipping Policy* (Princeton, 1938, 1946); *Boleslaw Adam Boczek, *Flags of Convenience* (Cambridge, Mass., 1962). More general business aspects are discussed in: *Clinton H. Whitehurst, *The U.S. Merchant Marine* (Annapolis, 1981); *Lane C. Kendall, *The Business of Shipping* (Cambridge, Md., 1973), and in the older Emory R. Johnson, Grover G. Heubner, and Arnold K. Henry, *Transportation by Water* (New York, 1935). *C. Bradford Mitchell, *A Premium on Progress* (New York, 1970), sketches the history of the American maritime insurance industry; his *Touching*

The Adventures and Perils (New York, 1970) covers the American Hull Insurance Sydicate; and *Without Prejudice* (New York, 1971) deals with the U.S. Salvage Association. T. C. Chubb, *If There Were No Losses* (New York, 1957), recounts the history of a leading insurance firm.

Index